SOCIAL PROBLEMS 92/93

Twentieth Edition

Editor

LeRoy W. Barnes
Middlesex Community College

LeRoy W. Barnes is a professor of social science at Middlesex Community College in Connecticut. He holds degrees in history, political science, and education from Lawrence, Wesleyan, and Harvard. He has headed the Center for Teaching, which seeks to improve classroom instruction within Connecticut's community/technical college system. Recently he was cited by the state Board of Trustees for teaching excellence and distinguished service, an honor providing funds for research and educational innovation.

Outside school, he is an accomplished musician and participates in community efforts to upgrade adult learning and to restore landmark buildings and antique pipe organs.

Annual Editions
A Library of Information from the Public Press

Cover illustration by Mike Eagle

The Dushkin Publishing Group, Inc.
Sluice Dock, Guilford, Connecticut 06437

The Annual Editions Series

Annual Editions is a series of over 55 volumes designed to provide the reader with convenient, low-cost access to a wide range of current, carefully selected articles from some of the most important magazines, newspapers, and journals published today. Annual Editions are updated on an annual basis through a continuous monitoring of over 300 periodical sources. All Annual Editions have a number of features designed to make them particularly useful, including topic guides, annotated tables of contents, unit overviews, and indexes. For the teacher using Annual Editions in the classroom, an Instructor's Resource Guide with test questions is available for each volume.

VOLUMES AVAILABLE

Africa
Aging
American Government
American History, Pre-Civil War
American History, Post-Civil War
Anthropology
Biology
Business and Management
Business Ethics
Canadian Politics
China
Comparative Politics
Computers in Education
Computers in Business
Computers in Society
Criminal Justice
Drugs, Society, and Behavior
Early Childhood Education
Economics
Educating Exceptional Children
Education
Educational Psychology
Environment
Geography
Global Issues
Health
Human Development
Human Resources
Human Sexuality
International Business
Japan

Latin America
Life Management
Macroeconomics
Management
Marketing
Marriage and Family
Microeconomics
Middle East and the Islamic World
Money and Banking
Nutrition
Personal Growth and Behavior
Physical Anthropology
Psychology
Public Administration
Race and Ethnic Relations
Social Problems
Sociology
Soviet Union and Eastern Europe
State and Local Government
Third World
Urban Society
Violence and Terrorism
Western Civilization,
 Pre-Reformation
Western Civilization,
 Post-Reformation
Western Europe
World History, Pre-Modern
World History, Modern
World Politics

Library of Congress Cataloging in Publication Data
Main entry under title: Annual Editions: Social problems. 1992/93.
    1. United States—Social conditions—1960.—Periodicals. I. Barnes, LeRoy W., *comp.*
II. Title: Social problems.
309′.1′73′092′05   73-78577   ISBN 1-56134-099-5
HN51.A78

Twentieth Edition

Manufactured by The Banta Company, Harrisonburg, Virginia 22801

To the Reader

In publishing ANNUAL EDITIONS we recognize the enormous role played by the magazines, newspapers, and journals of the *public press* in providing current, first-rate educational information in a broad spectrum of interest areas. Within the articles, the best scientists, practitioners, researchers, and commentators draw issues into new perspective as accepted theories and viewpoints are called into account by new events, recent discoveries change old facts, and fresh debate breaks out over important controversies.

Many of the articles resulting from this enormous editorial effort are appropriate for students, researchers, and professionals seeking accurate, current material to help bridge the gap between principles and theories and the real world. These articles, however, become more useful for study when those of lasting value are carefully *collected, organized, indexed,* and *reproduced* in a *low-cost format,* which provides easy and permanent access when the material is needed. That is the role played by *Annual Editions.*

Under the direction of each volume's *Editor,* who is an expert in the subject area, and with the guidance of an *Advisory Board,* we seek each year to provide in each *ANNUAL EDITION* a current, well-balanced, carefully selected collection of the best of the public press for your study and enjoyment. We think you'll find this volume useful, and we hope you'll take a moment to let us know what you think.

Welcome to *Annual Editions: Social Problems 92/93.* I hope you will find this year's articles as interesting as my students have. Each article has been chosen for its timeliness and capacity to capture interest. You will find a wide selection of topics and opinions taken from a broad range of publications. Each of these readings can spark class discussion or make a surefire start for an essay.

Our collection begins with problems that are "close to home" and progresses through nationwide problems to global concerns. This arrangement is rather arbitrary and intentionally loose in the hope of accommodating the numerous course outlines that use *Annual Editions.* To help you locate articles that will fit your needs, we offer two useful aids. In the Table of Contents, you will find short descriptions of each article to give you a summary of the content up front. Another aid is the Topic Guide, which lists articles by topics. If you seek articles on a given theme—as when starting a research paper—be sure to check the Topic Guide first.

This edition stresses two important recent developments within our society: Our neglect of children, and the widening gap between the rich and the poor. Together these developments mean we are raising our next generation in poverty and without full benefits of traditional social institutions such as family. Today's children—tomorrow's leaders—have been born after our society accepted as commonplace the previously unfamiliar terms "single parent" and "homeless." Many articles address the questions—Are we bringing up tomorrow's leaders in conditions worse than were once used to rear their parents? Are we silently accepting future social problems by not preparing tomorrow's adults for success? Certainly we should try for better conditions.

This year's collection finds many authors challenging the United States to clean up its act. Many want the United States to solve domestic problems such as the disintegrating family, crumbling infrastructure, drugs, ineffective schools, poverty. Significantly, many authors see social links among such problems. They tie weak family relations to poverty, and both to weak schools and crime.

Further, authors seem worried about the place of our deteriorating nation among the world's leaders. They notice that social problems are increasingly global. Keeping the peace, lessening pollution, and easing poverty will require an international effort. Authors recognize that the balance of power among leading nations is being reshuffled, and, thus, added together they might ask, When world politics settle, will the United States have the internal stability and world outlook to succeed against global social problems?

I am sure you will find such issues fascinating and will want to discuss them with friends. I wish you success in your studies and good reading. If you have suggestions for articles or topics to include in future editions of this series, please use the article rating form provided on the last page of this book, or write and share your views.

LeRoy W. Barnes

LeRoy W. Barnes
Editor

Contents

Unit
1

Close to Home

Four selections review some of the dynamics of personal problems. Topics include divorce, unplanned parenthood, and drinking.

Unit 2

Racial and Ethnic Diversity

Six articles discuss some of the problems encountered by ethnic and racial minorities.

The concepts in bold italics are developed in the article. For further expansion please refer to the Topic Guide and the Index.

Unit 3

Nonethnic Minorities

Seven articles discuss the problems faced by minorities, including America's underclass, homosexuals, the elderly, single parents, and the disabled.

The concepts in bold italics are developed in the article. For further expansion please refer to the Topic Guide and the Index.

Unit 4

Politics, Public Policy, and Priorities

Eight selections examine the current state of American politics. Topics include the politics of social policy, education, drugs, the homeless, and abortion.

The concepts in bold italics are developed in the article. For further expansion please refer to the Topic Guide and the Index.

Unit
5

National and Global Economy

Four articles review the current state of the American economy. Topics include the economic problems we will face in the next decade.

Unit 6

Global Peace or War

Five articles consider the national and global concerns of peace and war.

The concepts in bold italics are developed in the article. For further expansion please refer to the Topic Guide and the Index.

Unit 7

Global Environment

Four selections examine the national and global problems of humankind's impact on the environment. Topics include the current state of the Earth, global consumption, and the greenhouse effect.

The concepts in bold italics are developed in the article. For further expansion please refer to the Topic Guide and the Index.

Topic Guide

This topic guide suggests how the selections in this book relate to topics of traditional concern to students and professionals involved with the study of social problems. It is useful for locating articles that relate to each other for reading and research. The guide is arranged alphabetically according to topic. Articles may, of course, treat topics that do not appear in the topic guide. In turn, entries in the topic guide do not necessarily constitute a comprehensive listing of all the contents of each selection.

TOPIC AREA	TREATED IN:	TOPIC AREA	TREATED IN:
Abortion/Right to Life	24. Abortion in a New Light	Elderly	3. Unplanned Parenthood 4. What Triggers Their Drinking? 16. Story of a Nursing Home Refugee
African Americans	3. Unplanned Parenthood 4. What Triggers Their Drinking? 7. New Black Politics	Europe	31. Myths of European Unity
Asian Americans	9. Japan's Influence on American Life 33. Roots of Muslim Rage	Family	1. America's Family Time Famine 2. Divorce 3. Unplanned Parenthood 11. Why Is America Failing Its Children? 12. Children in Peril 13. Everyday Life in Two High-Risk Neighborhoods 14. Feminization of Poverty
Business/Industry	26. High Cost of America's Economic Ignorance 27. Income Distribution Disparity 28. Will the Third Great Wave Continue? 29. Deadly Migration		
		Foreign Policy	30. America's Century Will End With a Whimper 31. Myths of European Unity 32. CIA Connection 33. Roots of Muslim Rage 34. Military Victory, Ecological Defeat
Children	1. America's Family Time Famine 3. Unplanned Parenthood 11. Why Is America Failing Its Children? 12. Children in Peril 13. Everyday Life in Two High-Risk Neighborhoods 14. Feminization of Poverty		
		Future	25. Big Messes
Conservation	37. Deforestation in the Tropics 38. Rethinking the Environment	Grandparents	3. Unplanned Parenthood
		Greenhouse Effect	37. Deforestation in the Tropics
Crime	13. Everyday Life in Two High-Risk Neighborhoods 25. Big Messes 32. CIA Connection	Health	16. Story of a Nursing Home Refugee 24. Abortion in a New Light
Divorce	2. Divorce	Homeless	15. Prejudice Against Men 18. American Nightmare: Homelessness
Drugs	4. What Triggers Their Drinking? 13. Everyday Life in Two High-Risk Neighborhoods 32. CIA Connection	Housing	22. Infrastructure
		Immigration	8. Immigration Reform 9. Japan's Influence on American Life
Education	6. America the Multicultural 21. Education: Ideas & Strategies 25. Big Messes 26. High Cost of America's Economic Ignorance	Infrastructure	22. Infrastructure

Close to Home

Let us start with some problems you may already know through your own experiences. While you might not think like a sociologist, you probably do know about people. You know about disagreements over values and priorities, about cultural differences, about denial and being ignored. You probably sense that social groupings like family and government are very important when studying society. You may have figured out that a problem within one home may be part of a national trend. You may also know that within one small home, a problem can be monumental to the people involved.

In this section, you will learn how families try their best to raise responsible children, but find their time wrenched away by society's demands for two-parent careers. And you may be saddened to learn of aging citizens, never before heavy drinkers, turning to alcohol to dull the neglect of an unappreciative society. Personal pain, value conflicts, and denial, you will find them all in these articles.

To get the most from this first section, read the articles quickly, then take time to think about each problem as a "student of society." Draw on your personal experiences and your best reasoning skills. How does a problem connect to society at large? How do social institutions, values, and prejudices interplay with a problem? What changes within society will be needed to resolve a problem?

Family is an important theme in this year's collection. "America's Family Time Famine" outlines basic value problems: parents torn between careers, families disrupted, children raised without siblings. As we have raised our social value for adult workers, we have traded in our emphasis on quality childhood. The trend against parenting seems nationwide, yet for each child and for each parent it is clearly "close to home." Here is a very local problem involving personal priorities, which at the same time is part of a national social trend.

"Divorce: Sometimes a Bad Notion" calls broken marriages a "rite of passage," meaning they are almost expected of every citizen. But is divorce good for society? Is it good for those leaving a broken family? This article poses questions about a basic social institution, the family, and asks you to decide.

"Unplanned Parenthood" deals with grandparents who thought they had completed their duties as child-rearers only to start afresh with raising grandchildren. Imagine yourself after thirty years of supervising and loving your children, having to start over again because your own children have failed as parents! Imagine yourself as a little

child having to worry that death or severe illness might take you away from the only responsible family you have left!

About twenty years ago, researchers began to study alcohol abuse among the elderly. "What Triggers Their Drinking?" introduces us to seniors who may not have experienced problems with alcohol until after retirement. What pressures, what neglect does society place upon senior citizens that triggers alcoholic drinking? The article also shows how a social problem can be ignored—even by researchers because the people who suffer do not fit the socially accepted image of someone in trouble.

Looking Ahead: Challenge Questions

What personal experience have you had with a social problem close to home? How did it make you feel?

From your experience, do people suffering a social problem usually notice the large aspect of the problem? Do they sense they are part of a national or global problem?

What social values compete with families spending time with children? If you had to choose between advancing your career and raising your child, which would you place as your top priority?

Is our current high divorce rate good or bad for society? For individuals?

What are the causes that could require grandparents to have to raise their grandchildren? Is having grandparents raise children good or bad for society?

What social pressures or neglects trigger senior citizens to drink after years without alcohol abuse? What questions should researchers in sociology ask in order to understand elderly alcohol abuse?

How does "thinking like a sociologist" differ from "everyday thinking?"

America's Family Time Famine

William R. Mattox, Jr.

William R. Mattox, Jr. is a policy analyst who focuses on work and family issues for the Family Research Council. This article is adapted from a piece published in the Winter, 1991 edition of the Heritage Foundation's Policy Review.

Many parents in America today are out of time. Out of gas. Running on empty. "On the fast track of two-career families in the go-go society of modern life, the most rationed commodity in the home is time," observes syndicated columnist Suzanne Fields. And the children of today's overextended parents are starving — starving from a lack of parental time, attention and affection.

Parents today spend 40 percent less time with their children than did parents in 1965, according to data collected from personal time diaries by sociologist John Robinson of the University of Maryland. In 1965, parents spent approximately 30 hours a week with their kids. By 1985, parent-child interaction had dropped to just 17 hours a week.

These changes are presenting significant challenges to American family life. Parents today employ a variety of time-management strategies to meet their work and family responsibilities. In roughly one-third of all two-income families today (one-half of those with preschoolers) spouses work complementary

Mom and Dad on their way to work

 By William R. Mattox, Jr., from *Children Today*, November/December 1990, pp. 9-11, 31. Reprinted by permission.

Here Sis and I are doing homework

shifts to maximize the amount of time children are cared for by at least one parent. The most common ''tag-team'' arrangement is one in which the father works a standard 9-to-5 job and the mother works part-time in the evenings or on weekends.

Other two-income households work concurrent shifts. Families in which the youngest child is of school age often choose this strategy to minimize the amount of time parents are unavailable to children during non-school hours. Same-shift arrangements are also common among families in which both parents have a high attachment to their careers and in those in which limited employment opportunities leave few alternatives.

Whether couples adopt a tag-team arrangement or a same-shift strategy, two-income households spend considerably less time with their children than do breadwinner-homemaker households. (Although there are certainly some traditional families that suffer from father absence due to the time-demanding nature of the sole breadwinner's work.)

This discrepancy is most pronounced in maternal time with children. In fact, research by University of Virginia sociologists Steven Nock and Paul William Kingston shows that employed mothers of preschool children on average spend less than half as much time with their children as full-time mothers at home. Moreover, Nock and Kingston show that employed mothers do not compensate for this shortage in quantity of time by devoting a higher proportion of the time they do spend with children to ''high quality'' child-centered activities such as playing with dolls, going to the park, or reading.

Time pressures can be especially daunting for single parents—and especially harmful to their children. Children in single-parent homes usually receive less parental attention and supervision than other children. Not only is one parent absent from the home (and research by sociologist Frank Furstenberg shows that three-fourths of all children of divorce have contact with their fathers less than two days a month), but the other parent is overloaded with money-making and household tasks. Indeed, Robinson's

data show that, on average, single mothers spend 33 percent less time each week than married mothers in primary child-care activities such as dressing, feeding, chauffeuring, talking, playing, or helping with homework.

Moreover, children in single-parent families often have very irregular schedules. One study found that preschool children of single mothers sleep two fewer hours a night on average than their counterparts in two-parent homes, in part because harried mothers find it difficult to maintain a consistent bedtime routine.

Sibling Revelry

Kids aren't just missing out on time with their parents. Thanks to the ''birth dearth,'' they are also missing out on interaction with siblings.

In 1975, 62 percent of all women aged 40-44 had given birth to three or more children over the course of their lifetimes. In 1988, only 38 percent had done so. The percentage of those giving birth to just one child rose from 9 to 15 percent during this same time period.

Some regard the decline in family size

as a positive development because it means children today receive more individualized attention from their parents than did children a generation ago.

Even if this were true—and sociologist Harriet Presser reports "not only are Americans having fewer children than ever before, they are spending less time with the children they have"—it can hardly be argued that a one-child family generally has as rich a family experience as a larger family. Even if an only child receives more individualized parental attention, he still misses out on the intimate joys of having brothers and sisters—playing wiffle ball in the backyard, exchanging gifts at Christmas time, double-teaming Dad in a wrestling match on the family room floor, attending a sibling's ballet recital, and (later in life) reminiscing about old times at family reunions.

Today's fast-paced family life is also eroding the development of other aspects of what sociologist David Popenoe of Rutgers University says "is arguably the ideal child-rearing environment":

a relatively large family that does a lot of things together, has many routines and traditions, and provides a great deal of quality contact time between adults and children; regular contact with rela-tives, active neighboring in a suppor-tive neighborhood, and contact with the world of work; little concern on the part of children that their parents will break up; and the coming together of all these ingredients in the development of a rich family subculture that has lasting meaning and strongly promulgates such family values as cooperation and sharing.

Eating dinner together is one time-honored family tradition some believe is on its way out. "The family meal is dead," columnist Jonathan Yardley has written. "Except on the rarest occasions—Christmas, Thanksgiving, certain religious holidays—when we reach down to the innermost depths of the tribal memory and summon up turkeys and pies, roasts and casseroles, we have given up on what was once a central element in American domestic life."

Research on the prevalence of regular family mealtimes is mixed. Some reports claim as many as 75 percent of all families regularly dine together, while others suggest less than 35 percent do so. Whatever the case, polls taken by the Roper organization show that the proportion of families that dine together regularly declined 10 percent between 1976

and 1986. This helps explain why heat-and-eat microwavable dinners for children to prepare alone are "the hottest new category in food products," according to a food industry spokesperson.

Whatever the virtues of microwavable meals and other convenience foods, there is reason to be concerned about children routinely feeding themselves. As Suzanne Fields observes, "The child who grazes, standing in front of a microwave eating his fried chicken, biscuits, or refried beans, won't starve, but he may suffer from an emotional hunger that would be better satisfied if only Mom and Dad were there to yell at him for every pea he slips onto the knife."

So Many Bills, So Little Time

So how did American families run out of time? Growing economic pressures have a lot to do with the American family time crisis.

One of the supreme ironies of recent economic developments is that while America has experienced steady growth in its gross national product, the economic pressures on families with children have risen significantly. How can it be that at the same time we hear so much about the longest peacetime economic expansion in our nation's history, we also hear talk that economic pressures have grown so much that many families today must have two incomes?

Wage stagnation is one big reason. During the 1970s and '80s, constant dollar earnings of American husbands grew at less than 1 percent per year compared to a real growth rate of 3 percent per year in the 1950s and '60s. Moreover, for some occupational and demographic groups—particularly non-supervisory workers and males under age 25—real wages have actually fallen since 1973.

While wages have stagnated, taxes have risen dramatically. In 1950, a median-income family of four paid 2 percent of its annual gross earnings to the federal government in income and payroll taxes. Today, it pays 24 percent. In addition, state and local taxes, on average, take another 8 percent from the family's gross income.

Moreover, the erosion in the value of the personal exemption (the tax code's

Mom fixing dinner, calling for pizza, my favorite!

chief mechanism for adjusting tax liability to reflect differences in family size) has shifted more of the federal income tax burden onto the backs of families with dependents. Had the exemption kept pace with inflation since 1950, it would now be worth close to $7,000. Instead, it stands at $2,050.

On top of this, families are finding their take-home pay does not go as far as it once did. As economist Sylvia Ann Hewlett puts it, families today are "like hamsters on a wheel," running hard just to keep up.

Over the past 25 years, increases in the cost of several major family expenses—housing, health care, transportation, and higher education—have significantly outpaced the general inflation rate. For example, Joseph Minarik of the Congressional Joint Economic Committee has calculated that the typical 30-year-old man could get a mortgage on a median-priced home in 1973 with 21 percent of his income. By 1987, a median-priced home mortgage would take 40 percent of a typical 30-year-old's gross income.

The cost of housing, which is typically a family's single greatest expense, is tied directly to crime rates and school districts. As crime rates have risen and school performance has declined, an under-supply of housing in good school districts with low crime rates has driven the price of housing in such neighborhoods way up. Thus, parents who value safety, education, and time with children must either live in areas with poorer schools and higher crime or divert time from children to market their labor in order to purchase a home in a safe neighborhood with good schools. That is a quintessential Hobson's choice.

Perrier and Teddy Bears

Growing economic pressures aren't the only reason families have less time together. A number of cultural factors have also played a major role.

"Unbridled careerism" is partly responsible for the decline in family time, says Karl Zinsmeister of the American Enterprise Institute. "For years, one of the most cogent criticisms of American sex roles and economic arrangements has been the argument that many fathers get so wrapped up in earning and doing at the workplace that they become dehumanized, losing interest in the intimate joys of family life and failing to participate fairly in domestic responsibilities," he writes. "Now it appears workaholism and family dereliction have become equal opportunity diseases, striking mothers as much as fathers."

The devaluation of motherhood stands behind such trends. As Zinsmeister notes, "Today, women are more likely to be admired and appreciated for launching a catchy new ad campaign for toothpaste than they are for nurturing and shaping an original personality." Ironically, this has a detrimental impact on fatherhood as well. So long as child-rearing is viewed as a low calling for women, it is unlikely that it will take on increased significance for men.

Apart from unbridled careerism, some of the reduction in family time has been driven by a rampant materialism that places a higher premium on obtaining or retaining a "Perrier and Rolex life-style" than on investing time in a larger kin group.

"Increasingly, Americans are pursuing a selfish individualism that is inconsistent with strong families and strong communities," writes University of North Carolina sociologist Peter Uhlenberg. "This movement is fueled by the media, most especially television (both in its programming and advertising), which suggests that personal happiness is the highest good and that it can be achieved by pursuing pleasure and material goods."

Indeed, it has become all too common for parents to buy material goods for their children in an attempt to compensate for their frequent absence from the home. Harvard University child psychiatrist Robert Coles calls this the "teddy bear syndrome":

Some of the frenzied need of children to have possessions isn't only a function of the ads they see on TV. It's a function of their hunger for what they aren't getting—their parents' time. The biggest change I have seen in 30 years of interviewing families is that children are no longer being cared for by their parents the way they once were. Parents are too busy spending their most pre-cious capital—their time and their energy—struggling to keep up with MasterCard payments. They're depleted. They work long hours to barely keep up, and when they get home at the end of the day they're tired. And their kids are left with a Nintendo or a pair of Nikes or some other piece of crap. Big deal.

Swimming Upstream

Of course, not all parents are trying to "buy off" their children with Teenage Mutant Ninja Turtles gear or overpriced sneakers. Many are struggling to raise responsible children and to transmit family values such as sharing, responsibility, commitment, and self-control. But these families are finding themselves swimming upstream against an increasingly unfriendly culture that instead promotes casual sex, instant gratification and selfish individualism.

Whereas once institutions outside the family, such as schools, churches, the mass media, and businesses, formerly reinforced the inculcation of traditional values, today they are often indifferent or downright hostile to family values and the rights of parents to pass on such values to their children. Many parents sense that they are being undercut by larger institutional forces. And they recognize that children who lack the self-esteem that comes from parental attention and affection are especially vulnerable to negative peer and cultural influences.

"Doing Things Together"

Some opinion leaders in government, academia, and the mass media view initiatives designed to increase family time—especially those that recognize the legitimacy and strengths of the breadwinner-homemaker family model—as an attempt to "turn back the clock" rather than "facing the realities" of modern family life. These leaders overlook the fact that concerns about family time are not limited to those who believe the traditional family model is ideal.

A 1989 Cornell University study found that two-thirds of all mothers employed full-time would like to work fewer hours so that they could devote more time to their families. And when respondents to a 1989 survey commissioned by the Mass Mutual Insurance Company were asked to identify "extremely effective" ways to strengthen the family, nearly twice as many opted for "spending more time together" than listed "full-time parent raising kids."

Moreover, most Americans do not sneer at the past the way elitists do. As Whitehead observes:

In the official debate (on family issues), the remembered past is almost always considered a suspect, even unhealthy, guide for the present or future. . . . But for the parents I met, the remembered past is not a dusty artifact of the good old days; it is an important and vital social resource. Parents take instruction from their own family's past, rummaging through it for usable truths and adopting—or modifying or occasionally rejecting—its values. . . . In the official language, the family isn't getting weaker, it's just "changing." Most parents I met believe otherwise.

Americans believe "parents having less time to spend with their families" is the most important reason for the family's decline in our society, according to a recent survey. And most parents would like to see the work-family pendulum swing back in the direction of home.

To be sure, most children would not object to spending more unhurried time with their parents. Indeed, when 1,500 schoolchildren were asked, "What do you think makes a happy family?" social scientists Nick Stinnett and John DeFrain report that children "did not list money, cars, fine homes, or televisions." Instead the answer most frequently offered was "doing things together."

Divorce:
Sometimes a bad notion

FRED MOODY/*SEATTLE WEEKLY*

D ivorce, along with high-school graduation, marriage, and death, is now an established American rite of passage. Everyone, either directly or indirectly, is touched by it. A first marriage undertaken today stands (avert your eyes, squeamish reader) a 66 percent chance of ending in divorce. For the first time in history, an American marrying now is more likely to lose a spouse through divorce than through death.

Divorce most often is portrayed as liberating. The ease with which we divorce is regarded as a proof of the individual freedoms Americans enjoy. It

---

"Quite often, divorce is much more devastating than people who go into the process anticipate."

---

is one more means we have of achieving self-fulfillment—the *raison d'etre* of the baby-boom generation. When no-fault divorce was ushered in 20 years ago, it was hailed as a quick and easy solution to relationships gone sour. Now, a generation later, legions of divorced parents and their children are emerging to paint a far different picture: one of financial travail, psychological devastation, and endless emotional turmoil. Study after study documents so much discontent surrounding divorce that it now appears to be an even greater source of disillusionment than marriage is.

Divorce is particularly disillusioning for women and children. No-fault reforms have robbed women of alimony, and no-fault's lax child-support enforcement has allowed men to default on their obligations to the point where many divorced women and

children are reduced to poverty. Instead of reducing inequality between the sexes, no-fault divorce has widened the gap in status between men and women, and is the leading cause of the well-documented feminization of poverty in America.

There's no question that the fundamental right to divorce should be available to anyone; the ability to divorce a monster or an addict, or to get out of a marriage that is an incurable mistake, is a humane and civilized right. But the notion that every unhappy marriage is a bad one, or that individuals are morally as well as legally entitled to place their own pursuit of happiness above the well-being of their offspring, is ruinous. Opting for divorce before having exhausted every effort at preserving a relationship is self-destructive.

We need to re-examine our motives and consider reforms—from marriage education to legal representation for children in divorce proceedings. But first we need to look more closely at the path we have taken from the strict protection of marriage as a social institution to its severe weakening by our now-inalienable right to divorce.

I n England, birthplace of the American legal tradition, divorce didn't even exist until 1857, and not until 1900 had most of the United States legislated, under stringent guidelines, grounds and procedures for divorce. From then on, so gradually that no one noticed for nearly 40 years, the divorce rate crept steadily upward. After World War II it took a huge leap, then crept up gradually again until the mid-1960s, when it took off on a sharp upward curve that is still rising. In 1965, there were 10.6 divorces for every 1,000 married women in the United States; by the early 1980s, that number had nearly doubled, to 22.6 per 1,000.

Until the early 1970s, divorce in nearly all instances was universally acknowledged as a hor-

From *Utne Reader*, November/December 1990, pp. 70-78. Excerpted from *Seattle Weekly*, November 22, 1989. Subscriptions: $29.95/yr. ($39.95 out-of-state) from *Seattle Weekly*, 1931 2nd Ave., Seattle, WA 98101.

rible event. Divorce proceedings were ugly, detailed airings of connubial crimes, as husband and wife squared off in court to fight over money, children, and one another's morals. Then came the 1970 advent of no-fault divorce in California, followed by its almost instant acceptance nationwide.

With no-fault, couples had only to declare their marriage irretrievably broken, reach an agreement over division of assets, custody of children, and child-support payments, and have the agreement ratified by a court. Proponents even asserted that it would reduce the nation's rising divorce rate, for by eliminating the issue of guilt from marital disputes, no-fault divorce would facilitate reconciliations. People would use divorce proceedings as a forum for solving problems rather than exacerbating or creating them. Reasoning like this led such conservative groups as Christian fundmentalists and the Catholic Church to join liberals in supporting California's proposed no-fault laws.

In theory, divorce was supposed to be liberating for men and women alike as well as demonstrably better for children than living with unhappily married parents—another milestone on America's most-traveled road, the path to self-fulfillment.

Alas, none of those hopes has been realized. Even with the nationwide adoption of no-fault legislation, the American divorce rate continues to rise at the same rate. In all likelihood, nothing could have slowed the divorce rate's climb, but it would have been interesting to see what might have happenened had California lawmakers agreed to fund a proposed "family court," in which divorce issues would have been debated and sometimes resolved. Without that feature, the court system became a mere rubber-stamp reviewer of agreements hammered out between spouses and their lawyers.

The emotional fallout of divorce is easy to see. Legions of divorced people, their attorneys, their therapists, their children, and their children's therapists have learned that divorce is shattering.

"Quite often, divorce is much more devastating than people who go into the process anticipate," says Seattle psychiatrist Dr. Herbert Wimberger. "They are surprised by how painful it is, by how long the pain lasts. Divorce very often is a serious loss, bringing on a severe grief reaction." Adds Seattle psychotherapist Diane Zerbe, "Everybody knows somebody five years later who is still emotionally invested in their failed marriage, still angry at their ex-spouse, and their bitterness is a major part of their life. They haven't been able somehow to come to terms with what happened and go on to find a more satisfying relationship."

The evidence also seems to suggest that second marriages are no happier, with even less likelihood of working than first marriages (for some reason, third ones have better odds).

No-fault has also become a source of no-limit frustration and bitterness for wronged spouses, by shifting the power overwhelmingly from the spouse who wants to stay married to the spouse who wants a divorce. It offers an amoral solution to a problem many people regard as moral. It also has backfired psychologically. The idea that a procedure providing no outlet for anger would somehow do away with anger has proven an illusion. "I keep telling my lawyer," says one furious woman currently going through a divorce, "that my husband is sleeping with other women, that he won't even talk to me, that he neglects our children, and the lawyer keeps answering, 'Irrelevant! Irrelevant!' It isn't fair!"

In many divorces, the rage that formerly came out during the debate over grounds for divorce now is redirected into interminable custody disputes and negotiations over child support. In one recent case, the husband, being divorced by his wife, was determined to get sole custody of their children, even though he had had little to do with them during his marriage. He made extravagant accusations against his wife—of abandonment, child abuse, and incest—all of which were dutifully investigated and dismissed by the court.

As all this suggests, no-fault also failed to deliver on its promise of convenience and lower cost. "People are spending more time and money on divorce than ever before," says Seattle family-law attorney Nancy Hawkins.

Worst of all has been the disastrous impact of no-fault divorce on women and children. In Washington state, for example, property is divided equally between divorcing spouses, regardless of who is primarily responsible for the failure of the marriage. Before 1973, the wounded party—usually the wife—was awarded a greater share of a couple's property as a form of compensation for pain and suffering. No-fault's attempts to make divorce law gender-neutral, and therefore more fair, have created a raw deal for women. It has led to the virtual elimination of alimony payments to wronged or financially disadvantaged wives, and to drastic reductions in the amount and duration of maintenance payments to wives who gave up career goals for their families.

Judges have further disadvantaged such women by refusing to regard a husband's future earnings as community property, even in cases where a wife could demonstrate that her support and the sacrifice of her own career contributed to her husband's success and earning power.

Consequently, divorced women who win custody of their children now suffer, on the average, a 33 percent decline in their standard of living, while their ex-husbands enjoy a corresponding rise in theirs. This is largely due to the dismal complexities of court-ordered child support. In Washington, research shows that court orders for child support are almost always too low to cover the actual costs of raising children. Further, only 50 percent of divorced dads in Washington pay the full amount of their child-support judgment; 25 percent pay part of what they're ordered, and the remaining 25 percent simply ignore the order and pay nothing at all.

The effect on children is enormous. According to University of Washington sociologist Diane Lye, more than 70 percent of America's black children and 50 percent of its white children will live in single-parent homes by the time they are 16 years old. "There are 18 million poor children in our country now," she says, "and over half of them are living in single-parent homes caused by divorce."

This immense sociological problem is rooted in a psychological quagmire. Marriage in our society is a swamp too mysterious to be charted by lawyers, judges, and legislature. Particularly given our uniquely American preoccupation with the self, a married couple's individual psychological needs are at odds with their common need. "Some sociologists argue," says Lye, "that the American ideology of love is completely incompatible, and clashes head-on, with continued self-fulfillment."

Says Wimberger, "Marriage in some ways can be described as an impossible proposition to begin with. There are these divergent needs: People want companionship, closeness, and so on, but at the same time they want to be themselves, so they are constantly negotiating." The negotiation is made all the more tense, in Wimberger's view, by a society in which everything is transitory. In the past, a person's innate fears about the changes such negotiations would entail could be overcome by the need to make a marriage livable, for he or she had no other choice. In the no-fault present, married people often find it easier simply to flee the marriage. Spouses are disposable.

Much of Wimberger's counseling work is with couples, and over the years he has seen certain distinct patterns take form in one marriage after another. American marriages are so imbued with romanticism that most people enter into them blissfully blinded to practicality. "So many people take marriage for granted," he explains. "You tie the knot and everything is supposed to go happily ever after. People don't realize that relationships need a lot of work. Then when things start to go sour, they don't know what's wrong, because they don't know how to talk to each other, and they don't have any support from an extended family."

As marriages deteriorate, couples tend to think more wistfully of divorce than of reconciliation. As Zerbe sees it, "It's such a pleasant fantasy if you're having problems in your marriage. To think that you can go out and find somebody better and have dates and have all that excitement. And that if only

Children of divorced parents have a much higher incidence of divorce.

you were free to find the right person, who would appreciate how great you are.... Each partner assumes that the problem is with the other partner."

Recognized early enough, these patterns can be broken. Too often, however, couples are too lost

in their anger by the time they seek help. Where once they might have recognized that they had workable emotional problems, now one or the other is simply convinced that he or she is no longer in love.

Divorce brings with it a whole new set of problems—particularly if the divorcing couple has children. While research until very recently has implied that children of divorced parents are better off than children of unhappily married parents, new studies, such as those cited in Judith Wallerstein's book *Second Chances* (Ticknor & Fields, 1989), suggest the opposite. Wimberger is convinced that the adverse effects of divorce on children are grossly understated. "I think the literature is a little bit slanted," he says. "Too many of the researchers perhaps are divorced and trying to make the best of things. Even when children accept sort of superficially that their parents are divorced and that they might be better off after divorce, they usually continue to have the fantasy of Mom and Dad getting back together. Children of divorced parents have a much higher incidence of divorce. And, of course, a great deal depends on what their relationship is with the parent who leaves after a divorce. If a child loses a parent, that is a loss that people don't get over."

In Zerbe's view, divorce very often robs children of both parents, whatever the custody arrangements. "Part of it," she observes, "is not so much the divorce itself but the fact that both parents are so devastated by it that their parenting abilities are interfered with. So that really the kids are struggling not just with the divorce but with the fact that they've lost both parents' emotional availability."

When fathers are often physically absent (since mothers more often get full or primary custody), there emerges one of divorce's most constant and

Young people need to be made aware of the dire consequences of marriages carelessly undertaken.

classic patterns. There is something about the lack of continual contact between fathers and children, through routine and traumatic moments alike, that dramatically heightens the child's feelings for the father and just as dramatically dulls the father's feelings for his child. In her 10-year study of 60 middle-class divorced families, Wallerstein sees this terrible pattern played out everywhere, in nearly every divorce. "One of the great tragedies of divorce is that many fathers have absolutely no idea that their children feel rejected," she writes in *Second Chances*. "Although the fathers seem indifferent or uncaring, this may not be the case at all. I have talked with many fathers who genuinely think that they have good relationships with their children, while the children feel rejected and miserable."

This rampant paternal blindness adds to one of our society's most profound problems: the emotional and financial neglect of children. Fathers, unable to see their children's need for their love and their lucre, may simply default on both counts,

leaving the state and the schools to try to pick up the pieces. As a result, as Seattle University economics professor Peter Nickerson points out, "the taxpayers pay a tremendous burden. In this state, more than half a billion dollars are paid out in AFDC [Aid to Families with Dependent Children] payments, and as much as half of that may be going to children of divorce. And that doesn't include the fact that the schools are so screwed up—kids there are hungry

Does work cause divorce?

In the years 1977 to 1985, researchers at the Institute for Labor and Mental Health interviewed several thousand working people from a wide variety of work situations. These were people whose lives were not "in crisis"—they were workers who were facing the normal stresses of the work world.

What we discovered was that beneath the surface, very widespread pain pervades thousands of families. In general, the pain springs from the illusion that their personal life should make up for everything else that is unfulfilling; that it should be a "haven in a heartless world" unaffected by the daily frustrations of the working world. Most importantly, people believe that the "right" relationship will provide that haven. Yet most people in this society fail to find the magical relationship that they believe will compensate for the alienation of the larger world.

People typically return home from work feeling tense, often upset, sometimes depressed, almost always with a deep sense of frustration, for which they blame themselves. Typically, these feelings are buried beneath a surface level of relief at getting home, and most workers attempt to present themselves as not "letting it get to them." They try to pretend that they are unaffected by stupid bosses, arrogant supervisors, new processes that they aren't sure they can master and feel they must, sales that didn't go through, people they aren't sure they have impressed enough, co-workers with whom they must compete for praise or promotions, or changes in the economy that may make their product less desirable and their jobs less secure. Most frequently I found that people don't want to know about the psychic costs of work, or even begin to think about them. They tell themselves that all this can be quickly forgotten in some form of "relaxation" at home.

Some people are so successful at building a set of psychic defenses around themselves that they're literally unaware of the tensions they bring home. Some of these people end up suffering from chronic stress-related illnesses in their late forties and early fifties. Others show nothing more than a slight feeling of being tired.

But these are the exceptions. Stress shows up in

the lives of most people in more obvious ways. They try a wide variety of strategies to bury their feelings. TV helps to recreate a world of fantasy and escape from self-paralyzing work thoughts, while alcohol and drugs can deaden the pain. (Ironically, those who try to combat alcoholism or drug abuse often engage in therapies that reinforce the very dynamics that led to the abuse. Patients are taught to "take responsibility" for their addictions and "take charge of their lives"— an orientation that denies the social roots of our personal problems. Of course, getting people away from addictive behavior is a valuable thing to do, but denial of its cause is likely to lead to recurrence of other self-destructive behaviors.) People sometimes engage in frenetic activity in sports, sexual conquests, religion, and politics, using them to escape from feelings of pain. When one's emotional life is consumed by these activities, it leaves no time for introspection.

The huge amount of emotional energy that gets put into repressing the alienation, self-blaming, and anger that we experience at work leaves us too little energy to develop the emotional connectedness necessary to maintain a relationship. When we are regularly out of touch with our feelings, we simply don't have the skills to be loving and open and honest partners in a relationship.

Add to this another reality factor: As families become increasingly nuclearized, they actually have to take on a greater set of support functions than in the past. Without the extended family networks that used to engage in child-rearing, taking care of elderly parents, and coping with demands for entertainment and recreation, the very same burdens that once were distributed among a large clan are suddenly heaped on the shoulders of every two-adult nuclear family.

Also, most relationships—even among progressive-minded couples—are hampered by expectations that women are responsible for nurturing both children and husband, as well as for keeping the household running. For homemakers, there's still little recognition that housework and child care are often every bit as exhausting as and ornery and their parents are fighting."

What little is being proposed in the way of solutions to this mess generally falls into two approaches, one seeking to buttress the family and the other seeking to replace it. In Washington, state senator Ellen Craswell, noting that 26,000 Washington marriages each year end in divorce, and that 14,000 of those divorces involve children, introduced a bill during the last legislative session that

work done by the male breadwinner. Women with jobs in the workplace must often cope with the same dynamics of repressed anger and self-blame that men experience, and then return to a home where a second job of home and child care awaits them. As if this were not enough, they are expected to be therapists, nursemaids, and sexual goddesses for their husbands, fulfilling male fantasies about being taken care of and receiving compensation from the world of work.

It would be foolish to argue that all families share all these dynamics to the same extent. Not every workplace is equally stressful. Some couples have learned to recognize that the tensions they generate are often a reflection of external realities—so they can have a good fight, then use it as a springboard to deeper levels of intimacy. Some people have learned how to deal with their anger—and not to fear it.

Still, there is a widely shared reality of pain in family life, and it is unrealistic to expect that it can be relieved by anything less than a massive restructuring of the world of work. And a first step is for us to recognize that the pain is a reflection of a social reality we did not construct and that we as individuals cannot change without the creation of a very large movement for social change.

In the meantime, we must also develop a deeper level of compassion for ourselves and each other, once we truly understand how powerful the forces are that work against loving relationships. If we approach each other with an adequately developed sense of compassion, we may begin to understand the other side of the picture: how truly incredible and powerful are the forces of beauty, dignity, and worth within each of us.

—Michael Lerner

Michael Lerner is editor of Tikkun *magazine, a bimonthly Jewish critique of politics, culture, and society, published in Oakland, California. A new edition of his book* Surplus Powerlessness, *from which this article was adapted, was published by Humanities Press in the spring of 1991.*

would have eliminated no-fault divorce. Her reasoning was simple: If divorce is harder to get, there will be less of it, and more families will opt to find a way to remain intact.

But it is probably impossible to turn back the clock, as the conservative Craswell has proposed. Washington's divorce rate, save for a brief blip immediately after the 1973 introduction of no-fault divorce, has risen along a steady curve from the mid-1960s to the present, which suggests that no-fault was more a recognition of reality than its cause. "When we think about families," says Diane Lye, "we have to think about the diversity of family life in America. Whatever we might like, and however much we feel that the family is the best place for children, the reality is that that is not what's happening. We need not so much to force families to stay intact as to separate out the negative consequences of divorce. Ours is not a problem of rising divorce rates—it's a problem of inadequate financial support for mothers and children."

The Washington legislature implemented a new child-support program in 1988 designed not merely to help children subsist, but to preserve their standard of living after divorce. Divorcing parents fill out detailed income forms that have led to payments far higher than what courts had been ordering in the past; more importantly, it serves as a guideline that judges must follow instead of using their discretion in setting a payment amount.

Clearly, far more sweeping reforms are called for. At the very least, courts need enough time and money to study divorce decrees and determine whether they adequately provide for women and children. As things stand now, they simply rubber-stamp agreements reached between people who are in no shape to keep their children's best interests in mind.

There should also be lawyers representing children in divorce hearings, as they do in child-abuse hearings. A child's lawyer should be able to argue on behalf of the child's best interests—that the divorce be denied, that parents undergo further counseling, that children be compensated for the emotional and material damage divorce will bring down on them.

Rampant divorce is dangerous not only to children—it also harms, often permanently, the husbands and wives who suffer through it. It lowers the moral tone of the entire nation, as society seconds the motion that we are entitled to look first of all after ourselves. Since the mid-1960s, divorce has had almost unremittingly good press, and the better divorce's public image, the greater priority many people give to self-fulfillment over obligations to others. Those who shape and mold opinion in this country—writers, reporters, moviemakers, and advertisers, to name a few—need to de-romanticize divorce.

Young people need to be made aware of the dire consequences of marriages carelessly undertaken: Marriage and divorce education is as critical to our society's health as sex education. Divorce's romanticized image as a harmless quick fix is a lie. That fantasy has led legions of naive and discontented people into even greater unhappiness than they had suffered in their marriages.

Since the advent of no-fault, one of the fundamental truths about divorce has been discounted: that love or marriage may be fleeting, but divorce is forever. Those contemplating divorce should understand that it often affords not a new beginning, but only a new form of anguish. "You never get divorced for real," says one woman, who left her husband six year ago. "You never get rid of that person." Another woman concurs: "I thought divorce would be like jumping through a hoop," she says. "But it's not a hoop—it's a tunnel."

UNPLANNED PARENTHOOD

David Larsen

The author recently retired after many years as a reporter/writer with the Los Angeles Times.

Raising your grandchildren is a lot different than raising your own kids," says Mary Etta Johnson of Anaheim, California. "We hadn't had children in our home for years; suddenly they were there almost 24 hours a day."

Johnson and her husband, Albert, took their two grandchildren into their home after their daughter and son-in-law became involved in drugs and the marriage broke up. They've had the youngsters, now nine and seven, for five years now; in 1986, they got permanent custody.

In Media, Pennsylvania, Diane Warner decided she'd had enough and told her drug-addicted live-in daughter to move out. Her little grandson stayed.

Three years ago Melody Hudgins' daughter left her two-year-old son in a Hollywood motel room and went out to buy drugs. The tot was found by police, who turned him over to his grandmother. The boy's father? As in most of these cases, he simply isn't in the picture.

At an age when they least expect it, when they had other plans for their later years, an increasing number of grandparents nationwide are finding themselves being recycled as parents—to their children's children.

There are many reasons: death, abandonment, incarceration, mental illness, physical and/or sexual abuse. But the main cause is drug or alcohol addiction. And the burden, ironically, falls on a generation that played virtually no role in the drug scene.

There are no statistics to define the scale of the problem, which affects families in middle-class suburb and inner-city alike. But social-service agencies agree the number is rising.

Barbara Kirkland, an activist grandmother in Colleyville, Texas, says talks with family counselors nationwide lead her to conclude that about 5 percent of American families comprise a grandparent raising a grandchild.

Kirkland and husband Gerald are raising their ten-year-old grand-daughter. Their son was killed in an industrial accident; their former daughter-in-law (the couple were divorced) has made no attempt to contact her child. "Friends suggested we attend parenting courses," says Kirkland of those first anxious months in her new role. "But this is different from being a young parent. That's why I founded a support group of my own: Grandparents Raising Grandchildren."

Across the country other grandparents in similar situations are using support groups to help them cope with the special challenges they face.

In a neon-lit conference room in Long Beach, California, visitors find a scene Norman Rockwell would never have painted. Nine grandmothers sit on couches and chairs facing each other. They aren't swapping recipes or travel tales. They're attending their weekly meeting of Grandparents As Parents. Sylvie de Toledo, the licensed clinical social worker who runs the sessions, started GAP three years ago after seeing firsthand the trials her own parents went through when her sister died and they took in her eight-year-old son.

"Older people in this situation feel cheated out of the traditional doting-grandparent role," she says. "And the children are also deprived of the relationship. The word 'grand' has been taken out of the experience for both generations."

De Toledo leads GAP groups at the Psychiatric Clinic for Youth in Long Beach and at the Reiss-Davis Child Study Center in Los Angeles; in between, she spends a lot of time on the phone helping grandparents in other states start their own organizations.

Judy Kingston and Peggy Plante started GAP in Quincy, Massachusetts, in November 1989. Judy and Larry Kingston are raising a nine-year-old grandson; Peggy Plante and husband Frank are raising their four-year-old granddaughter. The Plantes have permanent guardianship of their granddaughter and are in the process of adopting her.

Their group meets once a month in a nearby seniors' hall with anywhere from seven to 17 people attending. Sessions often feature guest speakers such as psychologists, social workers and attorneys who offer professional insights into members' problems. Between meetings, group members call each other when things get rough; there's also a monthly newsletter.

"I was surprised at how many of us there were," recalls Kingston. "I'm sure there must be even more people out there in this situation who aren't aware we exist."

In Shreveport, Louisiana, Betty and Ralph Parbs had already raised their own four children when they found themselves with three live-in grandchildren—all under age ten. One day Parbs remarked to her husband, "You know, honey, we can't be the only people in this position."

All it took to find the others was a small ad in the local paper.

"We got four responses," says Parbs. "Then it kind of snowballed." Now, five years later, GAIN (Grandparents Against Immorality and Neglect) draws some 50 people to meetings held twice monthly in the community room of a nearby mall.

Diane Warner founded her Pennsylvania group, Second Time Around Parents, in anger. "I'd been watching yet another television show about the drug problem," she recalls, the frustration rising in her voice. "They were talking about the millions of dollars the government is pouring into the war on drugs and into building new rehabilitation centers. And I *know* some addicts use rehab centers as a way to avoid jail—almost as a vacation—I've seen it in my own home! And I thought, 'God! Why isn't any of this money going to the victims—to the children of these drug addicts and their caregivers? What about *us?*' "

Second Time Around's weekly meetings attract some 20 grandparents. But Warner doesn't intend to stop there. Says she: "We've got a lot of political work to do. There isn't one law in this country that protects people in our position."

In Milwaukee, Wisconsin, child psychotherapist Carole Stewart started From Generation to Generation after noticing how many of her young clients lived with their grandparents.

"A lot of these people thought this would be their time in life," says Stewart. "And though they love their grandchildren, they didn't expect this responsibility. Raising children is the most stressful job in the world. Here, grandparents give each other advice on how to cope."

"For sure it helps us—we've learned how to laugh again," agrees Paula Browne of GAP in California. "But it also helps the kids. They'll ask why they don't have a normal family like other children. Then they go to our outings and realize they aren't the only ones living with their grandparents."

Support-group meetings fulfill the same general purpose. They're especially helpful, says de Toledo, because members are often in different stages of acceptance and draw emotional support from those with more experience.

Florence Gilmore, who flew to Washington state to collect her three young grandsons after their parents, both drug addicts, were declared unfit, was overwhelmed by practical matters: "When I first came to GAP I was emotionally and spiritually exhausted," she recalls. "I didn't know what shots the boys had had, where to find a good doctor. Eddie [my husband] and I spent all our time changing diapers. It was terrible. And for several months Eddie worked nights then babysat while I worked during the day. He was really wonderful."

"I was angry when I first came to these meetings," admits Melody Hudgins. "I resented having to raise a child again and I was angry at my daughter for putting me in this position."

Grandparents also feel guilty. "They say to themselves, 'What did I do to cause this?' " says Barbara Kirkland of GRG. "They have to acknowledge these feelings and that it's okay to have them. The fact is," she stresses, "probably nothing they did caused the situation."

That familiar lament, "Where did we go wrong?" hits hard at these times, especially when the adult children grew up in stable, loving homes. "The kids see some terrible things," says Diane Warner, whose home was wrecked when her daughter was beaten up by a companion—in front of the daughter's child.

Their own anxiety aside, recycled grandparents have to cope with the reactions of others: "People tell me I'm too old to be doing this," says Elinore Simmons, who's raising a seven-year-old boy and a four-year-old girl. "I tell them I have no choice."

As a result, social lives suffer.

"Other older people don't want to see you come around with little kids," says Johnnie Mae Short, who's raising three grandchildren. "They don't stop being your friends—they just don't have you over like they used to."

"Your social circle does change," agrees Kirkland. "Friends whose kids are in college don't understand when they phone and you have to put them on hold while you get Tommy a glass of water. Or they'll call you at 6 o'clock and invite you over, not realizing it's too late for you to get a sitter or that you're just too tired to make the effort. Soon the phone calls and the invitations stop."

Some grandparents are active in Girl or Boy Scouts, attend PTA meetings or do their part toward school events. "But they don't fit into that younger, more energetic group of parents who are confident they're going to change the world," says Kirkland. "They've already been there."

Though often it is widowed grandmothers who take in the children, there are many actively involved grandfathers. Frank Plante, for one, sees only opportunity in the situation. Says he: "It's like starting over again."

Other grandfathers, however, may feel neglected. Albert Johnson confesses to some resentment: "We'd just learned to play golf and were planning a trip to New England," he says."But it won't happen now. Maybe a little later—with the kids."

Few grandfathers attend support groups; when they do, it's usually out of curiosity.

"The burden of raising a child at this stage of life and also coping with the loss of an adult child—for whatever reason—often causes problems between couples who've spent most of their lives together," says de Toledo. "It's important that grandparents share the responsibility. But it's imperative they set aside time for themselves away from the grandchildren; a time to give to each other."

That can be hard. All agree they don't have the energy they once had.

In Wisconsin, Virginia Walker, a regular at From Generation to Generation sessions, has good reason to be tired. As nursing secretary at a Milwaukee hospital her shift doesn't end until 11:30 P.M., she usually doesn't get to sleep before 2 A.M., and less than five hours later she's laying out clothes for the eight-year-old grandson she's raising as a single grandparent.

"He stays with the babysitter weeknights and she brings him over before she leaves for work in the morning," Walker says. "He and I see each other mostly on weekends, when we go to the library or the movies or maybe the park."

Says Charlotte Ellison, who is up before 7 A.M. and usually still doing laundry late at night, "I don't know whether it's killing me or keeping me alive."

Then there's the financial drain. Some grandparents have adult children as well as grandchildren dependent on them. Some have had to stop working, since the cost of child care negates their earnings.

Ellison gave up her highly successful career as a commercial artist, and she and her husband were forced to dip into savings they'd planned to use for retirement. Johnnie Mae Short and her husband have no savings left. Says Short: "We eat a lot of spaghetti and meatloaf." Diane Warner lost her $42,000-a-year job while trying to help her daughter fight her drug addiction. "But then she'd take off with my car and leave the boy at home," Warner recalls. She and her grandson are on welfare: now she's afraid she'll lose her home, too. For those like Warner who have custody of their grandchildren, there's the extra burden of court costs.

Unlike foster parents, grandparents raising their natural grandchildren receive minimal federal or state support. Some may qualify for Aid to Families With Dependent Children, but this is not as comprehensive as foster-care benefits. Foster-care payments are higher, include a clothing allowance, and increase as the child grows older. However, not all states allow relatives to be eligible for the foster-care program; some argue that "grandparents already have adequate incentive to care for their grandchildren." Social Security assistance is limited, available only when natural or adoptive parents have died or are disabled.

Senator John Heinz* (R-Pennsylvania), ranking Republican on the Senate Special Committee on Aging, is studying the impact of the nation's drug epidemic on America's families, and in particular on older citizens. He is exploring legislation that would help grandparents who must intervene to protect their grandchildren. One possibility: That when working grandparents have legal custody of one or more grandchildren, employers be required to extend group health insur-

[*Senator John Heinz died in a plane crash, April 4, 1991.—Ed.]

ance coverage to those children. Heinz is also looking at the foster-care program with an eye toward creating a new assistance category to accommodate the special circumstances that exist when a grandparent assumes the role of parent.

Says Heinz: "I plan to examine this issue closely for the sake of grandparents who have put their lives on hold to parent a second family, and for the children—the hidden victims of drug abuse. We should reward grandparents for stepping in to care for a needy child. They deserve the same support and respect foster parents receive."

And if all that weren't enough, the grandparents worry about their grandchildren's social and academic well-being. Some of the kids are embarrassed by their situation, particularly by the age gap. Their peers may tease them, thus emphasizing the difference between their families and those of their friends.

Betty Parbs likes to tell other grandparents who are raising their grandchildren not to dwell on ages. "That'll kill you, right there," she maintains. But sometimes the youngsters are the first to point it out. When Parbs accompanied her granddaughter to a school carnival, the girl remarked brightly, "You're a *lot* older than the other mommies."

Schoolwork itself proves a challenge. "Quite a lot of these children are behind academically because they missed school while living with their parents," says de Toledo. "They have difficulty learning and require special programs. They may have a hard time concentrating because they're constantly worrying about their parents"—to whom they still feel a strong attachment regardless of how badly they were treated. They're reluctant to give up hope their parents will change and return to take care of them.

Unfortunately, this fantasy is often shared by grandparents, who become easy targets for emotional and financial exploitation by their adult children.

The relationship that develops between grandparents and grandchildren in these situations is unique, resulting in a dependency on the part of the child that can be quite touching.

Johnnie Mae Short had a heart attack five years ago. "My granddaughter worries about me," she reports. "At school she uses the excuse that she's sick so she can call home—to see how *I'm* doing."

"Kids worry, consciously or unconsciously, that they'll be abandoned again, this time by their grandparents," says de Toledo. "They feel insecure when the grandparent taking care of them becomes sick. They think: If this grandparent dies, who will take care of me? It's a scary thought for a youngster."

In these dramas, all the players who are old enough recognize the alternative is usually a foster home, and few consider that acceptable.

For the grandparents it's a labor of love, but all reach a point where they need time out for themselves. Paula Browne takes a painting class at a nearby college. Simmons plays bingo once a month. Johnnie Mae Short takes refuge in Nintendo video games. Patricia Westfall, who had seven grandchildren living with her at one time, used to get up at 4 A.M. to crochet "because it was the only time when I had peace and quiet."

"Take time out for such things as exercise," advises Peggy Plante of GAP in Massachusetts. "Go to the hairdresser's. It will make you more fun to be with. When you're good to yourself, you can be good to others."

"It's important to have someone to talk with who is in the same situation," says Kirkland. "Most of the time your own family will tell you it's not your responsibility. And it's devastating to take your kid to court and have him or her declared an unfit parent. That's when you really need another grandparent for support."

It's not hard to find support if you're prepared to take the initiative.

"When you go to your grandchild's school, watch to see who's accompanying the other kids," says Paula Browne. "You'll see some grandparents and you can strike up a conversation." Other grandparents suggest similar tactics in supermarkets, malls and buses.

"We won't be hard to spot," says Hudgins. "We all look stressed."

Yet with all the tribulations and heartbreak, re-parenting does have its rewards, says Browne: "These kids give you so much more love than your own kids because you've taken them out of the depths they've been in."

Hudgins says grandparents put more into their new role than they did the first time around. "I had my own child in my 20s," she says. "I'm older and wiser now."

"When I come into the room and get a big hug," says Johnnie Mae Short, "it makes up for a *lot*."

It's no picnic—but, as Ellison says earnestly, "We don't want to see our grandchildren turn out the way our kids did."

Perhaps these grandparents' feelings are best summed up by Short. "I'd rather have them," she says, "than worry about them."

Older Problem Drinkers—
Long-Term and Late-Life Onset Abusers:
What Triggers Their Drinking?

U. of South Fla. Treatment Program Focuses on Age-Related Problems

**Lawrence Schonfeld, Ph.D.
and Larry W. Dupree, Ph.D.**

Lawrence Schonfeld is Chair, and Larry W. Dupree is former Chair and currently a research faculty member, of the Department of Aging and Mental Health of the Florida Mental Health Institute at the University of South Florida in Tampa.

G rowing older exposes an individual to many forms of stress uncommon to younger individuals. While the majority of older people may be relatively healthy and living independently, others experience difficulties in coping with the changes associated with aging. One such indication may be excessive or problem drinking.

About 20 years ago, researchers began to investigate the problem of the elderly alcohol abuser. In the late 1960's and early 1970's, surveys and descriptive studies began to differentiate two major categories of older problem drinkers (Gaitz and Baer, 1971; Rosin and Glatt, 1971; Simon et al., 1968; Zimberg, 1974). The "Early Onset" elderly alcohol abuser was described as an aging alcoholic who has demonstrated significant alcohol-related problems for many years, often beginning abusive drinking by his or her 30's or 40's. This individual is often well known to the medical profession, social services, and the community. According to Zimberg (1984), early onset alcohol abusers have similar personality characteristics to younger alcoholics.

In contrast, the "Late-Life Onset" elderly alcohol abuser may begin abusing alcohol in his or her 50's or 60's. This person is often viewed as a reactive drinker, i.e., one whose problem began after the occurrence of such events as the death of a spouse, retirement, moving away from their original home or state, reduction in income, and impaired health. It is less likely that this individual will be seen as a public inebriate, and more likely that he or she will drink at home and alone.

Early investigations often produced estimates or projections related to the prevalence of the problem, a problem in itself since relatively few elderly utilize mental health or substance abuse treatment services. Previous estimates of elderly living in the community who abuse alcohol range from 2 to 15 percent.

Current literature often adds little to the implications for treatment and simply cites the early researchers in the field. Brody (1982) called for an end to simply repeating these original estimates and stressed the need for new investigations. In the last few years there has been increased interest in the study of the older alcohol abuser.

Problems with Screening

One problem that may cause the older drinker to be overlooked is that many of the instruments used to investigate potential alcohol or drug abuse have been based on younger populations, relying on indicators that may not be relevant for the older individual (Graham, 1986). Brief screening instruments often inquire about a potential alcohol abuser's problems at work, difficulties with the family or marriage, problems with the law (driving while intoxicated), or drinking in the morning.

However, for many of the older problem drinkers, these items would not apply. Despite age of onset (early or late-life) of the drinking problem, most elderly who have been admitted to our treatment programs drank at home, alone, and in response to depressive states. Few were employed, few were active drivers, and many were widowed or divorced, and socially isolated. Thus, there appears to be a need for items on screening assessments which relate to more later-life issues.

Even if we were able to accurately predict or identify alcohol-related problems through a screening instrument, few older individuals enter treatment for alcohol abuse. There are numerous reasons for this underutilization. Substance abuse treatment programs, especially those that are publicly funded, are inundated with young people who abuse illegal drugs. Private substance abuse treatment is expensive, especially for those on limited incomes, with limited insurance coverage.

In addition, we must consider the person's reluctance to enter treatment and difficulty in "navigating" through social services for the first time, as well as service providers' difficulty in identifying older problem drinkers. Dementia or other cognitive impairment may be identified as problems, when in fact alcohol abuse may be responsible for changes in mood, physical functioning, or cognition.

From 1979 to 1981, the Gerontology Alcohol Project (Dupree, Broskowski, and Schonfeld, 1984), admitted late-life

From *Aging*, No. 361, 1990, pp. 5-9. Reprinted by permission.

21

onset elderly alcohol abusers into a treatment program using cognitive/behavioral, skills building techniques within a Relapse Prevention framework (Marlatt and Gordon, 1980, 1985). Each individual was assessed for the events and emotional states that preceded the consumption of the *first* drink on a "typical" day of drinking, i.e., high-risk situations. In most cases, loneliness and depression preceded the first drink. Treatment often focused on rebuilding the social support network, self-management approaches for overcoming negative emotional states, and general problem solving.

Almost three quarters of the individuals who completed the program and a subsequent one-year follow-up maintained their drinking goals (in most cases abstinence). From this program, additional questions were raised, primarily: Would the program be as effective with early onset individuals? What differences would be observed between the two categories of elderly alcohol abusers? And, would there be a need for separate treatment modalities based on age of onset, just as there may be differences in treatment needs for young and elderly alcohol abusers?

A newer program, the Substance Abuse Program for the Elderly, began in 1986. This program is aimed at elderly alcohol abusers (regardless of age of onset) and individuals who abuse or misuse medications. Because of the program's wider admission criteria, comparisons of the antecedent conditions to recent drinking for early onset and late-life onset alcohol abusers were possible (Schonfeld, Dupree, and Merritt, 1987).

Schonfeld and Dupree (in press) compared the admission data from 23 early and 23 late-life onset alcohol abusers over age 60, matching pairs of individuals for age and sex. Results indicate that the early onset elderly alcohol abuser had significantly higher depression scores (Mean = 17.1) on the Beck Depression Inventory (Beck, 1972) than did their late-life counterparts (Mean = 6.6). Similarly, as indicated by life satisfaction scores (Neugarten, Havighurst, and Tobin, 1961) and trait anxiety scores (Patterson, O'Sullivan, and Spielberger,

1980), more severe psychological problems were present in the early onset group.

All 46 people had been asked to focus on their drinking in the 30 days before their last drink prior to admission. Both groups consumed alcoholic beverages on an average of about 22 of those 30 days. Both groups consumed substantial quantities on a "typical day" of drinking. Alcohol consumption was measured in terms of Standard Ethanol Content units or SECs. One SEC is the equivalent of one ounce of 100 proof liquor. On a typical day of drinking, the early onset group consumed 17.5 SECs and the late-life onset group consumed 12.4 SECs. Although the difference in quantity consumed was not statistically significant, frequency of intoxication was. The early onset group reported that they were intoxicated an average of 16 days out of the 30-day period as opposed to 8 days for the late-life onset group. Finally, the individuals in the early onset group were more likely to drop out of treatment (56 percent dropped out) than late-life onset individuals (only 26 percent dropped out).

Previous literature suggested similarities in personality between the early onset individual and young alcohol abusers (Zimberg, 1984). If this were true, perhaps they would use alcohol in a similar manner, i.e., in response to interpersonal problems, peer pressure, conflicts with spouse, etc., rather than depression or isolation. Because such findings would have implications for treatment, the determinants of drinking on a "typical day" of drinking for the early and late onset older alcohol abusers were investigated as derived from a structured interview (the GAP Drinking Profile; Dupree, et al., 1984).

What the interviews revealed were many similarities—not between early onset older drinkers and young drinkers—but between the early onset and late onset older drinkers. Most were steady (daily) drinkers, who drank at home and alone, and in response to such negative emotional states as sadness, loneliness, depression, and boredom. Many were widowed, divorced, and retired. Social support networks were minimal. If such similarities hold true for

elderly alcohol abusers as a general population, it may indicate that while the etiology and duration may differ, the antecedents to current drinking behavior are similar.

The similarity of current drinking behavior in the two groups of elderly individuals may be due to the age-related problems (increased losses, death of a loved one, retirement, etc.) predominating in their lives. A second possibility is that the two groups experience alcohol abuse and the diminution of social support through different avenues. The late-life onset individual may begin to abuse alcohol in response to the losses, whereas, the early onset individual may have caused some of the losses or alienation of family and friends by continued alcohol abuse over many years.

Age-Specific Treatment?

As indicated by our 1-year follow-up data, cognitive behavioral approaches seem to be effective with older individuals, but similar results have been found with younger treatment groups (Chaney, O'Leary, and Marlatt, 1978). Some have suggested, without supportive data, that we "mainstream" the older person with the younger individual, rather than develop age-specific programs (Brown, 1986). However, many of the treatment plans developed in our program through identification of each individual's personal antecedents to drinking were aimed at increasing socialization, decreasing negative self-statements, and improving self-esteem, rather than dealing with interpersonal conflicts and peer pressure. If we were to combine different age populations into group therapy, the older, less vocal and perhaps less self-disclosing individual might not have an opportunity to express his or her needs and learn skills for overcoming losses and coping with problems.

The issue of age-specific programs has been addressed in several studies. Janik and Dunham (1983), using data gathered by the National Institute on Alcohol Abuse and Alcoholism, indicated that elderly alcoholics were just as successful as younger individuals in treatment programs, implying that age-specific programs were unnecessary. However, this finding only indicates the relative effectiveness of treatment for the two age groups. To further investigate the potential benefits of specific programs, Atkinson, et al., (1985) and Kofoed, et al., (1984, 1987) compared elderly alcoholics who were entered into a mixed-age group treatment with a group of elderly subjects in age-specific treatment. They found that those in the age-specific group treatment remained in treatment longer and completed treatment more often.

Age-specific treatment has some advantages. The approach should promote more cohesiveness in group treatment. Whereas confrontational approaches have been used with younger populations, less confrontive and more supportive approaches would serve to focus on the needs of the older individual. The needs and issues of younger individuals often relate to peer pressure, interpersonal conflicts, work-related problems, marital difficulties, and parental responsibilities. For the older individual, drinking appears to be a reaction to losses. Treatment would emphasize rebuilding of the social support network (Dupree, et al., 1984; Zimberg, 1984) and coping with problems common to later life. For instance, group treatment could discuss adjustment to retirement, loss of income, widowhood, and coping skills to handle feelings of loneliness and boredom when finances and transportation are limited.

Few of the elderly we have treated were working, many were widowed or divorced, and lived at a considerable distance from their adult children. If the elderly were entered into mixed-age group treatment or support groups, the common denominator of discussion would most likely become the consumption of alcohol. The potential danger is that while abstinence might be stressed, the high-risk situations that led to alcohol abuse prior to treatment, if not attended to, would result in relapse after treatment. These high risk situations seem to be different for the elderly population.

The disadvantages for the specific programs for the elderly alcohol abuser are largely in terms of cost. The elderly as a population underutilize substance abuse services (Kola, Kosberg, and Joyce, 1984; Kosberg and McCarthy, 1985) making it difficult to justify the

cost of personnel, time, and money, when client census is low. Low utilization rates might be due to an inability of the "system" to identify alcohol problems; the reluctance of social service workers to label someone as an alcohol abuser; or to the amount of resources which need to be devoted to younger populations of substance abusers. Whatever the reason, given the low admission rate and the reality of budgets, specific programs for the elderly may be a low priority.

It would be repetitious with other researchers if we were to say the problem of elderly alcohol abuse needs further verification of its extent and treatment implications. The problem may continue to be overlooked due to the older problem drinker's lack of visibility. However, as the number and proportion of older people increases, alcohol abuse in the elderly is likely to become less hidden.

REFERENCES

Atkinson, R.M., Turner, J.A., Kofoed, L.L. and Tolson, R.L. (1985) Early versus late onset alcoholism in older persons: Preliminary findings. *Alcoholism*, 9, 513-515.

Beck, A.T. (1972) *Depression: Causes and treatment.* Philadelphia: University of Pennsylvania Press.

Brody, J.A. (1982) Aging and alcohol abuse. *Journal of the American Geriatric Society*, 30, 123-126.

Brown, N. (1986) Mainstreaming reduces elderly isolation. *Alcoholism and Addiction*, 7 (1), p. 41-42.

Chaney, E.F., O'Leary, M.R., and Marlatt, G.A. (1978) Skill training with alcoholics. *Journal of Consulting and Clinical Psychology*, 48, 305-316.

Dupree, L.W., Broskowski, H., and Schonfeld, L. (1984) The Gerontology Alcohol Project: A behavioral treatment program for elderly alcohol abusers. *The Gerontologist*, 24, 510-516.

Gaitz, C.M. and Baer, P.E. (1971) Characteristics of elderly patients with alcoholism. *Archives of General Psychiatry*, 24, 372-378.

Graham, K. (1986) Identifying and measuring alcohol abuse among the elderly: Serious problems with existing instrumentation. *Journal of Studies on Alcohol*, 47 (4), 322-326.

Janik, S.W. and Dunham, R.G. (1983) A nationwide examination of the need for specific alcoholism treatment programs for the elderly. *Journal of Studies on Alcohol*, 44, 307-317.

Kofoed, L., Tolson, R., Atkinson, R., Toth, R., & Turner, J. (1984) Elderly groups in alcoholism clinic. In R.M. Atkinson (Ed.) *Alcohol and drug abuse in old age.* Washington D.C: American Psychiatric Press, Monograph Series, 35-48.

Kofoed, L., Tolson, R., Atkinson, R., Toth, R., Turner, J. (1987) Treatment compliance of older alcoholics: An elder-specific approach is superior to "mainstreaming". *Journal of Studies on Alcohol*, 48 (1), 47-51.

Kola, L.A., Kosberg, J.I. and Joyce, K. (1984) Assessment of policies and practices of local programs for the aged toward the problem drinker, *The Gerontologist*, 24 (5), 517-521.

Kosberg, J.I. and McCarthy, E.J. (1985) Problem drinking participants in programs for the elderly: Programmatic considerations. *Journal of Applied Gerontology*, 4 (2), 20-29.

Marlatt, G.A. Gordon, J.R. (1980) Determinants of relapse: Implications for the maintenance of behavior change. In P.O. Davidson & E.O. Davidson (Eds.) *Behavior therapy assessment: Diagnosis, design, and evaluation.* N.Y.: Springer.

Marlatt, G.,A. & Gordon, J.R. (1985) *Relapse Prevention: Maintenance strategies in the treatment of addictive behaviors.* N.Y.: Guilford Press.

Neugarten, B., Havighurst, R., and Tobin, S. (1961) The measurement of life satisfaction. *Journal of Gerontology*, 16, 134-143.

Patterson, R.L., O'Sullivan, M.J., and Spielberger, C.O. (1980) Measurement of state trait anxiety in elderly mental health clients. *Journal of Behavioral Assessment*, 2, 89-97.

Rosin, A.J. and Glatt, M.M. (1971) Alcohol excess in the elderly. *Quarterly Journal of Studies on Alcohol*, 32, 53-59.

Schonfeld, L., Dupree, L.W., & Merritt, S. (1987) Alcohol abuse and the elderly: Comparison of early and late-life onset. Presented at the 95th Annual Convention of the American Psychological Association, New York.

Schonfeld, L. and Dupree, L.W. (in press) Determinants of drinking for early and late-life onset elderly alcohol abusers. *Journal of Studies on Alcohol*.

Simon, A., Epstein, L.J., and Reynolds, L. (1968) Alcoholism in the geriatric mentally ill. *Geriatrics*, 23, 125-131.

Zimberg, S. (1974) The elderly alcoholic. *The Gerontologist*, 14, 221-224.

Zimberg, S. (1984) Diagnosis and the management of the elderly alcoholic. In R.M. Atkinson (Ed.) *Alcohol and drug abuse in old age.* Washington D.C: American Psychiatric Press, Monograph Series, 23-34.

Racial and Ethnic Diversity

The racial and ethnic makeup of the United States is changing dramatically. Not only have conditions of racism changed since the 1960s, but percentages of types of peoples have shifted. For a long time the term "immigrants" applied to Americans whose families came from European lands. Today the new wave of immigration is coming from Latin America and Asia. Furthermore, racial and ethnic groups are moving up the social-class ladder, which makes for a society much in flux and different from only a generation ago.

The selections in this unit begin by addressing the population shifts, and then examine three basic social institutions: education, jobs, and government. Then the importance of labels in studying how people see themselves racially and ethnically is discussed.

"Beyond the Melting Pot" addresses shifts in ethnic makeup. Within a generation, white Americans will be a mathematical minority. The new "typical American" will trace ancestry not to Europe, but to Asia or Latin America. In New York City, this shift already exists among school children. The new multiracial society will pose interesting challenges. For example, the elderly will be mainly white, while the working class upon which the elderly will depend will be nonwhite.

"America the Multicultural" raises educational questions about the new multiethnic society. Whose history should schools teach? What values from the past should we hold up for our children to cherish? Changes in current society involve what we emphasize about our past. Will we honor all past cultures, or only some?

"A New Black Politics" calls for blacks to rethink their political traditions in light of racial changes in society. What constitutes an economically productive, socially pluralistic, and democratic urban community? Should new political ties be forged to support the people of cities—at the expense of old-time Democratic party politics? Even "black" itself must be redefined to include Asian and Latin American urban citizens.

"Immigration Reform" focuses on federal government policies toward immigrants. Deciding who is accepted into our society and who is rejected is indeed difficult. What should be our policy toward children of undocumented parents that are born on U.S. soil? Should families who have lived within the United States for years be forced to return to homelands they no longer recognize? Here is an article likely to challenge your thinking about how to act fairly in a social context.

"Japan's Influence on American Life" looks at the influence that 200,000 Japanese that have recently arrived in the United States are having on American culture. From stimulating the United States to change its schools, to management practices, the Japanese impact has already made important differences in American thinking.

" 'Return' of Native Americans Challenges Racial Definition" shows how an ethnic label can shift in popularity as a people increase self-identity and pride. Native Americans gained in the 1990 census mainly by responding positively to census takers. The implications are being felt by federal benefit programs and affirmative action, raising questions about how to update federal policies.

Looking Ahead: Challenge Questions

How will the shifts in ethnic percentages change the culture of U.S. society?

If our society increases its multicultural makeup, what approach should schools take when teaching history? Should schools attempt to teach about all cultures equally?

What changes should blacks make in traditional "black politics" to place more political power in the hands of urban people?

How should the federal government decide who can stay in the United States, who must leave, or who must never enter? Should the government seek to develop a multicultural society?

What positive cultural influences are the recent immigrants from Japan having on our society?

Why were so many Native Americans willing to register by that title in the recent federal census? What problems or challenges does this willingness to self-identify pose for government programs?

Unit 2

Beyond The Melting Pot

In the 21st century—and that's not far off—racial and ethnic groups in the U.S. will outnumber whites for the first time. The "browning of America" will alter everything in society, from politics and education to industry, values and culture

WILLIAM A. HENRY III

 Someday soon, surely much sooner than most people who filled out their Census forms last week realize, white Americans will become a minority group. Long before that day arrives, the presumption that the "typical" U.S. citizen is someone who traces his or her descent in a direct line to Europe will be part of the past. By the time these elementary students at Brentwood Science Magnet School in Brentwood, Calif., reach midlife, their diverse ethnic experience in the classroom will be echoed in neighborhoods and workplaces throughout the U.S.

Already 1 American in 4 defines himself or herself as Hispanic or nonwhite. If current trends in immigration and birth rates persist, the Hispanic population will have further increased an estimated 21%, the Asian presence about 22%, blacks almost 12% and whites a little more than 2% when the 20th century ends. By 2020, a date no further into the future than John F. Kennedy's election is in the past, the number of U.S. residents who are Hispanic or nonwhite will have more than doubled, to nearly 115 million, while the white population will not be increasing at all. By 2056, when someone born today will be 66 years old, the "average" U.S. resident, as defined by Census statistics, will trace his or her descent to Africa, Asia, the Hispanic world, the Pacific Islands, Arabia—almost anywhere but white Europe.

While there may remain towns or outposts where even a black family will be something of an oddity, where English and Irish and German surnames will predominate, where a traditional (some will wistfully say "real") America will still be seen on almost every street corner, they will be only the vestiges of an earlier nation. The former majority will learn, as a normal part of everyday life, the meaning of the Latin slogan engraved on U.S. coins—E PLURIBUS UNUM, one formed from many.

Among the younger populations that go to school and provide new entrants to the work force, the change will happen sooner. In some places an America beyond the melting pot has already arrived. In New York State some 40% of elementary- and secondary-school children belong to an ethnic minority. Within a decade, the proportion is expected to approach 50%. In California white pupils are already a minority. Hispanics (who, regardless of their complexion, generally distinguish themselves from both blacks and whites) account for 31.4% of public school enrollment, blacks add 8.9%, and Asians and others amount to 11%—for a nonwhite total of 51.3%. This finding is not only a reflection of white flight from desegregated public schools. Whites of all ages account for just 58% of California's population. In San Jose bearers of the Vietnamese surname Nguyen outnumber the Joneses in the telephone directory 14 columns to eight.

Nor is the change confined to the coasts. Some 12,000 Hmong refugees from Laos have settled in St. Paul. At some Atlanta low-rent apartment complexes that used to be virtually all black, social workers today need to speak Spanish. At the Sesame Hut restaurant in Houston, a Korean immigrant owner trains Hispanic immigrant workers to prepare Chinese-style food for a largely black clientele. The Detroit area has 200,000 people of Middle Eastern descent; some 1,500 small grocery and convenience stores in the vicinity are owned by a whole subculture of Chaldean Christians with roots in Iraq. "Once America was a microcosm of European nationalities," says Molefi Asante, chairman of the department of African-American studies at Temple University in Philadelphia. "Today America is a microcosm of the world."

History suggests that sustaining a truly multiracial society is difficult, or at least unusual. Only a handful of great powers of the distant past—Pharaonic Egypt and Imperial Rome, most notably—managed to maintain a distinct national identity while embracing, and being ruled by, an ethnic mélange. The most ethnically diverse contemporary power, the Soviet Union, is beset with secessionist demands and near tribal conflicts. But such comparisons are flawed, because those empires were launched by conquest and maintained through an aggressive military presence. The U.S. was created, and continues to be redefined, primarily by voluntary immigration. This process has been one of the country's great strengths, infusing it with talent and energy. The "browning of America" offers tremendous opportunity for capitalizing anew on the merits of many peoples from many lands. Yet this fundamental change in the ethnic makeup of the U.S. also poses risks. The American character is resilient and thrives on change. But past periods of rapid evolution have also, alas, brought out deeper, more fearful aspects of the national soul.

Politics: New and Shifting Alliances

A truly multiracial society will undoubtedly prove much harder to govern. Even seemingly race-free conflicts will be increasingly complicated by an overlay of ethnic tension. For example, the expected showdown in the early 21st century between the rising number of retirees and the dwindling number of workers who must be taxed to pay for the elders' Social Security benefits will probably be compounded by the fact that a large majority of recipients will be white, whereas a majority of workers paying for them will be nonwhite.

While prior generations of immigrants believed they had to learn English quickly to survive, many Hispanics now maintain that the Spanish language is inseparable from their ethnic and cultural identity, and seek to remain bilingual, if not primarily Spanish-speaking, for life. They see legislative drives to make English the sole official language, which have prevailed in some fashion in at least 16 states, as a political backlash. Says Arturo Vargas of the Mexican American Legal Defense and Educational Fund: "That's what English-only has been all about—a reaction to the growing population and influence of Hispanics. It's human nature to be uncomfortable with change. That's what the Census is all about, documenting changes and making sure the country keeps up."

Racial and ethnic conflict remains an ugly fact of American life everywhere, from working-class ghettos to college campuses, and those who do not raise their fists often raise their voices over affirmative action and other power sharing. When Florida Atlantic University, a state-funded institution under pressure to increase its low black enrollment, offered last month to give free tuition to every qualified black freshman who enrolled, the school was flooded with calls of complaint, some protesting that nothing was being done for "real" Americans. As the numbers of minorities increase, their demands for a share of the national bounty are bound to intensify, while whites are certain to feel ever more embattled. Businesses often feel whipsawed between immigration laws that punish them for hiring illegal aliens and anti-discrimination laws that penalize them for demanding excessive documentation from foreign-seeming job applicants. Even companies that consistently seek to do the right thing may be overwhelmed by the problems of diversifying a primarily white managerial corps fast enough to direct a work force that will be increasingly nonwhite and, potentially, resentful.

Nor will tensions be limited to the polar simplicity of white vs. nonwhite. For all Jesse Jackson's rallying cries about shared goals, minority groups often feel keenly competitive. Chicago's Hispanic leaders have leapfrogged between white and black factions, offering support wherever there seemed to be the most to gain for their own community. Says Dan Solis of the Hispanic-oriented United Neighborhood Organization: "If you're thinking power, you don't put your eggs in one basket."

Blacks, who feel they waited longest and endured most in the fight for equal opportunity, are uneasy about being supplanted by Hispanics or, in some areas, by Asians as the numerically largest and most influential minority—and even more, about being outstripped in wealth and status by these newer groups. Because Hispanics are so numerous and Asians such a fast-growing group, they have become the "hot" minorities, and blacks feel their needs are getting lower priority. As affirmative action has broadened to include other groups—and to benefit white women perhaps most of all—blacks perceive it as having waned in value for them.

The Classroom: Whose History Counts?

Political pressure has already brought about sweeping change in public school textbooks over the past couple of decades and has begun to affect the core humanities curriculum at such élite universities as Stanford. At stake at the college level is whether the traditional "canon" of Greek, Latin and West European humanities study should be expanded to reflect the cultures of Africa, Asia and other parts of the world. Many books treasured as classics by prior generations are now seen as tools of cultural imperialism. In the extreme form, this thinking rises to a value-deprived neutralism that views all cultures, regardless of the grandeur or paucity of their attainments, as essentially equal.

Even more troubling is a revisionist approach to history in which groups that have gained power in the present turn to remaking the past in the image of their desires. If 18th, 19th and earlier 20th century society should not have been so dominated by white Christian men of West European ancestry, they reason, then that past society should be reinvented as pluralist and democratic. Alternatively, the racism and sexism of the past are treated as inextricable from—and therefore irremediably tainting—traditional learning and values.

While debates over college curriculum get the most attention, professors generally can resist or subvert the most wrong-headed changes and students generally have mature enough judgment to sort out the arguments. Elementary- and secondary-school curriculums reach a far broader segment at a far more impressionable age, and political expediency more often wins over intellectual honesty. Exchanges have been vituperative in New York, where a state task force concluded that "African-Americans, Asian-Americans, Puerto Ricans and Native Americans have all been victims of an intellectual and educational oppression. . . . Negative characterizations, or the absence of positive references, have had a terribly damaging effect on the psyche of young people." In urging a revised syllabus, the task force argued, "Children from European culture will have a less arrogant perspective of being part of a group that has 'done it all.'" Many intellectuals are outraged. Political scientist Andrew Hacker of Queens College lambastes a task-force suggestion that children be taught how "Native Americans were here to welcome new settlers from Holland, Senegal, England, Indonesia, France, the Congo, Italy, China, Iberia." Asks Hacker: "Did the Indians really welcome all those groups? Were they at Ellis Island when the Italians started to arrive? This is not history but a myth intended to bolster the self-esteem of certain children and, just possibly, a platform for advocates of various ethnic interests."

Values: Something in Common

Economic and political issues, however much emotion they arouse, are fundamentally open to practical solution. The deeper significance of America's becoming a majority nonwhite society is what it means to the national psyche, to individuals' sense of themselves and their nation—their idea of what it is to be American. People of color have often felt that whites treated equality as a benevolence granted to minorities rather than as an inherent natural right. Surely that condescension will wither.

Rather than accepting U.S. history and its meaning as settled, citizens will feel ever more free to debate where the nation's successes sprang from and what its unalterable beliefs are. They will clash over which myths and icons to invoke in education, in popular culture, in ceremonial speechmaking from political campaigns to the State of the Union address. Which is the more admirable heroism: the courageous holdout by a few conquest-minded whites over Hispanics at the Alamo, or the anonymous expression of hope by millions who filed through Ellis Island? Was the subduing of the West a daring feat of bravery and ingenuity, or a wretched example of white

imperialism? Symbols deeply meaningful to one group can be a matter of indifference to another. Says University of Wisconsin chancellor Donna Shalala: "My grandparents came from Lebanon. I don't identify with the Pilgrims on a personal level." Christopher Jencks, professor of sociology at Northwestern, asks, "Is anything more basic about turkeys and Pilgrims than about Martin Luther King and Selma? To me, it's six of one and half a dozen of the other, if children understand what it's like to be a dissident minority. Because the civil rights struggle is closer chronologically, it's likelier to be taught by someone who really cares."

Traditionalists increasingly distinguish between a "multiracial" society, which they say would be fine, and a "multicultural" society, which they deplore. They argue that every society needs a universally accepted set of values and that new arrivals should therefore be pressured to conform to the mentality on which U.S. prosperity and freedom were built. Says Allan Bloom, author of the best-selling *The Closing of the American Mind:* "Obviously, the future of America can't be sustained if people keep only to their own ways and remain perpetual outsiders. The society has got to turn them into Americans. There are natural fears that today's immigrants may be too much of a cultural stretch for a nation based on Western values."

The counterargument, made by such scholars as historian Thomas Bender of New York University, is that if the center cannot hold, then one must redefine the center. It should be, he says, "the ever changing outcome of a continuing contest among social groups and ideas for the power to define public culture." Besides, he adds, many immigrants arrive committed to U.S. values; that is part of what attracted them. Says Julian Simon, professor of business administration at the University of Maryland: "The life and institutions here shape immigrants and not vice versa. This business about immigrants changing our institutions and our basic ways of life is hogwash. It's nativist scare talk."

Citizenship: Forging a New Identity

Historians note that Americans have felt before that their historical culture was being overwhelmed by immigrants, but conflicts between earlier-arriving English, Germans and Irish and later-arriving Italians and Jews did not have the obvious and enduring ele-

ment of racial skin color. And there was never a time when the nonmainstream elements could claim, through sheer numbers, the potential to unite and exert political dominance. Says Bender: "The real question is whether or not our notion of diversity can successfully negotiate the color line."

For whites, especially those who trace their ancestry back to the early years of the Republic, the American heritage is a source of pride. For people of color, it is more likely to evoke anger and sometimes shame. The place where hope is shared is in the future. Demographer Ben Wattenberg, formerly perceived as a resister to social change, says, "There's a nice chance that the American myth in the 1990s and beyond is going to ratchet another step toward this idea that we are the universal nation. That rings the bell of manifest destiny. We're a people with a mission and a sense of purpose, and we believe we have something to offer the world."

Not every erstwhile alarmist can bring himself to such optimism. Says Norman Podhoretz, editor of *Commentary:* "A lot of people are trying to undermine the foundations of the American experience and are pushing toward a more Balkanized society. I think that would be a disaster, not only because it would destroy a precious social inheritance but also because it would lead to enormous unrest, even violence."

While know-nothingism is generally confined to the more dismal corners of the American psyche, it seems all too predictable that during the next decades many more mainstream white Americans will begin to speak openly about the nation they feel they are losing. There are not, after all, many nonwhite faces depicted in Norman Rockwell's paintings. White Americans are accustomed to thinking of themselves as the very picture of their nation. Inspiring as it may be to the rest of the world, significant as it may be to the U.S. role in global politics, world trade and the pursuit of peace, becoming a conspicuously multiracial society is bound to be a somewhat bumpy experience for many ordinary citizens. For older Americans, raised in a world where the numbers of whites were greater and the visibility of nonwhites was carefully restrained, the new world will seem ever stranger. But as the children at Brentwood Science Magnet School, and their counterparts in classrooms across the nation, are coming to realize, the new world is here. It is now. And it is irreversibly the America to come.

— Reported by Naushad S. Mehta/New York, Sylvester Monroe/Los Angeles and Don Winbush/Atlanta

AMERICA THE MULTICULTURAL

ROBERT J. COTTROL

Robert J. Cottrol is a specialist in American legal history and an associate professor of law at Rutgers School of Law in Camden, New Jersey. He is the author of The Afro-Yankees: Providence's Black Community in the Antebellum Era *and many articles about race and law in the United States. This article is drawn from a speech he delivered at the AFT conference, "Building Alliances for Youth at Risk."*

I GREW UP in the fifties, in an era when public schools, with few exceptions, presented a picture of the world that was relentlessly monocultural and, I might add, monochromatic. World history classes presented us with an impressive array of European heroes and villains, King John I (who I confess made a greater impression on me as the villain of numerous Robin Hood movies than as the grantor of the Magna Carta), Charlemagne, Columbus, Louis XIV, Napoleon, Kaiser Wilhelm, Adolf Hitler, Winston Churchill, and the list goes on. Rarely did the standard world history class examine the lives of the great figures from Africa, Asia, Latin America, or the indigenous populations of the Americas. Likewise, in American history class it was possible to go through the school year learning about Washington, Jefferson, Adams, Lincoln, Roosevelt, Wilson and other great men of U.S. history, with only a pause, in February, during what was then called "Negro History Week," to spend a brief moment on George Washington Carver and his experiments on the peanut.

So my views on multicultural education are informed, in part, by childhood memories. But my views also have been informed by my adult experiences. I have spent my adult life studying the role of race in American legal and social history. This study has left me with an appreciation for the diversity of American culture and for America's opportunity to contribute further to global civilization.

LET ME first say what multicultural education is not, or at least should not attempt to be. It should not simply be a program designed for minority students. There is a temptation to believe that multicultural education can somehow provide a quick fix for the ills that plague inner-city education. If only we teach inner-city students about the African Kingdom of Mali in the Middle Ages instead of dwelling on Medieval England, if we present less Abraham Lincoln and more Frederick Douglass, if we offer more of the writings of Malcolm X and less discussion of the Eisenhower administration, then students who previously had been turned off by school will suddenly become scholars, enthusiastic and interested in their school work. Would that this were so! We then could easily switch to a more Afro-centric or Hispano-centric or Asia-centric curriculum, confident that a change in subject matter would produce diligent, enthusiastic students. The increase in language and analytical skills alone that would result from their new studiousness would more than justify any subject matter deficiencies such a curriculum might produce. These could be corrected later.

Unhappily, multicultural education has only a marginal ability to bring about such a transformation. The students most at risk—those from decaying inner city neighborhoods, those from broken families, those who join gangs in fear of their lives, those who are the heirs of a culture of despair that has developed in all too many of our ghettoes in the last generation—will not be inspired nor have their lives radically changed by the addition of a multicultural dimension to their educations, however much we might hope so. The addition of black, or Hispanic, or Asian, or Indian heroes and role models might inspire a few such students, but multicultural education cannot be seen as a remedy for society's neglect of its cities, the poor people that dwell in them, and the urban schools that will shape the next generation of Americans.

Reprinted with permission from the Winter 1990 issue of the *American Educator,* the quarterly journal of the American Federation of Teachers.

2. RACIAL AND ETHNIC DIVERSITY

Nor should multicultural education be the occasion for building up false ethnic pride or for substituting myths about people of African, Asian, or Latin American descent for myths concerning people of European descent. Multicultural education should not be an excuse for replacing the myth of "America the Perfect" with "America the Reprobate." In an honest, serious multicultural education, one in which students encounter the rich diversity of the American heritage, our students should learn about the greatness of Thomas Jefferson's ideas *and* that, as a slaveholder, he betrayed America's ideals. Our students should learn about the great achievement that was the opening of the American West *and* about the tremendous price America's indigenous populations paid in the process.

The fact is that American history—like any history—offers no simple, pure truths. Our history is neither great nor terrible, but a complicated mix of both, with good growing from evil, and evil growing from good. It is this complexity that makes history interesting and challenging. We shouldn't deny students of any color the richness of this American dilemma.

THE TEACHING of history is probably the most important part of multicultural education because it is the major means by which the culture, values, and legacy of our civilization are passed from one generation to the next. American history, like history generally, tells us the ways in which our civilization is unique, and yet, properly taught, it reminds us of our kinship with others who share the human experience.

Every student who passes through our school system needs to be made aware that the cultures of peoples from every corner of the earth have made significant contributions to the American experience. This means teachers must bring some of the newer historical scholarship into the classroom. At one time those who wrote about and taught history believed their mission was to relate the stories of the great men and public events of each age and to ignore the day-to-day lives of ordinary people. We would learn about George Washington but little about the lives and motivations of the farmers, shopkeepers, and artisans who served with him in the Continental Army. Or we would learn about the Lincoln-Douglas debates but little about the agonies of the slaves who were at the heart of those debates. We learned about the building of the transcontinental railroad but nothing about the day-to-day living conditions of Irish and Chinese laborers who carved that railroad out of the American wilderness.

> *At every point in our nation's history, American culture has been transformed, and our democratic ideals tested and strengthened, by America's black, brown, red, and yellow citizens.*

Much recent scholarship—by focusing more on the lives and contributions of minorities; on the political and social lives of ordinary Americans; and by exploiting such historical sources as census data, court records, and voting statistics—has given us a more complete picture of the American past. It is important that this new, more historically accurate picture be painted for our students as early in their education as possible. The incorporation of that scholarship will tell us and our students much concerning the civilization that we Americans of all colors have built on the North American continent.

Our civilization began with an English base. We need not deny nor underplay this fact even when we are teaching children of African, Latin American, Asian, American Indian, and I might add, Eastern and Southern European descent. Our notions of law and politics, of constitutionalism in the broadest sense of that term, are English in origin. It was in England that modern concepts of limited, representative government, due process in criminal trials, the rights to organize politically and challenge the government through orderly political processes took their modern form. These ideas have captured the imagination of the world; they have been adopted as ideals and, increasingly, as practices by people of every race. The great Latin American liberator Simon Bolivar took American ideas of constitutionalism and incorporated them into the fundamental charters of a number of South American countries. He went the American Constitution one step better by, in many cases, abolishing slavery immediately upon attainment of independence. And these constitutional ideals have been spread by Americans of every race. Japanese-Americans helped draft Japan's postwar democratic constitution. The great African-American lawyer and jurist Justice Thurgood Marshall helped draft Kenya's first constitution as an independent nation.

The spread of Anglo-American constitutionalism has been a multiracial enterprise as was the creation of English as a universal language. The English language was spread by British colonial administrators and by Americans of every description, by Jewish-American tourists, by Polish-American students studying in foreign universities, by Hispanic Peace Corps volunteers, by the Negro and Nisei GIs who played a large part in liberating Italy and France during World War II.

BUT THE story of America is not just about how Anglo-American ideas were spread by a multicultural citizenry. At every point in our nation's history, American culture has been transformed, and our democratic ideals tested and strengthened, by America's black, brown, red, and yellow citizens. This is a story all students need to know. We should tell students about anthropological historian Peter Wood, whose work on eighteenth-century South Carolina, *Black Majority,* shows us that much of the American cowboy culture had West African origins. Our students should know that at the time of the Constitution's formation that the issues of slavery and black citizenship were hotly debated, and they should know that black people were not passive bystanders in that debate. The odyssey of early Amer-

30

ican freedom is not complete unless students learn of Paul Cuffee's successful struggle to attain black suffrage in eighteenth-century Massachusetts or that Richard Allen established an independent black church in eighteenth-century Philadelphia because he and his congregation refused to participate in a segregated church. A student who walks away from an American history class unaware that the nineteenth-century war between the United States and the Seminole nation of Florida occurred because Seminole chief Osceola regarded the fugitive slaves who lived among the Seminole as an integral part of the Seminole nation and refused to return them to their former masters has missed an important chapter in the history of the struggle for freedom in this country. Nor should we neglect to tell our students that the Texas War for Independence (the war in which the battle of the Alamo was fought) occurred, in part, because Mexico had abolished slavery and refused to allow American settlers in Texas to maintain slaves.

The struggles to end segregation and slavery and to build a more just society in their aftermath, provide the most vivid examples of how a multicultural population changed this country and helped enlarge the definition of freedom here, and indeed around the world. An Afro-American culture was formed in slavery, a culture different from the West African culture from which its people were descended—a fact we should never lose sight of, for if we do, we run the risk of asking black students to substitute an ersatz African culture for the rich African-American culture that is theirs. The Afro-American culture formed in slavery was an American culture and one that influenced not only black Americans but white ones as well. Who can look at American music, storytelling, and cooking without seeing this Afro-American culture? Who can look at southern white Protestantism and its fervent religiosity and deny the Afro-American influence?

But the impact of black people on the story of American freedom is broader and deeper than these examples. No student should leave our schools without having encountered the life of Frederick Douglass, preferably in one of his magnificent autobiographies. Douglass, one of nineteenth-century America's great statesmen and men of letters overcame handicaps even greater than those of his legendary friend Abraham Lincoln. Born a slave, he had a bootlegged education as a child, clandestinely taught to read and write by his master's wife. He escaped and had an incredible career as an abolitionist, journalist, and statesman. His concern for human freedom extended far beyond the precincts of slavery and race. He was an early advocate of women's suffrage and the betterment of working class whites. While still a fugitive, he stayed in England for a time. Notwithstanding his gratitude to his English hosts and his appreciation for their support of the American abolitionist cause, he did not hesitate to criticize England's treatment of Ireland and to befriend the Irish statesman Daniel O'Connell. During the Civil War, Douglass played a courageous role in persuading Lincoln to move beyond simple unionism to embrace the antislavery cause. No American student can truly be said to have had a complete education without studying the life of this remarkable man.

But there are others who must be studied. The slaves and free black men who rallied to the American cause and served with the Union forces during the Civil War helped write a new chapter in American constitutionalism. Students should become familiar with these lives, and I would heartily recommend the movie *Glory* as one way to discover that chapter in American history. We need to teach our students about former slaves who in the aftermath of Appomattox worked to unite and rebuild the many families that had been separated during slavery. We must tell our students about how much freed men valued education. Whole families would till the soil for twelve or fourteen hours a day and then go to school because they believed that education would bring about a better life for their children. We also need to tell our students that the dashing of those hopes led to the frustration that is at the root of many of today's urban problems. Our students also need to be taught that one of the most important cases establishing the principle of equal treatment under law came when a Chinese immigrant named Yick Wo insisted on an equal right to run his small business—a laundry.

Students studying twentieth-century America need to learn of A. Philip Randolph's struggle to bring dignity and economic justice to black workers. We must tell them about Walter White's attempts to stop lynchings, of Judge William Hastie's efforts to bring a measure of justice to the Jim Crow army of World War II, and of the incredible heroism of the Japanese-Americans of the 442nd regiment in that war and how they and black troops, two groups singled out for second-class military and civilian citizenship, helped to liberate Dachau. Students' knowledge of America will be enriched immeasurably by studying the lives of Americans of all races who were active in the civil rights movement. Children cannot appreciate the richness and poverty of the twentieth-century American experience without examining the world through the eyes of labor leader Cesar Chavez, or walking down the mean streets of East Harlem with Piri Thomas.

These too are part of the American story. They are the legacy of all Americans as much as are our more familiar memories of Washington and Lincoln. These stories should not be put to one side, reserved for students of some races but not others or marginalized as sidebars to American history. This *is* American history.

WE ARE coming to the end of a remarkable, and in many ways terrible, century. In this period, we have seen extraordinary technological progress, moving testimony to the human capacity for the acquisition and application of knowledge. But we have also seen another, darker side of human character. We have seen the rise of totalitarian forces made more potent and more terrible by that same technological progress. I do not know how the history of the world in the twentieth-century will be written in the future. I suspect that future historians will note that the United States played an admirable, indeed leading, role in vanquishing those totalitarian forces—Imperial Germany in the first World

2. RACIAL AND ETHNIC DIVERSITY

War, Nazism, Fascism, and Japanese militarism in the Second, and more recently Communism, in what was once termed by John Kennedy the long twilight struggle of the Cold War. Our record in this regard has by no means been perfect. There were compromises between our ideals and our policies. We have, for example, been slow to anger over the tyrannies that rule in China, and South Africa, in Uganda and Iraq. But still the American people—through great expenditure of resources, including our most valuable resource, the lives of the nation's sons and daughters—have not only done much to vanquish tyranny but much to advance the cause of freedom as well. Ours is a remarkable record for a nation that was not counted among the great powers at the beginning of this century.

But there is another great contribution we can make to the world. At the beginning of this century, W. E. B. Du Bois said that the problem of the twentieth-century would be the color line. How prophetic he was. With slight modification, we can see that the problem for the next century remains the same. The problems of ethnic strife and multiculturalism plague nations around the globe. We need not look beyond our northern neighbor, Canada, to see language and ethnicity dividing a peaceful and prosperous country. Our former adversary, the Soviet Union, now faces ethnic conflict that may engulf the country in a civil war that could threaten the entire world. Eastern Europe's difficult road to democracy is made more so by the release of long pent-up ethnic hatreds. Western Europeans who once looked with amazement and scorn at American racial problems have suddenly become very quiet on the subject in the face of large-scale immigration from Asia and Africa. The nations of Africa are divided by tribalism. The problem of South African racism and tribalism still mocks universally held values. Japan has scarcely begun to address the question of justice for Koreans and other ethnic minorities. Irish Protestants and Catholics still quarrel over issues that had their origins during the reigns of Tudor and Stuart monarchs.

For all its faults and for all the faults that a multi-cultural education will uncover and report, the United States remains the most successful multi-ethnic and multiracial society of our time, perhaps of all time. This too is the American story. And so we return to the real teaching challenge: telling the very complicated story of American history to students—complicated because it includes so much that is terrible and so much that is remarkable. It is a history of contradiction and dilemmas. Ultimately, we should judge the quality and success of our multicultural education programs not strictly according to how many individuals of color are noted—such an approach could easily lead just to more sidebars, which is not the point. In judging a particular multicultural education effort, we should ask whether it tells the story of how American culture was shaped and transformed by a multicultural population. And we should ask whether it helps our students come to grips with the contradictions at the core of our history.

Moreover, multicultural education should include, as part of its fundamental *corpus*, the teaching of the democratic ideas—tolerance, justice, rule by law, individual rights, majority rule, and more—that have made possible our incredibly diverse, prosperous and—relatively speaking—amicable society.

Perhaps our most important contribution to the twenty-first century will be to demonstrate that people from different races, cultures, and ethnic backgrounds can live side by side; retain their uniqueness; and, yet, over time form a new common culture. That has been the American story. It is a history that has much to tell the world. It must be told by American educators.

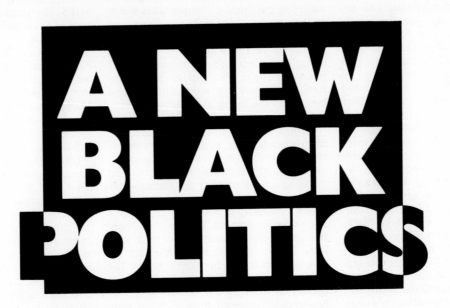

A NEW BLACK POLITICS

'We must rethink the concept of blackness itself'

W e have reached the end of a long, historical phase of the black political experience in America. Well-worn political assumptions no longer are effective or meaningful. Even Jesse Jackson's unprecedented electoral mobilizations of 1984 and 1988 seem slightly anachronistic when compared to the elections of Douglas Wilder as governor of Virginia and David Dinkins as mayor of New York City. There is an awareness that the system of institutional racism has changed in the past two decades, but civil-rights leaders have failed to alter their general strategy or tactics.

MANNING MARABLE

Manning Marable, professor of political science and sociology at the University of Colorado, Boulder, is the author of many books. His most recent is a political biography of Malcolm X, to be published in 1991, and he is now at work on a major study of black political thought in the Twentieth Century.

The black movement's disarray and apparent fragmentation stem from the convergence of three great crises which it has failed to address comprehensively—the crisis of ideology, the crisis of politics, and the crisis of consciousness or historical imagination.

These three great crises have not been addressed by black politicians, civil-rights officials, and other leaders of black society because this elite is a prisoner of its own historical successes. Its finest triumph, the dismantling of the system of legal segregation and the selective integration of minorities into the political mainstream of American society, has proved to be its last hurrah on the national stage.

In the aftermath of his great civil-rights achievements, and in the midst of his opposition to the Vietnam war, Martin Luther King Jr. tried to challenge his followers to move beyond their traditional civil-rights agenda.

"Where do we go from here?" King asked. None of his lieutenants, not even Jesse Jackson, was willing to go where he was prepared to take the movement. A quarter of a century later, we must answer King's question with new strategies and programs. But we cannot use old theoretical tools to build a new movement.

The first and most important measure we must take to restructure and resurrect a viable black protest movement is to forge a new synthesis of an old feud.

The organizational structures of black protest movements from abolitionism to the present have been based on two fundamental racial ideologies that guided nearly all strategies and tactics: integration and black nationalism.

Racial integrationists, beginning with Frederick Douglass and culminating with King, have consistently advocated the elimination of all restrictions that kept blacks from participating fully in the mainstream of society. They perceived racial designations of any type as a stigma and hoped for the ultimate elimination of the ghetto. Their primary strategic weapons were legal challenges in the courts and activism in the political system to elect politicians favorable to liberal goals. Integrationists consequently emphasized the construction of multiclass political coalitions and, after the New Deal, promoted a strategic long-term alliance with the Democratic Party. Culturally, they wanted to believe in the myth of the melting pot. They perceived themselves first as Americans and only secondarily as members of a discriminated-against racial minority.

There were important differences of opinion within the ranks, but they all could agree that a color-blind society was their immediate goal.

Confronting the integrationists were their ideological rivals, the black nationalists, who bitterly rejected integration as a political and cultural hoax designed to deepen the levels of exploitation and economic oppression. They were suspicious of alliances with whites and preferred the development of political linkages to nationalists in Africa and the Caribbean. They advocated black community-controlled schools and viewed busing for school integration as a liberal racist plot to fragment their neighborhoods.

The black nationalists' most important difference with the integrationists was over economics. The nationalists were unpersuaded that desegregation of the business establishment and trade-union movement would actually translate into black economic empowerment. Instead, they favored the use of legal segregation as a catalyst for the mobilization of land, labor, and capital. Black-owned insurance companies would sell policies to blacks; black-owned farms would provide fresh produce to black-owned inner-city grocery stores for black consumers. The insight that segregation could provide the basis for the growth of a black entrepreneurial elite was the heart of Booker T. Washington's strategy of early Twentieth Century black capitalism and Marcus Garvey's Universal Negro Improvement Association. Today, it is the central economic plank of the nationalist platform of Louis Farrakhan.

Despite their differences, a subterranean unity existed between both ideological paradigms. Both essentially followed a race-based strategy for societal change. The integrationists used race as a means of organizing liberal constituencies toward the goal of abolishing race; the nationalists used race as a technique for building group solidarity. Both sides, for different reasons, minimized the growing class divisions among blacks.

Only one major figure in black political history, W.E.B. Du Bois, tried to bridge the chasm of racial ideologies. His approach was a search for synthesis; he sensed correctly that a dialectical approach for black activism must include two components: the nationalists' reaffirmation of black identity, culture, and values, and the integrationists' demand for full rights within a democratic political system. But Du Bois's approach was never accepted or fully understood.

Now, however, we must refocus. Instead of emphasizing electoral politics above all other activities or pursuing purely separatist objectives, we must turn to the practical problems experienced by the majority of African-American people in the central cities.

The basic question for the early Twenty-first Century must be: What constitutes an economically productive, socially pluralistic, and democratic urban community?

I am not suggesting a hasty updating of Saul Alinsky's community-organizing strategy. The current socioeconomic crisis

experienced by millions of Hispanics, African-Americans, and working-class whites in our cities no longer takes shape in the context of old-style Jim Crow segregation. Nor do the basic conflicts occur primarily in the workplace, although struggles against job discrimination remain important. The greatest manifestations of oppression now occur in what can be termed the living place, or the urban, postindustrial community.

Struggles over housing, health care, day care, schools, jobs, and public transportation all revolve around this question of the future of the postindustrial city. The urban and working poor are second-class citizens, denied access to a quality of life which a minority of white, affluent Americans take for granted. Both political parties ignore their demands, and their material conditions continue to deteriorate.

According to the Economic Policy Institute, the share of the nation's wealth owned by the highest one-tenth of all households increased from 67.5 per cent in 1979 to 73.1 per cent in 1988. The percentage of all after-tax income earned by the richest one-tenth of all American families increased from 29.5 per cent in 1980 to almost 35 per cent today. Conversely, the Business-Higher Education Forum reported in June that the median wealth of black households is only 9 per cent of that of white households. Even with the increase in the minimum wage legislated earlier this year, the inflation-adjusted buying power for those earning minimum wage has declined by one-fourth since 1981. In the absence of significant change, the deterioration of black communities and family life will continue.

A new community-based agenda will require detailed social-science research on the particular problems of dozens of cities, particularly the medium-sized ones—those that used to be manufacturing and industrial towns with significant minority populations.

Advances in progressive urban planning and policy must be based on empirical research, not rhetoric. One outstanding model for future work comes from the Center for Applied Public Affairs Studies at the State University of New York at Buffalo. Directed by Henry Louis Taylor Jr., its recent comprehensive study of the changing socioeconomic status of Buffalo's African-American community provides the foundation for a series of innovative economic, social, and educational proposals for progressive activity.

This refocus on practical problems is, once again, the first and foremost measure we must take.

Second, we must discard the idea that electoral activity is the only form of politics, or even that it is the most

important arena for political conflict. And we must discard the theory that the Democratic Party can be "humanized," or "reformed from within," or transformed into a labor party.

The leftist version of the Democratic Party's realignment finds its origins in both Stalinism and unorthodox Trotskyism. The strategy was echoed by the late Michael Harrington, Bayard Rustin, and many leftists who worked hard for Jesse Jackson in 1984 and 1988.

But it won't work.

Understanding the collapse of the old liberal coalition of minorities, organized labor, and the Democratic Party is critically important to understanding the new political environment—the period since the demise of "black power." Race was transformed into more complex structures of domination, and the influence or leverage on public policy of such integrationists as the NAACP was greatly reduced.

As the majority of America's white electorate shifted from the cities to the suburbs, becoming better educated and reflecting entrepreneurial values, the social base for New Deal liberalism declined. The AFL-CIO's influence on national Democratic Party politics fell sharply. Traditionally liberal constituencies divided with blacks over a broad range of issues—Jewish-Americans, for example, over affirmative action, Israeli connections with South Africa, and Jesse Jackson. As the white electorate became more conservative and elitist, candidates for public office increasingly reflected these trends. The relative political and social weight of both national parties declined, as candidates became more independent of partisan affiliations.

Over time, a rough division of labor developed between the Republicans and the Democrats. The Republicans projected themselves as the party of "national management," capable of running the Executive Branch and making decisions in foreign policy. White upper-middle-class Americans consistently favor Republicans to reduce taxes on income and capital gains, expand opportunities for capital, and push back demands by minorities, workers, and the poor for redistribution of income.

The Democrats are now perceived as the party of "parochial interests," the politicians who are best at defending the local interests of various constituencies. Because Democrats still control most state legislatures, they have managed to gerrymander many Congressional districts to maximize their ability to compete electorally. Then, with the advantages of incumbency, most Democrats are able to win handily. The re-election rate in the House of Representatives was 98 per cent in 1986 and 1988.

In effect, we have been experiencing a coalition government of "national unity," a marriage operating more from consensus than from competition. Both national parties now have a vested interest in maintaining this electoral partnership, which is the principal reason the Democrats have ceased to function as a loyal opposition in anything but name.

Many Democrats recognize that they could probably win the Presidency by the route advocated by Jesse Jackson—expanding the electoral base to include millions of nonvoting blacks, Hispanics, poor, and working-class voters, and advancing an American version of leftist social democracy, attacking the power of corporations. This would force the Democrats into a truly antagonistic relationship with the Republican Party and with virtually all elites in corporate America.

It would also require the organizational restructuring of the party, an idea that party bureaucrats everywhere find abominable. Democratic Party leaders would rather lose a Presidential election, and cooperate with George Bush and Robert Dole in coordinating national policies, than permit the ranks of the poor and powerless, minorities and liberal feminists, to assume authority within their party.

The ideological transformation of the party system is largely responsible for the small but growing cohort of "post-black politicians"—elected officials, recruited largely from the professional classes, who are racially and ethnically "black" but who favor programs with little kinship to the traditional agendas of the civil-rights movement. One prominent example is Virginia Governor Douglas Wilder, who is already being touted as a possible candidate for Vice President in 1992 or 1996. Yet another likely post-black candidate is Philadelphia Congressman William Gray.

Post-black political candidates generally favor the death penalty, oppose new taxes, and support corporate interests. They are presented to working-class and poor blacks as their symbolic victories, direct proof that racism has declined in significance. Their election can be viewed as a psychological triumph for African-Americans, but they represent no qualitative resolution to the crises of black poverty, educational inequality, crime, and unemployment.

Conversely, another group of black politicians has also emerged lately, largely based in the ghetto. They opportunistically manipulate racial symbols and language to enlist constituencies among the poorest blacks. These charlatans rely on the old nationalist rhetoric of racial solidarity, but lack any progressive content because they are detached from any social protest movement for empowerment or resistance. A few examples are Washington Mayor Marion Barry, Chicago Congressman Gus Savage, and Atlantic City Mayor James Usry.

In the past decade, many of Barry's chief advisers have been indicted, convicted, imprisoned, or forced to resign because of various improprieties. Barry himself is on trial for use of crack cocaine. Yet for months, he held the city hostage to his own blind ambition, rallying his supporters by emotional appeals to racial unity. His public antics have reversed and set back the progressive campaign for District of Columbia statehood for the next twenty years.

Long known as the least effective member of the Congressional Black Caucus, Savage used anti-Semitic smears against a black challenger in the recent primary, deriding his opponent for accepting campaign contributions from Jews.

Particularly shameful was the rhetoric of Usry, the Republican incumbent who had been endorsed by New Jersey Governor Thomas H. Kean in 1986. Challenged by city councilman Jim Whelan, a white Democrat with significant support among blacks, Usry resorted to crude racial slogans to polarize Atlantic City's electorate. His campaign literature exhorted African-Americans to vote for him because of "the color of my skin" and because the Lord wanted him to "make life better for you—my people." Usry won the endorsement of the Nation of Islam's local representative and the backing of activist Dick Gregory, who asserted that whites had "rigged" voting machines to steal the election.

The opportunism and poverty of so many black elected officials are rooted in the bankruptcy of black political ideas and electoral organization. Most poor and working-class blacks sense this, which explains the recent popularity of those who advocate extreme, militant solutions.

In Milwaukee last February, alderman Michael McGee threatened to create an armed militia of street-gang members, trained for urban race war, unless the city government funneled $100 million for job programs into the ghetto. McGee was widely denounced as "irresponsible" by more moderate blacks. Yet even the head of the local NAACP chapter, Felmer Cheney, admitted, "McGee is probably as frustrated as everybody else. Where in hell do we go?" The black middle-class leaders' inability to address this issue indicates the limitations of their theoretical and programmatic perspective.

The only viable alternative generated within black politics since the end of the civil-rights movement has been Jesse Jackson's Rainbow Coalition. But after two notable Presidential campaigns, the idealism that inspired thousands of progressives has disintegrated. In 1984, Jackson entered the fray without any serious hope of winning the Presidential nomination. His campaign was essentially a social-protest movement that used the Democratic primaries to increase black voter turnout and reinforce the liberal-left wing of the Democratic Party. By 1988, Jackson had shifted closer to the center, permitting black officials who had campaigned vigorously against him in 1984 to dominate municipal and statewide mobilizations.

But the Rainbow Coalition failed to develop a coherent national apparatus, with a national newspaper, regional political organizers, and trained cadre on campuses and in communities. Local activists drawn into the Jackson campaigns weren't encouraged to develop autonomous coalitions independent of the national electoral effort. Jackson's frenetic, larger-than-life personality and his chaotic organizational style, consisting largely of a coterie of loyalists who rarely disagree with the boss, work against genuinely democratic decision-making. Leftists who were members of the national leadership of the Rainbow recognized these problems but were reluctant to voice even mild criticisms of Jackson, who offered them a path out of their own sectarian political ghetto.

Part of the problem was the bitterly ironic relationship that developed unexpectedly between Jackson and such newly prominent post-black politicians as Wilder. Jackson's Rainbow had been responsible for elevating black politics to the national arena, illustrating that a black candidate could compete successfully, winning Presidential caucuses and primary elections in states without sizable minority groups. It was Jackson, not David Dinkins, who proved that a black candidate for high office could win a plurality of votes against more conservative white candidates in New York City.

Jackson's candidacy forced the Democratic Party to liberalize its posture toward women—witness the Vice Presidential nomination of Geraldine Ferraro in 1984—and toward blacks—witness the 1989 selection of Ronald Brown as head of the Democratic National Committee. His campaigns opened the political space for local African-American officials to seek statewide and mayoral positions, although their challenges were ideologically to Jackson's right.

Wilder's success in Virginia was based on a Rainbow-style approach, controlling nearly all black votes plus about one-third of the state's white electorate. But his political program was substantially more conservative than Jackson's. Once elected, Wilder lost little time endorsing centrist policy positions and repudiating liberal activism. Andrew Young's gubernatorial campaign in Georgia, in which he has endorsed the death penalty, faithfully follows Wilder's model, not Jackson's. Jackson's continuing flirtation with Presidential politics, and his refusal to run against Marion Barry in the District of Columbia's mayoral race, is attributable, at least in part, to his legitimate fear that Wilder or Gray is being groomed to eclipse him on the national stage.

Complicating matters is Jackson's tense and ambiguous relationship with Louis Farrakhan. Jackson has known Farrakhan intimately for more than a quarter of a century; Chicago was the political base for both men. In 1984, especially in the early days of the primary season, Jackson relied heavily on the Nation of Islam for security. People in Jackson's inner circle state candidly that he is intensely afraid of alienating Farrakhan personally or his black-nationalist constituency. Farrakhan has developed an extremely loyal cadre which expounds a conservative version of racial separatism and entrepreneurialism. Jackson fears a split with the nationalists that would repeat the hostilities that separated Martin Luther King from Malcolm X a generation ago.

Personally repelled by the crude anti-Semitism and authoritarian elements of the Nation of Islam's ideology, Jackson still believes he cannot denounce them for fear of turning this militant movement against him. In the absence of principled or decisive action condemning Farrakhan's anti-Semitism and sexist and chauvinist statements, the impression lingers that Jackson tolerates bigotry.

Thus a stalemate exists in black politics: Rainbow activism has reached a dead end, while post-black, centrist politicians are beginning to take the decisive initiatives. The failure here is not simply tactical but strategic. Jackson's political perspective is still frozen in the lessons of the civil-rights era. His basic instincts are to pressure the Democratic Party to the left, not to map a strategy for effective counter-hegemonic power.

But the grand realignment of the Democratic Party is a grand illusion. It is in the interests of both parties in our national-unity government to maintain the electoral status quo regardless of the destructive social and economic consequences for millions of Americans. We should not play cards with a stacked deck; rather, we should change the rules of the game.

Black and left activists must revive the traditions and tactics of non-electoral political protest; they must develop new institutions of creative resistance.

Freedom schools, for example. Open, multiracial academies, held during late afternoons and on weekends for secondary-school and college students, could offer a public protest curriculum. Learning how to organize street demonstrations, selective buying campaigns, and civil disobedience, reading about the personalities and history of American protest—such activities would help revive the radical consciousness of this generation.

Changing the rules requires innovations in the electoral process itself. The traditional plurality system in American elections gives the victory to the candidate with the most votes. This system is not only easily usurped by corporate interests, but also, by its nature, manipulates public preferences in time-worn outcomes. In multicandidate, citywide elections, in which minority constituencies represent one-third of the total vote or less, it becomes virtually impossible to elect candidates who represent their interests. Two results are predictable: Either the turnout rate of blacks gradually declines in national elections, which has occurred for the past fifteen years, or candidates emerge who are more conservative and thus politically palatable to the white upper middle class and corporate interests.

A better idea would be to restructure voting procedures to permit minority interests to be expressed democratically. Civil-rights attorneys in several states have pushed for changes in local elections that give each voter several votes in each multicandidate race. The votes could be clustered behind one candidate or shared in blocs with coalition partners. The result would be to give minorities a much greater chance of being represented even in citywide races, yet the system would not discriminate against white majorities.

The best research in this area is being done by Lani Guinier of the University of Pennsylvania Law School. Her soon-to-be-published manuscript, "Black Electoral Success Theory and the Triumph of Tokenism," provides a blueprint for innovative challenges to the concept of democratic representation.

Instead of worrying about whether Jackson will contest the Democratic Party's Presidential nomination in 1992, progressives should refocus electoral efforts on other priorities. More resources should be devoted to increasing the size of the electorate. The National Voter Registration Act, passed last February by the House of Representatives, should be a major legislative priority for civil-rights groups. The bill calls for automatic updating of voting rolls with information provided by drivers' license and renewal applications and reports of address changes given to motor-vehicle departments. Since nonvoters are disproportionately nonwhite, poor, unemployed, and/or working-class women, any significant increase in turnout should shift the electoral results leftward.

We must rethink our current organizational forms and our approach to building coalitions. Has the NAACP, created during the nadir of Jim Crow segregation, outlived its political utility? To raise the question, and to answer it affirmatively, by no means denigrates the organization's outstanding contributions to the freedom struggle. Both reform-minded integrationists and separatist-oriented nationalists presume a form of race-based politics that does not recognize the subtle ways in which political, economic, and social institutions are assuming a nonracialist form, but nevertheless perpetuate the prerogatives of domination.

The passage of the Civil Rights Act of 1964 marked not the end of institutional racism but its transformation. The new, mutant version of inequality began to employ a race-neutral discourse while maintaining the objective of minority domination. It soon became difficult for civil-rights veterans to distinguish allies from antagonists, since nearly all adhered to the language of equality. Integrationists sensed that the rules of the game had changed but did little to modify their tactics. The habits and reflexes of five consecutive generations socialized by traditional segregation were too deeply ingrained to be questioned.

Black legal scholar Kimberle Crenshaw accurately characterizes the political environment since the demise of Black Power as the "post-reform period." Among the new elements of social inequality are such economic factors as the steady erosion of jobs, falling real incomes, and the swollen ranks of the poor, unemployed, and homeless in the ghetto. Thousands of African-American young people who are seeking work are unable to find it at an income level that could support a family. For the first time in recent history, a majority of young black women and men have never had or expect to have meaningful, rewarding employment any time in their lives.

A second element of the new political economy of domination is the set of intractable social problems proliferating inside urban black neighborhoods: high infant mortality rates and declining health standards, the growing numbers of juvenile pregnancies and female single-parent households, the increase in crime, street-gang activity, and use of hard drugs. These social problems are invoked by conservative intellectuals and politicians to undermine blacks' traditional demands for equality. Thomas Sowell, Charles Murray, Glen Loury simplistically attribute them, *ad nauseam*, to the welfare system, the black family, sexual promiscuity, and/or the lack of a work ethic among blacks.

The social crisis of the inner city is far more likely caused by the deindustrialization of urban areas, the flight of capital to the suburbs and overseas, and the absence of a comprehensive Federal policy for families and neighborhood development which could include expansion of public transportation systems, free child care, well-staffed public health clinics, adequate and affordable housing, and job-training programs.

The cruelest example of urban under-development may be the Government's attitude toward public education and child development. A rapidly emerging educational underclass is unable to compete successfully for the new jobs requiring computer-related skills. This generates a tremendous amount of bitterness and frustration among young people.

Yet another byproduct of urban decay and disruption is fear. Most middle- and upper-class whites employed in the financial and commercial districts of major cities flee to the suburbs after dark, seeking the safety of elaborate burglar-alarm systems and private security guards. Black and Hispanic working-class families living next door to crack houses aren't as fortunate. Blacks have long been the chief victims of violent crime. A typical white male's statistical chance of becoming a murder victim is one in 186; a black man's odds are one in twenty-nine. Black women are nearly twice as likely to be rape victims than are white women. Fear means that elderly black people and young single mothers with children are reluctant to leave their homes at night to attend civic meetings. Fear paralyzes a segment of the black middle class living in the suburbs, which wants to engage in socially constructive projects inside the ghetto but also wants to avoid crime.

These new forms of domination are not exclusively applied to blacks—they are used to hold down other minorities as well. The changing forms thus require activists to shift ground, from a racial to a truly multi-ethnic focus.

The development of constructive relations between African-Americans and Hispanics, Native Americans, Asian/Pacific-Americans, and other ethnic minorities is foremost. Neither the traditional civil-rights groups nor the Congressional Black Caucus has continuing dialogues with parallel groups among Puerto Ricans or Mexican-Americans. Black-Hispanic political relations in many cities have become more fractious than fraternal. Cooperation between Hispanic and black caucuses in most state legislatures and city councils is, at best, inconsistent. African-Americans make few gestures to learn Spanish or to appreciate the unique perspectives and problems articulated by progressive La-

tino groups. Even Jackson's notable overtures to the Latino community didn't go far beyond the expression of political platitudes, without subsequent programmatic cooperation among these urban ethnic constituencies after the Democratic primaries ended.

African-Americans have to recognize demographic trends and the new multi-ethnic realities. Until the middle of the Twentieth Century, "race relations" in America meant black-white relations. This is no longer true. Today, one in four Americans is nonwhite. Three decades from now, the nonwhite population will have doubled, to 115 million, while the white population will remain the same. But Hispanics, not African-Americans, will make up the dominant group.

Any progressive urban policy agenda must emphasize the many economic, educational, and social problems shared by blacks and Hispanics. Despite the perception among some blacks that the majority of Hispanics are middle class or relatively privileged, statistics show a different reality. In 1988, the Census Bureau reported a poverty rate for whites of 10.1 per cent; for Hispanics and blacks, the rates were 26.8 per cent and 31.6, respectively.

In recent months, Asian-black tensions have erupted in many urban areas. The well-publicized economic boycott by black activists of Korean merchants in Brooklyn's Flatbush neighborhood is projected superficially as a manifestation of "black racism." But, as ethnic studies scholar Ronald Takaki observes, the "harmful myth of Asian superiority" is used to divide people of color with common interests.

Like African-Americans, Asian-Americans have experienced racial discrimination and vigilante violence. The tragic 1982 case of Chinese-American Vincent Chin, who was killed by Detroit auto workers who thought he was Japanese, is only one example of a disturbing trend. Many Asians are working-class or poor. One-fourth of New York's Chinatown population in 1980 was below the poverty level. And middle-income Asians frequently confront the same problems faced by middle-class blacks. Asian professionals complain about the "glass ceiling" inside corporations and academic institutions, limiting their upward mobility. The "affluent, hardworking" Korean shopkeepers, according to Takaki, have household incomes of between $17,000 and $35,000 annually, hardly ranking them with the idle rich. The reality behind the image of Asian-American affluence is that there is economic and social common ground with other people of color, and the foundations for coalitions exist.

We must refocus our tactical approach toward the majority of white Americans

as well. Liberalism and appeals to moral suasion are no longer effective. The recent electoral behavior of the white middle and upper classes is largely dictated by perceptions of narrow, material self-interest. Whites will have to be shown in concrete terms that they have a direct stake in the consequences of the urban crisis. Investments in economic development, public transportation, public housing, and health care which benefit people of color are absolutely necessary for the productivity of society as a whole.

In *The Burden of Support*, sociologist David Hayes-Bautista notes that more than one-half of all children in California will be Hispanic by the year 2030, but whites will total about 60 per cent of the elderly. A similar situation will exist across the United States within forty years: the existence of a retired leisure class over age sixty-five which will be largely white, subsidized by the growing wage deductions paid by an increasingly nonwhite labor force. It's easy to envision a political revolt against Social Security and other Federal programs for the elderly, by racial and ethnic minorities.

Finally, we must rethink the concept of blackness itself, as a political category and as it relates to the construction of coalitions.

In the Caribbean, radical scholar-activist Walter Rodney used the term "black power" to connote a strategic alliance among people who were racially and ethnically designated as black, East Indian, and Chinese to struggle against neo-colonial rule. In the United Kingdom in the 1970s, the antiracist mobilization of Asians, Africans, West Indians, and even radical whites was fought under the rubric of "black power."

We must recognize that black oppression is not biologically or genetically derived; it is driven by the systematic exploitation of black people in the economic system, and through their political and social domination within society. Perhaps the term "people of color" could be the basis of a new strategic unity of Chicanos, Puerto Ricans, African-Americans, West Indians, Native Americans, Asian/Pacific-Americans, the unemployed and poor of any race who experience second-class citizenship because of corporate greed and a nonresponsive Government.

Black politics must go beyond the notion of a Rainbow Coalition—essentially an electoral mobilization with sporadic and uneven connections between multi-racial and multiclass constituencies—to a more advanced level of organization based on the struggles to improve the quality of urban life and labor and build a truly democratic, pluralistic society for the majority of Americans.

IMMIGRATION REFORM

OVERVIEW OF RECENT URBAN INSTITUTE IMMIGRATION POLICY RESEARCH

The past five years have been a time of unusual ferment in immigration law and policy. In 1986 Congress passed the landmark Immigration Reform and Control Act (IRCA), which was intended to give the government the tools required to bring illegal immigration under control. Four years later Congress enacted the Immigration Act of 1990, which increased the number of visas to be awarded and substantially transformed the legal immigration system by revising the labor, family, and other grounds for admitting immigrants into the United States.

With a Ford Foundation grant, The Urban Institute and The RAND Corporation embarked on a joint Immigration Research Program in 1988 to address continuing issues and problems pertaining to immigration and immigration policy. Some of their findings on changes introduced by the 1986 and 1990 legislation are presented in this special section on immigration.

New Tools

Taken together, the 1986 and 1990 immigration laws have introduced major new tools and approaches for U.S. immigration policy. IRCA, for example, established employer sanctions, the penalizing of employers hiring undocumented immigrants or committing associated violations. IRCA also authorized a series of legalization programs intended to regularize the immigration status of undocumented aliens residing in the United States.

New Enforcement Policies and Pressure for Compliance

The new laws substantially expanded the reach of immigration law and policy. The legislation assigned new responsibilities to the Immigration and Naturalization Service (INS) and mandated that

> The articles that follow place the 1986 and 1990 immigration laws in historical perspective. They also provide information about the effectiveness of the legalization and employment sanction programs of IRCA; and the projected effects of the 1990 Immigration Act on the size and composition of the immigrant population in the United States. An article on the changing role of the INS, a review of immigrant policies in Western Europe, and a selected bibliography of Urban Institute Immigration Research Program books, reports, and papers round out this special section on immigration reform.

the business community comply with IRCA. IRCA's employer sanctions brought all U.S. employers under a new regime of labor regulation; and the legalization provisions of the law altered the status of several million immigrants residing in the United States.

New Influx of Immigrants

These laws have contributed to increased migration to the United States. More than 2.5 million people have attained legal status under IRCA's amnesty provisions. The Immigration Act of 1990 not only increases the number of annual legal admissions by 40 percent, it also provides several avenues for regularizing the legal status of many in the United States who remain undocumented. As these demographic changes occur, the question arises whether the nation needs an immigrant policy that better protects newcomers' social and economic integration to complement immigration reform initiatives.

New Rationale

The new laws also alter the rationale used for selection of immigrants. Perhaps the most notable change is the gradual shift in emphasis that the 1990 legislation embodies. It moves away from the social goal of family unification to the economic goal of meeting the labor force requirements of employers. At the same time, though, the 1990 immigration law counterbalances this trend by increasing the number of family members admitted through the creation of a temporary "safe haven" for undocumented Salvadorans already in the United States.

New Problems

But recent legislation has inadvertently introduced a number of new immigration-related problems. Most debated has been the expansion in discrimination against foreign-sounding or -looking job applicants. Another less noticed problem involves the proliferation of taxing new responsibilities assigned to an already overburdened INS and a diffusion of the agency's mission. These emerging areas of concern are the focus of Institute research now underway.

 From *Policy and Research Report*, Winter/Spring 1991, pp. 11-20. Reprinted by permission of The Urban Institute, 2100 M Street, NW, Washington, D.C., 20037.

RECENT TRENDS AND LEGISLATIVE RESPONSES

Although other nations may receive larger numbers of immigrants in relation to their population, no other nation willingly accepts as many new settlers as does the United States. Significant changes in U.S. immigration law in 1986 and 1990 have reaffirmed this country's openness to immigrants. The legislative acts address significant changes in the numbers, origins, and legal status of the nation's immigrant population that have occurred in the past three decades. Recent work by Urban Institute researchers Michael Fix and Jeffrey S. Passel puts both laws into historical context and assesses the likely effects of the 1990 legislation.

Legal immigration to the United States has increased steadily over the past five decades, from about 1 million immigrants in the 1940s to some 6 million in the 1980s. More immigrants live in the United States now than at any time in history— more than 17 million. But the rate of immigration in the 1980s was not the highest our nation has experienced. The number of arriving immigrants peaked at 8.8 million in the first decade of the twentieth century, when our population was about one-third of what it is today.

Moreover, while recently the proportion of foreign-born persons in the United States has been increasing steadily, from about 4.9 percent in 1970 to about 7 percent in 1990, this does not even approach the levels of the nineteenth century. Then, about 1 person in 7, or almost 15 percent of the population, was foreign-born. This ratio of foreign-born to native-born began a steady decline in 1932. The immigration cutbacks can be traced to a number of factors, including the restrictive immigration laws of 1921 and 1924, the inhibiting effect of the great depression and world war II, and the aging of earlier groups of immigrants.

1986 IMMIGRATION ACT IN HISTORICAL PERSPECTIVE

The impact of immigrants on the labor force also is less today. In 1907 alone, for example, the number of immigrants who found jobs when they arrived added about 3 percent to the U.S. labor force. An equivalent amount of immigration today would mean an annual flow of 9 million persons into the United States — more than ten times current numbers.

In the nineteenth century, virtually all immigration to the United States was from Europe and Canada; this trend continued into the 1950s. By the 1980s, however, only 14 percent originated from Europe and Canada.

The most dramatic change is an increase in the proportion of Asian immigrants, which rose from 13 percent in the 1960s to 44 percent in the 1980s. In this same period, immigration of Mexicans and other Latin Americans remained steady, at 14 percent and 26-27 percent, respectively.

The explosive increase in the immigration of Asians to the United States—2.6 million arrived in the 1980s—can be traced to the legal changes incorporated into the Immigration Act of 1965. That law put immigrants from all countries on essentially equal footing and eased restrictions in force since 1885 against immigration from Asia.

As total immigration increased during the 1980s, so did the number of illegal immigrants. The estima-

ted number of illegal aliens in this country rose from 2.5 to 3.5 million in 1980 to 3 to 5 million by 1986.

Enactment of the Immigration Reform and Control Act (IRCA) in 1986 authorized legalization of immigrants who had resided illegally in the United States since before January 1, 1982. Since the law's passage, some 2.5 million formerly illegal aliens have attained legal status; the estimated number of illegal aliens remaining is 1.8 to 3 million.

These estimates of the undocumented population are lower than might be expected, considering recent media publicity given to apprehensions of illegal aliens along the U.S.-Mexico border. Such publicity, however, obscures two important factors: First, much of the inflow from Mexico consists of temporary labor migrants; and second, there is a large, unreported reverse flow from this country back into Mexico.

The impact of immigration, both legal and illegal, is uneven across the country. Three-quarters of all immigrants who arrived in the United States in the 1980s came to only six states—California, New York, Texas, Florida, Illinois, and New Jersey. During this period two states— California and New York—received more than half, about 3.3 million of the total 6 million. Of these, 2.3 million arrived in California and 1 million in New York.

This uneven impact played a key role in the redistribution of U.S. population during the 1980s, a decade of considerable population growth. For example, California's huge population increase, confirmed in the 1990 census, was fueled mainly by immigrants. Texas received significant numbers of both immigrants and internal migrants. But the arrival of large numbers of immigrants in New York and Illinois nevertheless failed to offset the exodus of residents out of these states in the 1980s.

These shifts in the numbers, origins, and geographical distribution of immigrants provided the impetus for the Immigration Act of 1990, which addresses primarily the issue of legal immigration. The act defines the family unit, labor, and other criteria for admitting immigrants to the United States.

1990

IMMIGRATION

ACT AND ITS

LIKELY

EFFECTS

The Immigration Act of 1990 was enacted at a time of extreme economic uncertainty, when the nation was poised on the brink of a recession and the outbreak of war in the Persian Gulf. In an era when other industrialized countries are making their immigration laws more restrictive, the 1990 act authorizes an *increase* in legal immigration to the United States. In so doing, it complements the 1986 attempt of the Immigration Reform and Control Act (IRCA) to close the "back door" of illegal immigration with a legislative strategy for keeping open the "front door" of legal immigration.

This liberalization allows entry of many more family members of immigrants and creates a temporary "safe haven" for as many as 500,000 undocumented Salvadorans already in the United States. Thus, it stands in sharp contrast to IRCA, which focused primarily on limiting illegal immigration.

Passage of the 1990 act was driven by three imperatives:

• **Economic**—to forge a closer link between immigration and human resources policy, in order to avoid the anticipated mismatch between the numbers and skill requirements of future U.S. jobs and the numbers and skill levels of future immigrants.

• **Cultural**—to encourage more diversity in the immigrant stream.

• **Social**—to promote family unity.

The provisions of the 1990 law, according to Fix and Passel, signal two important conceptual shifts in U.S. immigration policy: a stronger focus on labor market concerns and an interest in diversifying the immigrant stream, principally by increasing the number of immigrants from Europe.

Cap on Immigration. The new law places a yearly cap on total immigration for the first time since the 1920s. For 1992-95 the limit is 700,000 persons; for the years thereafter, 675,000.

The cap, however, may be more symbolic than real because the law allows an unlimited number of visas for immediate relatives of U.S. citizens (now about 220,000 per year), while at the same time setting a floor of 226,000 visas for other family-based immigration.

Employment-Related Immigration. The number of visas reserved for workers under the new law will increase significantly—from the current level of 58,000 per year to 140,000. However, only about 40 percent of the total is expected to be workers; the others are likely to be members of workers' families. The new law emphasizes admission of skilled workers by capping the number of visas for unskilled workers at 10,000, about half the number allowed under previous law.

Diversity. Perhaps the most interesting innovation in the Immigration Act of 1990 is the class of diversity visas it creates to "seed" immigration from countries that have sent comparatively few migrants to the United States in recent years. However, the diversity criteria are not demanding enough to ensure such an outcome. In fact, during the three years following the law's enactment, national origin and not human capital considerations will largely determine who obtains a visa.

Family-Based Immigration. An important sign of the new law's pro-immigrant character is its approach to family-based immigration. These provisions are driven by congressional interest in promoting the nuclear family, by an interest in eventually diversifying the immigrant stream, and by a less publicized interest in reducing the size of the nation's illegal population.

The provisions increase the number of persons who may enter based on the family categories. Admissions of immediate family members of United States citizens remain unlimited under the act; the preexisting preference system has been updated; and 55,000 visas per year for three years will go to immediate family members of immigrants who have attained legal status under IRCA's so-called amnesty programs.

Thus, despite public attention given to the increase in employment-based immigration, the bill did not increase workers at the expense of family-based admissions.

Reducing the size of the Undocumented Population. Several lesser-known provisions of the new law best demonstrate its generous, inclusionary nature. The legislation, for instance, prohibits the deportation of, and grants work authorization to, all spouses and children of the 2.5 to 2.8 million persons who will eventually attain legal status under IRCA, if the spouses and children were in the United States before May 5, 1988.

Another provision creates a temporary "safe haven" for a minimum of 18 months for an estimated 350,000 to 500,000 Salvadorans who, although living in the United States, were generally ineligible for legalization and remain undocumented.

Agencies in Charge of the Implementation. The liberal values that characterize the bill are striking, especially in areas related to public health. Whereas in IRCA the principal agency of enforcement was the Immigration and Naturalization Service, under the 1990 bill responsibility for implementation is assigned to Health and Human Services, which is given the authority to determine whether a person "has a communicable disease of public health significance" or "has a physical or mental disorder that could or has in the past posed a threat to others." The former made possible a recently announced, sweeping revision of the nation's policy on immigration and AIDS. The latter substantially eliminates most grounds for excluding those with a physical or mental disability.

Passage of the 1990 act should quiet the concerns of many who feared that enactment of IRCA in 1986 signaled a new, restrictive era of immigration policy. The various programs have the power to change the legal status and work eligibility of more than 1 million persons. In terms of sheer numbers, immigrants in the United States under the legalization and safe-haven provisions clearly outnumber the 34,000 new skilled workers admitted annually under the bill.

Future Research Focus

Urban Institute demographers and immigration analysts are taking a close look at the impact of the 1990 law on the size and makeup of the immigrant stream entering the United states. This work in turn will contribute to Institute assessments of the future effects of immigration on the composition of the U.S. population. Another focus will be the family structure of different immigrant groups both within the United States and within the immigrants' countries of origin in order to predict future immigration trends.

Institute research is also addressing a broad range of economic impacts. For example, how do new immigrants fare economically? What impact do they have on the native-born work force? An analysis of the community impacts of immigrants is forthcoming, with research addressing the fiscal and other costs engendered by recent immigration.

Finally, another set of under-researched issues—those relating to immigrant policy—is an area of focus. Should the United States have a deliberate policy for integrating immigrants into society and for providing them specialized services? The Institute's program on immigration policy is developing a taxonomy of state and local immigrant policy and trying to determine how the state and local governments respond to increases in the number of immigrants and reductions in federal support for immigrant services.

A conference in summer 1991 will examine some of these issues, specifically immigrant integration, adaptation, and policy.

For further information see "The Door Remains Open: Recent Immigration to the United States and a Preliminary Analysis of the Immigration Act of 1990," by Michael Fix and Jeffrey S. Passel, available from the Institute's Research Paper Sales Office for $8.00.

ILLEGAL IMMIGRATION: ARE EMPLOYER SANCTIONS WORKING?

Newly available research on undocumented immigration indicates that one of the major goals of the 1986 Immigration Reform and Control Act (IRCA)—to reduce the flow of undocumented migrants into the United States—was achieved, at least in the short term. Border apprehensions and undocumented immigration declined substantially in the years immediately following enactment of the legislation.

However, much of the decrease in the flow of undocumented immigrants through 1989 appears to result from the 1986 IRCA legislation *legalizing* formerly illegal residents, not from the legislatively mandated employer sanctions. The legalization of more than 1 million agricultural workers and 1.7 million other illegal immigrants removed many individuals from the flow. Yet, recent evidence of a resurgence in illegal immigration in 1990 calls into question the effectiveness of employer sanctions. If the number of illegal aliens is rising, even after successful implementation of legalization efforts, are the IRCA sanctions working?

The Paper Curtain, a book of essays edited by Institute researcher Michael Fix, helps answer this question. It provides a series of perspectives on the impact of these sanctions, their implementation, and potential reforms in light of the growing controversy about employer sanctions and whether they should be retained and reformed, or repealed.

In a concluding chapter, Fix summarizes three arguments for repealing employer sanctions:

1. *Flows of illegal immigrants*. The analysis of flows, based on apprehensions along the southern border of the United States, indicates that the comparatively steep decline in illegal immigration through FY89 reversed itself sharply in FY90, when the number of apprehensions per linewatch hour rose 22 percent. The reversal tends to reinforce the contention of co-researcher Jeffrey S. Passel and others that the decrease before 1990 was largely due to the

effects of the legalization program and would continue to erode over time.

2. *Farm labor stability* . If sanctions were having their intended effect, there would have been less worker turnover and more regular employment of authorized workers in California agriculture. Philip Martin and Edward Taylor demonstrate in one of the book's chapters that this has not been the case. Instead, turnover among farm workers is increasing, not decreasing, as new immigrant workers continue to be drawn to seasonal farm work, largely through the recruitment of farm labor contractors.

3. *National origin and citizenship discrimination.* Given supporting evidence in numerous studies , it is reasonable to conclude that some new employer discrimination can be tied to IRCA.

Overall, sanctions appear to be ineffective in reducing undocumented immigration, stabilizing turnover in low-wage industries such as California agriculture, and avoiding the unintended costs of additional discrimination. The case against sanctions is strengthened further by recent regulatory developments that will increase the burden borne by law-abiding employers.

Proponents of employer sanctions, on the other hand, claim that they reflect a consensus, at least among lawmakers, that tolerates increased admission of immigrants as long as the perception of control remains in place. Moreover, they contend that there is no good policy alternative to sanctions and that sanctions are a necessary part of any long-term strategy to control illegal immigration, albeit one that may need to be reformed.

Among the book's suggested reforms:

• Substantially increased resources for employer education regarding discrimination.

• A federally funded follow-up study of sanctions-related discrimination, using both audits and surveys.

• More systematic oversight of sanction practices and penalties, together with expedited development of a national data base that permits enforcement officials to monitor implementation for fairness and consistency.

• Rapid transition to requiring two identification documents for immigrants (reducing the potential for fraud).

• Substantial expansion of the Department of Labor's role in enforcing employer sanctions.

The last reform is the most challenging and potentially far-reaching. It is based on European success in linking sanctions to labor law enforcement, and would permit enforcement of workplace regulations by an experienced inspection staff. The strategy also has the advantage of identifying employers who violate both immigration and labor laws and coordinating their prosecution. Shifting responsibility to the Department of Labor may help link the administration of employer sanctions with a broad and effective employer education campaign and antidiscrimination mandates.

For further information see Undocumented Migration to the United States: IRCA and the Experience of the 1980s, *edited by Frank D. Bean, Barry Edmonston, and Jeffrey S. Passel, Urban Institute Press, 1990, $18.75;* The Paper Curtain: Employer Sanctions' Implementation, Impact, and Reform, *edited by Michael Fix, Urban Institute Press, summer 1991.*

LEGALIZATION PROGRAMS: A CAUTIOUS WELCOME

Implementing the legalization programs created by the Immigration Reform and Control Act of 1986 (IRCA) presented a multifaceted challenge to the Immigration and Naturalization Service (INS).

Congress authorized two temporary, one-time legalization programs— a general one for immigrants who had resided in the United States continuously since 1982, and the Special Agricultural Worker (SAW) program for undocumented agricultural workers who had resided in the United States for at least six months.

The INS was responsible for implementing both programs, each with its own requirements. The administrative burden was compounded by the fact that in each program some of the required steps for obtaining legal status posed complicated questions, including how to ensure both availability of and funding for the services.

The INS responded slowly, beginning its outreach effort only one month before the start of the application period for temporary residence (Phase I) under the general program, and publishing proposed regulations only four days before the program started. The regulations for Phase II—receipt of permanent resident status—were issued nine months after the first applicants became eligible for it. When the perception grew that the legalization program was not working, immigrant advocacy groups prodded the INS both through litigation and by working more closely with local INS officials. As a result of the legalization programs created by IRCA, more than 2.5 million undocumented immigrants have achieved legal status.

Former Institute researcher Susan González Baker reviewed INS implementation of legalization programs and analyzed remaining implementation problems as well as successes. Her findings are based on interviews with government and private officials and agencies responsible for program implementation and on first-hand observation by Urban Institute and RAND Corporation researchers at eight study sites: Los Angeles, San Jose, San Antonio, El Paso, Houston, Chicago, New York, and Miami.

The general legalization program has been more successful in processing applicants than the SAW program for undocumented agricultural workers, which has been plagued by charges of fraud as well as by a lack of resources.

Nationally, approval rates for the general program exceed 90 percent. But, two years after the close of the SAW program, over 400,000 of the 1.4 million applicants remain in limbo awaiting resolution of their petitions.

Although approval rates for the general program were high, turnout varied widely by region and city. Of the 1.7 million applicants, 1 million filed their petitions in the eight study cities, nearly 700,000 of them in Los Angeles. Aggressive publicity by Los Angeles INS officials and high-profile advocacy from immigrants' rights groups contributed to the city's large turnout.

By contrast, only 100,000 applications, half of the expected turnout, were filed in New York City. González Baker attributes this low turnout both to the difficulty of conducting publicity and outreach activities in areas with a more diverse immigrant population and to the commitment of fewer resources by the New York INS.

Turnout was heaviest among Mexican undocumented immigrants. Although a little more than 50 percent of the total undocumented population was of Mexican origin, about 75 percent of the immigrant population with legal status reported Mexico as their country of citizenship. Such heavy turnout is attributed at least in part to the INS Spanish language publicity campaign. When other ethnic groups also were mobilized through aggressive outreach strategies, early turnout was substantial, as evidenced by the 16,000 Polish applicants in Chicago.

Advocacy groups played a crucial and often under-appreciated role in sustaining the INS commitment to legalization. Even in communities where INS officials made legislation a top priority, immigrant advocates continued to play an important role. This included forging cooperative relationships with the agency, counseling applicants on how to file petitions, and filing class action lawsuits on behalf of applicants.

Assistance to newly arrived immigrants, particularly at the community level, will continue to be important as the United States shifts some of its focus from legalization efforts to ways to integrate newcomers more effectively into society.

For further information see The Cautious Welcome: The Legalization Programs of the Immigration Reform and Control Act, *by Susan González Baker, 1990, from The Urban Institute Press in association with The RAND Corporation, $19.00.*

THE CHANGING ROLE OF THE INS

In 1986, the landmark Immigration Reform and Control Act (IRCA) charged the Immigration and Naturalization Service (INS) with implementing two complex programs: Employer sanctions, subjecting 7 million firms to regulation by the INS for the first time, and legalization, offering amnesty to several million illegal immigrants. The reform law also expanded the INS Border Patrol, required states to use an INS data base to verify the legal status of immigrants applying for public benefits, and increased the INS budget.

How well has the agency coped with these dual responsibilities and expanded tasks? Urban Institute researcher Jason Juffras, whose recent study examined IRCA's effect on the INS, reports that the generally positive impact of IRCA on the INS was weakened by two developments.

First, the INS responded to congressional pressure to increase efforts to deport criminal aliens and interdict drugs. While these programs may have been worthwhile, they overstrained the INS staff and precipitated a budget crisis in the agency in 1989.

Second, because the agency grew so rapidly, the decentralized management structure of INS—consisting of a central office, four regional offices, 33 district offices, and 22 Border Patrol sectors—was unable to provide sufficient oversight and ensure consistent implementation of the new programs.

Effects on INS Enforcement

Juffras noted that the INS implemented employer sanctions mostly in a measured and cooperative way, emphasizing the education of employers and voluntary compliance. Sanctions represented a major stride for the INS toward becoming a regulatory agency controlling incentives instead of a police agency controlling people. These sanctions have promoted an enforcement process that is fairer, more predictable, and less intrusive than the workplace raids the INS had formerly employed. However, as described below, sanctions have been a less important enforcement priority for the INS than IRCA sponsors might have imagined.

The INS did a creditable job in implementing sanctions largely because Congress imposed constraints on the agency even as it expanded its enforcement power. The "sunset" provision ensuring three annual reviews of the impact of sanctions on employment discrimination was the most important constraint. Another factor in the successful implementation effort was the willingness of the INS to recruit special agents—the plainclothes officers who take the lead in enforcing sanctions—from outside the agency. The new agents made it easier for the INS to switch from a policy emphasizing workplace raids to one stressing employer education and voluntary compliance.

Yet sanctions were only one of several important changes in INS enforcement policy between 1986 and 1989. IRCA also set the target of a 50 percent increase in the Border Patrol. The cost of such an expansion, as well as the political appeal of the Border Patrol, ultimately meant that most of the added enforcement resources the INS received to implement IRCA were devoted to border control and not to employer sanctions. During the same period, two major antidrug bills enacted in 1986 and 1988 mandated that the INS do more to remove criminal aliens from the United States and interdict drugs at the border. Staff and money were funneled into these responsibilities, leaving sanctions with only one-third of INS's extra enforcement money in 1987 and 1988.

As a result of these changes in enforcement policy, the INS entered the 1990s as a diversified and more versatile law enforcement agency. INS investigators typically divided their time among sanctions, criminal alien removal, and antifraud efforts. The Border Patrol has also broadened its role and become more specialized. The patrol now serves as

both the leading drug interdictor along the land border and as a participant in more antidrug task forces with other agencies.

The downside of this growth in enforcement responsibilities is that it outstripped the agency's capacity for effective oversight. Regional and district offices had to be given considerable latitude, resulting in different priorities and procedures around the country. District offices and Border Patrol sectors often operated independently in pursuing sanctions and criminal alien cases. Overall, concern about sanctions seemed to decline as INS managers decided to stress criminal alien removal and drug interdiction.

The 1989 INS budget crisis reflected the inability of this agency to meet all of its new enforcement responsibilities. In trying to reach the target of 50 percent expansion of the Border Patrol, the INS exceeded its budget by $50 million, forcing an agency-wide hiring freeze and cuts in other programs.

Effects on INS Services

INS services also benefited from IRCA, although the positive impact of the legislation on INS services was the result of a long and difficult learning process. From the outset of the legalization programs, the INS was criticized for insufficient outreach services to illegal immigrants and for overly restrictive regulations on eligibility. Despite these problems, the INS eventually improved its outreach services, eased its regulations under pressure from advocacy groups, and gradually learned which groups immigrants tend to trust and how to target outreach to different ethnic communities. This learning process should help the INS communicate more effectively with immigrant groups in the future.

To implement legalization programs, the INS had to hire hundreds of new staff members and transfer staff from other divisions into the program. Many of the new staff received praise for their willingness to serve immigrants, and the expo-

sure of long-time employees to a service program provided them with the experience and increased the commitment needed for the INS to improve its other service programs.

Finally, the sheer challenge of the legalization program, which involved processing 3 million people through a two-step procedure—permanent residency and then citizenship—spurred the INS to improve the infrastructure and funding mechanisms for its service programs. To assist with these efforts the INS computerized its regional and district legalization offices, an important step for an agency criticized for its lack of automation. The INS also paid for legalization entirely through applicant fees. This experience with user fees led Congress to grant the INS authority to switch its services to user-fee funding, a change that will put the INS on firmer financial footing in the future.

Overall, IRCA increased the importance of service programs in the INS while retaining the dominance of enforcement programs. As the INS almost doubled its budget—from $570 million in 1986 to $1.12 billion in 1990—the service programs fared quite well, increasing by 166 percent. Yet, service programs still account for only 12 percent of the INS budget. In other respects, such as the allocation of attorneys to INS programs, enforcement continues to take precedence over services.

For further information see Impact of the Immigration Reform and Control Act on the Immigration and Naturalization Service, *by Jason Juffras, January 1991, from The Urban Institute Press in association with The RAND Corporation, $10.25.*

THE EUROPEAN EXPERIENCE WITH IMMIGRANT POLICIES

As the numbers of immigrants and refugees arriving on European and American soil increase, the need for a coherent set of policies addressing their specific needs takes on heightened importance. This is especially true for Western Europe, where the reunification of East and West Germany, dramatic changes in Eastern Europe, and the movement toward a single European market in 1992 prompt urgent consideration of immigrant and refugee issues.

The increasing cultural and linguistic diversity of the new arrivals is expected to expand the immigration debate beyond such traditional issues as the criteria for admission to

---

"While these countries have developed explicit immigrant policies [implementation] has been less than successful."

---

a particular country. Equally important will be the ability of the host countries to meet the educational and social service needs of various immigrant groups. What models exist for developing such a coherent approach and how relevant are they to the U.S. experience?

Three European countries— Germany, France, and the United Kingdom—have all received large numbers of immigrants since the turn of the century and will probably receive substantially more over the next ten years. Each of these countries has established policies aimed at integrating the immigrants and refugees already there, while pursuing other policies to restrict new arrivals.

Immigration to these countries began mostly as temporary labor recruitment that evolved into permanent immigration through ad

hoc but deliberate integration policies over time. Institute researcher Wendy Zimmermann and colleague Charles Calhoun, now at Fannie Mae, look at the experiences of France, Germany, and the United Kingdom and draw lessons, where possible, for U.S. immigrant policy.

Zimmermann and Calhoun base their findings on a series of interviews conducted during May and June of 1990 with immigrant officials, immigration researchers, and representatives from immigrant organizations in France, Great Britain, and the former Federal Republic of Germany. The interviews have been supplemented with a selective review of published research and current reporting on immigration and immigrant policy in Europe.

Despite differences in attitudes toward immigration, the fundamental principle governing policymaking in all three countries is to restrict newcomers while integrating those already in the country. Immigrants are generally granted access to education, housing, and social services by law, but in practice are often denied equal access to services, either because of political conflicts, discrimination, or competition for resources. For instance:

• In Germany, immigrants have equal legal access to government-subsized low-income housing; but the combination of a quota system, a general housing shortage, and the practice of giving priority to former East German migrants and ethnic Germans coming from Eastern Europe has in practice limited availability of housing.

• In the United Kingdom, local districts are less likely to build schools in low-income, heavily immigrant areas for fear of being perceived as pro-immigration.

• In France, although the government has developed language and integration programs in schools, these programs reach only a few

and often are not of high quality.

Thus, while these countries have developed explicit immigrant policies, even as they have followed a restrictionist approach to the admission of new immigrants, implementation of those policies has been less than successful. Moreover, increasing illegal immigration, a growing population of refugees and people seeking asylum, and political and economic developments in Eastern Europe have also begun to divert the attention and resources of the European governments away from integration and toward a policy of greater immigration control.

Despite different immigration histories and varying attitudes toward immigration and immigrants in Europe and in the United States, some comparisons can be made. For instance, although access to permanent residence and citizenship is somewhat easier in the United States, access to social services is more complex and restrictive. The best example of this is the five-year ban in the United States on eligibility for benefits facing the undocumented population that recently attained legal status.

Zimmermann and Calhoun suggest that U.S. policymakers turn their attention to creating deliberate policies and programs that meet the diverse needs of the country's immigrants and refugees. These policies will need to address, among other issues, immigrant education, housing, public benefits, employment, and vocational training. While the European countries may not provide the best example of how immigrant policies should be implemented, they offer a model for making integration and immigrant programs an explicit goal of public policy.

For further information see "Immigrant Policies in Western Europe," by Wendy Zimmermann and Charles Calhoun, available from the Institute's Research Paper Sales Office for $8.00.

SELECTED READINGS ON IMMIGRATION POLICY

Urban Institute Press publications are distributed by University Press of America. All other publications are available from the Institute's Research Paper Sales Office

The Cautious Welcome: The legalization Programs of the Immigration Reform and Control Act of 1986, *Susan González Baker.* Examines the implementation of the legalization programs of IRCA on the basis of extensive field research. U.I. Press, 1990, Paper $19.00; Cloth $36.75.

"Immigrant Policies in Western Europe," *Wendy Zimmermann and Charles Calhoun.* Examines immigration and immigrant policies, including welfare, education, citizenship, and employer sanctions policies in France, Germany, and the United Kingdom and draws implications for United States policy. U.I. Paper PRIP-UI-15, June 1991.

"The Door Remains Open: Recent Immigration to the United States and a Preliminary Analysis of the Immigration Act of 1990," *Michael Fix and Jeffrey S. Passel.* Discusses recent trends in immigration, their impact on different states, and the major provisions of the new law and how it may affect future admissions. U.I. Paper PRIP-UI-14, January 1991, $8.00.

Employer Hiring Practices, Differential Treatment of Hispanic and Anglo Job Seekers, *Harry Cross, with Genevieve Kenney, Jane Mell, and Wendy Zimmermann.* Analyzes results of hiring audits specifically designed to ascertain whether foreign-looking or -sounding Hispanics are treated differently from those perceived to be U.S. citizens. U.I. Press, 1990, $14.25.

Enforcing Employer Sanctions: Challenges and Strategies, *Michael Fix and Paul T. Hill.* Assesses the national implementation of IRCA's employer sanctions provisions and discusses what choices remain. U.I. Press, 1990, $13.00.

"Factors Affecting Refugee Emigration," *Barry Edmonston and Sharon M. Lee.* Reports a statistical analysis on how the situation in 74 countries affects the migration of refugees. U.I. Paper PSC-DPS-UI3, August 1990, $8.00.

The Fourth Wave, *Thomas Muller and Thomas J. Espenshade.* Analyzes the economic and social impact of Mexican immigration on southern California. U.I. Press, 1985, $16.25.

"Harvest of Confusion: SAWs, RAWs, and Farmworkers," *Philip L. Martin and J. Edward Taylor.* Explains California's labor-intensive agriculture; the Special Agricultural Worker, or SAW, legalization program; and the hypothetical calculations required to determine whether Replenishment Agricultural Workers, or RAWs, will be admitted to do farm work after 1990. U.I. Paper PRIP-UI-4, December 1988, $8.00.

"Immigration Policy in the United States: Future Prospects for the Immigration Reform and Control Act of 1986," *Thomas J. Espenshade, Frank D. Bean, Tracy Ann Goodis, and Michael J. White.* Discusses the influence of selected domestic and international considerations on the effectiveness of IRCA. U.I. Paper PRIP-UI-2, October 1988, $8.00.

The Impact of the Immigration Reform and Control Act upon the Immigration and Naturalization Service, *Jason Juffras.* Discusses the effects of IRCA on the Immigration and Naturalization Service, specifically the INS ability to enforce the immigration law and provide service to immigrants. U.I. Press, 1991, $10.25.

"The Initial Effects of Immigration Reform on Farm Labor in California," *Philip L. Martin and J. Edward Taylor.* Analyzes the results of a survey designed to provide data on employment, wages, and production practices in 1988. U.I. Paper PRIP-UI-7, March 1990, $9.00.

"Looking Back: Five Aspects of the Legalization Program," *David S. North.* Reviews five specific outcomes of IRCA's legalization program. U.I. Paper PRIP-UI-13, August 1990, $8.00.

Opening and Closing the Doors: Evaluating Immigration Reform and Control, *Frank D. Bean, Georges Vernez, and Charles B. Keely.* Outlines major historical features of immigration to the U.S., examines the provisions of IRCA, and provides an overview of IRCA's implementation and effects. U.I. Press, 1989, $10.25.

The Paper Curtain: Employer Sanctions' Implementation, Impact, and Reform, *Michael Fix* ed.. Examines the related issues of the implementation, impact, and reform of employer sanctions and selected programs authorized by IRCA intended to curb illegal immigration. U.I. Press, forthcoming, 1991.

"Remedying IRCA-Related Discrimination: Modest Proposals," *Michael Fix.* Discusses recent findings of IRCA-related discrimination in hiring practices and proposes nonintrusive policy responses. U.I. Paper PRIP-UI-9, October 1990, $8.00.

"SAVE and Automated Verification of Immigration Status," *Wendy Zimmermann.* Examines welfare use among immigrants and the Systematic Alien Verification for Entitlement system. U.I. Paper PRIP-UI-10, August 1990, $8.00.

"A Short History of U.S. Policy toward Illegal Migration," *Thomas J. Espenshade.* Discusses interplay of laws restricting entry into the United States and the number of illegal aliens apprehended within U.S. borders. U.I. Paper PRIP-UI-8, September 1989, $8.00.

Undocumented Migration to the United States: IRCA and the Experience of the 1980s, *Frank D. Bean, Barry Edmonston, and Jeffrey S. Passel* eds.. Presents the most up-to-date evidence available on the size of the illegal population in the United States and how it has changed in the 1980s. U.I. Press, 1990, $18.75.

"The U.S. Immigration Reform and Control Act and Undocumented Migration to the United States," *Michael J. White, Frank D. Bean and Thomas J. Espenshade.* Presents an assessment of the impact of IRCA on the flow of undocumented migrants across the U.S.-Mexican border by analyzing a monthly time series of INS Border Patrol apprehensions. U.I. Paper PRIP-UI-5, July 1989, $8.00.

JAPAN'S INFLUENCE ON AMERICAN LIFE

There's more to it than team building and sushi. The Japanese are changing Americans' self-image—and inspiring an urge to learn.

Stratford P. Sherman

REMEMBER when America was the greatest country in the whole wide world? After World War II a euphoric sense of supremacy—*No. 1, by God, and proud of it!*—seemed the birthright of U.S. citizens. But the feeling has faded, and even the whipping America gave Saddam Hussein couldn't quite bring it back. The changed mood accompanies a new respect for the Japanese, who rose to mastery and power while Americans were horsing around with LBOs, credit cards, and cocaine.

Suddenly, all around the U.S., Japanese are settling in as neighbors, classmates, and employers—over 200,000 at last count, with more coming all the time. Many are executives whose decisions affect thousands of workers. Unlike earlier arrivals on these shores, these people have no intention of becoming Americans. They

REPORTER ASSOCIATES *Mark D. Fefer and Jung Ah Pak*

come not as immigrants, but as expatriates—and conquerors.

Japan has much more to offer than the business ideas, such as just-in-time manufacturing, that already have altered the habits of many U.S. corporations. What most Americans don't yet see is Japan's deeper effect on their society. The barriers of language and race are formidable, and Japanese expatriates often seem more eager to fit in than impose their culture on the U.S.

But buy a round of drinks for the patrons at Rumors, a dimly lit bar on the outskirts of Lexington, Kentucky, and they'll talk your ear off about Japan's growing influence. The bar is a few miles down the road from Toyota's Georgetown plant—where 68 Japanese, 3,650 Americans, and a whole lot of robots build the Camry sedans that J.D. Power & Associates rates as the nation's top-quality auto. Rumors is a

blue-collar hangout where customers keep their caps on while they drink—beer, mostly, and Seven-and-Seven. Country-western music videos play on the cable TV; tacked to a rafter over the bar is a bumper sticker with an American flag that reads TRUCKERS FOR THE TROOPS.

These country boys aren't about to start wearing kimonos, but they are remarkably cosmopolitan and aware. Bartender Sam Thurman, 31, who wears one earring, a black T-shirt, and shorts emblazoned with the words "Rude Dogs," is a house framer by trade who works at Rumors to evade unemployment. "The Japanese come in here sometimes," he says. "They're down-to-earth people, and they've proved that they have a lot of good ideas." Counters Buck Arnett, 31, a union pipefitter who was working 60-hour weeks at a Dow Corning plant before being laid off in April: "I don't like the Japs." But when asked why Japan so often bests America in business, Arnett doesn't flinch: "It's our own damn fault." The others all nod and raise their brewskies in agreement. "Hell, yes!" they say.

THAT RECOGNITION represents a turning point for grass-roots America. Says David Halberstam, whose book *The Reckoning* explored U.S.-Japanese competition in autos: "It's the end of an illusion we've had since the Battle of Midway, that if America does it, it's the best." Now Americans are asking themselves why they can't do as well as the Japanese.

When folks in Kentucky and elsewhere first saw Japanese companies clobber their U.S. counterparts years ago, many reacted as if the Japanese had landed from Mars, equipped with some kind of extra-smart mutant genes. But as greater numbers of ordinary Americans meet Japanese face to face, many respond just like Barbara Tinnell, 26, a team leader at the Toyota plant, who has spent six weeks in Japan on training tours. Says she: "From how good they're doing you almost expect the Japanese to be superior people—but they're not different, really." Perceptions like hers are priceless because they imply a responsibility to measure up.

But how? Americans like Tinnell are finding one answer in the Japanese management practice of *kaizen*, or continuous improvement—and in the enthusiasm for learning that is the real force behind it. Japan's towering achievement in manufacturing is the sum of countless small advances by individual workers and companies. For Americans raised to regard learning as something that happens in school, that is a profoundly new way of looking at things.

The 1987 film *Tampopo* illustrates the Japanese attitude. The picture (available on videocassette) tells the story of a widow who runs an unsuccessful noodle shop. Inspired by a customer's fierce criticism, she painstakingly masters the art of making *ramen* soup. That's all there is to the plot, but it plays like an adventure. How different from, say, *Rocky*, in which the hero spends most of the time bulking his biceps.

JAPANESE-STYLE learning typically involves lots of personal contact. For Americans, there is now more opportunity to meet people from Japan than ever before. Japanese companies currently employ over 400,000 people in the U.S. Some 35,000 Americans are taking college-level courses in Japanese, and enrollment continues to rise. Over a million Americans visited Japan in 1990, 40% more than five years ago, while three million Japanese sojourned in the U.S., mostly as tourists or students.

Japan's expatriates are spread all over the U.S. More than a third live on the West Coast, particularly in California, where 20% of all Japanese-owned U.S. factories are located. Roughly a quarter have gathered in New York City and nearby suburbs. The rest are scattered in smaller groups from Wyoming to Georgia, where Yamaha makes golf carts. The Japanese Chamber of Commerce of Georgia has almost 300 members.

In California, where the influx of Asian peoples began more than a century ago, the influence of Japanese expatriates is diluted and blurred. They compete for attention with newcomers from countries as diverse as Cambodia and Peru, and with a large and well-assimilated population of Americans of Japanese descent. To see signs—often contradictory—of what lies ahead, one must go to towns like Fort Lee, New Jersey, and Georgetown, Kentucky, where, in an atmosphere of awkward affability, Japanese and Americans are learning to live together.

A disproportionate number of the Japanese expatriates around New York City have gathered in a couple of suburbs. In Fort Lee, across the Hudson River from Manhattan, Mayor Nicholas Corbiscello remembers the day when the only Asians he saw there were the people who pressed his shirts. Now 15% of the students in the public schools are citizens of Japan. That figure understates the Japanese presence, since many of the children transfer to Japanese schools in New York City after fifth grade.

"I don't think there's any question that the Japanese will change America. I've seen a change right before my eyes," says Alan Sugarman, Fort Lee's superintendent of schools. He is a fervent believer in multiculturalism, the idea that ethnic groups can no longer be expected to abandon their distinctiveness in the traditional melting pot: "We can't stampede newcomers into being Americans anymore." But that's okay, he says. The Asian kids' diligent study habits set the standard for everyone else, leading American students to work harder. Achievement scores in Fort Lee are rising, and 90% of high school graduates go to college, vs. 75% in the mid-Seventies.

Japanese and American cultures often clash. That is the case in Scarsdale, New York, where a fifth of public-school students are from Japan. Unlike Fort Lee, which includes diverse ethnic and immigrant groups, Scarsdale is wealthy, homogeneous, and somewhat stunned from the sudden influx from Japan. American and Japanese adults there lead mostly separate lives, in part because the expatriate group is large enough to sustain itself. Like U.S. expatriates of an earlier era, who earned the epithet "Ugly Americans" by herding together in ignorance of local ways, the Japanese are most comfortable with one another.

THE CHILDREN have no choice but to meet and compete at school. A college sophomore, who says he didn't often speak to the Japanese while at Scarsdale High, draws this broad lesson from his experience: "Racial tension between Asians and Americans is just inevitable." Principal Judy Fox is trying hard to promote harmony: Scarsdale High is preparing a course in Japanese language and culture, has put Japanese-English dictionaries in every classroom, and hired "bias-reduction consultants," who encourage students to talk out their differences.

The efforts, though well intended, have yet to bear fruit. "I don't think students here know much about Japanese culture, considering how many Japanese are here," remarked senior Jimmy Zednik, 18, who said he had spent a year in Yokohama. Indeed, a recent visit to the school—during an "International Day" festival, as it happened—suggests that only a few American students mingle with the Japanese.

The kids gathered in the gym at lunchtime to sample foods of their ancestral lands, from Africa to Korea. The U.S. table, offering pretzels, potato chips, and brownies, attracted almost nobody, while the Japan table, serving noodles and sushi, was mobbed. But when Americans and Japanese sat on the floor to eat, they stayed apart. Asked about the apparent conflict, an American girl gestured to a nearby Asian, saying, "*She's* my friend." Replied the Asian: "Yeah—but I'm not Japanese."

Across the room, a group of young Americans eagerly confessed their racist feelings to a visitor, all the while chowing down on Japanese food. Their bluntest remarks don't deserve to be printed, but the sources of their anger are plain. "They're smarter than us," said one, pointing with his chin to some nearby Japanese. Added another: "You hear your parents talking about how they're taking over."

A few feet away, Futa Sakamoto, a ninth-grader, sat with a group of Japanese. He said he does mix with Americans but wishes his schoolmates were more friendly: "*We'll* change, but the Americans don't want to." Part of the trouble, his companions acknowledge, is the language barrier that encourages the Japanese to stick together. Yoshi Ito, 15, gratefully remembered his experience as one of the few Japanese in an American summer camp: "It was very nice to be alone. If there were more Japanese people there, I wouldn't learn."

JAPANESE companies in the area are catching on to the problem. Hitachi, for one, now advises expatriate employees to spread out instead of congregating in the U.S. equivalent of the foreigners' ghettos that Japanese disdainfully call *gaijin mura*. The company also suggests that they take part in community activities, and the Japanese know how to take a hint: Yasushi Sayama, who was general manager of corporate administration before returning to Japan a few months ago, joined a local Lutheran church, even though he's not Christian.

Compared with the tensions of Scarsdale, multiculturalism comes easy in the beautiful state of Kentucky. For one thing, there aren't that many Japanese living around Georgetown or nearby Harrodsburg,

WHY MADONNA ISN'T JAPANESE

Ardent consumers of American popular culture, the Japanese have been largely unable thus far to enrich it. Sure, U.S. children play Nintendo and read Japanese-influenced comics like *Usagi Yojimbo*, which chronicles the adventures of a samurai rabbit. Rare is the American who doesn't own a Japanese VCR, Walkman, or car. And yes, Japanese cuisine is winning converts: According to Kenji Kishimoto of Suntory, which sells its beer in the U.S. mostly in Japanese restaurants, the States boasts roughly 3,500 such eateries. That's 40% more than in 1980, but so what? Even *Wendy's* has that many outlets.

In U.S. pop culture, Japanese ideas seem to succeed only when watered down. Ninjas are big, but you'd have to go into some kind of trance to find much Confucian thought in *Teenage Mutant Ninja Turtles II*. The last Japanese tune to reach *Billboard*'s hit parade was "Sukiyaki" in 1963. (Idiotically named for the U.S. market, it was actually about love, not lunch.) Hollywood has lavishly honored director Akira Kurosawa, whose film *Ran* was Japan's biggest U.S. box-office hit. Total ticket sales? Only $7 million, about what it costs to lure Jack Nicholson out of bed.

Nor has Japanese culture made major inroads into ordinary consumer marketing. Smith & Hawken, a specialized mail-order house, does well with Japanese garden tools. But despite a recent plug on *thirtysomething,* the highbrow Signals catalogue has sold only a few hundred of the desktop Zen rock gardens it offers for $45 each. Kellogg has introduced what it calls an "Oriental cereal" named Kenmei with a bold ideogram on the box meaning grain plant. The stuff is like Rice Krispies minus the snap-crackle-pop, and it isn't making much noise in the marketplace, either. Perhaps wisely, ads for Anheuser-Busch's successful Bud Dry beer don't mention that the lengthy dry brewing process, which causes extra fermentation, comes from Japan.

In time, all this may change. The trendy young tastemakers in New York and L.A. went Japanese years ago. They're drawn to artists like Masami Teraoka and fashion designers like Rei Kawakubo, who sells $100 million of clothing annually under her Comme des Garçons label. They admire the thoughtful spareness of Japanese design—and the way things work in America, that means someday you probably will too.

where Hitachi makes auto parts. Of that factory's 490 employees, only 14 are Japanese. The expatriates—managers and engineers—seemed to fit right in while eating lunch at the local Pizza Hut.

The other great difference here is that the Japanese provide a powerful boost to the Kentucky economy, and the Americans likeliest to meet Japanese are those who work for them. In this unprosperous corner of the world, people are thankful just to hold a job.

The Japanese are shrewd employers. In Kentucky, which lost many sons in World War II—Harrodsburg has a memorial to victims of the Bataan death march—the Japanese hire mostly young people with no memory of that war and little chance of finding a better job anywhere else. The Japanese can be more demanding than boot-camp drill instructors, but they pay well and reward outstanding performance. And the plants make products that sell, which translates into pride and job security for workers.

Some become enthusiasts. Dean Lee has been promoted twice in his three years at Hitachi; only 27, he manages the plant's production planning. An intelligent man who holds a degree in industrial technology from Morehead State University, Lee sounds like a Moonie when he says, with conviction, "We're an American company"—as if Japanese ownership and management counted for nothing.

Working for Hitachi, he says, "has just changed me totally." Among the lessons learned from his employers: patient deliberation in making decisions. Instead of just buying a car this year, Lee pondered his choices for four months before settling on a Mercury, which, he notes, uses Hitachi parts. He recently sold his house but plans to rent an apartment and carefully consider his options before buying again.

John Beets, 35, a Toyota team leader, learned a lot by observing the Japanese at play. "They know how to relax," he says, "but a party or a golf game with them lasts two or three hours at the maximum—then the schedule kicks in and they go off somewhere else. Now I tend to set schedules for myself more. I make sure I have flexibility but also try to get something done at certain points along the day."

FOR Karen Satterly, 24, a born-again Baptist who assembles circuitboards at Hitachi, the lesson is more personal. In her high school she says many Americans felt inferior to their few Japanese schoolmates, the offspring of expatriate managers. When she joined Hitachi, she felt uncertain of her ability to meet the company's standards. "The Japanese are such particular people," she explains. In time Satterly learned how to make the parts the precise way her employers want them. She's proud of her work now, and of herself. "I think a lot of people feel inferior, and that tends to make them a little mean," she says. "That's just something they have to overcome."

Experiences like these are the essence of Japan's influence in America: an accumulation of personal discoveries, small in themselves, that could add up to something big.

'Return' of Native Americans Challenges Racial Definition

SUMMARY: The 1990 census shows an increasing number of people who have identified themselves as American Indians. Observers attribute the surge to better social acceptance, growing ethnic pride and possible eligibility for affirmative action benefits. Meanwhile, racial preference and intermarriage have made the task of racial definitions more problematic.

Returns from the 1990 census reveal that several hundred thousand Americans reidentified themselves as American Indian after the 1980 count, apparently having changed their racial identification from white or other races to Indian when they filled out their census forms.

A continuing surge of pride in American Indian ancestry among those who previously disavowed it surely accounts for a large portion of the identity switch. As many as 10 million Americans, or one in 25, can claim at least some Indian ancestry. With social attitudes changing, many have begun to assert their lineage. Following a long history of anti-Indian discrimination, Indian culture has gained acceptance and even admiration among the public.

"It's OK to be Indian today," says A. Gay Kingman, executive director of the National Congress of American Indians.

Another factor may be at work too, however. As members of a minority group, American Indians are eligible for special benefits under affirmative action programs.

Given this fact, the census results highlight a troublesome social combination: The spread of racial preferences and the growing incidence of marriage across racial lines together make a person's racial classification economically more important but also more difficult to determine.

"Race is a socially constructed category," says Matthew Snipp, a rural sociologist at the University of Wisconsin. As intermarriage erodes the once-strict boundaries between races, and as people cross those boundaries more freely, racial definitions become fuzzier. "One of the things that we're beginning to see," Snipp observes, "is that when you go over racial lines, then the whole idea of what race means becomes more and more problematic, in the sense that we don't know what our race is, or what racial groups are, or how you define membership in one or another."

Is someone who is one-sixteenth Asian, for example, Asian enough for affirmative action purposes? Is an Argentine less Hispanic than a Mexican? Such classification disputes have begun cropping up across the nation with increasing frequency. The question is particularly open-ended among those of American Indian descent, because historically, intermarriage between those of European and Indian descent has been commonplace.

This switch in self-identification to American Indian continues a three-decade census trend that began in the 1960s and apparently crested in the 1970s, but proceeded with considerable impetus in the past decade. Since 1960, it has led to a tripling of the American Indian population, to some 1.8 million.

Even accounting for high American Indian birthrates, natural population growth alone cannot explain the increase. The phenomenon is "demographically impossible," according to Jeffrey Passel, a demographer at the Urban Institute, a Washington think tank.

"The only thing we know pretty much for sure is that you can't start with previous censuses, add births and subtract deaths, and get to the next census," says David Word, a statistician and demographer with the Census Bureau. The 1990 census for American Indians is about 10 percent higher than would be expected from natural population increases, Passel estimates; the 1980 count was 35 percent higher.

Moreover, the biggest increases in the American Indian population are showing up in such odd places as New Jersey and Alabama, states that have no large tribal groups, tribal lands or reservations. By contrast, in the so-called Indian states of the West such as Arizona, Wyoming, Oklahoma or South Dakota, where some two-thirds of American Indians live, the population increases come in closer to expectations.

"One of the interesting things about this," Passel says, "is that it's not happening by and large in the states that we think of as having a lot of Indians."

The population figures are far too high to be attributed to improved census counts.

Another Decade of Pride

Increase in residents identifying themselves as American Indian, Aleut or Eskimo from the 1980 census to the 1990 census

State	%	State	%	State	%
Alabama	117.7%	Kentucky	59.8%	North Carolina	24.0%
Arizona	33.2	Louisiana	53.7	North Dakota	28.6
Arkansas	35.5	Maryland	61.7	Ohio	66.3
California	20.3	Michigan	38.9	Oklahoma	49.0
Connecticut	46.8	Minnesota	42.5	Oregon	40.9
Delaware	52.0	Mississippi	37.9	Pennsylvania	55.7
District of Columbia	42.2	Missouri	61.0	Rhode Island	40.5
Georgia	75.3	Montana	27.9	South Dakota	12.5
Hawaii	84.2	Nebraska	35.0	Texas	64.4
Illinois	34.1	Nevada	47.6	Vermont	72.4
Indiana	62.3	New Hampshire	57.8	Virginia	61.6
Iowa	34.7	New Jersey	78.3	Wisconsin	33.5
Kansas	42.9	New York	58.3	Wyoming	33.6

SOURCE: U.S. Census Bureau; data on 12 remaining states not available

M. VEY MARTINI / INSIGHT

"Obviously, if you're going to create goodies by race, then people are going to try to sneak under the wire."

Nor can immigration, which is swelling the tally of Asians and Hispanics, be an important factor among the indigenous Indian peoples. The only explanation demographers can point to is a voluntary change in self-identification.

The Census Bureau has no regulations governing how one should answer the race or ancestry questions. "The census doesn't make you prove that you're a member of a tribe or anything," says Wayne L. Ducheneaux, a Cheyenne River Sioux and president of the National Congress of American Indians. "It just asks you if you're Indian, and if you say yes, you're counted as one."

People may answer the census questions however they choose, and apparently, says Passel, "people are now considerably more willing to identify their race as American Indian than they used to be."

Demographers can only speculate as to why this should be, lacking any concrete evidence of people's motives.

It would be fair to assume, says Passel, that census counts reflect some spillover from affirmative action programs. "You can attribute this in part to the fact that people perceive there may be some benefits to them of their Indian ancestry," he says. "Whether there are or not is a different question, but the fact that they perceive that there might be some is what's important."

To be sure, individual responses to census questions are confidential; the answers cannot make anyone eligible for any affirmative action benefits. "Checking yourself off as American Indian on the census form buys you absolutely nothing," Snipp says. However, given that the census form is an official government document, there may be a perception, however erroneous, that how one answers the census has a bearing on one's racial classification for employment or other purposes.

Pride in Indian ancestry is also a major factor, Passel and other demographers believe. The 1960s civil rights movement kindled greater respect for nonwhite races. Before that time, American Indian culture was widely disdained. Such brutal episodes as the forced removal of the Cherokee from the Southeast to Oklahoma in 1838 and 1839 color much of early American history.

From the late 19th century until the 1960s, Snipp notes, the U.S. government believed Indians should be assimilated into the wider culture. "The federal government in particular implemented a number of fairly repressive policies designed basically to stamp out Indian culture," he says. These included a Court of Indian Offenses, administered by the Bureau of Indian Affairs, that existed until 1935. Its purpose, Snipp says, was to prosecute Indians who practiced traditional tribal culture, who wore traditional dress, lived in traditional homes or practiced traditional religion. Schools were also used as tools of forced assimilation and indoctrination.

As late as the 1950s, Congress legally "terminated" several tribes by taking them off the government's list of recognized tribes. As a result, the terminated tribes lost their sovereignty rights and other legal protections. Among those tribes were several California Indian rancherias, or communities, the Catawba of South Carolina and the mixed-blood Ute of Utah. Although most of them have since been restored to the government list, some remain unrecognized. The Ponca tribe of Nebraska was restored to the government list only last October. The federal government now recognizes 507 tribes.

In fact, says Ducheneaux, "We're in one of the cycles again where it's kind of fashionable to be an Indian. Characterizations of Indian culture in television and film have swung from disparaging to admiring, as a comparison between 1950s westerns and the recent film "Dances with Wolves" clearly illustrates.

In light of the general — not to say complete — shift in public attitudes, it is hardly surprising that more Americans would declare Indian lineage.

Reidentification can also work in reverse, say census analysts. For example, if the 1940 census had been taken in 1942, fewer people probably would have listed their ancestry as German.

The census patterns themselves indicate a rise in a kind of romantic fascination with American Indian ancestry among those who never claimed it before, notes Passel. The largest shifts in self-identification are showing up mainly in Eastern states, which account for just one-third of the Indian population. The 1990 counts there came in 30 percent above estimates based on birth and death rates, Passel says.

By contrast, in the states that account for two-thirds of the Indian population, the census count came in only 3 percent above expectations. Analysts believe that in the West even people who claim some Indian ancestry generally consider American Indians to be those who are enrolled members of a tribe.

Tribal requirements for membership are far more strict than the simple self-designation asked on the census form. Each tribe determines its membership criteria, much as nations set their own requirements for citizenship. Many tribes require some fixed percentage — one-half or one-sixteenth, for example — of Indian ancestry.

The certification process is often quite formal. The Cherokee Nation of Oklahoma, for example, requires that individuals trace and legally document their lineage back to the "final enrollment" of 43,000 Cherokee that took place from 1899 to 1906, says tribal registrar R. Lee Fleming.

Some federal benefits, including social services, welfare and health care, are directed specifically to American Indians, but people who receive tribal benefits must be enrolled members of a federally recognized tribe.

Moreover, beneficiaries must also live on or near a reservation, says Steve Gleason, assistant to the assistant secretary for Indian affairs. While the Bureau of Indian Affairs receives a few calls each week from people claiming to be Indian and asking where they can sign up for benefits, Gleason says there has been no unusual increase in such requests.

Eligibility for affirmative action, however, is determined by individuals' self-identification, and such benefits are much more widespread and valuable. A shift in self-identification, at least as reflected in the census, would be far more likely to appear among those of American Indian descent than those of African or Hispanic ancestry, most of whom are already identifying themselves as such. A large pool of people can claim American Indian ancestry but do not identify themselves racially as such; many of these can switch their racial identification if they decide to do so for whatever reason.

The census questionnaire itself reflects a greater social sensitivity to racial identification. The 1960 census, for example, had one race question with seven categories. In 1970, the race question expanded to a dozen categories, and a trial question on Hispanic origin was added.

By 1980, the race question had expanded to 14 categories. The question on Hispanic origin was extended to the entire census, and a new question on ancestry was added, with space allowed for open-ended responses.

"There's clearly a recognition in the census that this data is important," Passel says, "and the census usually doesn't lead

A shift in self-identification would be far more likely to appear among those of American Indian descent than those of African or Hispanic ancestry.

in this regard. The census content follows."

As the use of racial preferences spreads, the definition of race becomes increasingly important to an individual's economic status; at the same time, intermarriage makes such definitions hazier. Reports of racial impostors are becoming more common, as are disputes over who exactly is entitled to preferences on the basis of ancestry. In San Francisco, a Hispanic fire fighter is even calling for a review board to determine racial eligibility.

These trends follow a typical pattern that has emerged in countries using racial preferences — from India, which grants special benefits to the untouchables and other "backward castes," to Malaysia, which favors Malays over Chinese, and South Africa, which discriminates in favor of whites. Walter E. Williams, an economist at George Mason University and author of a book on South African racial policies, argues that racial preferences create incentives to fraud and so beget legal rules delineating racial identity.

"Obviously, if you're going to create goodies by race," Williams says, "then people are going to try to sneak under the wire."

The proposal in San Francisco to set up a racial review board, Williams says, bears an unsettling resemblance to schemes used to defend South African apartheid. Early on in the apartheid regime, he notes, population registry laws were instituted to provide definitions of race. The government had a particular classification problem with so-called coloreds, people of mixed descent. Racial classification boards were also put in place, where individuals could legally challenge the racial classification of another person.

So far, U.S. preferences still rely on self-identification. Eventually, however, "you're going to have to give that up" to maintain the integrity of the system, Williams warns. Because affirmative action policies award jobs, contracts, admission to college and other economic benefits on the basis of race as well as individual competence, they inevitably create strong incentives to claim those benefits among those whose connection to the protected group may be tenuous at best.

The 1990 census results, showing a huge increase in those reidentifying themselves as American Indian, may reflect people responding to these incentives.

— *Carolyn Lochhead*

Nonethnic Minorities

Let us think beyond the notion that it is impolite to discriminate against minorities. Discrimination is not merely rude, it is theft of social power. In sociology, the term minority means lack of power, sometimes termed powerlessness. Those who discriminate seek to keep minorities weak in power: lacking money, lacking political voice, lacking good paying jobs, lacking education, and lacking good housing. Discrimination is literally a put-down. Do not think of discrimination as bad manners; think of it as social aggression.

This section looks at some of the groups remaining after we subtract racial and ethnic minorities: children, women, homeless men, the elderly, and gays and lesbians. Each of these groups experiences difficulties with social power. Some are denied quality jobs because of gender or because they are too old or too young. Some are denied privacy and dignity. Some are denied the right to the benefits of religion and family. Discrimination seeks to push people out of the mainstream of society, to pay them less, to educate them less, and to give them less voice and protection. As you read the articles, try to understand how minorities are denied power, and where within our society they may find strength to maintain their dignity.

Our first article, by television pediatrician T. Berry Brazelton, asks "Why Is American Failing Its Children?" Children, he contends, endure more deprivation than any other segment of society. Some children know as early as age nine months that society expects them to fail.

As a helpful parallel to Dr. Brazelton's article, "Children in Peril" provides statistics we can use to describe the plight of children. Did you realize that the United States has the highest infant mortality rate in the industrialized world? Data are presented showing how children are victimized through substances and diseases transmitted by their parents, how they are poisoned by lead, and injured by automobiles, burns, and gunshot wounds.

"Everyday Life in Two High-Risk Neighborhoods" provides two short research field reports from inner-city neighborhoods. Philippe Bourgois lived with a family in a tenement in East Harlem. He used classical participant-observer methods, spending hundreds of nights on the streets and in crack houses. Linda Burton focused on the impact of illicit drug trafficking on families. The paired articles picture how social problems, in this case drugs and poverty, touch inner-city children.

"The Feminization of Poverty" uses a scholarly approach to support the contention that female-headed households, that is, women with children, are a large and growing portion of our nation's poor. She charges that sexism and racism within an unjust economy perpetuate a minority position for such families.

"The Prejudice Against Men" asks us to consider whether the social problem of homelessness might be compounded by society's attitude toward males. Perhaps the cultural belief that men ought to fend for themselves and not ask for help causes males to live on the streets instead of seeking shelters. This article poses an interesting cultural question about a continuing social condition.

"The Story of a Nursing Home Refugee" will introduce you to a person with spunk. Katharine Butterworth has a great deal of experience with nursing homes—first with her husband, and most recently herself. In her nineties, she prefers to live alone rather than give up her privacy and her dignity. The article is lively, yet it gets to the problems of providing quality care for our oldest citizens.

Should couples who love and are committed to one another have the right to a Christian marriage? "Rights Issues Split Protestant Churches" discusses how questions of marriage and ordination for gays and lesbians are challenging mainline Protestant denominations. Since religion and marriage constitute basic institutions, having church leaders seriously discuss gay and lesbian concerns is a clear sign of social change.

Looking Ahead: Challenge Questions

Is America actually failing its children? If so, what social measures ought to be taken to reverse the failure?

How has drugs caused the social institutions of inner-cities to deteriorate? How might we protect children from the deprivations of living within a drug environment?

What evidence exists to support the contention that female-headed households are victims of racism and sexism?

How does our cultural attitude toward men contribute to the sad conditions of homelessness?

What are the problems of nursing homes? Are there ways to preserve human dignity within an institutional setting?

Unit 3

Why Is America Failing Its Children?

Children endure more deprivation than any other segment of society. Yet, says the author, the U.S. could reduce this tragedy with remedies that are available right now.

T. Berry Brazelton

T. Berry Brazelton, a pediatrician at Harvard Medical School and Children's Hospital Medical Center in Boston, is the author of numerous books on child care and a columnist for Family Circle magazine.

Frightened children crowd the chaotic, steamy hall outside a Los Angeles courtroom. Some are crying. Others can only muster the energy to whimper. Most are dirty, with sallow skin and dull expressions, and they cling to their mothers' skirts.

In succession, the mothers and a few fathers are called to appear before a sympathetic but harried judge, who has already studied the pile of reports from welfare workers and now allots 30 minutes to hear and decide each case. The question: Which children can stay with their parents and which ones cannot?

The children in the courthouse have been living at a shelter that tries to rehabilitate families. Their stories have a pathetic sameness. A family of four had been wandering for two years after relatives threw them out. When the father succeeds in panhandling money, he drinks and becomes abusive and violent. The mother, haggard and slow-moving, appears half-witted. Her file says she is incapable of caring for her two children. The

daughter, age 8, was failing second grade and has changed schools five times. Her 5-year-old brother has bad dreams. At the welfare hotel where the family lived for a while, he was scared that "a mean man" would take him away from his mother. When asked how that made him feel, he replied "itchy." The reason, his mother said, was that there were not enough beds and that the children slept on the bug-infested floor.

What choice do the courts have with such families? Often, the judges will deem the case hopeless and try to salvage children by putting them in foster care—"before it is too late."

But, in too many cases, it already seems too late to me. The families are locked into a system that is not working for anyone—the family or the courts—and judges and social workers can offer only Band-Aids.

I was at the courthouse several months ago with other members of the National Commission on Children, a group appointed by the White House and Congress in 1989 to study the status of America's future generation. The panel's 36 members come from all professions, all political persuasions and all parts of the country. In the first year of its two-year tenure, the commission has been visiting prisons, court-

rooms and neighborhoods, and holding hearings and meetings in cities and towns from Connecticut to California. What it learns will shape its recommendations, due next spring, for private and public initiatives for the 90's.

As a pediatrician with 40 years' experience with 25,000 children, mostly middle class, I have begun to regard the growing neglect and poverty of the young as the biggest threat to the nation's future. I also see evidence that we could start preventing this terrible waste, with remedies available right now—but we seem to have lost the will even to think about it.

Consider the reaction when the commission reported its first-year findings last month. Children are the poorest group in society, with more than one in five living in a household whose income is below the poverty level, $12,700 for a family of four. Despite medical advances, the United States infant mortality rate is worse than in some third world countries, and every *day* more than 100 American babies die before their first birthday, and as many as 18 percent of newborns in some city hospitals are born exposed to alcohol, crack and other hard drugs.

On hearing all this, the press asked, "So, what's new?" The panel could only reply, alas, that

nothing is new. Americans have become numb to reports of the hopelessness of their children.

Are we really so cynical or are we afraid to face the problem? As the commission has noted, the figures are widely reported, but too rarely followed up by action. Taxpayers and legislators are not yet determined to insure that every child has the opportunity to grow up healthy and whole, to be secure, and to become literate and economically productive.

Certainly, the uneven face of American poverty is a factor. Although at least 21 percent of all children are needy, the problem is more intense in city neighborhoods and rural pockets. Forty-five percent of black children and 39 percent of Hispanic children were poor in 1987, compared with 15 percent of whites. More than half the children in households headed by single women are impoverished.

Employment does not guarantee escape from poverty. Forty-four percent of poor two-parent families have at least one full-time worker, and 25 percent of these households have a parent who works part time. The prevalent bias—that those who are destitute deserve it—is not borne out by the commission's investigations.

Needy children are in double

From *The New York Times Magazine*, September 9, 1990, pp. 41-42, 50, 90. Copyright © 1990 by T. Berry Brazelton. Reprinted by permission of Lescher & Lescher, Ltd.

jeopardy. They have the most health problems, and the least access to care. Poor women do not receive prenatal care or adequate preventive care for their infants. When they do seek help, no one seems to care about them as people. Thus, they go to doctors and hospitals only in emergencies. In general, the families that suffer the most social stress receive the least social support. The widening gap in this country between rich and poor makes it even more likely that these children will repeat their parents' poverty. They will not be prepared to contribute to society— except in an antagonistic, often violent, way.

WHEN I TESTIFY ABOUT the problems of middle-class, two-career families, I find the news media attentive. The increasing pressure on such families is enormous. But even there, in pressing for decent day care, maternity and paternity leaves from work and other initiatives related to children's well-being, I have learned how little commitment there is at the national level to family issues.

We are the least family-oriented society in the civilized world. If you asked any citizen, "Does America believe in families and children?" the answer would be, "Of course." But how much denial and distortion is couched in that answer!

If there is an implicit bias in the United States, it is this: Families should be self-sufficient, and if they're not, they deserve to suffer. That outlook appears to dominate political and private decisions. Only for the group of desperate families willing to label themselves hopeless — unwed, unemployed, homeless — do we have handouts, like Aid to Families with Dependent Children. To qualify for help, a family must first identify itself as a failure. The labels stick. Treated as such, people will feel and act like failures. Despite the huge amount spent on welfare, the efforts are generally counterproductive, offering money without real support.

Programs like Head Start and Women, Infants and Children (a supplemental food program) have often succeeded because they reached out to parents. Families are educated together. As children succeed, their parents begin to feel successful. This progress has a lasting effect. Unfortunately, few programs take such an approach, and the human and financial commitment required is considerable. To succeed, a program has to make people feel as if they are individuals worthy of help. How is that done? It might mean that someone has to enter the bleak, often dangerous, world of poor families to help clean up their house, for example, to buy the groceries and to play with their children.

SEVERAL MONTHS AGO, I was hurrying to an appointment in lower Manhattan. I saw a typical homeless man approaching. He had long, matted hair and dirty, slept-in clothing. I was relieved to see that his eyes were fixed on the ground. I averted mine to avoid contact, which would have added guilt to my feelings about his condition.

As we passed each other, he said, "I sure like your show, Doc."

Startled and unbelieving, I asked, "Do you watch it?"

"When I can find a free TV," he replied.

"Do you have any children?"

"Yeah, a baby. She's right over here, if you want to see her."

He took me over to the protected corner of a bank building, where a young woman was tenderly nursing her 4-month-old baby. The father, whose image had already changed in my eyes, picked up the infant, cradled her and began to play.

Soon they were locked in a reciprocal exchange of "Yeah," "Coo," "That's right," "Coo," "Come on, one more time." He turned to me and said, "That's how you do it on your television show."

I was completely won over. We were on the same wavelength and talked about baby and family issues for several minutes. All the ingredients for being a successful parent were there, needing only adequate support.

I didn't give them housing or money, but they welcomed my respect and empathy. Their gift to me was insight into the depth of my prejudices.

When I returned to my Cambridge, Mass., office that afternoon, a young father brought me his 4-month-old baby. He was as proud and committed as my friend of the streets. He demonstrated the same tender communication as he looked down at his daughter. "How is my girl?" he said. She cooed. He cooed back. Their communication was a replica of the powerful bonds I saw growing in the homeless family in New York.

Families do care about one another. What an opportunity we have to strengthen and cement young families around a new baby.

MEMBERS OF THE National Commission on Children went to a high-security prison in rural South Carolina to talk to teen-agers serving sentences of 15 to 20 years for rape, murder and armed robbery.

Many of the young men, white and black, carried the signs of intractable poverty: the shifty, gaze-avoiding look with head half-cocked that says, "Hit me again, I'm no good." The looks of others, however, were clear-eyed, direct and confident. They sat in a ring next to us in the room where we met. The armed guards who surrounded us were as unobtrusive as possible. We wanted to find out what brought these children there.

As we talked, the questions became more personal. Their responses seemed to fall into two categories.

One group became sullen and lifeless. Their shoulders sagged. Their hands shifted uneasily in their laps. Their dirty hair and sallow complexions gave the impression that they had given up. Only their eyes belied this, becoming steely as they watched the more verbal members talk with us. They were angry, not hopeless.

The verbal teen-agers were alert and carried themselves with the confidence of athletes. Their complexions were clearer, their hair was likely to be clean and thick. Their responses were open and charming, and had none of the ominous hostility of those of the other group. They used body language to capture our attention. One could easily imagine offering a home to one of them, though their histories included murder and rape.

A handsome youth in this group told us his story. He grew up in poverty in rural South Carolina, raised by a struggling single mother. Even as a child, he felt sorry for her. He saw her as overwhelmed — with too many kids, no support, no hope in her job. No one ever had time to do anything but scold or swat him. He couldn't wait until he reached the age of 12. Then, he figured, he could be on his own and be as angry as he always wanted. He could rob, vandalize, even murder, if anyone got in his way. He could get all the things he wanted, trying to banish the empty feeling he always had. He spoke as if this had been his destiny, and he had fulfilled it.

Others spoke of anger and crime as an antidote to boredom and emptiness. They told us how sure they were that they needed to be incarcerated. A curly headed boy said, "I knew that if they didn't put me in jail the first time, I'd keep on until they did."

A commission member asked, "What will you do when you finish your term here?"

"Get put back in, I guess," he replied. His energy and air of self-confidence covered his underlying turbulence.

I felt this boy had the capacity for what physicists call escape velocity. As particles circle a central focus, centrifugal force holds them in their orbit. A few particles spin out of orbit and shoot off into space with escape velocity. These particles are endowed with unusual force. They continue on a long trajectory.

Some young prisoners had that kind of personal force. If they had been salvaged early and had had this energy channeled more positively, they might have become the children who escape from poverty. But no one had stood by to help or guide them. No one had given their families individual attention or expert advice.

WHEN I SAW THESE TEEN-agers in the Bennettsville, S.C., prison, I thought: From years of experience, I know that we have the knowledge to recognize this expectation of failure, when a child is as young as 9 months. Can we avert it if we start to help them then?

In our work at Children's Hospital in Boston, where I founded the Child Development Unit, we assess babies of all ages and from all sectors of society. By 9 months of age, the babies who show signs that they expect to fail for the rest of their lives can be identified by various tests. For instance, we can tell a lot when we hand them two blocks to play with. A child who expects to succeed in demanding situations will take one block, mouth it, rub it in his hair, drop it over the side of the table, looking up to see who will retrieve it. Finally, he'll show his cognitive capacity to match size and shape by putting the two blocks together. At that point, he'll look up at the examiner with a twinkling, bright-eyed look. He *expects* to be praised.

By contrast, a child who expects to fail may dutifully take the two blocks. He won't dare to experiment. His repertory is already limited by the realization that no one will care. He slides the two blocks close to each other, demonstrating appropriate cognitive capacity. But, as if compelled, he slides them past each other. As he

fails in the task, he looks up at us with a dull look of failure. He cocks his head to one side, as if to say: "Hit me again. I'm no good, and I deserve it." At 15 months, he'll trip as he walks. Then he'll look up vacantly to receive the recognition of his failure. At 18 months, he'll make the adults who take care of him so angry, with temper tantrums and other provocations, that they'll want to strangle him. He already feels it is his destiny to fail.

We don't know whether he expects to fail because he comes from a chaotic, unrewarding environment, or whether learning disabilities or hyperactivity have held him back. Either factor produces such a pattern. A hyperactive child senses his failure long before it can be diagnosed. He already experiences the damaged self-image that will be the most serious hurdle for any potential remedial action. Poor children sense that hopelessness in their parents and learn to fail. No one in their surroundings has the time or the energy to observe them as they work to master a developmental task. No one supports them as they struggle toward a goal. If they do master something, there is no one to say: "Look what you just did! You did it yourself!" The rewards to fuel future success are not present.

Some children need help from the day they are born. The newborns who are exposed to alcohol and hard drugs like crack and heroin are potentially handicapped by the disorganization of their nervous systems, a condition that is hard to establish medically but is apparent to anyone who sees the baby. They are either limp and unresponsive or are hypersensitive and behave chaotically. They have difficulty receiving and responding to the stimuli of a soothing voice or face. When they are cuddled or rocked, they react with piercing wails and jerky motions. Few people could love these babies. They are likely to suffer later from learning disabilities and to be either hyperactive or emotionally flat. They also tend to be at the mercy of their impulses. The social programs re-

> Some children need help from the day they are born. The programs required to educate them will require billions. Then, billions more to incarcerate them.

quired to educate them will cost billions of dollars. Then, eventually, it will cost billions more to incarcerate them. A new generation will have to live with them, as well as pay the price of our generation's insensitivity to their parents' hopelessness.

What would help? Special centers for fragile infants and mothers would allow two generations a safe haven, a place to withdraw from their addiction and despair. A new mother has a rare incentive to re-evaluate her own life. Early intervention in teaching mothers how to care for their babies could help.

Recently, I assessed a premature infant at Boston City Hospital. She was one of twins born to a drug addict. The other baby was still on life support, but at 1 week of age, this one was now out of the oxygen unit and could be evaluated. She still had an intravenous line dripping into her right hand for feeding. The intestinal tracts of such babies cannot tolerate food, and they must be fed artifi-

cially. Meanwhile, they are at high risk.

The neonatologist told me she and the other doctors thought that the baby was blind, because her eyes wandered independently. They weren't sure if she could hear, and her muscle tone was so poor that they thought she had a damaged nervous system. Newborns of mothers addicted to cocaine are unresponsive. During pregnancy, the drug crosses into the placenta and remains in a fetus's system for two to three hours after a 20-minute hit for the mother.

As I tried to arouse this limp infant, she suddenly began to stiffen and scream, changing from a listless state to a hyperactive one. Her screams, coupled with her scrawny, wrinkled body and frowning face, made her extremely unattractive. What would an addicted parent in an addicted environment do to such a baby? The ingredients for child abuse were all there. When I tried to swaddle her, she fought her way out of the wrappings with frantic motions of arms, legs and torso. When I tried to give her a pacifier, she spit it across the room.

Finally, in desperation, I forced her left thumb into her mouth and held it there. She gagged, and the onlookers winced. I held it in her mouth until she finally began to suck on it. At that point, her eyes, which had been wandering, came together. She seemed to focus all of her kinetic energy on her sucking. Her eyes opened to follow my face and voice, as I rocked her gently and talked quietly to her. She followed a bright red ball that I held about 18 inches in front of her eyes. Her face brightened and softened, her features became babyish and pretty for the first time. Her entire body relaxed in my hands, as she followed me with her eyes and turned to my voice. She had become an engaging baby. No longer did we think she was blind, or even brain-damaged. She was saving herself.

The nurses who had cared

for her were amazed. They brought in the mother, a depressed, fragile-looking woman who had been indicted on charges that she had abused her fetus. As she watched her transformed baby responding to my face and voice, relaxed and responsive, sucking on her fist to control herself, the mother began to weep and said: "What I've done to my baby!"

The woman, addicted to crack, heroin and methadone, is in treatment and is showing signs of progress. Her baby is in an early intervention program and is doing well. She probably does not have permanent brain damage, though she may eventually have various physiological problems.

But a lot is known about remedial treatment for fragile premature babies, knowledge that could also be applied to drug-exposed babies. In a recent study in eight cities of high-risk premature infants, sponsored chiefly by the Robert Wood Johnson Foundation, it was demonstrated that intervention for the infant and personal care and attention for the families paid off. At age 3, the I.Q.'s of the babies who received help increased by 6 to 13 points, enough to provide them with the basis for making it in society.

Many of these babies will have learning disabilities, attention disorders like hyperactivity and, eventually, im-

pulse disorders, meaning they will lack all sense of self-control. If they are sent home to a parent who is addicted or to an otherwise chaotic environment, they have little hope for recovery.

Can some addicted mothers be salvaged for their babies' sake? The effort needs to be made, because there are not enough foster homes for the lost children. If this isn't addressed as a national emergency, the country will throw away two generations — the babies and their mothers.

The course of American poverty can be changed. We must identify what endangers children and what protects them. We must begin early to enhance parents' desire to nurture their children. A few programs follow this approach, and they are outlined in Lisbeth B. and Daniel Schorr's excellent book, "Within Our Reach: Breaking the Cycle of Disadvantage" (Doubleday, Anchor).

Take two outstanding programs, in Tacoma, Wash., and New Haven.

In Tacoma several years ago, a group from Catholic Community Services was bemoaning the tragedy of troubled families who were on the verge of giving up their children. The families received aid from a patchwork of services, but needed more concerted help. The group created a program, with the help of financing from the National Institute

of Mental Health, that offers the services of social workers, psychologists and counselors for any family in imminent danger of losing their child or children. The worker has only two families at a time and meets frequently with them at home, even occasionally helping with daily problems like balancing checkbooks. Gradually the family learns to trust this counselor, who can then help them with the harder task of rebuilding their lives. The success of the Tacoma program is demonstrated in the number of preserved families. Ninety percent of the families in the program are together after nine years.

The New Haven program is for school-age children. Starting two decades ago, Dr. James P. Comer, a Yale child psychiatrist, reorganized communities around efforts to improve elementary schools in devastated neighborhoods. The parents work with the teachers, principal and other school staff as part of a team. Children do better in school when they see that their parents are involved in their education. At the same time, the parents find allies who can help them with the problems of living in the inner city.

More than 100 schools across the country have adopted the parent-partnership approach, and they have reported impressive gains in students' test scores. With support from the Rockefeller

Foundation, Dr. Comer's approach will be tried in the District of Columbia public schools.

According to the Schorrs, the programs that succeed in helping children have four things in common, all seemingly self-evident but all difficult to achieve with the current Band-Aid system. Help must be available at all times and in many different ways. There must be provision, missing from current welfare policies, for meeting individual needs. The staff must be trained and, just as important, build trust among the people. The program must also be accepted in the community.

The challenge for the National Commission on Children is to come up with ways to strengthen families and to support them as they nurture their children's development. We can do it, but it will be expensive and difficult. American leaders seem able to focus only on danger from outside the country, not yet recognizing in any committed way that the greatest threat is from within, in the breakdown of families and in the growing numbers of poor. The anger and addictions of the impoverished and the harm being done to their children are a national crisis. If we want poor children — and therefore all children — to have a future in this country, we have no choice but to make families our top priority.

CHILDREN in PERIL

GEOFFREY COWLEY

American kids remain the most neglected in the developed world

C hildren have never had it easy. A fair proportion have always been beaten, starved, raped or abandoned, and until quite recently even the loved ones faced daunting obstacles. At the beginning of this century, one American child in 10 didn't live to see a first birthday. Today, thanks to major strides in nutrition, sanitation and medical care, 99 out of 100 survive infancy. Yet astonishing numbers continue to die or suffer needlessly. Nearly one child in four is born into poverty, a formidable predictor of lifelong ill health, and a growing number lack such basic advantages as a home, two parents and regular access to a doctor. Every year thousands die violently, from abuse or preventable accidents. Millions go unvaccinated against common childhood diseases. Millions more are poisoned by cigarette smoke or household lead.

Decrying the situation has become a national pastime. Panels are assembled, studies conducted, articles written, speeches made. Yet by vital measures, American children remain the most neglected in the developed world. Their health and welfare are simply "not high on the agenda of this country," laments Dr. Reed Tuckson, a former Washington, D.C., health commissioner and now a vice president at the March of Dimes Birth Defects Foundation. "The federal government doesn't think this is as important as the savings and loan crisis." Here's proof.

Infant mortality

According to newly released government figures, 9.1 out of every 1,000 American babies died during infancy last year (down from 9.7 per 1,000 in 1989). Such rates are a far cry from India's 97 deaths per 1,000 or Guinea's 143, but they're among the highest in the industrialized world—and they don't apply equally to all Americans. The death rate for black infants (17.6 per 1,000 births as of 1988) is more than twice that for whites (8.5 per 1,000). And some regions remain what the National Commission to Prevent Infant Mortality calls "disaster areas." Washington, Detroit and Philadelphia suffer higher infant-death rates than Jamaica or Costa Rica. Parts of the rural South fare even worse. "What we have here in the Mississippi delta is a Third World situation," says Mike Gibbs of Mississippi's Sharkey-Issaquena Health Alliance. Indeed, a baby born in Sharkey or Issaquena county is less likely to survive infancy than one born in Chile.

The main reason children die during infancy is that they're born too soon or too small. Babies with low birth weights (under 5.5 pounds) are 40 times more likely than others to die during their first month, and 20 times more likely to die within a year. Those who survive often grow up deaf, blind or mentally retarded. The problem has eminently preventable causes, including drug and alcohol abuse, smoking, poor nutrition and a lack of prenatal care. Yet low birth weight is as common today as it was a decade ago. Nearly 7 percent of all U.S. babies—a quarter million a year—are born too small. The rate is far higher, and rising, among minorities. In 1988 fully 13 percent of all black children came into the world dangerously underweight.

Substance abuse

Low birth weight is not the only effect of parental substance abuse. Fetal alcohol exposure is the nation's leading known cause of mental retardation, surpassing both Down syndrome and spina bifida. Cigarette smoke not only poisons developing fetuses—causing a quarter of all low birth weights and a tenth of all infant deaths—but disables children who breathe it growing up. Smokers' kids are at increased risk for many respiratory diseases, including asthma. And babies born to cocaine users suffer devastating neurological problems.

The number of fetuses exposed to tobacco and alcohol hasn't changed much lately; America produces 5,000 to 10,000 children with full-blown fetal alcohol syndrome each year, and 10 times that number may suffer the similar but less severe symptoms of fetal alcohol effect. By contrast, cocaine use rose ominously among young women during the 1980s. Though recent findings suggest the problem has peaked, experts guess that a million women of childbearing age use the drug and that 30,000 to 100,000 deliver cocaine-exposed babies each year. At New York's Harlem Hospital, the frequency of cocaine use among expectant mothers jumped from 1 percent in 1980 to 20 percent in 1988. A 1989 survey suggested that 17 percent of Philadelphia's babies were born exposed.

Contagion

Syphilis, gonorrhea and AIDS may sound like adult afflictions, but children are paying dearly for the surge in sexually transmitted diseases over the past decade. They're paying, too, for the decline of childhood immunization efforts. For less than $100 a child can gain immunity against polio, whooping cough, diphtheria, tetanus, measles, mumps and rubella. Virtually all America's kids receive these basic vaccines by the time they start school. Yet vast and growing numbers of 1- to 4-year-olds remain unvaccinated, especially in poor areas. Dr. Antoinette Eaton, president of the American Academy of Pediatrics (AAP), calls the situation "disastrous."

The government stopped tracking early-childhood immunization rates six years ago, but signs of trouble abound. As of 1985 the proportion of preschoolers receiving particular vaccines was 23 percent to 67 percent lower in this country than in Europe. Only half of America's 1- to 4-year-olds were being immunized against polio, according to the AAP, and a quarter received no vaccinations. Recent studies have identified inner-city neighborhoods where 50 to 70 percent of preschool children are unvaccinated. Not surprisingly, these lapses have triggered a major resurgence of once rare childhood diseases. Whooping cough is twice as common today as it was in 1970. Measles cases rose from 1,500 in 1983 to an astounding 25,000 last year.

Lead poisoning

This summer federal health officials are expected to acknowledge formally what researchers and activists have long maintained: that 3 million youngsters—one in six children under 7—have dangerous levels of lead in their blood. A standard ingredient in wall paint until the late 1970s, lead still pervades many households, and mounting evidence suggests that blood levels once considered safe can cause neurological damage. Many experts now consider it the nation's foremost environmental hazard.

Children don't have to eat paint chips to be poisoned; a more common source is the dust that falls from old walls and window panes. Experts are also wary of water systems, lead crystal and imported cans and ceramics. Babies exposed to low doses of lead in the womb tend to be under-weight and underdeveloped at birth. During

grade school, lead-exposed kids exhibit behavioral problems, low IQ and deficiencies in speech and language. And research has shown that teenagers with histories of lead exposure drop out of school seven times as often as their peers.

Lead poisoning is most prevalent among the least privileged—a 1988 study suggested that more than half of low-income black children are afflicted—yet the hazard extends far beyond the ghetto. The study found that in the group with the *lowest* risk—whites living outside central cities—one of every 11 children had high levels of lead in his blood. Officials at the federal Centers for Disease Control in Atlanta have recommended lead screening for all children under 6, yet only one in 10 receives it. If the agency redefines lead poisoning as expected, the demand for a national testing program will surely grow.

Injuries

No disease, drug or environmental hazard rivals traumatic injuries as a killer of children. Every year mishaps claim the lives of 8,000 American youngsters and permanently disable 50,000. Car and bicycle accidents are the main menace, with a death toll of 3,400. Burn injuries kill 1,300—and 1,200 drown. Others die from choking or falls or gunshot wounds. Though most of these injuries are unintentional, child advocates resist calling them accidents. "Our contention," says former surgeon general C. Everett Koop, now chairman of the national Safe Kids Campaign, "is that 90 percent of permanent childhood injuries can be prevented."

The challenge is simply to make parents more vigilant. Koop's campaign stresses such basic precautions as installing smoke alarms (9 out of 10 fire deaths occur in houses that lack them), keeping toddlers away from swimming pools, turning pot handles toward the back of the stove where kids can't reach them and getting children to wear bicycle helmets. According to the National Center for Health Statistics, nearly 70 percent of all hospitalized bicyclists are treated for head trauma. Helmets reduce the risk of brain injury by almost 90 percent—yet only 5 percent of young bike riders wear them.

Injury would seem an equal-opportunity hazard, yet black children die from injuries at nearly twice the rate of others. Koop blames inadequate supervision and a lack of medical care—which is to say he blames poverty. "When I look back on my years in office," he says, "the things I banged my head against were all poverty."

Poverty

Kids under 5 suffer more poverty than any other age group in America. Roughly one in four is poor, versus one in eight adults, and the consequences are manifold. Poor children are more likely to suffer from low birth weight, more likely to die during the first year of life, more likely to suffer hunger or abuse while growing up and less likely to benefit from immunizations or adequate medical care. Moreover, notes Dr. Peter Boelens of the Sharkey-Issaquena Health Alliance, poor kids grow up without ever "understanding what is necessary for healthy living."

Infant Mortality Rates

As of 1988, infant death was twice as common in the U.S. as in Japan. American black children were dying at twice the rate of whites. Selected rankings:

Country	Deaths per 1,000 live births
Japan	5.0
Switzerland	6.8
Singapore	7.0
Canada	7.3
France	7.7
East Germany	8.1
U.S. Whites	**8.5**
United Kingdom	8.8
All U.S.	**10.0**
Czechoslovakia	11.9
China	12.0
Nigeria	13.8
U.S. Blacks	**17.6**

SOURCES: STATISTICAL OFFICE OF THE UNITED NATIONS; NATIONAL CENTER FOR HEALTH STATISTICS

The First to Suffer

Young children endure more poverty than any other age group in the population.

25%

Percent of children under 6 years who are poor

Percent of all people in U.S. who are poor

1966 70 75 80 85 89

SOURCE: NATIONAL CENTER FOR CHILDREN IN POVERTY

Healthy People 2000, the federal government's public-health blueprint for the rest of the decade, seeks to reduce the nation's infant mortality rate to 7 deaths per 1,000 (from today's 9.1), to reduce the frequency of low birth weight to 5 percent (from today's 7 percent) and to ensure that 9 out of 10 (instead of 3 out of 4) expectant mothers get early prenatal care. Modest goals, yet few children's advocates expect them to be met. Too many better-armed interests are competing for the available federal dollars. "Children don't vote," says Florida Gov. Lawton Chiles, chairman of the National Commission to Prevent Infant Mortality, "and they do not contribute to political campaigns."

There are glimmers of hope. The Bush administration recently proposed a five-year, $171 million initiative to reduce infant mortality by half in 10 hard-hit cities—but proposed paying for it by taking money away from existing maternal and child-health programs. Congress blocked that move and has appropriated $25 million to fund the 10-city effort next year. No one is complaining, but the effort is only a start. "We want to encourage and celebrate Mr. Bush's initiative," says Tuckson, of the March of Dimes. "But if we recognize that reducing infant mortality is important, why not 20 cities?"

Or 40? There is no economy in neglecting children's health. Kids born underweight end up in intensive-care units, often at state expense. Many remain lifelong burdens to society. "Forget the humane reasons for providing prenatal health care," says Jennifer Howse, president of the March of Dimes. "There is a cold, hard business reason. It saves money."

With LARRY WILSON *in New York,* MARY HAGER *and* STEVEN WALDMAN *in Washington and* JOE DELANEY *in Carey, Miss.*

EVERYDAY LIFE IN TWO HIGH-RISK NEIGHBORHOODS

Growing Up

PHILIPPE BOURGOIS

Philippe Bourgois is an assistant professor of anthropology at San Francisco State University and a visiting scholar at the Russell Sage Foundation in New York. He is writing a book entitled, In Search of Respect: Selling Crack in Spanish Harlem, *which will be published by Little, Brown & Co.*

I live with my family in a tenement in East Harlem opposite a large complex of public housing projects where I have been engaged since 1985 in ethnographic research. I am using the classical anthropological methodology of participant-observation fieldwork, focusing on a network of youths and adults who participate intensively in the underground economy—primarily street-level, retail crack distribution. This means I have spent hundreds of nights on the streets and in crack houses observing and tape recording dealers and addicts. I visit their families, attend their parties and intimate reunions—from Thanksgiving dinners to New Year's Eve celebrations—in order to collect life history interviews and to befriend their children, spouses, lovers, siblings, mothers, grandmothers, and—when possible—fathers and stepfathers. This allows me to situate the street dealing scene in its larger family and community context.

East Harlem, also referred to as "*El Barrio,*" or Spanish Harlem, is a 200-square-block neighborhood in New York City's upper East Side. Although the population is between 40 and 45 percent African-American, it is considered by both its residents and outsiders to be New York's quintessential Puerto Rican community. Most of the individuals I interact with are second- or third-generation New York-born Puerto Ricans.

According to 1980 census data, 29 percent of the population in East Harlem was at 75 percent of the poverty level, 48 percent at 125 percent, and 68 percent at 200 percent. In other words, if one were to adjust for New York City's exorbitant cost of living, well over half of the population would fall into the ranks of the "working poor." One in three families in East Harlem is dependent on public assistance, and approximately half of all households are headed by women. The schools in the neighborhood have one of the highest drop-out rates in the country.

The neighborhood is visibly poor. Abandoned buildings, vacant lots, and streets strewn with rubbish are the rule here rather than the exception. My block is not atypical: I can get heroin, crack, powder cocaine, hypodermic needles, methadone, Valium, PCP, and mescaline within a two-block radius of my apartment.

Despite this active street scene and the visible social and economic crisis it reflects, the majority of the adult population of East Harlem abhors drugs. Most heads of households work nine-to-five-plus-overtime at entry-level jobs and shun illegal activity. Nonetheless, this majority, mainstream, working-class and working-poor sector is in retreat. Many residents, especially the elderly, live in terror, venturing outside only during daylight hours.

The street-level drug dealers I study are resented and shunned by the majority of the community. Unfortunately, however, they control the streets. Worse yet, they are offering on a daily basis an all-too-persuasive, violent, and self-destructive alternative to the youths growing up in the neighborhood.

Most of the hard-core inner-city "unemployables" have, in fact, worked at legitimate pursuits at some time or other in their lives. All of the crack dealers and addicts whom I have interviewed have worked at one or more legal jobs in their early youth. In fact, most entered the labor market at an earlier age than the typical teenager. Before their twelfth birthday, many were bagging groceries at the supermarket for tips, stocking beers (off the books) in local "*bodegas*," or shining shoes. In fact, many dropped out of school in order to make money to obtain the childhood "necessities"—candy, sneakers, basketballs, baseball cards—that most preteens throughout the rest of America are able to buy with their allowances. What happens to these "eager-beaver" 12-year-olds that transforms them into the adult felons who terrorize their neighbors?

Income-Generating Opportunities: School Versus Drugs

The drug economy, especially retail crack sales, is currently out-competing the legal, entry-level economy for the "hearts and minds" of inner-city youth. Tragically, crack/cocaine is the only growing, dynamic, equal-opportunity-employer industry in East Harlem today. According to police records, millions of dollars worth of drug sales are going on within a stone's throw of the youths living in my building. Why should we be surprised when they drop out of school to "get some of mine's"? And why should we wonder why they refuse low-prestige jobs in the service sector in favor of building up crack/cocaine enterprises where their identities, rooted in street culture, become an asset rather than a liability?

The youths on my block are not disorganized or apathetic. On the contrary, they are overly organized and energetic. Their mobilization, however, is destroying them and their community. The most determined, lucky, and ruthless of the children on my block are running thousand-dollar-a-day drug sales networks and are not yet 18. They keep regular hours and supervise half a dozen employees who work on consignment or on an hourly wage.

The most successful drive their Mercedes, Jaguars, and Porsches up to the fire hydrant

WHAT OPPORTUNITIES FOR THE YOUNG?

on the block to be washed and waxed by local crack addicts while they stand triumphantly ten yards away and watch the neighborhood kids ogle their "ride" (car). To be this successful, they have to cultivate an aggressive and violent presentation of self or else they will lose credibility and be forced out of business, perhaps even killed. They believe with a vengeance in the traditional American dream: rags to riches through private entrepreneurship.

At the same time, contrary to what we hear in the media, the vast majority of the street sellers are not, in fact, making much money—on an average night, they might get $6 or $8 an hour. Of course, that is already twice minimum wage. But what is more important is that they are able to earn these "good wages" without having to demean themselves in jobs they believe compromise their sense of personal dignity. They do not want to adapt to the rules of a hostile outside world that is uncomfortable with their form of dress, their language, and their culture in general. In the crack economy, there is also a real possibility for dramatic advancement that is not easily replicated in the entry-level service sector, which is where the jobs available to them are located once they drop out of high school.

During the course of their lives, most of the street sellers cycle in and out of legal, just-above-minimum-wage jobs. Even the most hard-core sellers frequently talk about "going legit." In fact, one young man left the crack business when he was given a temporary job over the holidays with the Postal Service. Another street dealer recently took a union job as a porter for Woolworths; another now works as a bus driver for the New York City Transit Authority; yet another joined the Army. This shows that despite the strength of the underground economy, the situation is not hopeless. There is still an arena within which the mainstream economy can compete for their allegiance.

The Crack House: Youth Center and Day-Care Facility

In this neighborhood after 8:30 p.m. on a hot summer night, the only air-conditioned place open to teenagers is the crack house. Most teens do not yet use drugs or even drink beer, but they hang out in the crack house hallways to escape the heat and to watch the excitement: the money changing hands, the power plays of rising entrepreneurs, the well-dressed people coming and going, the emaciated addicts flitting by in various stages of cocaine psychosis. There is no mainstream institution competing with the crack house for their attention after dark.

One hot June evening, I walked into a crack house and saw three baby carriages parked near the video machines at the entrance. The mothers were teenagers vying to be noticed by the manager of the night shift. These girls were typical of those who are there every night: they are not only looking for someone to supplement their AFDC checks, they are also seeking excitement and searching for an identity that does not compromise their status as young mothers. They turn their backs on their babies to dance or to talk in private outside. When out of sight from their infants, they remain "confident" that should their babies wake up or start crying, one of the dozen or so crack-house habitués will attend to them.

The situation for the babies of the young mothers who resist the seduction of crack and who get jobs in the mainstream economy is often not that much better. The mothers' wages (even if combined with the fathers' income) will not pay the market rate for licensed day care in New York City. (As a point of reference, I pay $900 a month for first-class care at a full-time day-care facility!) If a relative is not able to care for the babies while the parent works, then they are left with a neighbor in an often inadequate, bootleg "family day-care setting." In one such "day-care" arrangement that a colleague of mine happened upon, the "caregiver" had just locked a two-year-old in a broom closet because the baby was "crying too much." We cannot expect working-class children to grow up unscarred in those kinds of situations. The irony is that these are precisely the families that are trying to "do the right thing": they work hard at legal jobs and refuse public subsidy.

The Breakdown of the Public and Private Sectors

The telephone company took six weeks to install my phone; the garbage trucks don't make their rounds at least once a month; about as often, the letter carrier fails to appear; and careless oil truck operators frequently spill heating oil all over the sidewalk when they fill the underground storage tanks of the tenement buildings. Neither Express Mail nor Federal

> **THE TELEPHONE COMPANY TOOK SIX WEEKS TO INSTALL MY PHONE; THE GARBAGE TRUCKS DON'T MAKE THEIR ROUNDS ... THE LETTER CARRIER FAILS TO APPEAR. IN SHORT, NOTHING WORKS ADEQUATELY.**

Express deliver on time in my neighborhood. In short, nothing works adequately—regardless of whether it is publicly or privately owned. Market mechanisms should normally be able to come into play to encourage providers of services, but the infiltration of organized crime into the local economy is an obvious obstacle to this process in East Harlem. Even 12-year-olds know that the Mafia controls the private contracting companies, the garbage collection services, and a critical proportion of the private-sector labor unions.

The miles and miles of abandoned buildings are powerful testimony to a profound infrastructure crisis. For the second summer in a row, the public swimming pool two blocks away that was the one healthy, popular, city-run activity center for youths in the neighborhood has been closed down while a corrupt construction company "renovates" it at a snail's pace. For the third year in a row, the basketball courts hedged in between the public housing towers are marred by deep potholes; only every other hoop on the courts is still in place, and the lighting systems for nighttime play never operate. Broken beer bottles, human feces, crack vials, and an occasional hypodermic needle litter the jungle gym where I take my two-year-old son to play on weekends.

It is unrealistic to expect most of the eight-and ten-year-olds playing tag in the ruins of the abandoned buildings or the preteen-agers sifting through mounds of garbage piled on the sidewalks to develop healthy notions of public good and personal responsibility. The "common sense" emerging among this newest generation is that "The System" hates them. A disproportionate number of adults and teenagers believe virulent conspiracy theories about "The Plan"—that is, the evil intentions of the wealthy white-power-structure elite toward poor African-Americans and Puerto Ricans living in Manhattan. A fringe group has even postered the bricked-up abandoned buildings along several blocks with a picture of a black family struggling into the distance, carrying their possessions on their backs. The word "Genocide!" is written above the picture in red ink. This kind of rage and frustration will filter down in one form or another to the bulk of the children in the neighborhood, including those living in stable working households.

Perhaps the most ironic failing of the public sector is that the biggest crack-house landlord is the City of New York. Crack is most frequently sold out of abandoned building storefronts or in housing project stairways. Most people in the neighborhood assume that the police are paid off to ignore this activity, but in fact they do not need to be. The police are overwhelmed by the magnitude of crime; their morale is low; they cannot relate culturally to the community; and inadequate budgets are poorly managed.

Our tax dollars are not spent as effectively in the inner city as they are in the suburbs. How else can one explain the chipped paint and dirty floors of the local post offices, or the complaint scrawled on the blackboard in my neighborhood's police precinct last January: "No more arrests until we get some heat in here!"

The schools offer the most blatant testimony of an irrational public-sector breakdown. Why is the beautiful but abandoned turn-of-the-century school building around the corner from me being renovated with tax incentives into commercial lofts? Two blocks away, my neighborhood's primary school is so overcrowded that special-education classes are being held in "renovated" broom closets. (On a more positive note, the extraordinary energy and commitment of New York's new chancellor of schools, Joseph Fernandez, is a hopeful sign. He is cleaning up school board corruption, ousting incompetent managers, and attempting to fire dysfunctional principals. More important, if his management technique is more than media hype, then he could be a public-sector model for the revitalization of crucial services without politically unrealistic infusions of new funds.)

It is not a question of providing a "special opportunity" or an "easy street" for the youths on my block. Instead, the necessity is to guarantee them what the rest of the nation takes for granted: streets where they do not have to witness gunfights; hot and cold running water in their homes; heat at recreation centers; public safety officers who do not curse at them when they stand on the corner; child care that is not abusive; schools where they do not have to peer through the keyhole of the bathroom before entering for fear of being raped; principals and teachers who do not smoke crack; regular garbage pickups and mail deliveries; abandoned buildings that are either renovated or ripped down rather than left standing for

years; a local economy and job structure that is not perversely distorted by narco-dollars; and supervisors in the entry-level economy who do not subject them to cultural ridicule because of their inner-city ethnic identity. In short, let us begin by offering them a level playing field.

Conclusion

Scholars studying urban America are debating whether or not the structural transformations of the 1970s and 1980s have created a qualitatively as well as quantitatively new dynamic of poverty different from the one faced by new immigrants at the turn of the century or prior to World War II. As our cities have shifted from manufacturing to service economies, high school graduates can no longer find stable, unionized jobs that provide health and retirement benefits and pay a family wage. The debate over the social implications of these long-term structural transformations in our nation's economy is not academic; it has important policy ramifications. The inner-city crisis is "Made in the U.S.A."; it is not caused by new immigrants or by residual cultural influences. Right now, we are not even reaching out to the boys and girls who want to play by the rules.

Because I come from a discipline that systematically analyzes cultural processes, I have reached the conclusion that the experience of second-generation urban poverty in America today is qualitatively different from what it was in the recent past. Political and socioeconomic forces have coalesced, rendering street culture more persuasive and "economically logical" than it was in past generations. Concretely, this means that a much higher percentage then ever before of our best and brightest inner-city youths are pursuing careers with rugged determination that lead to violence and drug addiction. Worse yet, current public-sector policies and private-sector practices are merely compounding this crisis rather than addressing it.

I HAVE REACHED THE CONCLUSION THAT THE EXPERIENCE OF SECOND-GENERATION URBAN POVERTY IN AMERICA TODAY IS QUALITATIVELY DIFFERENT FROM WHAT IT WAS IN THE RECENT PAST.

Caring For Children ■■■■■■

LINDA M. BURTON

Linda M. Burton is associate professor of human development at the Pennsylvania State University. Her primary area of research focuses on the effects of teen pregnancy on multigeneration family systems.

The continuing debate about the underclass has intensified the interest of scholars and policymakers in the child-care strategies of poor families who live in high-risk neighborhoods. Much of the research explores how census

DRUG SHIFTS AND THEIR IMPACT ON FAMILIES

tract data on the rates of crime, male joblessness, welfare dependency, and nonmarital fertility are related to a narrowly defined range of child-care arrangements these families use. While the research offers important information on the suggested link between the characteristics of the neighborhood and how families are faring, it provides little insight into neighborhood and family child-care *processes*—that is, how day-to-day activities in high-risk communities influence child-care arrangements in families.

Because of its impact on families, illicit drug trafficking is one ongoing activity in high-risk neighborhoods that has received considerable attention. High-volume drug activity in neighborhoods affects the lives of families, particularly children, in several ways. It provides local opportunities for recruiting children, adolescents, and their parents as drug dealers and users. It also increases the type and frequency of dangers that families are exposed to in the neighborhood. Exposure to these temptations and dangers prompts families to develop arrangements for taking care of their children that are appropriate to the situation.

The range of strategies used by these families is influenced by other factors as well as the dangers related to the local drug trade: the number of available and responsible child-care providers among local kin (such as grandparents) and friendship networks, parental work schedules, and parental drug use.

Using preliminary data from a community-based ethnographic study, this article describes several child-care strategies used by families consisting of two or more generations living in a neighborhood where there is considerable illicit drug activity. The types of strategies outlined are linked specifically to the daily timing of drug sales in the neighborhood, the work schedules of parents and grandparents, and parental illicit drug use.

The data here are from a larger ongoing study of the effects of teenage childbearing on persistent and working-poor black multigeneration families. The data on drug-trafficking schedules and child-care strategies

were obtained fortuitously—it was not my intention at the outset of the larger study to focus on these issues. After only one month of field research, however, it became apparent that understanding the connection between drug-trafficking schedules and child-care strategies was essential to being able to understand the day-to-day routines of young families that live in one particularly high-risk neighborhood.

The data were collected during the first year of the study. The study is being conducted in a poor, predominantly black neighborhood encompassing eight city blocks in a moderate-sized northeastern city. The drug trafficking and other related dangers in this neighborhood are extreme. The neighborhood is the only one of its kind in the city. The vast majority of poor black families in this city do not live in such environments.

To date, 127 males and females, 5 to 78 years old, have been interviewed in this neighborhood. In addition to these interviews, I have used a variety of qualitative field research techniques to collect data, including direct observation of neighborhood activities at various times of the day (8:00 a.m., 3:00 p.m., and 2:00 a.m.), focus group discussions with neighborhood residents, and informal observation of community and family events.

Neighborhood Drug-Trafficking Schedules

In industry, there is shift work; similarly, in this particular neighborhood there are daily shift-like patterns in the sale of illicit drugs and related environmental dangers. Three distinct drug activity shifts operate in this neighborhood: a morning shift (7:00 a.m.–4:00 p.m.), an afternoon/evening shift (4:00 p.m.–10:00 p.m.), and a night shift (10:00 p.m.–6:00 a.m.).

The morning shift is best described as having a low level of drug activity and the dangers such as crime that accompany it. Participants in the study indicate that this is the time of day when most drug dealers and users sleep. Consequently, neighborhood residents who are not involved in the local drug trade (which is the majority of families) use the safe morning hours to do their grocery shopping and banking, visit with friends in the neighborhood, attend church activities, deliver and pick up children from school, and take toddlers and preschool children out for walks. Community residents describe this as the "family time of day."

At approximately 4:00 p.m., the neighborhood "climate" changes. Around this time, the small-time drug dealers open for business on neighborhood corners. Older residents, parents not involved in the local drug economy,

3. NONETHNIC MINORITIES

and their children retreat inside their homes. Young children and adolescents who have no adult supervision hang out on the street. The local automobile traffic increases dramatically as people who live outside the neighborhood stop on their way home from work to purchase drugs. Uniformed police officers are nowhere to be found. As night falls, the stench of urine and vomit emanates from the local bars, alleys, and church steps. Community residents call this the "p.m. shift"—it is the time that dealers have "stolen" from families to promote the drug economy.

At 10:00 p.m., the neighborhood undergoes yet another transformation. Hard-core drug dealers make their appearance on the street. Young-adult, heavily addicted drug users lie around, seemingly dead, in alleys and doorways of churches and local businesses. The presence of undercover police officers is easily discernible. The stench of urine and vomit becomes more intense. Community residents agree that this is the most dangerous time of day in their neighborhood. They call it "the night shift."

Drug Shifts and Child-Care Strategies

In each of the drug-trade shifts described above, I observed a number of distinctly different child-care strategies that families in the neighborhood use. The arrangements involve a range of providers (parents, grandparents, teenage siblings, and elderly and young-adult males who are friends of the family) and child-monitoring activities. Participants in the study describe these strategies as responses to the dangers in the area associated with local drug activity, the work schedules of parents, and drug use among some of the neighborhood children's parents.

During the morning shift, employed and unemployed parents, grandmothers, retired "surrogate grandfathers," and a few young unemployed males take care of infants, toddlers, and school-age children of drug-addicted parents. A number of these caregivers offer insightful explanations about why they are child-care providers and why they monitor the children the way they do. A fairly common situation was described by Mary, a 68-year-old great-grandmother who is currently caring for her drug-addicted 36-year-old daughter's eight children. The children range from 1 to 20 years of age. Four of the children have mental and physical handicaps possibly related to their mother's drug use. Mary told me quite candidly why she was the child-care provider: "I ain't no different than any of the other grandmommas in my neighborhood that has a dopehead for a kid. We all have to take care

of our children's mistakes. If we don't, ain't nobody else gonna do it. Who cares how it affects us? I'm real sick. I got heart trouble and diabetes. I'm tired myself. But there ain't nobody else to do it."

Mary explained how she takes care of her grandchildren: "In the morning, I get up early, get the babies ready, and hits the streets. At 7:00 in the morning, I let the kids go out to play—them that don't have school. Then about 10:00 o'clock, I pack up the babies, and we go to the store and the doctor. I'm always home by 2:00 in the afternoon so we can all go inside. That's when shit starts to change around here. Them no-good women and men dope dealers takes over the streets. I done lost one child to dope. I ain't letting her babies get lost too."

Sam, a 65-year-old retired factory worker who currently takes care of his three nieces, had this comment: "We gets ready really early in the morning. I comb the girls' hair. I dress and feed them. Then I take them to school. Then I go and hang out with my buddies until it's time to pick my babies up. We hurry up and walk home because I want to be in the house by three o'clock. I don't want them to see the trash on the street. I don't want them to turn out like the low-life drugheads their momma and daddy are."

Shirley, a 27-year-old mother of three, also engages in close monitoring of her children but she speaks more defiantly than Mary and Sam about allowing the neighborhood drug trade to dictate the structure of her life and that of her children: "Sometimes I get so mad. It's not right to have to keep your kids inside after school. Sometimes I take my kids outside anyway . . . but I'm right there with them the whole time. I dare anyone to mess with them."

When Mary, Sam, Shirley, and others like them go inside with their children, and the parents and grandparents who work the swing shift in local factories leave for work, a second type of child-care strategy becomes apparent in the neighborhood for families without providers like Mary, Sam, and Shirley. It involves child-care provided by neighborhood teens or older siblings.

Ordinarily, this kind of child-care would be considered a safe, natural alternative for families. Unfortunately, however, in a high-volume drug-trafficking neighborhood, this strategy is often very risky. A few of the teens and older siblings who are responsible for the care of younger children "hang out" on the street from 4:00 p.m. to 9:00 p.m.—the time of day when children on the streets are exposed to heightened dangers related to the drug economy, including increased automobile traffic and street fighting. It is quite common to see young children and adolescent child-care

> "I'M ALWAYS HOME BY 2:00 IN THE AFTERNOON SO WE CAN ALL GO INSIDE. . . . THEM NO-GOOD WOMEN AND MEN DOPE DEALERS TAKES OVER THE STREETS. I DONE LOST ONE CHILD TO DOPE. I AIN'T LETTING HER BABIES GET LOST TOO."
> —Mary, Age 68

"SINCE THEY AIN'T GOT IT TOGETHER, I GOT TO TAKE CARE OF THE LITTLE ONES. I FEED THEM ALL. CHANGE DIAPERS. PUT THEM TO BED. I KNOW HOW TO DO ALL OF IT. . . . I HAVEN'T BEEN TO SCHOOL FOR A LONG TIME."

—Tameka, age 7

providers being solicited by small-time dealers to buy or sell drugs. When I asked Walter—a 14-year-old who was babysitting for his three younger siblings on a street corner—what impact the neighborhood drug activity had on his child-care responsibilities, he said: "I got to be out here where it's happening. I'm out here learning them the streets. Just 'cuz I got to watch my sisters and brother don't mean I got to stay inside with them."

Walter, his friends, and their siblings are usually in the house by 10:00 p.m.—just in time for their parents' arrival home from work. For families in which there are working parents, the child-care responsibilities of teens and older siblings are usually turned back to parents when they return from work. These parents are deeply concerned about the dangers their children are exposed to while they are at work. Walter's mother, for example, stated: "I know he is out there [on the streets] when I'm at work. I don't have any other way right now to have someone watch my children . . . . I hope and pray that I taught Walter the right things, though. He knows too that when I'm home he better be straight. The Lord only knows, I have to believe that what I taught him, the good I taught him, will bring him through and make him a good man."

Steven, a 37-year-old single parent of three teenage boys expressed his concern for his children and talked about the arrangements he makes for their care: "Yes, I worry about them. There is so much here to get into, too . . . . But I call my boys every hour and come home on my break. They know they better be here when I come."

For a small number of families in which parents are unemployed and both parents and grandparents have serious drug addictions, there is no available adult supervision for children and a third child-care strategy prevails. This is a strategy of the "night shift" and, fortunately, is not a frequent pattern in the neighborhood I studied. Children as young as five take care of their younger siblings during the late night to early morning hours while their parents or grandparents buy and

get high on "serious drugs" (crack, cocaine, heroin, ice). Tameka, a seven-year-old who takes care of her five-year-old brother, two-year-old twin sisters, and two-month-old brother, described her child-care responsibilities to me: "My momma and my grandmomma have to go out every night so they can feel better. They take something that makes them sleep and feel better sometimes. Sometimes they get sick. I know they take drugs. I'm not stupid. Since they ain't got it together, I got to take care of the little ones. I feed them all. Change diapers. Put them to bed. I know how to do all of it. In the morning, I get my brother dressed for school. I stay home all the time to take care of my real little sisters and brother because everybody is sleep. I haven't been to school for a long time."

I visited with only three children like Tameka in the neighborhood but was told by community residents and school officials that other children in the community live in similar circumstances. Children like Tameka are extreme cases and are clearly the most at risk. They receive very little, and rarely continuous, care themselves, they are subjected to myriad household and neighborhood dangers, and they miss, on average, 80–100 days of school per year.

Implications of Preliminary Findings

How many children are there like Tameka in the nation? How do we identify them, and how do we help them and the other children in these neighborhoods? Although the data presented here are preliminary and focus on child-care arrangements used by families who live in one small, high-risk neighborhood, they nonetheless call attention to three issues that policymakers, social service providers, and community leaders should consider in developing child-care programs for communities like these. First, the relationship between child-care strategies and neighborhood drug-trafficking shifts indicates that children whose parents work swing shifts or are addicted to drugs are at greater risk of exposure to dangers in the neighborhood during the late afternoon, night, and early morning hours when they have no responsible adult supervision. Clearly, programs designed to fill the gaps in responsible child care should be implemented in these high-risk neighborhoods.

Second, we observed that in order to protect children in high-risk neighborhoods, responsible caregivers feel that they have to literally lock children indoors to keep them safe. We need to know what the implications of this child-monitoring strategy are for children's healthy development. Can safe pro-

3. NONETHNIC MINORITIES

grams be instituted in these neighborhoods to allow children to have positive experiences outside after 3:00 p.m.?

Third, this research highlights the efforts of several important child-care providers—grandmothers, retiree surrogate grandfathers, and young unemployed black males. Although these people perform valuable services for children and families, it is important to note that, particularly in the case of grandmothers, the care they provide is not without personal cost. Many of the older-generation caregivers experience social, psychological, and physical problems in caring for the young children. If these caregivers are to continue providing this

valuable service for children, it is clear that they, too, must have support from local community groups and social-services agencies to meet their own needs as well as the children's.

We do not know how prevalent this type of neighborhood and the child-care strategies employed within it are in other inner-city communities throughout the nation. Further research is needed. But certainly, social scientists, policymakers, and community leaders need to look more closely at how activities in high-risk neighborhoods affect the lives of families and children who are trying to survive and thrive.

The Feminization of Poverty: Myth or Reality?

Martha E. Gimenez

Martha E. Gimenez is an Associate Professor in the Department of Sociology, University of Colorado, Boulder, CO 80309. The author would like to thank Val Burris, Dave Elliott, Richard Rogers, and the Insurgent Sociologist Collective for their helpful suggestions. An earlier version of this article appeared in the Insurgent Sociologist 14, 3 (Fall 1987).

Introduction

The "feminization of poverty" is a phenomenon of great concern to the government, social scientists, politicians, and feminists of all political persuasions, becoming popular in the early 1980s in the wake of deep cuts in social spending by the Reagan administration. The phrase "feminization of poverty" attempts to capture the essence of the following facts: in the United States, the fastest-growing type of family structure is that of female-headed households and, because of the high rate of poverty among these households, their increase is mirrored in the growing numbers of women and children who are poor; almost half of the poor in the U.S. today live in families headed by women. In 1984, 16% of all white families, 25% of all families of Spanish origin,[1] and 53% of all Black families were headed by women (Rodgers, Jr., 1986: 5); the poverty rate for white, Spanish-origin and Black female-headed households was 27.1%, 53.4%, and 51.7% respectively (*Ibid.:* 12).

Poverty affects not only young and adult women with children but also older women; in 1984, the median income of women 65 years and over was $6,020 (the corresponding figure was $10,450 for men in the same age category) and 15.0% of all women age 65 and over had incomes below the poverty line (Sidel, 1986: 158). The poverty of women is reflected in the poverty of children. In 1984 there were almost 13 million poor children in the U.S.; 52% of them lived in families headed by women and the poverty rate for

white, Black, and Spanish-origin children living in female-headed households was 46%, 66%, and 71% respectively (Rodgers, Jr., 1986: 32–33). In 1988, the poverty rate among female-headed families with children under age 18 was 44.7%; the poverty rate for white, Black and Spanish-origin female-headed households with children under 18 was 38.2%, 56.3%, and 59.2% respectively (Bureau of the Census, 1989: 62–65).

Facts and figures documenting the growing immiseration of women and children are available in many informative publications (see, for example, Stallard, Ehrenreich, and Sklar, 1983; Sidel, 1986; and Rodgers, Jr., 1986), together with analyses that put forth the notion that it is women, as women, who are peculiarly vulnerable to poverty. Poverty is being feminized and this idea is nowhere expressed more clearly than in an often quoted statement from the President's National Advisory Council on Economic Opportunity (1981):

> All other things being equal, if the proportion of the poor in female-householder families were to continue to increase at the same rate as it did from 1976 to 1978, the poverty population would be composed solely of women and their children before the year 2000 (Rodgers, Jr., 1986: 7).

Critics have rightly pointed out that the statement suggests that " . . . by the year 2000 all of those men who are presently poor will be either rich or dead" (AAWO, 1983: 6). Although those who quote the passage acknowledge that society does not remain still, and that poverty also affects men and falls more heavily upon non-whites, the main thrust of the analysis of present trends nevertheless continues to interpret them as the "feminization of poverty."

Is this a theoretically adequate notion? What can we learn from it? What are its shortcomings? Does it adequately convey the nature of the processes it describes? Is the "feminization of poverty" a real phenomenon or a mystification that obscures the unfolding of other processes? These are some of the questions I will seek to answer in this article. I will

From *Social Justice*, Vol. 17, No. 3, 1990, pp. 43-69. Reprinted by permission of *Social Justice*, P.O. Box 40601, San Francisco, CA 94140.

examine, from the standpoint of Marxist feminist theory, the strengths and shortcomings of current explanations to establish whether recent changes in the size and composition of the poor population, growth in female-headed families, and the increased vulnerability of women to poverty can be adequately understood as the "feminization of poverty." I will also assess the extent to which these trends are likely to change during the 1990s and, if so, in what directions. The feminization of poverty, I will argue, is a readily observable effect of a larger process: the growing immiseration of the U.S. working class, which makes family formation difficult, if not impossible, among its most impoverished sectors.

Factors Accounting for the Feminization of Poverty

The definition of a social phenomenon shapes the questions that can be asked about its possible determinants and, of course, the questions in turn shape the answers. In this case, it is unavoidable to center such questions on women: Why are women more likely to be poor than men? Why are female-headed households and families more likely to be poor? Why is the number of those households and families increasing? This leads researchers to focus on factors that are specific to the situation of women in modern society and to conclude that women, as a group and regardless of class, are more vulnerable to poverty than men and that, consequently, women's poverty has different causes than the poverty of men. These are some representative statements of this view:

While there is clearly much truth to the statement that race and class have been major determinants of poverty in this country, women as a group, including middle- and sometimes even upper-middle-class women, have recently become far more vulnerable to poverty or near poverty than their male counterparts. . . . It is clear that some of the key causes of poverty among women are fundamentally different from the causes of poverty among men (Sidel, 1986: 25).
There is a fundamental difference between male and female poverty; for men, poverty is often the consequence of unemployment and a job is generally an effective remedy, while female poverty often exists even when a woman works full-time. . . . Virtually all women are vulnerable—a divorce or widowhood is all it takes to throw many middle-class women into poverty (Stallard et al., 1983: 9).
Race may well be the principal determinant of poverty in this country. . . . And it is redundant to say that class causes poverty. . . . [T]o account for a trend that specifically involves women, we need an explanation in which gender is the determining factor. . . . [T]o explain the feminization of poverty we have to invoke some of the things that many women have in common—such as motherhood and low-paying jobs. . . . [L]ooking at commonalities, we are not attempting to understand how gender—as one factor—can affect one's economic status (Ehrenreich, 1987: 12).

The conceptualization of women *as a group* or a primary focus on gender characterizes most discussions of the feminization of poverty. Census data do not differentiate between social classes; researchers have information about income, sex, and racial and ethnic categories of analysis and this reinforces the tendency to frame the discussion in terms of statistical rather than theoretically significant categories of analysis. The determinants of women's poverty, it is therefore implied in the analysis, are factors that affect all women and place all women at risk.

What are these factors? Changes in mortality and marriage rates, divorce and separations, and out-of-wedlock births contribute to the increase in female-headed households (Rodgers, Jr., 1986: 38–42). Women's higher life expectancy contributes to the increasing number of women over 65 years of age living alone, many of whom are poor. Younger women become heads of households through out-of-wedlock childbearing, separation, divorce, or the decision to live alone while they work and postpone marriage until they consider it appropriate.

While young and old single women are found among poor female-headed households, the majority of these households consists of women and their children. Poor young women, particularly minority women, are more likely to become single mothers, and teen-age motherhood is perhaps one of the most important correlates of poverty. The amount of child support women receive from their children's father is very low; the majority receives none and for those who do, the payments are very small. Welfare payments are also extremely low and cannot lift families above the poverty level; most families receiving Aid to Families with Dependent Children (AFDC) live below the poverty level. Furthermore, welfare rules contribute to the breakup of families because, in most states, two parent families do not qualify for AFDC. The plight of both poor families in general and of poor female-headed families was intensified by budget cuts during the Reagan administration, which excluded millions of poor people, including children, from badly needed help (Stallard et al., 1983: 27–51; Sidel, 1986: 77–99; Rodgers, Jr., 1986: 64–94; O'Hare, 1985; Piven and Cloward, 1985). The sex-segregated nature of the labor market also contributes to the poverty of women; most women work in low-paid, low-status jobs with little or no prospect of promotion, and lacking good pension and retirement plans. Poverty is also the result of unemployment; many women cannot find jobs while others cannot work because of their childcare responsibilities and the lack of affordable and reliable day care.

Male unemployment, layoffs, and decline in wages are also crucial correlates of women's poverty. Such factors correlate with marital stress and violence, separation or divorce, and can make family formation impossible. Poor men who are chronically unemployed or underemployed cannot form families or stay with their families, particularly in states where welfare policies deny eligibility to two-parent families.

Because of the heritage of racial and economic discrimination, these factors are intensified in Black and Spanish-origin populations, which have a higher proportion of poor, female-headed families than the white population. Unemployment among working-age Black men is extremely high; only 55% of Black men are in the labor force (The center for the Study of Social Policy, 1985: 232). This situation leads Ruth Sidel (1986: 24) to ask whether present trends depict the feminization or the minoritization of poverty; her conclusion is that both phenomena are taking place because, like Blacks, women are also an oppressed group. Acknowledging that the poverty of men is correlated with the poverty of women, Sidel is critical of policymakers who avoid the cause-effect relationship between extremely high rates of male unemployment and a high percentage of female-headed families within minority populations. She alerts the attention of those concerned with the feminization of poverty to "the *obvious correlation* between the lack of economic opportunities for millions of American men . . . and their lack of commitment to and steady participation in family life" (*Ibid.*: 110, emphasis added).

Besides these structural factors and the lack of adequate welfare policies, Sidel argues that women's poverty is also the result of ideological and structural constraints peculiar to women. Women who are socialized to put family obligations first, who see themselves primarily as wives and mothers, and who seek in marriage and the family their fulfillment as adult members of the society, are likely to neglect or overlook the need to develop occupational and educational skills that will help them support themselves if they remain single or their marriage breaks up. Women's domestic activities, in spite of their social, economic, and psychological significance, are devalued and time consuming, and interfere with their full participation in the labor force. The domestic division of labor thus interacts with the sex-segregated nature of occupations to restrict the economic and educational opportunities of women. The negative effects of this situation become more salient once women become single heads of families (see, for example, Sidel, 1986: 25–35).

As the preceding discussion indicates, the feminization of poverty is associated with many interrelated structural and ideological variables. Stallard et al. (1983: 51) sum up the determinants of the feminization of poverty as follows:

> [It] is a direct outgrowth of women's dual role as unpaid labor in the home and underpaid labor in the workforce. The pace has been quickened by rising rates of divorce and single motherhood, but the course of

women's poverty is determined by the sexism—and racism—ingrained in an unjust economy.

It seems that recent literature has produced not only a detailed description but also some plausible and perhaps obvious explanations of the feminization of poverty. That this is really the case, in spite of the impressive documentation and well-developed arguments, is not as self-evident as it may seem. The identification of the determinants of the feminization of poverty in sexism, racism, and the operation of the economy does not really tell us much beyond that which is empirically obvious and observable. What is questionable is the meaning given to the trends: Are we witnessing the feminization and the minoritization of poverty or something else? I will introduce some additional facts and figures about poverty to highlight the complexity of these issues as well as the problems inherent in the "feminization of poverty" perspective.

Who Are the Poor?

Although women are more likely to be poor than men and, in absolute numbers, in 1983 there were more poor women (20,084,000) than men (15,182,000), *"the female share of the overall poverty population was the same in 1983 as it was in 1966 (the earliest available data)—57%"* (O'Hare, 1985: 18; my emphasis). By 1985, the number of poor males had declined 6.9% (to 14,140,000) compared to a 5.8% decline (to 18,923,000) for females. In 1988, the poverty population had declined to 31,878,000 (Bureau of the Census, 1989: 2). In 1985, the female share of the poverty population increased slightly, to 57.2%, while the male share declined slightly from 43% in 1983 to 42.8% in 1985 (Bureau of the Census, 1986b: 29).

The female and male shares of the poverty population from 1966 to 1985 show remarkable stability: the female share increases gradually, rising to 59.1% in 1978, declining to 57% in 1983 and 1984, rising to 57.6% in 1986 and declining to 57.1% in 1988 (see Table 1 at the end of the article, for changes in the sex and age composition of the population below the poverty level during the same time period).[2] If only adults over 21 are considered, in 1983 women comprised 62%—the same figure obtaining in 1966—of the poor (O'Hare, 1985: 18); this percentage increased to 62.1% in 1984, 62.7% in 1985, and 64.2% in 1986, declining slightly to 63.5% in 1988 (Bureau of the Census, 1986a: 28; 1986b: 27; 1987: 30; 1989: 66).

Mortality differentials increase the numbers of older women living alone; 27.7 million of the 6.7 million women age 65 and over who in 1983 were living as "unrelated individuals" lived below the poverty level. In 1984, the number of women in that category increased to 6.8 million, but the percent below the poverty level declined to 25.2 (Bureau of the Census,

3. NONETHNIC MINORITIES

1985: 41; 1986a: 29). In 1984, 20.8% of "unrelated males" age 65 and over fell below the poverty level. In 1988, while the number of women aged 65 and over living as "unrelated individuals" increased to more than 7.2 million, 25.5% lived below poverty level. Among unrelated males, the poverty rate declined to 19.6% (Bureau of the Census, 1989: 76).

As suggested in Table 1, the overall poverty rate increased between 1978 and 1983 (from 11.4% to 15.2%), but declined to 14.4% in 1984 and 13.1% in 1988 (O'Hare, 1985: 11; U.S. Bureau of the Census, 1986b: 3; 1988: 2; see Table 1). Poverty increased faster for the 18 to 44 age category (70%) than for the 45 to 64 (26%) and 65 and over (14.8%) age categories. Taking into account male/female differences, *between 1978 and 1983 the number of poor men increased faster than the number of poor women at all ages (51.6% vs. 38.7%), ages 18 to 44 (93.3% vs. 56.9%), and ages 45–64 (33.0% vs. 22.5%).* Among those age 18 and under, the percent increase for males and females was somewhat similar (40.0% vs. 38.1%); only among those 65 and over was the percent increase in the number of poor women slightly higher (15.7% vs. 12.7%) (O'Hare, 1985: 14).

Given the mortality differentials between the sexes, it is to be expected that poverty among the elderly would increase faster for women; on the other hand, the fact that poverty increased faster for men in the other age groups, particularly among those between 18 and 44 years of age, is somewhat surprising, especially since public and scholarly concern with the "feminization of poverty" has given the impression that men are always better off than women and have been less affected by structural economic change. According to those figures, in that time period, poverty affected younger people primarily, and men in particular. The number of men aged 18 to 44 below the poverty level almost doubled between 1978 and 1983, increasing from 2,832,000 to 5,474,000. As such, one could make a case for considering age, rather than sex, to be the defining feature of current poverty trends.

It might be argued that the higher percent change in male poverty between 1978 and 1983 is an artifact of the particular years chosen to make a comparison. O'Hare's analysis reflects the sharp fluctuations associated with the 1981–1982 recession. However, an examination of the average annual percent changes in the number of men and women below the poverty level between 1975 and every year until 1985, for all ages, shows an increase in male poverty for every year from 1982 on. For ages 18 to 44, there is a higher rate of increase in male poverty for every year from 1979 on.[3] The lower proportion of men below the poverty level makes percent changes in male poverty higher than what they would have been had sex ratios been closer to unity.[4] On the other hand, the higher percent changes in male poverty cannot be dismissed lightly as statistical artifacts; it must be remembered that male

poverty is an important correlate of female poverty. The sharp increases in male poverty between 1978 and 1983 were real and seem to have lingered on after the "economic recovery" that followed the 1981–1982 recession; they reflect the vulnerability of men to unemployment at times of rapid economic decline, whereas women tend to work in "recession proof" sectors of the economy (Smith, 1990: 129; Sparr, 1987: 11).

As indicated earlier, the proportion of men and women in the 18 to 44 age group who become poor has been steadily increasing. While in 1983 the poverty rate for families with a householder aged 45 to 64 was 8.7% (up from 6.4% in 1978) and 14.2% (up from 10.2% in 1978) for families with a householder age 25 to 44, it was 29.5% (up from 18.5% in 1978) for families with a householder under 25 (O'Hare, 1985: 13). In 1988, the poverty rate for householders under 25 remained essentially unchanged (29.7%), while the rate for householders aged 25 to 44 declined to 12% (Bureau of the Census, 1989: 68).

The faster increase in the poverty rate of younger workers of both sexes indicates the working class is experiencing substantial downward mobility (O'Hare, 1985: 13–14; Harrington, 1984: 46–48). The increase in the poverty of children, usually linked to the increase in the number of female-headed families, is actually the result of the increase in poverty among young adult workers; in 1983, 49% of poor children lived in female-headed households, while 81% of children in poor families lived in families where the householder was under 45. Between 1978 and 1983, 4 million children under 18 joined the poverty population and only 25% of them lived in female-headed households (O'Hare, 1985: 13–17).

Real average earnings of young male workers aged 20 to 24 have declined 30% since 1973. A comparison between the earnings of men who turned 30 in 1973, and in 1983, shows that the average real income of the older men kept up with inflation while that of the younger men declined 35% (*Dollars & Sense*, 1987: 10). Income inequality among young men is related to education; those without a college degree are reduced to taking whatever the economy offers them. These days, that means jobs that pay relatively little. While college attendance by low-income men is declining, the gap in earnings between college graduates and high-school dropouts is growing:

> in 1973, the average earnings of a 20- to 24-year-old male high-school dropout were three-quarters of the earnings of a college graduate. By 1984, this fraction dropped to two-thirds (*Ibid.*: 11).

In light of this information, it must be acknowledged that the "feminization of poverty" is only one important dimension of a broader process that also affects men, children, and the elderly to different degrees and for reasons that are fundamentally interrelated. *Just as an exclusive focus on "women" leads to a one-sided analysis that seems to give lesser importance to other dimensions of poverty, it would be equally misguided to focus on the poverty of "men" or of "young adult workers."* These are simple descriptive categories that describe the composition of the poor population, but cannot serve as the basis for developing a theoretical analysis of the meaning of present poverty trends. Poverty is, then, only a descriptive concept that does not help us understand the nature of the phenomena captured by these and many other statistics.

An important statement critical of the "feminization of poverty" perspective (AAWO, 1983) convincingly argues that it offers an inaccurate empirical and political analysis of the situation because it ignores, for all practical purposes, the class differences between women and the common basis for class and racial and ethnic solidarity between men and women. Because the focus of analysis is the poverty of women *as women,* their class and race are considered as less crucial in determining their poverty than the fact they are women. It is the case, however, that not all women are in danger of becoming poor; only those who are working class or members of racial and ethnic minorities are thus threatened; many women are becoming richer and, of course, ruling-class women have never been at risk of becoming poor (*Ibid.*: 2). Poverty is not a phenomenon affecting primarily women; it is a structural component of the capitalist economy that affects people regardless of age and sex and falls disproportionately upon minorities. It is racism, not sexism, that determines who works in the worst sectors of the economy. Racism excludes large numbers of minority men from employment and the possibility of forming families, thus changing the conditions faced by working-class women of color in ways that the "feminization of poverty" perspective cannot adequately account for, as long as it views all women as an oppressed class (*Ibid.,* 1983; see also Staples, 1985; The Center for the Study of Social Policy, 1985; Sparr, 1987).

The critique of the "feminization of poverty" interpretation of current trends presented above does indeed identify important issues that require further theoretical and empirical investigation. Each insight considered so far has to be connected to the underlying capitalist structural determinants in production and reproduction, to more clearly understand the significance of these empirically observable phenomena. This process entails the examinations of the relationship between capitalist structures, processes, and contradictions, which are not readily observable, in addition to the empirically observable changes in the size and composition of the poverty population. It is my contention that the feminization of poverty is an important dimension of a larger process: the immiseration of the working class brought about by the profound structural changes undergone by the U.S.

economy during the 1980s. The limits of an essay confine me to making tentative statements that will provide guidelines for future theoretical and empirical investigation.

Beyond Women as a Category of Analysis: Class Differences among Women and Their Impact on the Poverty of Propertyless Women

The feminization of poverty perspective *focuses mainly on the poverty of women* as women. This starting point introduces problems in understanding why some women become poor, while others do not. In this section, I will argue that gender-related factors are relevant correlates (not determinants) of poverty only among women whose class location already makes them vulnerable to poverty. If no class differences (in the Marxist sense) are taken into account in the analysis of the feminization of poverty, it appears as if it were caused primarily by sexism. It is necessary, therefore, to examine the concept of social class and explore its implications for the life chances of women in different social classes.

According to Marxist theory, class is a relation between people mediated by their relationship to the means of production. Ownership of means of production, even on a modest scale, gives both political and economic control over others and economic independence. Lack of means of production places workers—male and female—in a dependent position, vulnerable to the decisions taken by those who, by controlling capital, control their access to the conditions indispensable for their physical and social daily and generational reproduction: employment. Changes in the occupational structure and quantitative and qualitative changes in the demand for labor divide the propertyless class in terms of occupation, income, and education, which are precisely the building blocks with which the average person and most social scientists construct socioeconomic status categories.[5] This is the material basis for the common-sense division of people into a variety of "classes," in a ranking that ranges from "the poor" and the "lower class" at the bottom, to the "upper class" at the top, with the "working class," "middle," and "upper-middle class" in between. This is an empiricist understanding of social class that mystifies the sources of women's poverty; it is a simple ordering or gradational concept of class, which focuses only on the different power and resources individuals bring to the sexual and economic markets (Ossowski, 1963: 41-57; Weber, 1982: 62-62).

It is a central contention in my argument that, if the social-class location of women (not their socioeconomic status) is taken into account, it becomes obvious that it is not sex but rather class that propels some women into poverty.

3. NONETHNIC MINORITIES

1. *Capitalist women and petty bourgeois women are not in risk of becoming poor.* Being a capitalist or a petty bourgeois woman entails, theoretically, having capital of one's own and, therefore, a source of income independent from marriage or from paid employment. Women who own wealth are unlikely to become poor for gender related factors, though inheritance practices and family accumulation strategies might deny them full control over their property.

Of the top wealth-holders with gross assets of $300,000 or more in 1982, 39.3% (1.85% of the total female population) were women. Between 1985 and 1986, the proportion of women aged 21 and over in the poverty population rose 1.5% (from 62.7% to 64.2%); in the same period, the number of women workers (full time and part time) earning more than $35,000 increased 32%; those earning between $50,000 and $75,000 increased 34.5%, while the number of full-time women workers earning more than $75,000 increased 55.4%. In 1988, the proportion of women aged 21 and over in the poverty population declined slightly to 63.5%. Between 1985 and 1988, the number of full- and part-time women workers earning more than $35,000 increased 128.6%; the number of full-time women workers earning between $50,000 and $75,000 increased 83%, while those earning more than $75,000 increased 171.6% (Bureau of the Census 1987: 19; 1986: 17; 1989: 53). As some women fell into poverty, others certainly became more affluent, although in 1988 only 7.3% of full-time women workers earned more than $35,000 a year and only .48% earned more than $75,000 a year (Bureau of the Census, 1989: 53). Women earning over $35,000 a year are certainly far less likely to fall into poverty if they become single mothers, divorce, or separate. On the other hand, if they lose their jobs, *lack an independent source of income,* and are unable to find a job with similar pay, they will experience downward social mobility and might even become poor.

Patterns of income distribution and wealth ownership indicate the existence of extreme socioeconomic status differences (income based) and class differences (based on wealth ownership) among women, which constitute the underlying material basis for the notion that almost all women are vulnerable to poverty: that is so because most women (and most men as well) are propertyless.

2. *Propertyless women (and propertyless men) are always at risk of becoming poor.* As economist Ferdinand Lundberg trenchantly observed:

> . . . anyone who does not own a substantial amount of income-producing property, or does not receive an earned income sufficiently large to make substantial regular savings or does not hold a well-paid securely tenured job is poor. . . . By this standard at least 70% of Americans are poor, although not all of these are by any means destitute or poverty stricken (Lundberg, 1969: 23).

Propertyless women may attain, at the level of market relations, through family-transmitted advantages (e.g. real estate property, higher education) and/or marriage, a socioeconomic status that appears to place them above the working class. When it is argued that the feminization of poverty places all or most women at risk, including middle- and upper-middle-class women, a very important observation is made that does not apply to women across social classes. The often-made statement, "most women are just a man or a divorce away from poverty," reflects the conditions of existence of most *propertyless* women whom the capitalist organization of production and reproduction makes dependent on marriage and/or employment for economic survival.

Working-class women with substantial "human capital" of their own are still a minority; they, and women with stable jobs, face a lower probability of poverty than do women with fewer skills or with precarious working conditions. Data on women's income and employment indicate that the vast majority of *propertyless* women are working class, both in terms of their place in the relations of production (i.e., they are propertyless and depend on a wage or salary for their economic survival and their families) and at the level of socioeconomic stratification (i.e., the vast majority of women work in low-paid, low-status, blue- or white-collar jobs). Of the 39,214,000 women who worked full time in 1986, 72.3% earned less than $20,000; 32.3% earned less than $10,000 (Bureau of the Census, 1987: 19). By 1988, women's earnings had noticeably improved; of the 41,573,000 women who worked full time, 66% earned less than $20,000 (a decrease of 6.3%) and 27.7% earned less than $10,000 a year (a decrease of 4.6%). On the other hand, there are more men than women in middle-class and upper-middle-class occupations and in the better-paid, skilled blue-collar jobs. Consequently, most women experience some form of "upward mobility" through marriage and, if they lack skills or resources of their own, are likely to return to their previous place in the socioeconomic structure in case of separation, divorce, or widowhood.

Most of the "social mobility" propertyless men and women experience in their life time is not social-class mobility in the Marxist sense (e.g., changing from being propertyless to becoming petty bourgeois, small or big capitalist, etc.) but rather occupational mobility. It is important to realize that men and women can experience mobility at the market level while remaining, simultaneously and regardless of their socioeconomic status, located in the working class or propertyless class. Intra-class differences (i.e., within the propertyless class) in the socioeconomic status and individual resources men and women bring to the market is at the core of women's greater vulnerability to poverty and the transformation of marriage into the major source of economic survival for vast numbers of women.[6]

The feminization of poverty is a market-level structural effect of intra-class differences in male and female socioeconomic status and mobility; it is fundamentally a class issue, although it is experienced and analyzed as an effect of sex and race discrimination. Sexism and racism unquestionably intensify the effects of economic changes upon the more impoverished layers of the working class (see AAWO, 1983; Sparr, 1987). Nevertheless, the ultimate determinant of individuals' relative vulnerability to poverty is their class location: "if sexism [and, I add, racism] were eliminated, there would still be poor women (and poor non-whites). The only difference is that women (and non-whites) would stand the same chance as men (and whites) of being poor" (Sparr, 1987: 11).

The Immiseration of the Working Class

Capital is indifferent to the reproduction of the working class as a whole; the extent to which workers can have access to the means necessary for their own reproduction and that of the future generation of workers is very much constrained by the demand for different kinds of labor power. The demand for certain kinds of skilled labor power may lead not only to good wages and salaries but also to special subsidies like public and private funding for the development of special training and educational programs and, sometimes, to the establishment of daycare facilities at the place of work. In general, however, the social and physical reproduction of the working class on a daily and generational level is left to the ingenuity of the workers themselves; left behind in poverty are those whose skills are no longer needed or whose birth in the reserve army of labor deprived them of the opportunity to develop skills.

In the U.S., the working class has suffered enormous setbacks in the last 15 years, reflected in high rates of unemployment, a general decline in real wages, the demise of the "family wage" for most workers, and qualitative changes in the economy and the organization of work that have significantly reduced the number of full-time, skilled, and relatively well-paid blue-collar male jobs that constituted the backbone of the U.S. "middle class." The "new poor" include not only working-class women but also many working-class men and their families. According to a 1982 survey of the U.S. Conference of Mayors, the "new poor" were created by economic decline, high unemployment, and cuts in federal programs. They are "people who are losing their jobs, exhausting their financial resources, exhausting their unemployment benefits, and losing their hopes" (Congressional Quarterly, 1983: 129). In times of economic crises, the illusory nature of middle-class and upper-middle-class statuses is clearly re-

vealed when social class reasserts itself through the powerlessness and untold suffering heaped upon men, women, and children by unemployment, under-employment, and cuts in social services.[7] A recent report indicates that:

more than half of the 8 million net new jobs created between 1979 and 1984 in the U.S. paid less than $7,000 a year while the number of jobs paying $28,000 or more actually fell. . . . [T]he biggest losers in the changing job market have been white men while the biggest winners have been white women. . . . [S]ince 1979, nearly 97% of net employment gains among white men have been in the low-wage stratum (incomes below $7,012). . . . [D]uring the same period, white men have experienced a net loss of 1 million jobs paying $28,000 or more in 1984 dollars. Among white women, 42% of the 5 million net job gains fell into the median-income range (incomes between $7,012 and $28,048) and 13.7% into the $28,000 or above category (Bluestone and Harrison, 1986; emphasis added).

The significance of this information becomes clearer when one considers that the official poverty line for an average family of four was $10,178 in 1983 (O'Hare, 1985: 6) and $11,000 in 1985; this means that more than half the jobs created between 1979 and 1983 did not cover even the minimum costs of the physical reproduction of workers unless those earning such a low wage had a working spouse. This information supports the results of a study of the Bureau of Labor Statistics:

. . . only 65% of the 3.8 million experienced workers aged 25 to 54 laid off between 1979 and 1983 were employed in January of 1984, some 25% were still unemployed, and 10% had dropped out of the labor force altogether. They averaged 23 weeks of unemployment and only half of them earned as much after their re-employment as they had earned before (Rose, 1986: 24–25).

The Bureau of Labor Statistics predicted that the largest job growth between 1984 and 1985 would be for jobs mainly at the top (e.g., lawyers, physicians, and surgeons) and bottom of the occupational hierarchy (e.g., orderlies, nursing aides, janitors and cleaners, waiters and waitresses, etc.), with relatively few in the middle (e.g., blue collar supervisors, registered nurses, computer programmers) (Bureau of the Census, 1986c: 394).

[S]ince 1973, one of the fastest growing occupations for men has been sales, increasing by 114% through 1986. . . . [B]etween 1973 and 1986, the number of blue collar workers . . . increased by only 4.4%. In contrast, men's employment in service occupations—for example, security guards, orderlies, waiters, daycare workers, and janitors—increased by 36.7% (Dollars & Sense, 1987: 10).

The notion that men can escape poverty by obtaining a job while women remain poor even if they work full time (Stallard et al., 1983: 9) is not entirely accurate. Male poverty increased while the "feminization of poverty" was taking place. Given these trends, full-employment policies would neither reduce the poverty of women (Ehrenreich, 1987: 12) nor even keep most men out of poverty or near poverty conditions.

The Bluestone and Harrison report seems to suggest that, while conditions are worsening for large numbers of working-class men (see also *Dollars & Sense*, 1987: 10–11), better opportunities are developing for at least some working women. The sex ratio of the population of full-time workers (24,099,000) who in 1986 earned less than $10,000 (below the 1986 poverty threshold for a family of four, $11,203) was 0.90 (0.86 in 1988); the sex ratio of those earning less than $20,000 in 1986 (52.2% of full-time workers) was 0.95 (0.90 in 1988) (Bureau of the Census, 1987: 19; 1989: 52–53). On the other hand:

[S]ince 1982, the gain in real earnings for women has been higher than for men. Between 1982 and 1986 women's median earnings rose by 9.8%. This increase compares with a 5.5% increase in men's earnings (Bureau of the Census, 1987: 2).

In 1986, among full-time male workers, 45.5% earned less than $20,000 and 23.2% earned between $20,000 and $29,999 (comparable percentages for full-time women workers were 72.3% and 19.3%) (Bureau of the Census, 1987: 19). In 1988, income distribution changed; the percentage of full-time male workers earning more than $30,000 a year reached 36.5% (up from 31.3% in 1986) while the percentage of full-time women workers with similar earnings almost doubled to 12.5% (up from 6.7% in 1986) (Bureau of the Census, 1989: 52–53). In 1988, among year-round, full-time workers, women's median earnings ($17,610) did not change in real terms if compared to the 1987 median; on the other hand, men's median earnings ($26,660) were 1.3% lower in real terms, "the first decline in the real earnings of men since 1982" (*Ibid.*: 4). Although men, on the average, earn more than women and a larger proportion of full-time male workers earns more than $30,000 a year, the information provided above shows that the vast majority of working men earn rather modest incomes.

Prospects for the 1990s

The 1980s witnessed a marked deterioration in the standard of living of the U.S. working class. This process was accompanied by tax cuts benefitting the capitalist class and an increased polarization in the distribution of income. In 1986, the top fifth of households received 52.4% of the total private-sector income, while the bottom fifth received only 1%. Inequality was modestly reduced by taxes and government transfers (means and non-means tested), but even after these are taken into account, extreme inequality remained: the top fifth received 45.7% while the bottom fifth received 4.7%. Without government transfers (taxes do not reduce income inequality signif-

icantly), the poverty rate would have been 19.9% instead of 13.6% (Amott, 1989: 10–11). Real wages have fallen since 1973 while per capita income has risen sharply. Median family income has also risen in comparison with real wages, indicating that families' economic well-being now depends on the labor of more than one member: between 1970 and 1986, the proportion of married couples with children and two full-time workers nearly doubled, from 14% to 26%. In contrast, top CEOs' earnings were higher than ever; the highest paid was J. P. Manzi (Lotus Development Corporation), who received $26.3 million, while those trailing behind made incomes above $10 million:

. . . between 1977 and 1988, corporate bosses' salaries and bonuses gained by 12.2% *each* year. At the same time, workers saw their hourly wages advance by only 6.1% annually. . . . Taking all income sources into account, a top CEO makes somewhere around $5,000 an *hour* (Aguilar-San Juan, 1988: 10–11).

As the rich got richer, the poor got poorer; because the minimum wage of $3.35 an hour remained unchanged since 1981, the gap between earnings at minimum-wage levels and the poverty level increased each year. After a great deal of congressional debate, it was finally changed in November 1989 to no less than $3.80 an hour until April 1, 1990, and no less than $4.25 an hour after March 31, 1991 (U.S. Government, Fair Labor Standards Amendments of 1989: 1).

Is this situation likely to change? Can workers expect a radical improvement in their earning power? Can female workers, particularly those who are single heads of households and support children on their own, expect the development and implementation of policies that will make it easier for them to earn a living and provide adequate care and education for their children? Can minority workers expect a closing of the wage gap between them and white workers, and better opportunities for themselves and their children? Will the number of well-paid, blue-collar and white-collar jobs increase, thus making it possible for more workers to form families? The answer to these and related questions has to be, at this point, negative.

The last months of 1989 brought about unexpected and profound changes in the balance of power between East and West and in the political and economic direction of Eastern Europe. The end of the Cold War generated the hope that a "peace dividend" would bring badly needed funds for social programs, education, the country's infrastructure, housing, and so forth. Such hope, however, was premature; military expenditures, albeit somewhat reduced, will continue to dominate the budget. Taking into consideration the magnitude of the deficit (that is likely to increase with the proposed cuts in capital gains taxes) and the burden of the savings and loans bail out, it becomes obvious that it would be unrealistic to expect increases in the funding of existing social programs, much less the development and implementation of new ones. On the contrary, retrenchment and cuts in social programs are likely to characterize the 1990s.

At this time, for example, increases in food prices for the last eight months have rendered insufficient the $2.1 billion the federal government allocates among the states to pay for WIC (Special Supplemental Food Program for Women, Infants, and Children). Almost half the states have been forced to reduce the amount of food they provide, or to eliminate thousands of recipients from their lists. This is a program that helps about one-third of all babies born in the US. as well as 4.5 million women (pregnant, or with new-born babies) who are at high risk of malnutrition. Texas will drop 27,000 people, Oklahoma 15,000, and Colorado 10,000 preschool-age children; in Texas, children will get less cereal; in California, they will get less orange juice and no cheese; and in Colorado, expensive peanut butter will be replaced with beans and legumes (Pear, 1990: 1–2; Cain, 1990: 1–5). All states face increasing demands on their funds not only for social programs like WIC, but also for infrastructure, education, and urban needs. To cope with those demands, without federal funds, they are forced to increase regressive taxes on consumption (e.g., California has recently passed an increase in gasoline taxes).

The country badly needs a comprehensive universal health care plan (there are over 31 million people without health insurance), which would provide coverage to everyone, young or old, able or disabled. There is a need for adequate and affordable housing for the poor and the homeless (many of whom are families), and for growing numbers of waged and salaried workers who are unable to find affordable homes in the communities where they work. There is a need for job training programs to enable men and women, especially minorities (whose rate of unemployment is extremely high), to leave poverty behind, as well as more jobs that pay a living wage to male and female workers. There is a need for better working conditions to reduce the toll that occupational accidents and exposure to hazardous and toxic materials take on the lives of workers and their families. Above all, there is a need for a family policy that will enable parents, particularly single mothers, to be able to work without neglecting the health and well-being of their children. There are, however, important structural barriers to the attainment of these goals, even on a modest level.

Besides the budgetary constraints mentioned above, the nature of the world-economy and the opening of Eastern Europe to foreign capital create unforeseen limits to what working people can expect in this decade. The world-economy has generated a new breed of corporation that, unlike its multinational and transnational predecessors, has shed the pretense of allegiance to a specific nation-state and its relative

dependence on state protection of its interests in foreign jurisdictions. While nation-states can bicker about protectionism and terms of trade, and the more powerful states can still impose their will upon the weak within their internationally agreed-upon spheres of influence, the "stateless corporations" (Holstein et al., 1990: 98–105) are rapidly establishing their own jurisdictions and acquiring a degree of global economic power and flexibility in their operations that place them above the control of even the most powerful nation-states.

Among American-based corporations on their way to becoming stateless, the process manifests itself through the extent to which their main markets and sources of profit are located outside the United States. Manufacturers such as IBM, Gillette, Xerox, Dow Chemical, and Hewlett-Packard find their main markets abroad, and almost 70% of General Motors' 1989 profits came from operations outside the U.S. (Ibid.: 99). Foreign capital, on the other hand, is coming to the U.S. in unprecedented quantities, creating jobs and transferring technology while simultaneously establishing relations of economic interdependence that could turn (depending on future changes in the world-economy and the balance of power between nation-states) into relations of economic dependence of the kind U.S. capital imposes on other countries. At any rate, the development of the stateless corporation is likely to make more difficult the government's ability to create favorable conditions for capital investment and concomitant growth in the demand for labor. Stateless corporations are already forcing nation-states to compete for their favors; given that what matters to capital is profits, rather than national prosperity, and given the more favorable conditions corporations can find in countries with a standard of living and wage levels lower than those in the U.S. efforts by the U.S. government to entice investments with lower taxes might result in increasing the government deficit and forcing even further cuts in social programs.

In this context, an improvement in the job opportunities opening up for most workers is not likely, regardless of gender and race/ethnicity. It is also unlikely that family-support policies will be enacted and implemented. The Act for Better Childcare didn't pass and the family-leave bill was vetoed. The lack of quality and affordable childcare imposes substantial economic and psychological burdens on working parents, especially on working mothers, and it is a contributing factor to the poverty of thousands of single mothers. In the absence of policies establishing universal entitlements to medical care and childcare, thousands of mothers have no choice but to stay on welfare because the low-paid jobs they could get would not cover health and childcare costs.

There are today 31.1 million working women with children who work outside their homes; this includes

50.8% of mothers with children one year old or younger; 56.1% of mothers with children under age 6 and 73.3% of mothers with children ages 6 to 17 (Darnton, 1990: 66). Those who can afford it can leave their children in private daycare centers; those who cannot afford to pay have to leave their children in less-than-optimal conditions or forego employment altogether. Despite the real need for childcare, under capitalism what matters is effective demand (i.e., needs backed by money); consequently, services catering to the needs of upper-middle-class women prosper.

A good example is Boston's Beacon Hill Nannies Inc., which, after requiring a $375 application fee and a $2,600 post-selection payment, supplies customers with "upscale" college-educated nannies, suitable as "role models to children of the professional class" (Duffy, 1990: 115). These nannies earn $20,000 a year, a salary well above the $17,606 median salary of full-time female workers who worked 50 weeks or more in 1988. Median earnings for all women workers that year were $11,096, and 75.7% of them earned less than $20,000 a year (Bureau of the Census, 1989: 53).

This highlights the class and socioeconomic differences among working women, and calls into question the usefulness of the feminization of poverty thesis for characterizing present trends. Even if the federal government were to finance quality childcare for all working parents who cannot afford it, and for single mothers seeking to leave welfare, this might be a mixed blessing, as the unintended effects might be an increase in the supply of cheap female labor and in the unemployment rate among unskilled or low-skilled male workers, thus perpetuating the poverty of female workers (especially those who are single mothers) and the barriers for family formation in the lower strata of the working class.

Lest I might be misinterpreted, my argument does not imply that I consider marriage to be the solution to the "feminization of poverty." My argument is that family policies, including childcare, would make the lives of working women easier but would not, in themselves, lift from poverty or near-poverty status millions of working women. Dual-earner families are better off than families headed by women and, while it is true that families are not problem free,

> [W]e cannot get so caught up in "women's" issues that we lose sight of the fact that the overwhelming majority of American women and men clearly believe in marriage and the two-parent family (Sidel, 1986: 192).

The foundation for these families is the availability of well-paid jobs for both male and female workers, so that women who by choice or necessity find themselves solely responsible for their children are not thereby necessarily condemned to poverty.

Given current changes in the world-economy and the trend within the U.S. toward the growth of poorly paid jobs in the service sector while well-paid manu-

facturing jobs are exported to the Third World or Eastern Europe, the 1990s do not so far seem to promise the working class a substantial improvement over the conditions established in the 1980s.

Conclusion

The data discussed earlier in this article show that the sex ratio of the poverty population has changed little since 1966; its age composition, however, did change. Today, the majority of the poor are children under 18 and adults under 44 (See Table 1). While in absolute numbers, there are more poor women than men, poverty increased faster among men between 1978 and 1983, and declined faster among men in 1984, 1985, and 1986. Between 1979 and 1980, both sexes experienced the highest poverty increase; the number of men below poverty level increased by 25.2% and the number of women by 23.5% (Bureau of the Census, 1981; 1982).

Theoretically, these trends are empirical indicators of the immiseration of the working class. The essence of this argument is that people do not fall into poverty because of their age, sex, or racial/ethnic characteristics, but rather because of their social class. Age, sex, and ethnic/racial groups are not socially homogeneous; they are divided in social classes that, in turn, are stratified by income, education, and occupation. The fact that poverty falls disproportionately upon the young, women, and minorities does not invalidate the analysis; those who become poor share a common relationship to the means of production that cuts across age, sex, and racial/ethnic differences.

Sexism and racism are important in determining who gets the worst jobs or is most likely to be affected by unemployment (AAWO, 1983). Yet sexism and racism are not unchanging entities that stand on an independent material base; instead, they are shifting structural effects of capitalist processes of labor allocation that is designed to increase profit margins and enhance economic and political control over the working class. The general determining dynamics of poverty are, from this standpoint, located in general capitalist processes that racialize, ethnicize, and sexualize the work force on national and world-system levels (processes whose ideological, political, and legal effects, in turn, perpetuate them through time, endowing them with a deceptive universality and antiquity) (Wallerstein, 1983, 1985).

The specific determinants of recent poverty trends, on the other hand, are to be found in the interplay between the historical effects of sexism and racism and recent political and economic changes that have drastically altered the economic structure in the U.S. Some sectors of the capitalist class are lowering the average price of labor to become competitive at the international level; cuts in wages, union busting, right to work laws, "give backs," cuts in social services, and recent changes in immigration laws that allow the legalization of undocumented workers under certain conditions are all efforts aimed at cheapening the overall costs of labor (Piven and Cloward, 1985; Harrington, 1984).

Lacking access to the material conditions for their physical and social reproduction on a daily and generational level, almost 32 million members of the working class living below the poverty level barely survive under the restrictive conditions imposed by the welfare state. Altogether, 42.6 million people live below 125% of the poverty level; this includes 9.2 million families (45.9% headed by women) (Bureau of the Census, 1989: 68). Nutrition levels and health among the poor have deteriorated; between 1982–1985, the food-stamp program was cut by $7 billion and child-nutrition programs by $5 billion. In spite of the large number of people below the poverty level, only 19 million receive food stamps, while 12 million children and 8 million adults suffer from hunger (Brown, 1987: 37–41).

Lack of access to the basic material conditions necessary for physical and social reproduction on a daily and generational basis threatens the intergenerational reproduction of the working class among all races, particularly among racial and ethnic minorities. The immiseration of the working class culminates in the breakdown of its intergenerational reproduction; poor parents, particularly poor single mothers, are compelled to live under conditions that deprive them of their ability to reproduce people with marketable skills. This situation may be "functional" for the economy, in so far as the demand for skilled and educated workers is not likely to rise dramatically in the near future. From the standpoint of the working class and especially of minority workers, this is a very serious situation that cannot be redressed by civil rights, better educational opportunities, and measures designed to help women combine work and parenting, *in themselves*.

Wilson (1978; 1987: 233–240) wrote of the "declining significance of race" and the need to recognize the primarily economic- and class-based determinants of the poverty and deprivation of most Black Americans; *the magnitude of the feminization of poverty should alert us to the declining significance of sex as a cause of women's poverty*. The feminization of poverty reflects the fact that women make up more than half the U.S. property-less class and that the standard of living of this class has noticeably declined in the last 10 years (for a thoughtful statement about the need to overcome the limits of an exclusive focus on sex, to the detriment of class and race as sources of women's oppression, see Thorton Dill, 1987: 204–213).

The media, social scientists, politicians, and activists give—depending on their specific concerns, political agendas, and theoretical commitments—greater importance to different sectors of the poor: *the notoriety of the "feminization of poverty," the poverty of minorities, the elderly, or children contrast with the relative silence about the erosion in the standard of living and the growing poverty of the working class*. Uncovering the correlates of poverty pertinent to each of these sectors is important, but the analysis must go beyond this to avoid the development of theoretically flawed explanations and policies that pit the interests of women against the interests of men, the young against the old, and whites against non-whites.

Stress upon the poverty of those who are disproportionately poor produces a misleading perception of poverty as something that affects mainly women, the elderly, ethnic/racial minorities, and welfare recipients and that could, theoretically, be effectively dealt with by measures addressing the needs of women workers, civil rights enforcement, and welfare reforms. In fact, most poor people are white (65.1% in 1988); 61.5% of the poor aged 18 to 64 worked during the year and 12% of them worked full time; only 12% of the elderly aged 65 and over are poor and 50% of the poor who live in families do not live in families headed by women (Bureau of the Census, 1989). Furthermore, of the 2.5 million families between poverty level and 125% of the poverty level, only 31.6% are headed by women (*Ibid.*: 68–74).

To speak of the immiseration of the working class does not entail the adoption of a mindless economic reductionism nor the callous denial of the plight of minorities, women, children, and the elderly. It simply entails the recognition of the fact that those sectors of the poor population, including men, do not live as isolated individuals but rather are linked to each other through common relations of production and reproduction. The fate of each sector is tied to the fate of the others because they are all part of the same social class, just as the fate of individuals is tied to the fate of those with whom they share kinship or emotional and social bonds. People are "an ensemble of social relations" (Marx, 1969: 198) and cannot be meaningfully understood in isolation from those relations that give them their historically specific place in the world in which they live.

It is not by reducing people to age, sex, racial or ethnic categories that poverty and its determinants can best be understood; people are poor or become poor because they are subject to common socioeconomic and political processes that deprive them of access to their material conditions of existence, tear families apart, or make family formation impossible for vast numbers of working-class men and women, particularly those who are also members of racial and ethnic minorities. Placed in its historical context, the feminization of poverty is a real, important—albeit partial—dimension of a vast process of social transformation

3. NONETHNIC MINORITIES

TABLE 1

Male-Female Share of the Poverty Population by Age and Sex 1966–1985 (numbers in 1,000s)

Year	Population Below the Poverty Level Both Sexes		% Female All Ages	% Male All Ages	% Female 16–44 (1966-74) 18–44 (1975-85)	% Male 16–44 (1966-74) 18–44 (1975-85)	% Female 45–64	% Male 45–64	% Female 65 and Over	% Male 65 and Over	Sex Ratio	Poverty Rate
1966	M	12,225	57.1	42.9	16.3	11.5	9.4	5.8	11.5	6.5	75.1	14.7
	F	16,265										
1967	M	11,813	57.5	42.5	16.4	11.3	9.5	5.5	12.7	6.7	74.0	14.2
	F	15,951										
1968	M	10,793	57.5	42.5	16.7	11.2	8.4	5.6	11.9	5.8	74.0	12.8
	F	14,578										
1969	M	10,292	57.6	42.4	16.8	11.0	9.5	5.7	13.0	6.7	73.6	12.1
	F	13,978										
1970	M	10,879	57.4	42.6	17.2	12.6	9.4	5.4	12.3	6.0	74.3	12.6
	F	14,637										
1971	M	10,708	58.0	42.0	18.6	12.6	9.4	5.6	11.7	5.0	72.1	12.5
	F	14,841										
1972	M	10,190	58.3	41.7	19.5	12.6	9.5	5.5	10.8	4.5	71.5	11.9
	F	14,841										
1973	M	9,642	58.0	42.0	20.1	12.4	9.4	5.7	10.0	4.6	72.4	11.1
	F	13,316										
1974	M	10,313	57.2	42.5	20.2	13.3	9.0	5.4	9.4	4.2	74.3	11.2
	F	13,881										
1975	M	10,908	57.8	42.2	18.8	11.1	8.7	5.6	8.9	3.9	72.9	12.3
	F	14,970										
1976	M	10,375	58.5	41.5	19.5	11.7	9.1	5.2	9.3	4.0	71.0	11.8
	F	14,603										
1977	M	10,340	58.2	41.8	19.8	11.5	8.9	5.5	9.0	3.9	71.9	11.6
	F	14,381										
1978	M	10,017	59.1	40.9	20.4	11.6	8.9	5.4	9.3	3.9	69.7	11.4
	F	14,480										
1979	M	10,535	58.4	41.6	19.8	11.8	8.9	5.4	9.9	4.3	71.1	11.7
	F	14,810										
1980	M	12,207	58.3	41.7	21.1	13.2	8.1	4.9	9.5	3.8	71.5	13.0
	F	17,065										
1981	M	13,360	58.1	41.9	21.6	14.0	8.1	4.9	8.7	3.4	72.4	14.0
	F	18,462										
1982	M	14,842	56.9	43.1	21.8	14.8	7.9	5.0	7.7	3.2	75.9	15.0
	F	19,556										
1983	M	15,182	57.0	43.0	22.2	15.5	7.6	5.0	7.5	3.0	75.6	15.2
	F	20,084										
1984	M	14,537	57.0	43.1	22.0	15.2	7.8	5.3	7.0	2.8	75.9	14.4
	F	19,163										
1985	M	14,140	57.2	42.8	22.4	15.0	7.6	5.2	7.6	2.9	74.7	14.0
	F	18,923										
1986	M	13,721	57.6	42.4	22.8	14.1	7.7	4.9	7.7	3.0	73.6	13.6
	F	18,649										
1987	M	14,020	56.1	43.9	22.2	14.3	7.3	5.1	7.6	3.0	75.7	13.5
	F	18,518										
1988	M	13,667	57.1	42.9	22.5	14.4	7.7	5.0	7.9	3.0	75.0	13.1
	F	18,211										

Source: U.S. Bureau of the Census, several reports; see footnote 2 for complete references.

resulting in a drastic decline in overall wage levels and in the standard of living of the U.S. working class, a significant increase in the size of the reserve army of labor and its pauperized sector, the intensification of the proletarianization of women,[8] and the undermining of the material conditions necessary for the maintenance of "middle-class" and even "upper-middle-class" illusions, and for the intergenerational physical and social reproduction of the lower strata of the working class—particularly its racialized, ethnicized, and feminized sectors.

Notes

1. Both "Spanish Origin" and "Hispanic" are, for political, theoretical, and methodological reasons, highly problematic labels. They misrepresent the determinants of the disproportionate poverty rate among people of Mexican and Puerto Rican origin and/or descent, and obscure the qualitative differences between

U.S. minority groups and Spanish and Latin American immigrants. Throughout this article, I choose to use ''Spanish Origin'' because, unlike ''Hispanic,'' it is a simple, descriptive label that does not create the presumption of some kind of ''Hispanic'' race or culture. Readers interested in this issue should consult the January 1987 issue of the *American Journal of Public Health*, in which the political and methodological problems inherent in the ''Hispanic'' label are examined, as well as my article, ''Latino/Hispanic: Who Needs a Name? The Case against a Standardized Terminology'' (*International Journal of Health Sciences* 19,3 [1989]).

2. Bureau of the Census, ''Supplementary Report on the Low Income Population: 1966–1972,'' *Current Population Reports* Series P-60, No. 95, July 1974, Table 1; ''Characteristics of the Low Income Population: 1973,'' *Current Population Reports* Series P-60, No. 98, January 1975, Table 6; ''Characteristics of the Population Below the Poverty Level: 1974,'' *Current Population Reports* Series P-60, No. 102, January 1976, Table 6; Table 11 in ''Characteristics of the Population below the Poverty Level'' for the years 1975, 1976, 1977, 1978, 1980, 1981, 1982, 1983, *Current Population Reports* P-60, No. 106, June 1977; No. 115, July 1978; No. 119, March 1979; No. 124, July 1980; No. 130, December 1981; No. 133, July 1982; No. 138; No. 144, March 1984; No. 147, February 1985; No. 152, June 1986; Table 8; ''Money Income and Poverty Status of Families and Persons in the United States: 1985,'' *Current Population Reports* Series P-60, No. 154, August 1986, Table 18; No. 157, July 1987; Tables 11 and 18; ''Money Income and Poverty Status in the United States: 1988,'' *Current Population Reports* Series P-60, No. 166, March 1989, Table 21.

3. The decline in the poverty rate after 1975 is reflected in the decline, for all ages and both sexes, in the numbers below the poverty level during the next four years. In 1978, the year chosen by O'Hare as the base year, the poverty rate was low (11.3%) and the number of poor men of all ages (10,017,000) was relatively low if compared to most of the preceding years, but certainly higher than the lowest number recorded since 1966: 13,316,000 in 1973.

4. The lower proportion of poor men in the population below the poverty level might be partially correlated with sex differential mortality. This is a complex issue that cannot be fully examined here, but it is possible, nevertheless, to present some pertinent observations. Occupationally caused mortality and disability are disproportionately high among working-class men and women (Berman, 1978; Chavkin, 1984). Death rates among working-age males (15 to 64) are considerably higher than among females of the same age. Death rates from accidents and violence are also exceedingly high for younger males, particularly for Blacks (Bureau of the Census, 1986: 72; 76). As mortality varies inversely with socioeconomic status, it is reasonable to suppose that death rates for occupational accidents, disease, and violence are likely to be higher for working-class men than the reported rates that do not take class differences into account.

5. I am aware of the complexity of the issue of class and class structure within Marxist and neo-Marxist theory. Nevertheless, for the purposes of developing my argument in this article, I consider that it is enough to point out the crucial differences between classes defined at the level of production, and classes defined at the level of the market, in a Weberian and sociological sense. If relationship to the means of production is overlooked, it is possible to argue that most women, regardless of social class, could become poor; if the impact of propertylessness is considered, it becomes obvious that it is working-class women who are at a greater risk of becoming poor.

6. Intra-class differences in the market resources of propertyless men and women reflect, in turn, differential patterns in the intergenerational transmission of socioeconomic status that, in turn, are determined by the articulation of production and reproduction within the propertyless class, a topic that cannot be examined within the limitations of this essay.

7. See Richard Parker (1972) for an excellent discussion of the distorted way in which social class is commonly perceived by social scientists and the general public.

8. This process is not equivalent to the ''feminization of the proletariat'' (Ehrenreich, 1987: 12). For demographic reasons (higher male mortality), women have always made up more than half of the proletariat, whether they were aware of it or not. I refer here to the erosion of ''middle-class'' and ''upper-middle-class'' statuses among growing numbers of propertyless women. It is

also true that working women are concentrated in the more poorly paid jobs and that the demand for female (and male) cheap labor is increasing. These trends can be best understood not in demographic terms (giving emphasis to the sex or age composition of the proletariat), but rather as effects of current processes of wealth concentration and relative immiseration.

References

Aguilar-San Juan, Karen, 1988, ''Feeding Time: Corporate Execs Go to the Trough.'' Dollars & Sense (July/August): 10–11.

Alliance Against Women's Oppression (AAWO), 1983, Poverty: Not for Women Only—A Critique of the Feminization of Poverty. AAWO Discussion Paper No. 3 (September).

Amott, Teresa, 1989, ''Re-slicing the Pie.'' Dollars & Sense (May): 10–11.

Berman, Daniel M., 1978, Death on the Job—Occupational Health and Safety Struggles in the United States. New York: Monthly Review Press.

Bluestone, Barry and B. Harrison, 1986, ''Most New Jobs in U.S. Low-paying.'' Boulder Daily Camera (Wednesday, December 10).

Brown, J. Larry, 1987, ''Hunger in the U.S.'' Scientific American 256,2 (February): 37–41.

Bureau of the Census, 1989, Current Population Reports, Series P-60, No. 166, Money Income and Poverty Status in the United States: 1988. (Advanced Data from the March 1989 Current Population Survey.) Washington, D.C.: U.S. Government Printing Office.

_____, 1987, Current Population Reports, Series P-60, No. 157, Money Income and Poverty Status of Families and Persons in the United States: 1986. Washington, D.C.: U.S. Government Printing Office (No. 2, February): 37–41.

_____, 1986a, Current Population Reports, Series P-60, No. 152, Characteristics of the Population below the Poverty Level: 1984, Washington, D.C.: U.S. Government Printing Office.

_____, 1986b, Current Population Reports, Series P-60, No. 154, Money Income and Poverty Status of Families and Persons in the United States: 1985. Washington, D.C.: U.S. Government Printing Office.

_____, 1986c, Statistical Abstracts of the United States: 1987 (107th Edition). Washington, D.C.: U.S. Government Printing Office.

Cain, Debra, 1990, ''State Drops 10,000 from Food Program.'' Colorado Daily (June 1–4): 1.

Chavkin, Wendy (ed.), 1984, Double Exposure: Women's Health Hazards on the Job and at Home. New York: Monthly Review Press.

Congressional Quarterly, 1983, ''Problems of the Unemployed.'' In Employment in America. Washington, D.C.: 129–156.

Darnton, Nina, 1990, ''Mommy vs. Mommy,'' Newsweek (June 4): 64–67.

Dollars & Sense, 1987, ''Even Young Men Feel the Pinch.'' Number 131 (November): 10–11.

Duffy, Robert, 1990, ''Beacon Hill Nannies: A Bull Market in Babysitting.'' Business Week (May 14): 115.

Ehrenreich, Barbara, 1987, ''Making Poverty a Women's Issue.'' Dollars & Sense Special Issue on Women and Work.

Harrington, Michael, 1984, The New American Poverty. New York: Penguin Books.

Holstein, William J. et al., 1990, ''The Stateless Corporation.'' Business Week (May 14): 98–105.

Lundberg, Ferdinand, 1969, The Rich and the Super-Rich. New York: Bantam Books.

Marx, Karl and F. Engels, 1969, The German Ideology, New York: International Publishers.

O'Hare, William P., 1985, Poverty in America: Trends and New Patterns. Population Bulletin 40,3 (June). Washington, D.C.: Population Reference Bureau.

Ossowski, Stanislaw, 1963, Class Structure in the Social Consciousness. New York: The Free Press of Glencoe.

Parker, Richard, 1972, The Myth of the Middle Class. New York: Liveright.

Pear, Robert, 1990, ''Many States Cut Food Allotments for Poor Families.'' The New York Times (May 29): 1.

3. NONETHNIC MINORITIES

Piven, Frances F. and R. A. Cloward, 1985, The New Class War: Reagan's Attack on the Welfare State and Its Consequences. New York: Pantheon.

Rodgers, Jr., Harrell R., 1986, Poor Women, Poor Families. New York: M. E. Sharpe.

Rose, Stephen J., 1986, The American Profile Poster. New York: Pantheon.

Sidel, Ruth, 1986, Women and Children Last—The Plight of Poor Women in Affluent America. New York: Viking Penguin Inc.

Smith, Joan, 1990, "All Crises Are Not the Same: Households in the United States during Two Crises." Jane Collins and Martha E. Gimenez (eds.), Work without Wages. Comparative Studies of Domestic Labor and Self-Employment. Albany: State University of New York Press: 128–141.

Sparr, Pamela, 1987, "Re-Evaluating Feminist Economics: 'Feminization of Poverty' Ignores Key Issues." Dollars & Sense, Special Issue on Women and Work.

Stallard, Karin et al., 1983, Poverty in the American Dream: Women and Children First. Boston: South End Press.

Staples, Robert, 1985, "Beyond the Black Family: The Trend toward Singlehood." R. Staples (ed.), The Black Family, Belmont, Cal.: Wadsworth: 99–105.

The Center for the Study of Social Policy, 1985, "The 'Flip Side' of Black Families Headed by Women: The Economic Status of Black Men." R. Staples (ed.), op. cit.: 232–238.

Thorton Dill, Bonnie, 1987, "Race, Class, and Gender: Prospects for an All-Inclusive Sisterhood." R. Takaki (ed.), From Different Shores—Perspectives on Race and Ethnicity in America. New York: Oxford University Press: 204–213.

U.S. Government, 1989, Fair Labor Standards Amendments of 1989. Public Law 107-157, 11/17/89 (103 Stat. 938). Washington, D.C.: U.S. Government Printing Office.

Wallerstein, Immanuel, 1985, "The Construction of Peoplehood: Racism, Nationalism, Ethnicity." Keynote address for Conference on "Ethnic Labels, Signs of Class: The Construction and Implications of Collective Identity" (October 11–12). Mimeographed paper, Fernand Braudel Center for the Study of Economies, Historical Systems and Civilizations. New York: SUNY Binghamton.

_____, 1983, Historical Capitalism. London: Verso Editions.

Weber, Max, 1982, "Determination of Class Situation by Market Situation." A. Giddens and D. Held (eds.), Class, Power, and Conflict. Berkeley and Los Angeles: University of California Press: 60–61.

Wilson, William, 1987, "The Black Community in the 1980s." R. Takaki (ed.), From Different Shores—Perspectives on Race and Ethnicity in America. New York: Oxford University Press.

_____, 1978, The Declining Significance of Race. Chicago: University of Chicago Press.

■ BORN TO LOSE

The Prejudice Against Men

PETER MARIN

Peter Marin, an essayist and novelist who has been research-ing and writing about homelessness for the past three years, currently has a grant from the Alicia Patterson Foundation. A version of this article is being simultaneously published in the A.P.F. Reporter.

For the past several years advocates for the homeless have sought public support and sympathy by draw-ing attention to the large number of homeless fam-ilies on our streets. That is an understandable tactic. Americans usually respond to social issues on the basis of sympathy for "innocent" victims—those whose blameless-ness touches our hearts and whom we deem unable to care for themselves. Families, and especially children, obviously fill the bill.

But the fact remains, despite the claims of advocates, that the problem of chronic homelessness is essentially a problem of *single adult men*. Far more single adults than families, and far more men than women, end up homeless on our streets. Until we understand how and why that happens, nothing we do about homelessness will have much of an impact.

Most figures pertaining to the homeless come from limited studies or educated guesses that tend, when examined, to dis-solve in one's hand. The most convincing figures I know can be found in James Wright's book *Address Unknown: The Homeless in America*. According to Wright's data, out of every 1,000 homeless people in America, 120 or so will be adults with children, another hundred will be children and the rest will be single adults. Out of that total, 156 will be single women and 580 will be single men. Now break that down into percentages. Out of all single homeless adults, 78 percent are men; out of all homeless adults, more than 64 percent are sin-gle men; and out of all homeless people—adults or children—58 percent are single men.

But even those figures do not give the full story. Our federal welfare system has been designed, primarily, to aid women with children or whole families. That means that most of the families and children on the streets have either fallen through the cracks of the welfare system or have not yet entered it. They will, in the end, have access to enough aid to get them off the streets and into some form of shelter, while most men will be left permanently on their own.

I do not mean to diminish here the suffering of families or children, nor to suggest that welfare provides much more than the meanest alternative to homelessness. It is a form of in-dentured pauperism so grim it shames the nation. But it does in fact eventually get most families off the streets, and that leaves behind, as the chronically homeless, single adults, of whom four-fifths are men. Seen that way, homelessness emerges as a problem involving what happens to men with-out money, or men in trouble.

Why do so many more men than women end up on the streets? Let me begin with the simplest answers.

First, life on the streets, as dangerous as it is for men, is even more dangerous for women, who are far more vulnerable. While many men in trouble drift almost naturally onto the streets, women do almost anything to avoid it.

Second, there are far better private and public shelters and services available to women.

Third, women are accustomed to asking for help while men are not; women therefore make better use of available resources.

Fourth, poor families *in extremis* seem to practice a form of informal triage. Young men are released into the streets more readily, while young women are kept at home even in the worst circumstances.

Fifth, there are cultural and perhaps even genetic factors at work. There is some evidence that men—especially in ado-lescence—are more aggressive and openly rebellious than women and therefore harder to socialize. Or it may simply be that men are allowed to live out the impulses women are taught to suppress, and that they therefore end up more often in marginal roles.

More important, still, may be the question of work. His-torically, the kinds of work associated with transient or mar-ginal life have been reserved for men. They brought in crops, worked on ships and docks, built roads and railroads, logged

From *The Nation,* July 8, 1991. This article was written under a grant from the Alicia Patterson Journalism Foundation. Reprinted by permission.

and mined. Such labor granted them a place in the economy while allowing them to remain on society's edges—an option rarely available to women save through prostitution.

And society has always seemed, by design, to produce the men who did such work. Obviously, poverty and joblessness forced men into marginality. But there was more to it than that. Schools produced failures, dropouts and rebels; family life and its cruelties produced runaways and throwaways; wars rendered men incapable of settled or domestic life; small-town boredom and provinciality led them to look elsewhere for larger worlds.

Now, of course, the work such men did is gone. But like a mad engine that cannot be shut down, society goes right on producing them. Its institutions function as they always did: The schools hum, the families implode or collapse, the wars churn out their victims. But what is there for them to do? The low-paying service-sector jobs that have replaced manual labor in the economy go mainly to women or high school kids, not the men who once did the nation's roughest work.

Remember, too, in terms of work, that women, especially when young, have one final option denied to men. They can take on the "labor" of being wives and companions to men or of bearing children, and in return they will often be supported or "taken care of" by someone else. Yes, I know: Such roles can often constitute a form of oppression, especially when assumed out of necessity. But nonetheless, the possibility is there. It is permissible (as well as often necessary) for women to become financially, if precariously, dependent on others, while such dependence is more or less forbidden to men.

Finally, there is the federal welfare system. I do not think most Americans understand how the system works, or how for decades it has actually sent men into the streets, creating at least some male homelessness while aiding women and children. Let me explain. There are two main programs that provide care for Americans in trouble. One is Social Security Disability Insurance. It goes to men or women who are unable, because of physical or mental problems, to work or take care of themselves. The other is Aid to Families with Dependent Children (A.F.D.C.). It is what we ordinarily call "welfare." With its roots early in this century, it was established more or less in its present form during the Depression. Refined and expanded again in the 1960s, A.F.D.C. had always been a program meant mainly for women and children and limited to households headed by women. As long as an adult man remained in the household as mate, companion or father, *no aid was forthcoming.* Changes have recently been made in the system, and men may remain in the household if they have a work history satisfying certain federal guidelines. But in poor areas and for certain ethnic groups, where unemployment runs high and few men have a qualifying work history, these changes have not yet had much of an impact and men remain functionally outside the welfare system.

When it comes to single and "able-bodied," or employable, adults, there is no federal aid whatsoever. Individual states and localities sometimes provide their own aid through "general assistance" and "relief." But this is usually granted only on a temporary basis or in emergencies. And in those few places where it is available for longer periods to large numbers of single adults—California, for instance, or New York—it is often so grudging, so ringed round with capricious requirements and red tape, that it is of little use to those in need.

This combination of approaches not only systematically denies men aid as family members or single adults. It means that the aid given to women has sometimes actually deprived men of homes, even as it has provided for women and children. Given the choice between receiving aid for themselves and their children and living with men, what do you think most women do? The regulations as they stand actually force men to compete with the state for women; as a woman in New Orleans once told me: "Welfare changes even love. If a man can't make more at a job than I get from welfare, I ain't even gonna look at him. I can't afford it."

Everywhere in America poor men have been forced to become ghost-lovers and ghost-fathers, one step ahead of welfare workers ready to disqualify families for having a man around. In many ghettos throughout the country you find women and children in their deteriorating welfare apartments, and their male companions and fathers in even worse conditions: homeless in gutted apartments and abandoned cars, denied even the minimal help granted the opposite sex.

Is it surprising, in this context, that many African-Americans see welfare as an extension of slavery that destroys families, isolates women and humiliates men according to white bureaucratic whim? Or is it accidental that in poor communities family structure has collapsed and more and more children are born outside marriage at precisely the same time that disfranchised men are flooding the streets? Welfare is not the only influence at work in all of this, of course. But before judging men and their failures and difficulties, one must understand that their social roles are in no way supported or made easier by the social policies that in small ways make female roles sustainable.

Is this merely an accidental glitch in the system, something that has happened unnoticed? Or does it merely have something to do with a sort of lifeboat ethic, where our scarce resources for helping people are applied according to the ethics of a sinking ship—women and children first, men into the sea?

I do not think so. Something else is at work: deep-seated prejudices and attitudes toward men that are so pervasive, so pandemic, that we have ceased to notice or examine them.

To put it simply: Men are neither supposed nor allowed to be dependent. They are expected to take care of both others *and* themselves. And when they cannot do it, or "will not" do it, the built-in assumption at the heart of the culture is that they are *less than men* and therefore unworthy of help. An irony asserts itself: Simply by being in need of help, men forfeit the right to it.

Think here of how we say "helpless as a woman." This demeans women. But it also does violence to men. It implies that a man cannot be helpless and still be a man, or that helplessness is not a male attribute, or that a woman can be helpless through no fault of her own, but that if a man is helpless it is or must be his own fault.

Try something here. Imagine walking down a street and passing a group of homeless women. Do we not spontaneously see them as victims and wonder what has befallen them, how destiny has injured them? Do we not see them as unfortunate and deserving of help and *want* to help them?

Now imagine a group of homeless men. Is our reaction the same? Is it as sympathetic? Or is it subtly different? Do we have the very same impulse to help and protect? Or do we not wonder, instead of what befell them, how they have got themselves where they are?

And remember, too, our fear. When most of us see homeless or idle men we sense or imagine danger; they make us afraid, as if, being beyond the pale, they are also beyond all social control—and therefore people to be avoided and suppressed rather than helped.

Here too work plays a crucial role. In his memoirs Hamlin Garland describes the transient farm workers who passed through the countryside each year at harvest time. In good years, when there were crops to bring in, they were tolerated: fed, housed and hired. But when the crops were bad and men weren't needed, then they were forced to stay outside of town or pass on unaided, having become merely threats to peace and order, barbarians at the gates.

The same attitude is with us still. When men work (or when they go to war—work's most brutal form), we grant them a right to exist. But when work is scarce, or when men are of little economic use, then they become in our eyes not only superfluous but a danger. We feel compelled to exile them from our midst, banish them from view, drive them away to shift for themselves in more or less the same way that our Puritan forebears, in their shining city on its hill, treated sinners and rebels.

One wonders just how far back such attitudes go. One thinks of the Bible and the myth of the Garden and the first disobedience, when women were cursed with childbirth and men with the sorrows of labor—destinies still, as if by intention, maintained by our welfare system and private attitudes.

And one thinks too of the Victorian era, when the idealized vision of women and children had its modern beginnings. They were set outside the industrial nexus and freed from heavy labor while being rendered more than ever dependent on and subservient to men. It was a process that obviously diminished women, but it had a parallel effect on men. It defined them as laborers and little else, especially if they came from the lower classes. The yoke of labor lifted from the shoulders of women settled even more heavily on the backs of certain men, confining them in roles as narrow and as oppressive as those to which women were assigned.

We are so used to thinking of ours as a male-dominated society that we tend to lose track of the ways in which some men are as oppressed, or perhaps even more oppressed, than most women. But race and class, as well as gender, play roles in oppression. And while it is true, in general, that men dominate society and women, in practice it is only *certain* men who are dominant; others, usually those from the working class and often darker skinned (at least 50 percent of homeless men are black or Latino), suffer endlessly from forms of iso-

At the heart of their troubles is a helplessness they cannot overcome on their own.

lation and contempt that often exceed what many women experience.

The irony at work in all of this is that what you often find among homeless men, and what seems at the heart of their troubles, is precisely what our cultural myths deny them: a helplessness they cannot overcome on their own. You find vulnerability, a sense of injury and betrayal and, in their isolation, a despair equal to what we accept without question in women.

Often this goes unadmitted. Even when in deep trouble men understand, sometimes unconsciously, that they are not to complain or ask for help. I remember several men I knew in the local hobo jungle. Most of them were vets. They had constructed a tiny village of half-caves and shelters among the trees and brush, and when stove smoke filled the clearing and they stood bare to the waist, knives at their hips, you would swear you were in an army jungle camp. They drank throughout the day, and at dusk there always came a moment when they wandered off individually to sit staring out at the mountains or sea. And you could see on their faces at such moments, if you caught them unawares, a particular and unforgettable look: pensive, troubled, somehow innocent—the look of lost children or abandoned men.

I have seen the same look multiplied hundreds of times on winter nights in huge shelters in great cities, where a thousand men at a time will sometimes gather, each encapsulated in solitude on a bare cot, coughing and turning or sometimes crying all night, lost in nightmares as terrible as a child's or as life on the street. In the mornings they returned to their masked public personas, to the styles of behavior and appearance that often frightened passers-by. But while they slept you could see past all that, and you found yourself thinking: These are still, even grown, *somebody's* children, and many fare no better on their own, as adults, than they would have as children.

I remember, too, a young man in my town who was always in trouble for beating up older drunken men. No one understood his brutality until he explained it one day to a woman he trusted: "When I was a kid my daddy ran off and my mother's drunken brothers disciplined me. Whenever I made a mistake they punished me by slicing my legs with a straight razor." And he pulled up his pant-legs to reveal on each shin a ladder of scars marking each childhood error or flaw.

This can stand for countless stories I've heard. The feeling you get, over and over, is that most men on the street have been "orphaned" in some way, deprived somewhere along the line of the kinds of connection, support and sustenance that enable people to find and keep places in the social order. Of course economics plays a part in this—I do not mean to suggest it does not. But more often than not, something else is also at work, something that cuts close to the bone of social and psychological as well as economic issues: the dissolution of family structures and the vitiation of community; subtle and overt forms of discrimination and racism; and institutions—schools, for instance—that harm or marginalize almost as many people as they help.

For decades now, sociologists have called our attention to rents in our private social fabric as well as our public "safety nets," and to the victims they produce: abused kids, battered women, isolated adults, alcoholics, addicts. Why, I wonder, is it so hard to see homeless men in this context? Why is it so hard to understand that the machinery of our institutions can injure men as permanently as it does women? We know, for instance, that both male and female children are permanently injured by familial abuse and violence and "normal" cruelties of family life. Why, then, do we find it hard to see that grown men, as well as women, can be crippled by childhood, or that they often end up on the edges of society, unable to play expected roles in a world that has betrayed them?

And do not forget here the greatest violence done to men, the tyrannous demand made upon them when young by older and more powerful males: that they kill and die in war. We take that demand for granted in our society and for some reason fail to see it as a form of oppression. But why? Long before the war in Vietnam had crowded our streets with vets—as far back as the Civil War—the male victims of organized state violence wandered across America unable to find or make places in the social world. The fact is that many men never fully recover from the damage done by war, having seen too much of death to ever again do much with life.

Nor is war the only form in which death and disaster have altered the lives of troubled men. They appear repeatedly in the stories men tell. Listening to these tales one thinks of Oedipus and Lear, of tragedy in its classical sense, of the furies and fates that the Greeks believed stalk all human lives and that are still at work among us, no matter how much we deny them.

Gene, a homeless man I know, was conceived when his mother slept with his father's best friend. Neither of his parents wanted him, so he was raised reluctantly by his mother's parents, who saw him only as the living evidence of her disgrace. As an adult he married and divorced twice, had two children he rarely saw later in life, and spent two years in jail for beating nearly to death a friend he found in bed with his second wife. When I first met him he was living in a cave he had dug by hand out of a hillside, and he spent the money he earned on dope or his friends. But then he met a woman on the streets and they moved together to a cheap hotel. He got her pregnant; they planned to marry; but then they argued and she ran off and either had an abortion or spontaneously miscarried—it was never clear which. When Gene heard about it he took to his bed for days and would not sleep, eat or speak. When I later asked him why, he said: "I couldn't stand it. I wanted to die. I was the baby she killed. It was happening to me all over again, that bad stuff back when I was a kid."

Homeless men feel a sense of betrayal at society's refusal to recognize their needs.

Not everything you hear on the street is so dramatic. There are a thousand quiet and gradual ways American lives can fall apart or come to nothing. Often it is simply "normal" life that proves too much for some men. Some have merely failed at or fled their assigned roles: worker, husband, father. Others lacked whatever it takes to please a boss or a woman or else decided it wasn't worth the trouble to learn how to do it. Not all of them are "good" men. Some have brutalized women or left families in the lurch or fled lives in which the responsibility and stress were more than they could handle. "Couldn't hack it," they'll say with a shrug, or "I had to get out." And others have been so cruel to women or proved so unreliable or sometimes so unsuccessful that women fled them, leaving notes on the table or refrigerator such as the one a man in Seattle once repeated to me: "Gone. Took the kids. So long."

Are such men irresponsible? Perhaps. But in working with homeless men over the years, I've seen how many of them are genuinely unable to handle the stress others can tolerate. Many manage, for instance, to steer clear of alcohol or drugs for a certain period of time and then return to them automatically as soon as they are subject again to the kinds of stress they once fled. It is as if their defenses and even their skins are so much thinner than those of the rest of us that they give way as soon as trouble or too much responsibility appears.

The fact is that most such men seem to have tried to make a go of things, and many are willing to try again. But if others have given up and said, inside, *the hell with it* or . . . *it*, is that really astonishing? The curious world we've compounded in America of equal parts of freedom and isolation and individualism and demands for obedience and submission is a strange and wearing mix, and no one can be startled at the number of victims or recalcitrants it produces or at those who can't succeed at it.

Finally, I must add one more thing. Whatever particular griefs men may have experienced on their way to homelessness, there is one final and crippling sorrow all of them share: a sense of betrayal at society's refusal to recognize their needs. Most of us—men and women—grow up expecting that when things go terribly wrong someone, from somewhere, will step forward to help us. That this does not happen, and that all watch from the shore as each of us, in isolation, struggles to swim and then begins to sink, is perhaps the most terrible discovery that anyone in any society can make. When troubled men make that discovery, as all homeless men do sooner or later, then hope vanishes completely; despair rings them round; they have become what they need not have become: the homeless men we see everywhere around us.

What can be done about this? What will set it right? One can talk, of course, about confronting the root causes of marginalization: the failure of families, schools and communities; the stupidities of war, racism and discrimination; social and economic injustice; the disappearance of generosity and reciprocity among us. But what good will that do? America is what it is; culture has a tenacity of its own; and though it is easy to call for major kinds of renewal, nothing of the sort is likely to occur.

That leaves us with ameliorative and practical measures, and it will do no harm to mention them, though they too are not likely to be tried: a further reformation of the welfare system; the federalization of assistance to single adults; increases in the amount and duration of unemployment insurance; further raises in the minimum wage; expanded benefits for vets; detox centers and vocational education for those who want them; the construction of the kinds of low-cost hotels and boarding houses where men in trouble once stayed.

And remember that back in the Depression when the welfare system was established, it was paralleled by programs providing work for men: the Civilian Conservation Corps and the Works Progress Administration. The idea seems to have been welfare for women, work for men. We still have the welfare for women, but where is the work for those men, or women, who want it? Why no one is currently lobbying for contemporary forms of those old programs remains a mystery. Given the deterioration of the American infrastructure—roads, bridges, public buildings—such programs would make sense from any point of view.

But beyond all this, and behind and beneath it, there remains the problem with which we began: the prejudices at work in society that prevent even the attempt to provide solutions. Suggestions such as those I have made will remain merely utopian notions without an examination and renovation of our attitudes toward men. During the past several decades we have slowly, laboriously, begun to confront our prejudices and oppressive practices in relation to women. Unless we now undertake the same kind of project in relation to men in general and homeless men in particular, nothing whatever is going to change. That's as sure as death and taxes and the endless, hidden sorrows of men.

The story of a nursing home refugee

KATHARINE M. BUTTERWORTH
WHOLE EARTH REVIEW

Taking care of the elderly is not something we do very well in our society. Most older people prefer to live out their last years on their own or with loved ones rather than in a nursing home, so the burden of caring for them falls squarely on their family and friends. But because there is little public support—either in financial help or in tangible services—for those caretakers, sometimes that burden becomes too great and a nursing home becomes the only option. That's what happened to 91-year-old Katharine Butterworth, and this is her spirited account of that time. Dollars & Sense magazine describes the mixed-up financial picture of aging policy in the United States and reminds us that with our rapidly growing population, the problem is only going to get worse.

Young families who have the responsibility of caring for old people find it hard to tuck them in the chimney corner, mainly because there is no longer a chimney corner in which to tuck them.

A bulletin from my college proudly lists 10 graduates who lived to be 100, but every one of them is in a nursing home. A nursing home used to be a halfway house between hospital and going home. Now too often it is the permanent home, the last resort for a family desperate to handle an elderly invalid. Nursing homes are expensive and to receive any financial aid from the government, such as Medicaid, one must be destitute, but that is another story.

I know about three nursing homes, two for my husband, one for myself. My husband and I had had a good and healthy life when in our mid-80s he became ill, a bladder operation leaving him in need of a permanent catheter, the infection sometimes affecting his mind. I became ill and had to enter a hospital myself, so our children insisted he go into a nursing home.

When I recovered and returned home, I visited him. He had been given a small room opposite a noisy laundry room, and a woman patient next door was moaning all night. He said he was going to jump out the window, and I told him he was on the ground floor and could walk out. I

sat with him in the dining room with three men who didn't talk; they had Alzheimer's disease. The trays were metal, and noisy when handed out. He was served a huge sausage, the kind he particularly disliked, no knife, and a little dish of stewed fruit with a limp piece of cake on top. No fruit juice or water, liquids he was supposed to have plenty of. In addition he was tied in a wheelchair, making it difficult for him to reach the table. It depressed both of us.

At a meeting with the head nurses and an accountant, in which I was asked to sign many papers to make my husband's acceptance in the nursing home permanent, plus pay a $3,000 deposit in case we got behind in our payments, I burst out, "He's coming home." The nursing home had started out as a solution to a problem but it had turned into a nightmare. We would both be home in our apartment, would manage some way and die together.

Our help at home was erratic and our children again insisted my husband be placed in a nursing home. He needed more care and often wandered at night, waking me up. Once he fell out of bed at 2 a.m., which entailed my calling the police because I could not lift him or help him to climb back in.

This second "home" was much more elegant, with Georgian-style architecture, trees, garden, the room itself large and pleasant, but help here was short and he was often left in bed most of the morning. The dining room had none of the clatter of metal trays and the varied food was attractively served, each person seated at an individual table or in a wheelchair with a tray. It seemed quietly civilized until one patient shoved his tray with everything from soup to dessert and it shot with a crash across the floor, requiring that some poor soul clean up the mess. The patients looked normal but, one could guess, often were not.

Then we found Sandy and a nursing home was no longer necessary. Sandy was with us part time for

From *Utne Reader*, January/February 1991, pp. 42-49. Excerpted from *World Earth Review*, Fall 1990. *World Earth Review*, Box 38, Sausalito, CA 94966-9924.

over a year until my husband died. She was going to college, wanted to earn extra money, and we paid her above the minimum wage. Never have I known a more dedicated, hard-working, cheerful, intelligent young girl. She likes old people, and plans to run her own nursing home some day. May her dream come true. She was ideal for us, permitting my husband to stay home where he was happiest. She was strong enough to give him a tub bath, for example, and because she was cheerfully persuasive there was little friction, and I began to relax. He died at home, which in itself was a comforting end.

Six months after my husband died I came down with pneumonia, and my son and daughter-in-law took me to the emergency room in the nearby hospital. Slowly I recovered physically. There were many complications, X-rays, medicines, a speech therapist and psychologist (which confused me, but apparently I had had a slight stroke that I didn't realize until later). The best medicine was my roommate, Ruth, a rollicking, cheerful woman who was seriously ill, but made everyone who came to our room—cleaning woman, nurse, or doctor—smile.

Eventually a physical therapist got me out of bed and walking, leaning on a walker. I was shocked at how wobbly I had become. I had been in the hospital two weeks and it was time for me to move out. My son, ever helpful and concerned, phoned, "Be ready, Ma, at nine, packed and dressed. The nursing home has a room for you." We decided that this was necessary because my son and daughter-in-law were away all day, and I could never manage alone.

This home was brand new, elegant and very expensive. The girl at the entrance desk was attractively dressed and gave the impression that we were being welcomed to some country estate although the two checks my son made out, one for a large deposit, the other for a week's stay in a double room, provided hard reality.

My first impression was that a great deal had been spent on decor—charming wallpaper, heavy pink bedspread, modern lamp at the bedside table, and a modern picture on the wall. All I wanted was to get undressed and into bed, and I promptly went to sleep.

Looking back I can see why I have been critical of my elegant surroundings. One loss was not having a telephone. In the hospital I could lie in bed and gossip with all my friends. My son usually called every day. Eventually I could use the nurses' phone down the hall, but I had to have the phone handed to me across the desk, stand up, and naturally the call had to be short.

I shared a room with Rose, a woman who had been there for some time and who was a favorite with all the nurses. Her dressing often needed changing at 2 a.m., a process that involved a great deal of nurse chatter, lights, and curtain noisily pulled for "privacy." That I was awoken was unimportant to everyone but me.

Rose had a telephone that her son had had installed. I asked Rose if I could use hers and would pay her and she agreed. I used her phone just once,

when she was taken for some test and I thought my conversation would not bother her. With my address book in hand I went to her bedside table to make the call. As I was dialing, a tall head nurse stalked in, accused me of using Rose's property when she was out, and snatched my address book, saying that I must have taken it from Rose's drawer. I was startled by this false accusation and angry that this woman could think I would use the phone without Rose's permission. Later I made a scene with a superintendent but nothing came of it. Rose laughed when she returned, and all that really happened was I couldn't sleep that night and was given a sleeping pill. It was a good example of the old and the weak versus the young and the strong.

Was I doomed to spend the rest of my life in this nursing home? For one thing I felt it was too expensive. How long would my money last, spent in this ridiculously extravagant fashion? It was up to me to get up and return to normal life. Weak, I got dressed and with my walker managed to make it to a big living room, where I had breakfast off a tray. There I found a dozen other more active people doing the same. The next day I carried in the portable radio my son had brought me and I came back to the world and listened to the news and my favorite classical music station. At lunch, again with my walker, I went to the dining room despite the 20 minutes it took me to travel the short distance down the hall. I began to feel that with determination I could grow strong.

The staff of this particular home worked hard to make things easy and pleasant for the patients—one could say they ought to for the price. There was an exercise class every morning, and I joined this. We sat in a big circle, some in wheelchairs, others in regular chairs. A young, peppy woman led us. She brought a huge lightweight ball that she would roll to each in turn and we would kick it back with right then left foot. Many of us were weak but one could see an improvement. There were exercises with arms, "pick the apple out of the tree, then put it down in the basket"; silly, but it got one's muscles moving.

The staff organized movies and an ice-cream party for those of us who could walk or get someone to push our wheelchairs to the parlor. I began to walk the corridors for exercise, and to explore different areas. There was one much more expensive-looking area that had a living room arranged with couches and easy chairs as in a private home. Here the public library had installed a wide choice of books in large print and this attracted me. Just by signing my name and room number I could help myself. I realized for the first time that my illness had been severe enough for me to give up reading. I took out a novel that looked lightweight and easy to follow, and this room became my favorite.

In my own area there was a music room that was not used much, and I would take my book here, pretending there were no hospital beds around the corner. This room had an expensive grand piano made in China. Here on Sunday afternoon there was a concert for piano and harp. A young lady brought in her harp, an undertaking that took more time than the concert itself. Unfortunately there were barely more than a dozen people who attended.

As I walked around more I became acquainted with more patients. There was one pleasant woman with one arm paralyzed, who was always in a wheelchair. She explained to me that when she and her husband found they had physical problems they could not solve, they sold their house and both entered this nursing home with the idea of ending their lives here. They had enough money to pay for the most expensive suite, brought their own furni-

Now, at 91, I live alone, moving about with family and friends.

ture, and often had special meals ordered. I never met her husband, but she was such a cheerful realist she was a pleasure to talk to.

There was another alert old gentleman whose son visited him every Sunday, and he was eager to talk. He knew the area, had been in business all his life, and would have preferred to stay home. His wife had died, and he needed too much care for his daughter-in-law to handle. Again there was enough money for him not to worry.

Many of these old people grumbled and complained and were dull to talk to. The patients whose minds were affected I found depressing. One attractive woman beautifully dressed in different outfits was like a flitting bird. She explained that her children had left her here, and she wanted to escape but she didn't know how to get out. Then she would jump up and run down the hall. There was one man with Parkinson's disease who would walk endlessly up and down the hall never meeting one's eye, looking vaguely for someone, something, perhaps his own identity.

There was a dumpy little woman with

Who cares for our elders?

"Why should a woman in her 60s feel she must use up her life savings—even sell her home—to keep her mother in a nursing home for less than two years?" asked American Association of Retired Persons vice president Robert Maxwell. "Why should a couple married for 30 years be forced to get a divorce in order to protect the wife's income and assets, while the husband impoverishes himself to qualify for Medicaid-funded nursing home care?"

They shouldn't, of course. These are consequences of government inaction on an issue that affects nearly all people at some time in their lives. Mention long-term care of older citizens to most Americans, and the first image that comes to mind is the nursing home. While nursing homes constitute a thriving industry in the United States, they are not where most care for elders takes place.

For elders who can no longer fully care for themselves, most care is provided at home by family members and friends. An estimated seven million older Americans require some sort of assistance—from once-a-week shopping help, to once-a-day meal preparation, to round-the-clock nursing care.

For incapacitated elders and their families, the choices are hard. Nursing home care is costly and of poor quality. Home care services are virtually non-existent in many states, and where they are available they are expensive. For most who quit their jobs to care for their parents, there is little income support. The lack of long-term

care is indeed a national crisis.

Though most surveys of elders indicate they would rather not be institutionalized in nursing homes, institutionalization is precisely what our present system of long-term elderly care encourages.

Given the demographics of the United States, nursing homes are a growth industry. Roughly 1.6 million nursing home beds were in use in 1986. Because the number of elders in the U.S. population is projected to rise through the year 2030, the demand for nursing home beds is expected to increase to over two million in 2000, and to nearly three million by 2030.

Nursing homes are now a $38 billion industry with more than 19,000 homes. Once dominated by "mom-and-pop" operators and charitable organizations, the industry is increasingly composed of large, for-profit chains.

For nursing home residents, absentee ownership brings negative consequences. The Massachusetts Department of Public Health, charged with monitoring nursing home care, reports that absentee-owned homes have significantly more code violations than locally owned and non-profit homes.

For the patient or the patient's family, nursing home care is extremely costly. Average costs per day run as high as $100. Annual costs range from $25,000 to $40,000. Unless residents are extremely poor—or until they reach that point—most of the cost of nursing home care is borne by elders and their families. Medicare will pay only up to 100 days of acute medical and rehabilitative services in a nursing home, leaving people needing long-term care completely uncovered. Medicare pays only 2 percent of the nation's nursing home bill.

Alzheimer's disease, and she too was a wanderer with fluttering hands. She liked my room and once tried to get into my bed, to my horror. Another time she stole a book I had carelessly left on my bed. I had a nurse search her room, but we never found it, and I wrote the public library apologizing, hoping someone would return it.

Unlike the pleasant woman and her husband who planned to make this their permanent home, my attitude from the beginning had been to get strong and to leave the nursing home as soon as possible. I was lucky that I had no debilitating disease, that I could walk, and that my mind was normal. My finances were not great enough to pay for this "hotel" (for a bed and meals were what it amounted to, with little mental stimulation). In a little over three weeks I persuaded my son and daughter-in-law to take me in.

When I got to their rather cold house (the nursing home had been overheated), and had to get my own breakfast and lunch, and be alone all day, I realized I had been too impatient. I was not as tough as I had thought I was. I often would crawl back in bed and sleep an uneasy sleep, but soon I would force myself, warmly dressed, to walk around the back yard or go out for the mail. There was plenty to read, too much, but the most endearing feature was the family cat, Brandy. She too was lonely during the day, and she and I would lie down together on my bed, or she'd sit in my lap, and we'd talk and purr and were close company. Evenings and weekends were wonderful, with the stimulating company of my son and daughter-in-law, and delicious meals where all I did was set the table. The nursing home seemed far away. The next jump was to my own apartment, but this was cushioned by the arrival of my daughter, who cooked for me and spoiled me. Without the help of my children could I have recovered so quickly?

Now, two years later, at 91, I live alone. How long can I hope to keep moving about with family and friends, to take walks around the pond in the neighboring park? Can I hope to escape the permanent nursing home? ∎

Medicaid, known as the long-term care insurance policy that requires impoverishment for a premium, is the major public payer for long-term care services. For the poor and those older Americans impoverished by the high costs of long-term care, Medicaid covers nearly all nursing home expenses. Medicaid pays nearly half the nation's nursing home bill, making it—by default rather than by design—the country's long-term care insurance policy.

Once on Medicaid, older people needing care are hardly free of worry. Medicaid sets a fixed payment rate for nursing home care that is on the average 15 to 20 percent lower than the rates charged private payers. This gives nursing home operators a strong incentive to discriminate against those on public assistance. Medicaid-supported elders seeking nursing home care typically wait four times as long for a bed in a nursing home as privately paying elders.

With all of the problems associated with nursing home care, it is perhaps not surprising that older people overwhelmingly prefer to be cared for in their own homes. Yet government spending for long-term care is heavily biased in favor of nursing homes. Neither Medicare nor Medicaid covers any significant part of home care services. As a result, 85 percent of home care is provided by friends and family members without institutional support. Of the 15 percent who receive care from paid providers, 60 percent pay the entire bill themselves. High turnover among home care workers, who are overworked and underpaid, further hampers the availability of adequate home care.

Not surprisingly, most of the caregivers—paid and unpaid—are women. Women frequently care for their infirm husbands, whom they outlive by six years on average. The burden of care also falls on adult children, usually daughters and daughters-in-law, who give up paid work to care for frail family members. The vast majority of paid home care workers are also women.

Ironically, although home care tends to be much cheaper than nursing home care, cost containment is one of the major reasons for the government's bias toward institutional care. Public officials, recognizing that the number of elders currently going without publicly supported services far exceeds the number receiving support, fear a surge in demand for home care if the government were to provide it.

According to a recent survey commissioned by senior advocates, the U.S. public is greatly concerned about the inadequacy of long-term care. Sixty percent of respondents said they had direct experience with family members or friends needing long-term care, and more than 80 percent said nursing home costs would be a major hardship on their families. Most significant, over 70 percent said they wanted a government program providing universal long-term care and would be willing to pay higher taxes to support it.

—*Dollars & Sense*

Excerpted with permission from Dollars & Sense *(Jan./Feb. 1988). Subscriptions: $19.50/yr. (10 issues) from Economic Affairs Bureau, 1 Summer St., Somerville, MA 02143. Back issues: $3 from same address.*

Elder care: How the U.S. stacks up

The United States isn't the only nation scrabbling to meet the needs of a growing elderly population. Our limited federal health insurance for the old and lack of a comprehensive respite-care program for caregivers puts us behind some countries. But our commitment to Social Security sets us ahead of others.

	UNITED STATES	JAPAN	CHINA	SWEDEN
PEOPLE 65 OR OLDER	30 million (12%)	13.3 million (11%)	53 million (5%)	1.5 million (18%)
WHERE THEY GET CARE	About 95% care for themselves or are cared for by family and friends. Some get assistance from in-home caregivers and adult day-care centers. The rest live in nursing homes.	About 65% of the elderly live with their children. The rest live in state-sponsored hospitals, geriatric health facilities, and nursing homes.	Adult children are subject to criminal penalties if they don't support their parents. State-supported services care for the 10% of elders who can't work and have no spouse or grown children.	More than 90% live alone or with their families and receive such services as delivered meals, transportation, and weekend care; 7% live in nursing homes; and 2% live in apartments with 24-hour nursing staffs. Adult day-care centers are available.
WHO PAYS	Less than 2% of long-term care and just 42% of nursing home care is paid for by the federal government. Home-delivered meal services and some day-care centers receive federal and state funding.	The national and local governments provide free or very-low-cost health care to older people including medicine, hospitalization, and transportation, as well as day care.	Work units (factories, farms, schools, etc.) provide all social services, including health and respite care.	All institutional care and social services are paid for by the municipal governments, with help from the national government, which also pays all pensions.
HOW THE GOVERNMENT HELPS	About 33% of the federal budget goes to Social Security, Medicare, and Medicaid.	In 1986, it spent about $29.6 billion on elder-care programs.	The government underwrites part of the cost of various welfare programs, including homes for the aged, community-based long-term care, and hospitals.	This year, $1.5 billion will be spent on elder care.
AVERAGE TAX RATE	34%	28%	Not available	51%
FUTURE PLANS	Congress is considering extending Medicare coverage of long-term health care, as well as the Family and Medical Leave Act, which would guarantee unpaid leaves for employees whose parents need care.	The government hoped to increase the number of adult day-care centers from 96 in 1989 to 3,000 by 1990.	By 2030, about 24% of China's population will be elderly, and there will be fewer young adults because of a current requirement that couples have no more than one child.	The government is increasing subsidies that will allow elders to stay in their own homes.

Rights Issues Split Protestant Churches; More Battles Expected

JOHN GALLAGHER

Long the focus of contentious debate, questions surrounding the place of gays and lesbians in mainline Protestant churches heated up in the opening weeks of June to become one of the most divisive issues facing the denominations.

The issue pits church leaders, who fear dividing their congregations during a period of declining church attendance, against gays and lesbians, whose demands for immediate, substantive reform have grown adamant.

"You get really tired of people saying, 'I hear your pain,'" said Rev. Lisa Bove, comoderator of Presbyterians for Lesbian and Gay Concerns (PLGC), a support group. "We want justice, not sympathy."

In Bove's denomination, the issue reached a head when the general assembly of the Presbyterian Church-USA voted June 10 to reject a report that would have allowed the church to sanction same-sex relationships and ordain openly gay or lesbian clergy members.

The Episcopal church will consider ordination of gays and lesbians at its annual convention in Phoenix July 10, and both the Evangelical Lutheran Church of America (ELCA) and the United Methodist Church are studying similar proposals. But vigorous opposition from conservatives has left the denominations unwilling to change stands against homosexuality and same-sex unions.

A recent gay rights battle has even been fought in the American Baptist Church, one of the most conservative Protestant sects. Many delegates to the denomination's annual convention in Charleston, W.Va., which began June 18, objected to the presence of a booth sponsored by American Baptists Concerned (ABC), a gay support group, even though ABC has operated booths at Baptist conventions in the past. The support group defused the conflict by operating its booth under the name American Baptists for a Biblical Life-style.

Officials at Protestant churches "know that all the issues around sex are absolutely not going to go away," said Rev. Daniel Smith, a member of the 17-member task force that produced the Presbyterian report on sexuality. "They're trying to buy time and put off decisions by recommending study after study."

Ruth Frost, an openly lesbian Lutheran minister in San Francisco, said many gays and lesbians are suddenly willing to risk ostracism to claim their rights. "I see more and more people coming to the recognition that gays and lesbians can no longer wait for the church to give its stamp of approval on their lives," she said. "If we wait for people to approve our lives, the stamp of approval will be so paltry that our lives won't be our own."

Frost tied the new attitude to AIDS activism. "People are getting more vocal," she said. "In the past, they were willing to exist on a survival level. We turned a significant corner with AIDS."

Protestant leaders, meanwhile, are dogged by a crisis of their own – sharp declines in church attendance and membership. "It worries church officials that there would be a mass exodus" if pro-gay reforms are made, Smith said. "With that goes a tremendous amount of money."

Rev. Morris Floyd, a spokesman for the gay Methodist group Affirmation, added, "In the big mainline denominations, the governing groups are becoming more reactionary. Anything that threatens the harmony of the institution is viewed as a more serious threat than it was five years ago. Churches are less willing to do the right thing for the right reason. Whatever else happens, church officials want their institutions to stay intact."

But Robert Cromey, rector of Trinity Episcopal Church in San Francisco, said, "If the church gets smaller, that's not bad. I'm not in the numbers game. If people leave because we do something just, then we have to say, 'Go find a comfortable pew somewhere else.'"

Teachings against same-sex intercourse and ordination of gays and lesbians have been issues in Protestant churches for years. But the release last February of the Presbyterian report on human sexuality raised the volume of the debate to a new level. The study rocked the denomination by outlining a concept called justice-love, a teaching that sexual relationships could be sanctioned outside of marriage.

"Where there is justice-love, sexual expression has ethical integrity," the report said. "That moral principle applies to single as well as to married persons, to gay, lesbian, and bisexual persons as well as to heterosexual persons."

Smith said the committee that prepared the Presbyterian report knew that justice-love would spur intense public debate. "We decided that the issues were so serious and significant to the life of the church that we would tell the truth and not worry about the ramifications," he said. "To appeal to the whole church would be to say nothing more than that sex is a mess."

The 200-page report, which sold more than 27,000 copies, generated an enormous backlash. More than half the church's 171 presbyteries urged that the recommendations be rejected, as did eight former presiding officers of the church's governing body. One fourth of the local groups demanded that mention of the report be omitted entirely from assembly minutes.

The report "was a big dose all at once," said PLGC comoderator Harlan Penn.

Reprinted by permission from *The Advocate*, July 16, 1991, pp. 14-16.

"Sexuality is very close to people's identities."

"Sexuality is very close to people's identities. It's very hard for people to think about something that threatens their self-image."

By the time the Presbyterians convened their meeting in Baltimore June 4, the report clearly had little chance of adoption. Furor over it had reached such proportions that Gordon Stewart, chairman of the assembly committee that was considering the report, said one of his objectives was simply to prevent a schism within the 2.9-million-member church.

Stewart's committee recommended the report be set aside, a stance that the convention approved 534-31. Hundreds of people attending the assembly cheered the vote. Then, in a protest that had the permission of the assembly moderator, about 20 gays and lesbians carried a large wooden cross to the front of the auditorium while several hundred people marched behind them. The protest ended with members of the group hammering nails into the cross.

In addition to rejecting the report on sexuality, delegates to the Presbyterian convention prepared a pastoral letter on homosexuality to be read in the denomination's 11,500 churches June 16. The letter

• affirmed the "sanctity of the marriage covenant between one man and one woman to be a God-given relationship to be honored by marital fidelity,"

• described homosexuality as "not God's wish for humanity,"

• forbade the ordination of "self-affirming, practicing" gays and lesbians, and

• reiterated the church's 1978 and 1979 statements on homosexuality, which condemned fear of gays and lesbians but called on them to either "transform their desires" or remain celibate.

Penn said the letter means that gays and lesbians "can be members of the church, but they are second-class members."

The single bright point for gays and lesbians at the convention was a vote that allows ministers to bless same-sex relationships in church as long as the unions are not considered comparable to matrimony. "It's somewhat ambiguous, but we take it as a first step," Penn said.

Smith said rejection of the sexuality report was not a complete defeat for gays and lesbians. "The report is still out there," he said. "People are still reading it and discussing it."

Penn agreed. "At least the report got people talking," he said. "Hopefully, they'll continue to talk. I can imagine that a more bland report could have been accepted, but it would not have made any impact on the church. The church's constant effort is to simply sweep gay and lesbian issues under the rug. Anything that prevents or disturbs that process is good in the long run."

But Bove said the time for discussion has passed and a change in policy is the only acceptable course now. "It's never going to be a perfect time for patriarchy to be dismantled," she said. "Church officials are never going to be ready for that."

While the Episcopal convention is unlikely to be as tumultuous as the Presbyterian meeting, several resolutions seem certain to cause heated debate. "There will be some nasty things said," according to Kim Byham, a spokesman for the Episcopal gay group Integrity. "Lots of our resolutions will draw fire."

Gay rights supporters will introduce about 20 resolutions, including one that asks the convention not to meet in states that have sodomy laws and another that condemns groups that allege they turn gays and lesbians into heterosexuals.

But the resolutions that promise to attract the most attention would allow the ordination of gays and lesbians and the blessing of gay unions. The convention is likely to decide to leave the ordination question up to individual local bishops and reject the resolution on gay unions outright, Byham said.

The convention was also scheduled to consider several proposals intended to reassert antigay interpretations of the Bible. Among them is one introduced by Bishop William Frye, a seminary dean, that would forbid Episcopal clergy members from engaging in sex outside of marriage. "That one is clearly antigay," Cromey said.

Cromey predicted that Frye's resolution will fail "not because of any great love of gays and lesbians but because there is a tradition in this church that you don't make morality different for the clergy than for the laity."

Like the Presbyterians, Episcopalians have had greater success in preventing approval of antigay resolutions than in passing pro-gay ones. "It's not always easy to get gay-affirming legislation through, but our system is such that the negative legislation

can't go through," Byham said.

The month after the Episcopal convention concludes, the United Methodist Church is scheduled to complete the final draft of its study on homosexuality for the denomination's quadrennial meeting in 1992. Current church policy says homosexuality is incompatible with Christianity, but a preliminary draft of the new study, released in February, would soften the position by saying that the church "is unable to arrive at a common mind on the subject."

Still, the change holds little appeal to gay and lesbian Methodists. "People I talk to are not interested in a gradual approach," Floyd said. "We've been studying this a long time. It's like being a teacher who can't make a student believe that two plus two equals four."

Incited by the debates in the Presbyterian and Episcopal churches, Methodists attending the denomination's regional conferences in May and June passed resolutions supporting the church's current condemnation of homosexuality. "The world's landscape today is littered with the debris of the homosexual life-style," said Carl Harris, author of a resolution passed by South Carolina Methodists.

Methodist gay rights advocates said they doubt they can overcome conservative attitudes at the upcoming convention. "Most traditional liberal supporters of gay rights adopt a conciliatory posture the minute it gets tough," Floyd said.

An early victim of the conflict among Methodists was James Hawk, an ordained minister who disclosed last year that he is gay. The 600 members of the church's western Pennsylvania regional conference voted almost unanimously June 13 to defrock Hawk because of his sexual orientation.

Hawk said he disclosed his sexual orientation because he realized that "who we are is so very good and our way of loving is a good gift from God and nothing to be ashamed of." After making the disclosure, Hawk was allowed to remain a minister because he swore he would remain celibate, but he eventually revoked the promise.

"I decided celibacy is a gift and special calling," he said. "Just because you're lesbian or gay doesn't mean you should be celibate."

In a similar case in the Lutheran church, Paul Johnson, an assistant to the bishop of the La Crosse, Wis., ELCA synod, resigned under pressure in May after church officials

"People I talk to are not interested in a gradual approach."

learned that he had told colleagues at a conference that he is gay. Johnson, an ordained pastor for nearly 20 years, refused to accept an ELCA rule that requires gay and lesbian clergy members to remain celibate.

"For those of us who are gay, the church requires a commitment to lifelong celibacy," Johnson said. "I am unwilling to make such a commitment, and I don't believe that the church should require it."

Just a few months before the Johnson incident, William Kunisch, a student at Pacific Lutheran Theological Seminary in Berkeley, Calif., was disciplined by his synod after he expressed disagreement with the ELCA celibacy requirement. Last year, two San Francisco congregations were put

on ecclesiastical trial and suspended for ordaining a lesbian couple and a gay man.

But the Lutheran picture was muddied June 8, when the Milwaukee ELCA assembly voted to encourage its congregations to accept gay and lesbian ministers. "The majority believed that the church is a welcoming place for all people," said Rev. Peter Rogness, the synod's bishop.

Affirmation's Floyd said that individual bishops in many Protestant denominations are quietly ordaining clergy members who they know are gay or lesbian without overt authorization from their denominations. "Issues of church policy are blinked at," he said. If the Methodist church suddenly dropped its ban on the ordination of non-

celibate gays and lesbians, "not a great deal would change," he said.

But by refusing to deal openly with gay rights issues, the churches may inadvertently cause their own declines, Presbyterian committee member Smith said. "The four more-liberal mainline denominations are still rooted in the family unit of the '50s, which is such a small part of the population now," he said. "If that's what the church wants in its members, it should get used to a shrinking membership real fast."

Smith added, "It's stupid. The gay and lesbian community is the only group that wants into the church, and the church won't open its doors. No one else is out there banging on the door to get in."

Politics, Public Policy, and Priorities

Society has so many social problems, where should we begin? With our society changing—new immigrants, new social classes, rising minorities, variations in family—how can we know what to do first? What should we, the public, tell our political leaders to place at the top of the list to receive government help?

When society wishes to attack a social problem, it usually turns to government because government tradi-

tionally has been a collector and director of society's resources. Through taxes, government pools our economic strength, and through civil service and the military, government gathers society's human talent so that money and human power can focus on a project.

In the United States, another reason we turn to government has to do with democracy. Because governments—national, state, and local—are designed to reflect the will of the majority, people believe government listens when society calls for solutions.

Which problems should be tackled first? This unit challenges you to think one step beyond merely wanting to address a favorite social problem. Priorities need to be considered, as well as new ways of thinking about problems and solutions.

"American Nightmare: Homelessness" blames homelessness on weak national policies regarding housing. Economic forces, not the lower classes, led to the S&L bailout, real estate speculation, and the shortage in housing available to meet the needs of all citizens.

In "Rural Poverty," we are reminded that poverty is not just an inner-city problem. The poverty rate in rural countries is as dismal as the inner cities. The poor are coal miners, people on the back roads of Maine, and in makeshift villages along the Rio Grande. What measures should we take against this social problem?

"Beyond the Stingy Welfare State" suggests an old-fashioned approach to dealing with poverty. A century or more ago, our society used approaches that required the needy to seek self-improvement and urged the wealthiest to involve themselves directly in helping the poor. Would you favor using these past approaches today?

"Education: Ideas and Strategies for the 1990s" challenges us to think of the best way to help school children. Although the 1980s saw nearly every state reform its schools, children today appear worse off than before. Are you ready to free local schools from state control? Would you support "second chance" schools?

Infrastructure means the basic facilities we need to keep our nation functioning, such as bridges, highways, dams, and airports. When we fail to keep infrastructure in good repair, we slow our economy. "Infrastructure: America's Third Deficit" blames the current economic decline on unwise skimping for public works. Where do you stand on more government spending for large capital projects?

What is our policy for "Energy for the Next Century?" If President Bush has his way, we shall focus our efforts on finding more petroleum. If Greenpeace is heard, we may be heading toward a postpetroleum society.

Should we legalize abortion? Currently we debate whether abortion is morally right, but "Abortion in a New Light" says we ignore the important issues of illegal abortions and women's health. Would society be better to legalize abortion in all countries and to protect the health of women and children?

"Big Messes" concludes this section on public policy. It summarizes our shortsightedness in permitting large-scale problems to continue, all the while engaging in typical American optimism that they would be overcome easily.

Looking Ahead: Challenge Questions

Should we remodel our social class system as a first step to dealing with other social problems? Can we succeed against other social problems if we permit part of our society, such as the homeless, to live in abject poverty?

What measures should our society take to improve housing so we can end homelessness?

What measures should our society take against the pockets of "forgotten" rural poverty?

Would you be willing to take a very poor person into your own home as a remedy against national poverty?

Are you ready to tell your state government to release local schools from state controls?

Do you favor increasing government spending for public works as an answer to our nation's social problems?

Which do you favor as an energy policy, increasing the amount of petroleum fuels even at the expense of the environment, or moving to a postpetroleum society?

Should abortion be fully legalized as a national policy to protect women's health?

Why have large problems been permitted to continue until they have become "big messes?"

American Nightmare: Homelessness

In the worst housing crisis since the Depression, many families face the spectre of homelessness. Restoring the homeownership dream means shifting national spending priorities and taking housing out of the speculative market.

Peter Dreier and Richard Appelbaum

Peter Dreier is Director of Housing at the Boston Redevelopment Authority. Richard Appelbaum is Chairman of the Department of Sociology at the University of California at Santa Barbara.

During the 1980s, a new ingredient was added to the landscape of America's cities—millions of people sleeping in alleyways and subways, in cars and on park benches.

The spectacle of homeless Americans living literally in the shadow of luxury condos and yuppie boutiques symbolized the paradox of the decade: It was a period of both outrageous greed and outrageous suffering. The media gave us "lifestyles of the rich and famous," but they also offered cover stories about homeless families. And while the 1980s were often characterized as the "me decade"—an orgy of selfishness and self-interest—more Americans were involved in social issues, as volunteers and activists, than at any time in recent memory.

These contrasts are even more striking in light of the billions of dollars invested in speculative commercial real estate during the 1980s, which has led, according to a recent Salomon Brothers report, to an unprecedented high office vacancy rate. Rampant real estate speculation also contributed to the savings-and-loan debacle. The S&L bailout, perhaps the biggest rip-off in American history, may cost taxpayers over $500 billion, a regressive burden that will divert funds from much-needed economic and social recovery programs. Meanwhile, housing starts—particularly construction of low-rent apartments—have reached a postwar low while, according to a new U.S Conference of Mayors survey, demand for emergency shelter continues to grow.

What will the 1990s bring?

Everyone from President Bush to the late advocate for the homeless Mitch Snyder has agreed that homelessness is a national tragedy and an embarrassment to America in the court of world opinion. Most Americans acknowledge that something must be done, that no great and affluent nation should tolerate such fundamental misery. And public opinion polls show that a vast majority of Americans now put solving the problem of the homeless near the top of the national agenda. According to these polls, Americans are even willing to pay higher taxes, if the funds go to assist the homeless.

It is clear to most Americans that "a thousand points of light" cannot stem the rising tide of homelessness. Public policy was responsible for creating this epidemic, and changes in public policy will be required to resolve

From *Challenge* Magazine, Vol. 34, No. 2, March/April 1991, pp. 46-52. Reprinted by permission of M. E. Sharpe, Inc., Armonk, New York 10504.

this mounting problem. But as long as politicians, housing activists, and academic experts disagree on how many people are homeless, who they are, and why America suddenly found itself with so many people living on the streets, it will be difficult to forge a consensus on what to do. In this article, we seek to answer these questions.

Middle class crisis

No other major industrial nation has such widespread homelessness. Even Canada, a country quite similar to ours in most political and economic features, has neither the slums to match the physical and social deterioration of our inner cities, nor the level of homeless people sleeping in shelters, streets, and subways. This suggests that there is something unique about the way the United States deals with its most needy citizens; but it also suggests that a solution is within reach. Indeed, there is no reason why the United States cannot solve its homeless problem by the end of the twentieth century, if we can mobilize the political will to do so.

The growing epidemic of homelessness is only the tip of the iceberg. The United States faces its worst housing crisis since the Great Depression. The underlying problem is a widening gap between what Americans can afford to pay and what it costs to build and maintain housing. This has always been a problem for the poor; now it is a growing problem for the middle class.

The "American Dream" of homeownership is fading fast for a large segment of the middle class. Thanks to postwar federal housing programs, the rate of homeownership rose steadily for three decades, from 43.4 percent in the late 1940s to 65.6 percent in 1980. Since then, however, it has steadily declined, reaching 64.0 percent in 1989. The problem is particularly troubling for young families. For example, among twenty-five to thirty-four- year- olds, the homeownership rate dropped from 52.3 percent in 1980 to 45.2 percent in 1989. The median price of a new single-family home climbed from $69,300 in 1982 to about $120,000 today. While in 1973 it took roughly one-quarter of the median income of a young family with children to carry a new mortgage on average-priced housing, today it takes over half of a young family's income. In some regions of the country, housing prices have started to drop, but because of wage and employment trends as well as interest rates, this has not made a significant dent in overall housing affordability.

High rents make it impossible for most young families to save money for a downpayment. As a result, about the only people who can afford to purchase a home are those who already own one. Even among those who manage to buy a home, a growing number are in danger of losing their homes to foreclosure by banks.

Rents have reached a two-decade peak, according to a recent Harvard University study. This is especially a problem for the poor, who are now competing with the middle class for scarce apartments. Some 85 percent of low-income renters (5.8 million households) are paying at least 30 percent of their income for housing. Two-thirds of the poor are paying at least half of their income just for housing. The typical young single mother pays over 70 percent of her meager income just to keep a roof over her children's heads.

Perhaps the most important statistic is this: Only one-quarter of poor households receive any kind of housing subsidy—the lowest level of any industrial nation in the world. The swelling waiting lists for even the most deteriorated subsidized housing projects are telling evidence of the desperation of the poor in the private housing market.

Is it any wonder that the ranks of the homeless are growing?

Fundamental economic shifts

The initial stereotype of the homeless person was an alcoholic or mentally ill middle-aged man or "bag lady"—many of them victims of deinstitutionalization resulting from the Community Mental Health Act of 1963. But when more low-rent housing was available, including many rooming houses that have since been lost to gentrification, even people on the margins of society could afford a roof over their heads.

The homelessness crisis is not, as some suggest, primarily a problem of personal pathology. It is, rather, a symptom of some fundamental shifts in the nation's economy.

The most important involves the deindustrialization and gentrification of our urban areas. The past fifteen years have been characterized by a tremendous flight of previously high-wage industries to low-wage countries. Since the early 1970s, the electronics revolution has hastened the development of a global economy. Footloose firms have moved their manufacturing operations to more favorable locations—with low wages, lax environmental laws, tax breaks, and other subsidies—whether these be in suburbs, rural areas, or Third World countries.

As a result of this geographic realignment, it is unlikely that American industry will soon again enjoy the once-privileged postwar position that enabled our standard of living to rise steadily for almost three decades. Many American cities have still not recovered from the

4. POLITICS, PUBLIC POLICY, AND PRIORITIES

loss of blue-collar industry and jobs. As factories closed down, tax bases declined, waterfronts were left vacant, and downtown department stores went out of business, some cities began to resemble ghost towns.

During the past decade, many observers have hailed the "services revolution" as the savior of cities. It is true that many cities have now shifted from what University of North Carolina sociologist John Kasarda calls "centers of production and distribution of goods to centers of administration, finance and information exchange." Cities sought to revitalize their downtown areas with new office buildings, medical and educational complexes, hotels, urban shopping malls, convention centers, and even sports complexes. But such efforts, even when successful, do not stem the growing tide of poverty only blocks away from the glittering glass and steel. In the shadow of its downtown skyscrapers, Los Angeles resembles a Third World city, its streets teeming with economically precarious low-wage workers and homeless men, women, and children.

Why? Because the services economy is predominantly a low-wage economy, and most of its jobs offer no career ladder or upward mobility. According to Bennett Harrison and Barry Bluestone, in *The Great U-Turn* (see For Further Reading), the majority of jobs created since the 1970s have offered poverty-level wages. Working full-time is no longer a guarantee of escaping poverty. Even relatively low levels of unemployment in some cities mask the deepening poverty and desperation.

As Robert Reich has noted, the American economy has two escalators—a small one moving upward and a much larger one moving downward. More than 33 million Americans—one out of seven—now live below the poverty line. The figure for children is even more alarming: one of every four (and one-half of all black children) live in poverty. Today's poor people are poorer and likely to remain poor for longer periods of time. During the 1980s, both the minimum wage and Aid For Dependent Children (AFDC) benefit levels fell far behind the rate of inflation.

Not surprisingly, more and more of America's homeless are families with children and people with jobs. A survey released in December 1990 by the U.S. Conference of Mayors found that almost one-quarter of the homeless work, but have wages too low to afford permanent housing. Apart from those who live on the streets or in shelters, there are millions more who live doubled-up or tripled-up in overcrowded apartments, and millions of others who pay more than they can reasonably afford for substandard housing. As a result of this situation, millions of low-income Americans are only one rent increase, one hospital stay, one layoff away from becoming homeless.

Things are getting worse for the middle class as well. In recent years, the average middle class American has seen family income stagnate. In 1960, the typical thirty-year old head of household could expect family income to increase by 50 percent during the next decade. Today, he or she can expect family income (real buying power) to decline. According to a recent Children's Defense Fund report, young families (headed by someone under thirty) have seen their incomes erode by one-quarter over the past fifteen years; among Hispanics, the decline has been one-third; among Blacks, one half.

For a small, but very visible, segment of the population, however, these new economic forces have led to the up-escalator. The services economy has created a stratum of highly-educated, well-paid management and professional workers. They, along with top-level executives and owners of wealth, did well during the decade of corporate takeovers and leveraged buyouts. The share of national income now going to the wealthiest 20 percent is the highest since World War II. Meanwhile, the share going to the poorest 40 percent is the lowest in that period. By dramatically lowering tax rates of the affluent and big business, the Reagan Administration exacerbated these trends and redistributed income from the working class to the wealthy. President Bush's proposal to cut capital gains taxes would continue this trend.

All this pertains directly to housing. While America was witnessing a growing disparity of incomes, the affluent began viewing a house less as a home than as an investment, as valuable for its tax benefits as for its Victorian details. Young baby boom generation professionals moved into urban neighborhoods, especially those close to the downtown core, where they found work in the growing service sector. Housing that had been abandoned or devalued decades earlier became more attractive to so-called "yuppies." As the affluent and the poor began to compete for scarce inner-city housing, prices skyrocketed. Low-rent apartments were converted to high-priced condominiums. Rooming houses, the last refuge of the poor, were torn down or turned into upscale apartments. Businesses catering to the poor and working class families were replaced by high-priced shops and restaurants.

The housing market failed to expand significantly overall number of apartments, because it simply isn't profitable to build housing for the poor. The situation was made worse when the Reagan Administration removed the two props that once served to entice some private investors into providing low-rent housing—subsidies which bring housing costs and poor peoples' incomes into line, and tax shelters which indirectly produce the same result.

102

The role of government

The dramatic escalation of housing prices during the 1980s—and the ongoing affordability gap—stems from three basic factors. First, nearly everyone involved in housing is trying to maximize profits—including land development, materials manufacture, construction, rentals, and capital gains. For example, the average price of a residential lot has increased 813 percent in the past twenty years, from $5,200 in 1969 to $42,300 in 1989; more than half of that increase occurred in the last five years alone. Second, the cost of credit (the money borrowed to build and buy housing) adds a large and permanent cost to every housing unit. For homeowners, roughly two out of every three housing dollars goes to pay off the mortgage. For renters (who pay these costs indirectly), the proportion is often higher. Third, because housing is viewed as an investment by developers, landlords, and most homeowners, home prices and rents are often much higher than what it actually costs to build and operate housing. Both homeowners and landlords expect to sell their buildings for much more than they paid for them—a psychological and economic factor known as speculation. Government policies can exacerbate or curb these market-driven forces.

One way for the federal government to help close the gap between incomes and housing expenses is through a variety of consumer and developer subsidies. The magnitude of federal housing resources was never adequate, but the Reagan Administration made the situation even worse. Housing shouldered the largest burden of the Reagan budget axe. Since 1981, federal housing assistance has been slashed from about $33 billion to less than $8 billion a year. The number of new federally subsidized apartments built each year dwindled from over 200,000 in the 1970s to less than 15,000 last year. To put this in perspective, in 1981 the federal government was spending seven dollars for defense for every one dollar is spent on housing. By 1989, it spent over forty dollars on defense for every housing dollar.

The increase in homelessness parallels these federal housing cuts. And although President Bush and Housing and Urban Development (HUD) Secretary Jack Kemp have promised to deal with the nation's homelessness scandal, the Bush Administration actually proposed further housing cutbacks in its 1991 budget proposal, but was rebuffed by Congress. Bush's 1992 budget proposed further housing cuts.

The single housing subsidy that did *not* fall to the Reagan (and now Bush) budget axe is the one that goes to the very rich. The federal tax code allows homeowners to deduct all property tax and mortgage interest from their income taxes. This cost the federal government $34 billion in 1990 alone—more than four times the HUD budget for low-income housing. Over three-quarters of the foregone tax revenue goes to the 15.1 percent of taxpayers who earn over $50,000 annually; one-third of this subsidy goes to the 3.1 percent of taxpayers with incomes over $100,000. Over half of all homeowners do not claim deductions at all. Tenants, of course, don't even qualify. In other words, our nation's housing subsidies disproportionately benefit homeowners with high incomes, often with two homes. The *Washington Post* recently revealed, for example, that Sen. John D. (Jay) Rockefeller of West Virginia receives a tax subsidy worth about $223,000 a year just on his $15.3-million Washington mansion.

Another housing role for federal and state governments is to regulate lenders in order to guarantee a supply of credit for builders and homeowners. The government can control interest rates, require banks to meet community credit needs, and protect savings-and-loans to guarantee credit for the average homeowner. The Reagan Administration, however, dismantled most of the federal policies designed to regulate lenders. Reagan's policies resulted in a frenzy of speculative lending, mismanagement, and corruption by the nation's savings-and-loan industry during the past decade. President Bush has proposed a bailout of failing savings-and-loans which will fall primarily on low- and middle-income taxpayers, and which now looks as if it will swell to over $500 billion. And Bush's new plan to restructure the nation's banks does nothing to promote lending for homeownership or to encourage community development.

Finally, state and local governments can regulate land use, through zoning laws, to promote affordable housing development. Instead, most localities, particularly suburbs, use these regulations ("snob zoning") to keep out the poor. They can establish codes regulating the safety and health of new and existing buildings, but few state or local governments allocate adequate resources to enforce these laws, particularly in poor neighborhoods. They can also protect consumers by regulating rents, evictions, and condominium conversions. However, only a few local politicians are willing to buck the powerful real estate industry.

The politics of housing

In the past, the major political force for housing programs was the real estate industry—developers, mortgage bankers, landlords, and brokers. They, of course, wanted Congress to enact policies to help build more housing for the middle class or to provide subsidies to make it lucrative to house the poor. Developers, realtors, and mortgage bankers have been the most generous contributors to congressional and presidential candidates, and their national associations have strong political action committees, deep pockets, and effective local networks. In turn, many members of Congress have ties to developers and have lobbied HUD or bank regulators on their behalf.

But even the housing industry's clout couldn't offset the Reagan Administration's determination to slash federal housing funds, which suffered the biggest cuts of any domestic program. Recently, some conservative politicians and editorial writers have cynically used the corruption scandal at HUD as an excuse to dismantle federal housing programs even further. House Minority Whip Newt Gingrich (R-Ga.), *The Wall Street Journal*, and *The New Republic* have called for folding up HUD's tent and replacing it with a voucher program, an approach long-advocated by HUD Secretary Jack Kemp. But rent vouchers, on their own, won't solve the problem. About one million low-income households already receive such vouchers, which are intended to help them pay rent for apartments in the private market. But in cities with low rental vacancy rates, handing out vouchers is like providing food stamps when the grocery shelves are empty. About half the low-income tenants who now receive vouchers return them unused because apartments are so scarce. Clearly, we must increase the overall *supply* of low-income housing.

The Bush Administration has never acknowledged that more affordable housing is the only workable solution to homelessness. His proposed budget significantly *reduced* funding for new housing, while providing only minimal increases for emergency shelters and vouchers. In October, Congress enacted legislation that called for a slight increase in new housing funds. In January, however, Bush unveiled a 1992 budget proposal that called for *reduced* funding for new housing, while providing only minimal increases for emergency shelters and vouchers.

Ironically, one hopeful sign is that Jack Kemp's political ambitions have made him the most vocal and visible HUD Secretary in memory. In sharp contrast to his predecessor, Samuel Pierce, Kemp has been a high-profile Cabinet member, although his clout within the Bush Administration does not appear to parallel his public visibility. He visits shelters, meets with advocates and builders, and testifies before Congress. Although his approach to urban housing problems (vouchers, selling off public housing, creating "enterprise zones" in inner cities) and his budget proposals are woefully inadequate, his enthusiasm and visibility have helped keep the hous-

ing issue in the media. History suggests that social movements and social reform are best sown in the soil of "rising expectations." Kemp's rhetoric is clearly setting the stage for a revolt against broken promises.

Grassroots organizing for housing

If there was one silver lining during the 1980's housing crisis, it was the emergence of locally based efforts to address community housing needs. A combination of community organizations, municipal governments, unions, and business groups developed a wide range of innovative local programs and strategies to cope with the impact of federal housing cutbacks, and the changes in local housing markets. These forces have gained momentum in the 1980s—in part, as a result of the growing visibility of homelessness.

The fledgling grassroots housing movement is composed of tenant groups, homeless advocacy organizations, shelters and soup kitchens, church-based institutions, community-based nonprofit developers, neighborhood associations, senior citizen groups, women's organizations, and civil rights groups.

These groups have spent much of the past decade working, primarily on the local level, to plug some of the gaps left by the federal government's withdrawal from housing programs. They fix up abandoned buildings and construct new homes for the poor. They apply pressure on local governments to protect tenants against unfair evictions. They lobby for stricter enforcement of health and safety codes, and for municipal funds to be placed in banks with good records of investment in low-income neighborhoods ("linked deposits"). They persuade banks to open up branches in minority neighborhoods and increase available mortgage loans for low-income consumers. They publish reports to dramatize the plight of the homeless, to highlight the widening gap between incomes and housing prices, and to expose the continuing practice of bank redlining. They pressure and work with city and state housing agencies to expand available funds for affordable housing and to target more assistance to community-based groups.

But these have been primarily defensive efforts—brushfire battles to keep things from getting worse. Only the federal government has the resources needed to address housing issues and the problem of homelessness in a significant way. Despite the good work of groups like the National Low-Income Housing Coalition, the Association of Community Organizations for Reform Now (ACORN), and the National Coalition for the Homeless, and despite periodic bursts of mobilization like the Housing Now march (which brought 200,000 Americans to

Washington in October 1989), the housing movement has been relatively weak at the national level.

For the housing issue to move to the top of Congress' agenda, advocates must broaden the constituency and organize more effectively. The housing movement must mobilize people to influence Congressmembers through meetings and public accountability sessions, and letter-writing campaigns. It must do a better job of shaping the public debate, particularly getting the attention of the mainstream media to discuss alternative policies and local success stories.

Equally important, the housing movement must address the growing housing concerns of the middle class as well as the poor. As homeownership declines, and as more young adults are forced to live with their parents, the potential for a broad-based agenda grows. As Cushing Dolbeare, founder of the National Low-Income Housing Coalition, has pointed out, ''political demographics'' work against an exclusively low-income focus.

''The majority of Congress represent areas where low-income problems are not a major issue,'' observed Dolbeare. ''[A]sking Members of Congress to vote for low-income housing is often asking them to vote against their own political interests.'' Last year, the National Housing Institute, a think tank based in Orange, New Jersey, issued a Congressional scorecard based on twenty key votes on housing issues. More than one-third of Congresspeople received an "F" for voting against affordable housing at least half the time.

The housing agenda has always made the most headway when the concerns of the poor and the middle class were joined. In the Progressive era, that meant improving health standards for tenements for immigrant workers in the teeming slums, as well as building apartment houses for the middle class. In the Depression and the postwar years, it meant building subsidized housing for the working class and shoring up homeownership for the middle class.

But the political vehicles to fashion this coalition need to be rebuilt if the issue is to move from the margins to the mainstream of the nation's agenda.

The plight of the homeless confronts millions of middle class Americans on a daily basis. Most, of course, pass them by as they walk through the downtown sections of our cities, occasionally handing them spare change out of compassion or guilt. But a growing number of middle class Americans meet the homeless in different settings, especially as volunteers in soup kitchens and shelters. They parallel the settlement house reformers who pushed for improved tenement conditions at the turn of the century and for public housing during the Depression.

While some of the more militant advocates for the homeless criticize the ''shelter industry'' as a new form of institutional oppression, most shelter staff and volunteers would like nothing more than to eliminate the need for shelters. Their concerns and political skills have yet to be effectively mobilized.

Some mayors and governors have felt the local political heat to address the homelessness problem. They have become vocal allies of anti-poverty and housing advocates for a stronger federal role.

The labor movement—once a formidable advocate for federal housing policy—has barely recognized that a renewed federal housing agenda would provide jobs, as well as homes, for its members and for those it seeks to recruit. A large-scale housing production and rehabilitation program should be a major part of our anti-recessionary effort for job and economic recovery. Unions are becoming increasingly involved in the housing issue, but it is still not near the top of the unions' agenda. In Boston, for example, the Hotel Workers Union recently negotiated a contract requiring the hotels to contribute five cents an hour to a trust fund which the union will use to provide housing subsidies for members. The local union waged a successful campaign to amend the Taft-Hartley Act to allow unions to bargain for housing benefits. A number of unions, including the Bricklayers, have become successful nonprofit housing developers in a few cities. And the AFL-CIO was a sponsor of the ''Housing Now'' march.

Some sectors of the business community are also beginning to recognize the importance of the housing problem for their own bottom lines. Like health care and child care, high housing costs are increasingly becoming a barrier to business profits. In recent years, a growing segment of the business community has become sympathetic to some version of government-sponsored universal health care and universal child care. As high housing prices make it increasingly difficult for employers to attract workers (creating a labor shortage in many parts of the country), key business leaders are potential advocates for a federal housing program to subsidize housing costs for low-wage workers. But the U.S. Chamber of Commerce, trade associations, and other business groups have not yet signed on to the housing agenda.

The progressive housing agenda

In light of the HUD scandal, the public is correctly skeptical of programs that offer big profits to politically connected developers and consultants in the name of housing the poor. However, the solution is not to scrap federal housing programs, but to build on the cost-effective successes that have recently emerged in communities across the country.

The key to a successful housing policy is to increasingly remove housing from the speculative market and transform it into limited equity, resident-controlled housing, funded through direct capital grants rather than long-term debt. That is how a significant segment of the housing industry in Canada, Sweden, and other social democratic countries is organized. In the United States, the non-profit (or ''social'') sector is relatively small but it has grown significantly during the past decade.

Congressman Ron Dellums of California already has sponsored legislation tailored to this goal. The National Comprehensive Housing Act, drafted by an Institute for Policy Studies task force, calls for an annual expenditure of $50 billion. The federal government would make direct capital grants to nonprofit groups to build and rehabilitate affordable housing, as well as to purchase existing, privately owned housing for transfer to non-profit organizations. These homes would remain in the ''social'' sector, never again to be burdened with debt. Occupants would pay only the operating costs, which would dramatically lower what poor and working class families are currently paying for housing. The Dellums bill is clearly a visionary program—a standard for judging progress on long-term housing goals—but not yet a winnable bill in the current political climate.

In fact, the major housing bill passed in Congress in October and signed by President Bush in November, if fully funded, is a mix of good and bad news. After a decade of housing cutbacks, Congress would finally increase the federal commitment to housing. After months of political wrangling, the House and Senate agreed on legislation to add only $3 billion to the current housing budget. The bill, a compromise of versions sponsored by Senator Alan Cranston (D-Cal.) and Rep. Henry Gonzalez (D-Tex.), would provide some funding to assist first-time homebuyers, to preserve the existing inventory of public and subsidized housing, to expand housing vouchers for the poor, and to expand the capacity of non-profit builders. But it would not even restore the commitment of federal government to the pre-Reagan level of housing assistance, much less move us forward. The bill incorporates a progressive initiative, the Community Housing Partnership Act, sponsored by Rep. Joseph Kennedy (D-Mass.) at the urging of Boston Mayor Ray Flynn. It targets federal funds specifically to the non-profit ''social'' housing sector.

This year, housing advocates hope to make the Mickey Leland Housing Assistance Act the centerpiece of their efforts. Named after the late Texas Congress-

man, the bill would add $125 billion in new housing funds over a five-year period.

In broad terms, there are five key areas in national housing policy that need attention:

• Expanding the supply of low- and moderate-income housing, particularly through the vehicle of non-profit housing builders. We need to build at least five million new units (500,000 a year) this decade.

• Preserving the existing inventory of public housing (1.3 million units) and subsidized private housing (two million units), which are at risk because of expiring subsidies and long-term neglect—and giving residents a greater role in management.

• Providing adequate income subsidies to the seven-to-eight million low-income families who currently receive no housing assistance and cannot afford market rents.

• Providing working class and lower-middle class young families opportunities for homeownership, in part by putting a cap on the homeownership tax subsidy for the affluent while expanding it for the rest.

• Strengthening the government's regulation of banks and other financial institutions, particularly in terms of allocating credit for homebuyers, eliminating discrimination in lending, making the wealthy pay for the S&L bail-out, and putting consumer representatives on the Federal Reserve Bank.

In light of the war in the Persian Gulf, there is no guarantee that we will see a ''peace dividend'' to invest in housing, child care, health care, education, rebuilding the infrastructure, and other much-needed domestic programs. Without it, however, the nation cannot address its other gulf crises—the widening gulf between the wealthy and the rest of America, as well as the growing gulf in competitiveness between the United States and the rest of the world. There is no question that we must shift national spending priorities to solve our formidable domestic crises, including the lack of adequate housing for our population. This is the most urgent political issue we face today. And whether the nation's leaders seize this historic moment to act effectively in our best domestic national interests, is a question of political will, not resources.

For Further Reading

Richard Appelbaum and John Gilderbloom, *Rethinking Rental Housing,* Temple University Press, Philadelphia, 1988.

Martha Burt and Barbara Cohen, *America's Homeless: Numbers, Characteristics, and Programs That Serve Them,* Urban Institute Press, Washington, D.C., 1989.

Peter Dreier and J. David Hulchanski, "Affordable Housing: Lessons from Canada," *The American Prospect,* Summer 1990.

Peter Dreier, David Schwartz, and Ann Greiner, "What Every Business Can Do About Housing," *Harvard Business Review,* September-October 1988.

Bennett Harrison and Barry Bluestone, *The Great U-Turn: Corporate Restructuring and the Polarizing of America,* Basic Books, New York, 1988.

Clifford M. Johnson, Andrew M. Sum, and James D. Weill, *Vanishing Dreams: The Growing Economic Plight of America's Young Families,* Children's Defense Fund and Center for Labor Market Studies, Northeastern University, Washington, D.C., 1988.

Paul A. Leonard, Cushing Dolbeare, and Edward B. Lazere, *A Place to Call Home: The Crisis in Housing the Poor,* Center on Budget and Policy Priorities and Low-Income Housing Information Service, Washington, D.C., 1989.

Sandra J. Newman, *Subsidizing Shelter: The Relationship Between Welfare and Housing Assistance,* Urban Institute Press, Washington, D.C., 1988.

RURAL POVERTY
THE FORGOTTEN POOR
LEE SMITH

Mr. Smith is on the Board of Editors of Fortune *magazine.*

Let us now praise famous men. More than 50 years ago, *Fortune* commissioned writer James Agee and photographer Walker Evans to memorialize the hardscrabble existences of Alabama tenant farmers; though their research never appeared in the magazine, it resulted in the classic book of that title. Since then, the lot of America's rural poor—men, women, and children—has improved greatly. Today few starve. Almost all have shelter of some sort, and life spans are considerably longer than in grandpa and grandma's day.

But . . . hidden in the hollows of Appalachia, in makeshift villages along the Rio Grande, in shriveled industrial towns in Pennsylvania, on the back roads of Maine, and at the edge of cotton fields in Mississippi, the world that Agee and Evans uncovered endures. What's changed is that, for most Americans, the rural poor are even more remote and invisible than they were in the 1930s.

Now it is the urban poor who are the insistent, troubling presence, never long out of mind. Day begins with fresh reports of the overnight death toll in ghetto drug wars. The homeless in the streets block our path and demand our help.

Yet their country cousins are no better off. The poverty rate in rural counties, those without a town of 50,000, has climbed to 16%, almost as dismal as the inner cities' 18%. And their future is equally bleak. Despite scattered bright patches—rustic counties where tourism is flourishing, the handful of communities that have flowered around transplanted Japanese auto factories—much of the U.S. countryside is quietly and painfully dying.

That wasn't the case in the 1970s, when the long-term migration of jobs from the backwoods to the cities briefly reversed itself as corporations moved electronic assembly, apparel, and other low-tech plants to the sticks to take advantage of cheaper land and labor. For a decade rural manufacturing jobs grew at twice the rate of those in the city. But in the 1980s industry discovered even greater savings in Hong Kong, Mexico, and other foreign lands, and the backwoods boom went bust.

With the world economy becoming ever more global, America's nearly nine million rural poor are stuck on the part turned away from the sun. Any policy to ease their plight must start with a basic principle: People, not places, matter. Compassion does not require that U.S. taxpayers save small towns for their own sakes, despite the sentimental view that such places are reservoirs of virtue. Sometimes they are. They can also be backwaters of misery.

Who are the rural poor? Put aside a misconception. The victims are not those farmers besieged by drought and debt who received so much attention from politicians, rock stars, and the media a few years back. "The world's biggest myth is that there are millions of poor farmers," says Agriculture Department economist Kenneth Deavers. Farm families, who make up only about 10% of the rural population of 23 million, are by and large doing well. Their average income reached an all-time high of $43,323 in 1989, aided by $11 billion in taxpayer subsidies.

The poor are farmhands, who never had any land to mortgage. They are also coal miners, sawmill cutters, foundry men, and Jacks of whatever trades are hiring. Or Janes. Women make up 45% of the rural work force. A "go-getter" in many places refers not to a striver but to a fellow who picks up his wife after her shift.

Walk with us through a few representative towns for a look at work and life at the bottom.

WHO ARE THEY?

Belfast, Maine. President Bush's home in Kennebunkport is the Maine that outsiders know—the one where New England patricians summer in rambling, weathered shingle houses. But Maine has the lowest per capita income in the Northeast ($15,092 in 1988, $1,398 below the national average). About 130 miles up the coast from the Bush spread is Belfast, where a typical dwelling is a secondhand mobile home on a bare patch of ground.

Storms from way off shore have battered Belfast, a port town of 6,200, for two decades. During the 1970s rising fuel prices made it too expensive to heat chicken coops through the frigid winters and to import Midwestern feed grain. By the mid-1980s, the town's two big poultry processing plants, which once employed 1,100 people, had both shut down.

One of Belfast's few remaining enterprises is the Stinson Seafood Co., which cans herring pulled from local waters. For a visitor accustomed to entering a suburban plant through a colonnade of comely shrubs and trees that lead to a smart, polished reception lounge, Stinson comes as a shock. Alongside the entrance, an enormous dumpster full of ripening fish heads and tails waits to be carted off for fertilizer. A flock of seagulls almost hides the door.

Inside, several dozen women with kitchen shears, their hands rarely pausing, snip heads and tails off the fish and slap the bodies into cans. Base pay at Stinson is $4 an hour—a tad above minimum wage. An experienced packer raises her wages to $5 or $6 by filling 350 tins or more an hour. If she's lucky enough to clock 40 hours a week for 50 weeks a year, she can gross $12,000—still $600 below the waterline that defines poverty for a family of four.

CRIPPLING WORK

But at two snips to a fish and four fish to a tin, earning $5 an hour requires some 20,000 scissor squeezes a day, a routine that over time can be crippling. Ruthie Robbins, 58, has been cutting fish for 20 years, makes $6 an hour tops, and suffers from chronic tendinitis. "The doctor could immobilize my arm," she says, "but then I couldn't work." Her arthritic husband earns a few extra dollars repairing lawn mowers.

Stinson's workers don't complain much. A steady job is not easy to find in Belfast. Across from Robbins sits her daughter Lisa, 19, who smiles but won't take time out to chat. Carrying on family tradition, she trims fish at a furious pace.

Tunica, Mississippi. About 30 miles south of Memphis where the cotton and soybean fields begin their long flat run down the Delta lies Tunica, which has long held the miserable distinction of being the poorest American county in the poorest American state.

More than half of Tunica's 8,100 people live below the poverty line. Two-thirds occupy what is euphemistically called substandard housing. That usually means an unpainted pine shack patched with asphalt tile and protected uncertainly by a rusted tin roof. Front porches rise and fall like waterbeds. Inside, the standard three small rooms may hold a cot, a stick or two of furniture, a hot plate, and a television set. Some dwellings have no running water, so occupants share an outdoor tap and privy with neighbors.

Tunica has one manufacturing plant, Pillowtex, where 300 workers earn $7 an hour on average making pillows and mattress coverings, primarily for Wal-Mart stores. But agriculture is still its mainstay.

Picking cotton is no longer cruel hand labor. It is hard but dignified. Black men pilot 16-foot-tall John Deere pickers that straddle two rows of cotton plants at once. Pay is $4.50 an hour with no fringe benefits, tolerable work if there were only more of it. One man on a machine can clear 400 acres in a week, a job that required 25 people or more a generation ago. At the peak, during the harvest from October through Christmas, Tunica's cotton and soybean industries employ only 1,000.

PICKING COTTON

After that the county lapses into a coma. The pulse beats once a month, during the first week, when the welfare, Social Security, and other transfer payments that sustain half the population arrive.

Tunica's children look as lively as those anywhere. Better nutrition has been one of the true advances in recent decades, so physicians no longer routinely encounter the near starvation common before the 1960s War on Poverty. Give much of the credit to food stamps and to the federal WIC (Women, Infants, and Children) program, which supplies pregnant women and preschool children with fruit juice, cereal, infant formula, and other protein.

But when these youths reach adolescence, their spirits start to die. "Their dreams are so small," says Tunica Chamber of Commerce president Lawrence Johnson. "A 16-year-old told me the other day that no one anywhere lives as well as the Cosbys on TV, not even white folks." Only one in three graduates from high school. Some leave town. Many more turn into the men who pop cans of Budweiser in the late morning and stare blankly from dusty stoops.

Las Milpas, Texas. All the wrecked cars and splintered lumber in North America eventually roll and tumble down to the strip of Texas that lies just above the Rio Grande from Brownsville to El Paso—or so it looks from the highway. Fields of mesquite and acres of vegetables alternate with vast junkyards that advertise: "We repair used tires, starters, windshield-wiper motors."

This frugal land is where migrant workers from Mexico spend their winters in hundreds of *colonias*, or unincorporated communities, whose collective population is roughly 140,000. Some are U.S. citizens; others are resident aliens with green cards. The rest have slipped across the border illegally. Whatever their status, they pick the California lettuce, Washington State strawberries, and Illinois broccoli that end up in the nation's refrigerators.

Life in the U.S. doesn't get any more meager than in Las Milpas. With a population of 8,800, it is larger than most other *colonias* but otherwise typical. The better homes of Las Milpas are made of sturdy cinder block, the worst are discarded school buses or huts a notch or two below even Tunica's wretched norm. When migrants return from their trek north, they push their broken '73 Mercurys and '75 Chevrolets into the welding shops for mending. Or junkman Antonio Hernandez buys the heaps for as little as $10 each and resells the serviceable parts for perhaps twice that.

Jesus Villagomez could not afford to fix his truck, so this past summer he had to skip the northern harvests, where he might have earned $200 or more a week. Instead he made about $30 a week picking vegetables on local farms. The walls of his home are rigged from odd pieces of plywood; the roof is a composite of broken tin and plastic sheeting held in place by a used tire.

HOVELS WITH ELECTRICITY

In a space about the size of a secretary's cubicle, Villagomez lives with his wife and five children, ages 4 to 14. The parents sleep on a cot, the children on a mat ripped from the floor of a ruined car, amid a jumble of faded clothes, mud-encrusted boots, kitchen pots—and a small black-and-white TV. Even the poorest hovels of Las Milpas are electrified, as are 99.1% of all U.S. homes. But the crude "cowboy wiring," as it is known locally, that hooks the hut to a power line is a mixed blessing. Homes in the *colonias* burn with distressing frequency.

The Villagomez family shares with neighbors an outdoor water tap and a toilet that empties into an overworked septic tank. Even this far south the temperature in winter frequently falls below freezing, so the family huddles even closer than the hut demands. Can this life be better than the one they left in Mexico? "Yes," says Mrs. Villagomez without hesitation. "At school the children get an education—and also lunch."

THE POVERTY SYNDROME

The notion persists that even at its worst, rural poverty is preferable to the urban kind. That's doubtful. True, poor families in the country are more likely to have both mother and father in residence (53%, vs. 38% in the cities) and at least one of those parents is more likely to have a job (65%, vs. 54%). There is also far less crime. No drug dealers terrorize Belfast, Tunica, or Las Milpas with nightly turf battles.

But alcohol is abundant, and cocaine use is increasing. Even little Tunica has an intersection known as Crack Corner. And guess what state leads the nation in marijuana production? Missouri, followed by Kentucky. Not all of this crop leaves for the big cities.

Nor is rural life necessarily healthier. Country folk have a slightly lower mortality rate than city dwellers. But they are more likely to suffer from chronic disease and disabilities. That's partly because much of their work is dangerous and also because they are less likely to be covered fully by Medicaid, which is jointly financed by federal and state governments. New York, for example, pays for physical therapy for all patients, Alabama only for some.

HOUSING COSTS

On balance, low wages probably stretch further in the country, but not much. The major edge is in housing, which is substantially cheaper, though often shoddier, than city quarters. A shabby three-room apartment in Belfast rents for less than $200 a month, compared with $450 in Boston's rundown Roxbury section. Shacks in Tunica go for less than $150 and hovels in Las Milpas for under $100. But even at those prices, three out of four poor rural families spend more than 30% of their income on shelter.

Food, surprisingly, is sometimes more expensive in the country. People without land don't grow their own, and groceries are pricey, driven up by the distance from distribution centers and lack of competition. On average, urban counties have 29 supermarkets each; their rural counterparts only four. A five-pound bag of Pillsbury all-purpose flour was recently selling for $1.39 at a Giant Food market in Washington, D.C., $1.59 at Junior's supermarket in Las Milpas, and $1.79 at the Piggly Wiggly in Tunica.

The sharp run-up in gasoline prices in recent months has been particularly burdensome for low-wage rural workers, who must commute over long distances in older cars that chug-a-lug fuel. At roughly minimum wage, four or five hours of toil a week go just to pay for the daily 50-mile round-trip routine in states like Kentucky, North Carolina, Maine, and, of course, Texas.

LOSS OF OPPORTUNITY

But the great—and growing—disadvantage for country folk, even in the many places where the work ethic remains solid, is that opportunity is vanishing. Bad roads have long been a barrier to manufacturers. Now rural telecommunications systems that lag in everything from Touch-Tone dialing to fiber optics are discouraging service companies, which are also shipping overseas low-wage, low-skill jobs, such as key punching. As for rural education systems, "They are mostly abysmal," says Susan Sechler of Washington's Aspen Institute, which studies rural poverty.

Small wonder the brightest and most ambitious youngsters leave. "They see the flour barrel is empty and know it's time to go," says Robert Simmons, 44, who fled Tunica for Memphis, where he sells real estate. "The ones who stay behind are afraid to take a chance." As the local talent pool dries up, outsiders become even more reluctant to locate a new plant in Smallville.

Is there any way to break this vicious cycle? Market forces offer a few glimmers of hope. Las Milpas is likely to benefit from the prospering *maquiladoras* just across the Rio Grande, where U.S. and other foreign companies assemble cars, TV sets, and other goods for the American market. Those plants need warehouses and support facilities on the Texas side.

Recreation and retirement will keep some areas alive. The Ozarks and the Great Smoky Mountains already draw the elderly who are looking for inexpensive and safe quarters surrounded by pleasant scenery. As the population ages, those places could boom. Jobs in construction, resort management, and nursing would multiply.

William Galston, a senior scholar at the University of Maryland's Institute for Philosophy and Public Policy, advises rural America to offer government services at lower cost than the cities. "If I were a small town," says Galston, "I'd look at the controversy about prison overcrowding in the population centers and offer my help."

Still, only a small fraction of the countryside will be required to fill those needs. For the rest, the best thing the government could do would be to persuade residents to migrate—not to a troubled megalopolis like New York, but to Columbus, Ohio; Jacksonville, Florida; Aus-

tin, Texas; and dozens of other promising smaller cities.

That's not likely to happen. By temperament Americans are reluctant to write off regions as finished. Says Agriculture Department economist Robert Hoppe: "It's anti-growth, defeatist." Legislators are also unenthusiastic about programs that encourage constituents to clear out. A final problem: The less educated people are, the more attached they tend to be to a place.

But while government cannot force such folk to move on, it should at least stop giving them incentives to stay where they have no future. In Tunica, for example, Washington and the Mississippi state legislature have spent almost $7 million over the past several years constructing and subsidizing apartments. Humane though it is, this program merely houses people more comfortably in a place that is unlikely to ever generate enough jobs for them.

Instead, new policy initiatives should focus on helping individuals. Some already do, most notably the earned-income tax credit. This tax break is especially beneficial to the rural poor, who are more likely to be working than their city brethren. In the recent budget bill, Congress and the Bush Administration agreed to enrich the credit, so that in 1991 a wage earner who makes as much as $11,250 and has two dependent children will be eligible for a cash payment from the U.S. Treasury of up to $1,235. That's a 30% increase over 1990.

Why not take a similar approach to housing? Rather than build apartments in dead-end towns like Tunica, give people housing vouchers similar to food stamps they could exchange for rent. Recipients would then at least have the choice of using them in places where they might find work.

For all of human history, people have migrated from where opportunity has died to where it is being born. For those unable or unwilling to face such hard economic realities, government can do little more than offer more resources and more encouragement. "This isn't living, it's existing," says PamaLee Ashmore, a 32-year-old food cooperative manager, of her life in Belfast, Maine. She hopes her two children will move on—someday.

BEYOND THE STINGY WELFARE STATE

What We Can Learn from the Compassion of the 19th Century

MARVIN OLASKY

MARVIN OLASKY, *on leave as a journalism professor at the University of Texas, is a Bradley Scholar at The Heritage Foundation.*

Conservative politicians have been complaining for years about a spendthrift modern welfare state—but they have been stating the problem backward. The major flaw of the modern welfare state is not that it is extravagant, but that it is too stingy. It gives the needy bread and tells them to be content with that alone. It gives the rest of us the opportunity to be stingy also, and to salve our consciences even as we scrimp on what many of the destitute need most—love, time, and a challenge to be "little lower than the angels" rather than one thumb up from monkeys.

Poverty fighters 100 years ago were more compassionate—in the literal meaning of "suffering with"—than many of us are now. They opened their own homes to deserted women and orphaned children. They offered employment to nomadic men who had abandoned hope and most human contact. Most significantly, they made moral demands on recipients of aid. They saw family, work, freedom, and faith as central to our being, not as life-style options. They did not allow anyone to eat and run.

Largest Charity Army in History

The work of compassion a century ago went on amid city scenes more squalid than the ghettoes and barrios of today. Thousands of orphans roamed the streets. Infant mortality rates were 10 times present levels. New York Police Commissioner Thomas Byrnes estimated that 40,000 prostitutes worked the city in 1890. A survey found 6,576 New York slum families living in tenement "inside" rooms—rooms without windows facing out, only airshafts, which many tenants used as garbage chutes. "Walk along the streets any day and you will meet opium slaves by the score," writer Lafcadio Hearn said of 1870s Cincinnati: "They are slaves, abject slaves suffering exquisite torture." One journalist, Oliver Dyer, calculated that if all of New York's post-Civil War liquor shops (5,500), houses of prostitution (647, by his count), gambling halls, and other low-life establishments were placed for a night on a single street, it would reach from City Hall in lower Manhattan to White Plains, 30 miles away, with a robbery every 165 yards, a murder every half mile, and 30 reporters offering sensational detail.

Yet, during this period a successful war on poverty was waged by tens of thousands of local charitable agencies and religious groups around the country. The platoons of the greatest charity army in American history often were small, and made up of volunteers led by poorly paid professional managers. Women volunteers by day and men by night often worked out of cramped offices and church basements. The names of some agencies (Olivet Helping Hand Society, Hebrew Sheltering and Guardian Society) were warm, and the names of others (Union for Homeless and Friendless Girls, Erring Woman's Refuge) remarkably non-euphemistic. Groups such as the Evangelical Aid Society for the Spanish and the Committee for Ameliorating the Condition of Russian Refugees worked hard to bring immigrants into the economic mainstream and familiarize them with the American cultural heritage. Often, volunteers helped others of the same religion or nationality, and sometimes scolded them. One group of Italian–Americans worked to "drive houses of ill fame, beer dives, and gangs of loafers, thieves, etc., from Italian quarters, and to stop the sale of decayed fruits and vegetables."

The Reconstruction of Human Life

Evidence of these platoons' effectiveness comes from thousands of eyewitness accounts and journalistic assessments. Liberal reformer Jacob Riis, author in 1890 of *How the Other Half Lives*, lived his concern for the New York poor by hauling heavy cameras up dozens of flights of tenement stairs day after day to produce striking photographs of dull-eyed families in crowded flats. Despite seeing much misery, Riis concluded that "New York is, I firmly believe, the most charitable city in the world. Nowhere is there so eager a readiness to help, when it is known that help is worthily wanted; nowhere are [there] such armies of devoted workers." Riis wrote of how one charity group over eight years raised "4,500 families out of the rut of pauperism into proud, if modest, independence, without alms." He noted that a "handful of noble women...accomplished what no machinery of government availed to do. Sixty thousand children have been rescued by them from the streets."

Other usually reliable sources came to similar con-

Reprinted from the Fall 1990 issue of *Policy Review*, pp. 2-14, the flagship publication of The Heritage Foundation, 214 Massachusetts Ave., NE, Washington, D.C. 20002.

Jacob Riis/The Library of Congress

A prayer in the nursery at the Five Points House of Industry, 1889. Christians and Jews emphasized that philanthropy must address spiritual as well as physical needs.

clusions. When the journalist Ray Stannard Baker visited slum missions, he saw "demonstrated again and again the power of a living religion to reconstruct the individual human life." Author Edward Everett Hale analyzed the success of the Boston Industrial Aids Society in reforming alcoholics: "These women were most of them poor creatures broken down with drink, or with worse devils, if there are worse. But...500 people in a year take 500 of these broken-down women into their homes, sometimes with their babies, and give them a new chance." A middle-class volunteer in the slums was astounded when "with my own eyes I saw men who had come into the mission sodden with drink turn into quiet, steady workers....I saw foul homes, where dirty bundles of straw had been the only bed, gradually become clean and respectable; hard faces grow patient and gentle, oaths and foul words give place to quiet speech." Writer Josiah Strong concluded in 1893, "Probably during no hundred years in the history of the world have there been saved so many thieves, gamblers, drunkards, and prostitutes as during the past quarter of a century."

Rejection of Social Darwinism

Jacob Riis and his contemporaries, however, were not arguing that the war on poverty a century ago was won, or was even winnable in any final sense. Riis wrote that "the metropolis is to lots of people like a lighted candle to the moth." Those who climbed out of urban destitution were replaced quickly by others awaiting trial by fire. But poverty fighters then saw movement and hope. They saw springs of fresh water flowing among the poor, not just blocks of ice sitting in a perpetual winter. This sense

of movement contrasts with the frustrating solidity of American poverty during recent decades, as multi-generational welfare dependency has become common. And the optimism prevalent then contrasts sharply with the demoralization among the poor and cynicism among the better-off that is so common now.

What was their secret?

Their secret was not neglect, either benign or malign. True, Social Darwinism, which equated the economic struggle among humans with the struggle for survival among animals, was popular in some circles at this time. Many American Social Darwinists agreed with the philosophy's intellectual leader, Herbert Spencer, that "the unfit must be eliminated as nature intended." As a logical extension of this thought, Social Darwinism led to the belief, as one analyst wrote, that the poor should "be allowed, nay, be assisted, to die." But most Americans who were active in charities and churches fought that trend. The Brooklyn Christian Union called Social Darwinism an enemy of "the spiritual law of sacrifice" taught in the Bible and summarized most completely in the mercy of "the Father who spared not His Son for us." Buffalo minister S. Humphreys Gurteen attacked Social Darwinists who scorned "the cries of the suffering." The monthly magazine *Charities Review* criticized the belief that "the only solution of this charitable problem is to let nature eliminate the poorer classes. Heaven forbid!"

Nor was the secret of their success a century ago the showering of money on the poor. Riis often argued, "Alms do not meet the emergency at all. They frequently aggravate it, degrading and pauperizing where true help should aim at raising the sufferer to self-respect and self-dependence." New Haven minister H. L. Wayland opposed "well-meaning, tender-hearted, sweet-voiced criminals who insist upon indulging in indiscriminate charity." Their secret was not government welfare: There were very few federal or state programs, and the Rhode Island Board of State Charities and Corrections was typical in arguing that the occasional city program "does more hurt than good, and makes more paupers than it relieves." *Charities Review* pointed out that private agencies could be just as bad as government ones, when it criticized "that miscalled charity which soothes its conscience with indiscriminate giving."

Instead, the charity workers of a century ago succeeded because they were inspired by seven ideas that recent welfare practice has put aside. For convenience of memory we may even put them in alphabetical order, A through G. *Affiliation:* Emphasizing the restoration of broken ties to family and friends. *Bonding:* Forging long-term, one-on-one contact between a volunteer and a needy person. *Categorization:* Using "work tests" and background checks to distinguish among different types of applicants. *Discernment:* Learning how to say "no" in the short run so as to produce better long-term results. *Employment:* Requiring work from every able-bodied person. *Freedom:* Helping the able needy to resist enslavement to the charity of governmental or private masters. *God:* Emphasizing the spiritual as well as the material.

Enforcing Family Obligations

Let's begin where poverty fighters a century ago began, by emphasizing *affiliation.* The prime goal of relief, in the words of New York charity leader Edward Devine, was not material distribution but "affiliation...the reabsorption in ordinary industrial and social life of those who for some reason have snapped the threads that bound them to the other members of the community."

When individuals or families with real needs applied for material assistance, charity workers began by interviewing applicants and checking backgrounds with the goal of answering one question: "Who is bound to help in this case?" Charity workers then called in relatives, neighbors, or former co-workers or co-worshippers. "Relief given without reference to friends and neighbors is accompanied by moral loss," Mary Richmond of the Baltimore Charity Organization Society noted: "Poor neighborhoods are doomed to grow poorer and more sordid whenever the natural ties of neighborliness are weakened by our well-meant but unintelligent interference." When material support was needed, charities first went to relatives and others with personal ties instead of appropriating funds from general income. "Raising the money required specially on each case, though very troublesome, has immense advantages," one minister wrote: "It enforces family ties, and neighborly or other duties, instead of relaxing them." Church groups and the United Hebrew Charities even hired detectives and lawyers to track down and bring into court husbands who deserted wives and children.

Affiliation was important for both old and young. A typical case from the files of the Associated Charities of Boston notes that when an elderly widower applied for help, "the agent's investigation showed that there were relatives upon whom he might have a claim." A niece "was unable to contribute anything," but a brother-in-law

> ## "Nothing creates pauperism so rapidly as the giving of relief to [able-bodied] persons without requiring them to earn what they receive by some kind of honest labor."

who had not seen the old man for 25 years "promised to send a regular pension," and he did. The brother-in-law's contribution paid the old man's living expenses and reunited him with his late wife's family. "If there had been no careful investigation," the caseworker noted, the man would have received some bread, but would have remained "wretched in his filthy abode."

Similarly, abandoned young people were to be placed in alternative families, not institutionalized. In Baltimore, the Memorial Union for the Rescue of Homeless and Friendless Girls offered teen-agers free rooms with private families; they were expected to do chores just like other members of the family. Orphans were to be placed with families as quickly as possible—a century ago that meant days or weeks, not months or years in foster care. The American Female Guardian Society and Home for the Friendless noted that its 1,000 children sheltered each year were "not consigned to institution life but were transferred by adoption to Christian homes." The New York Children's Aid Society alone found permanent homes for 70,000 children. Jacob Riis wrote, "The records show that the great mass, with this start given them, became useful citizens."

Affiliation could also mean reinvolvement with religious or ethnic groups. The New York Charity Organization Society asked applicants what they professed or how they had been raised, and then referred them to local churches and synagogues. Some groups, such as the Belgian Society of Benevolence, the Chinese Hospital Association, the French Benevolent Society, the German Ladies' Society, the Hungarian Association, and the Irish Immigrant Society, emphasized ethnic ties. Members of the same immigrant group tended to help each other on an individual level as well.

Warm Hearts and Hard Heads

When adult applicants for help were truly alone charities encouraged *bonding* with volunteers, who in essence became new family members. Charity volunteers a century ago usually were not assigned to paper-pushing or mass food-dispensing tasks, but were given the opportunity to make large differences in several lives over several years. Each volunteer had a narrow but deep responsibility. The Philadelphia Society for Organizing Charitable Relief noted: "A small number of families, from three to five, are enough to exhaust all the time, attention, and friendly care which one visitor has." The thousands of volunteers were not babied by promises of easy satisfaction and warm feelings. Instead, the Philadelphia Society warned that volunteers would have "discouraging experiences, and, perhaps for a time little else," but would nevertheless be expected to maintain "the greatest patience, the most decided firmness, and an inexhaustible kindness."

Woodyards next to homeless shelters were as common in 1890 as liquor stores are in 1990: charity managers could see whether applicants were willing to work, and the applicants could earn their keep.

Such personal involvement gave charity workers "a weight and influence that no amount of charitable gifts of food and money" could ever have brought. Volunteers were often called "slum angels" as they became welcome sights in many tenements. Slum angels minded babies, helped wash clothes, and made food for the sick. One charity leader noted that a visit "very often" meant "several hours spent in...hard and difficult work," and pointed out that if needs were *not* desperate, visitors could "rest assured" that they were "switching off the right track." There was a catch, however: those being helped had to work hard to help themselves. If, over time, those who needed to change their ways refused to do so, volunteers were instructed to shake the cockroaches off their feet and move on.

There were failures, but success stories also emerged. The magazine *American Hebrew* in 1898 told of how one man was used to dependency, but volunteers "with great patience convinced him that he must earn his living"— soon he was, regaining the respect of his family and community. Similarly, a woman had become demoralized, but "for months she was worked with, now through kindness, again through discipline, until finally she began to show a desire to help herself." A man who had worked vigorously but could no longer do so because of sickness was helped to develop a new trade in mending

broken china. Edward Everett Hale told of one woman who had been to the House of Correction 10 times and was heading for an 11th visit until a New Hampshire postmaster took her into his own home so that he and his wife could give her personal attention day after day; she finally straightened up. Speakers at the Indiana State Conference on Social Work regularly told of those "transformed from dependent to respectable citizens."

Not by Money Alone

The key was personal willingness to be deeply involved. Nathaniel Rosenau, manager of the United Hebrew Charities, noted that good charity could not be based on the "overworked and somewhat mechanical offices of a relieving society." Protestant minister Gurteen similarly asked whether the chief way for the better-off to help their neighbors was "by giving a handsome subscription from a full purse to this or that charity? By small doles of money or clothing to some favored individual? By doing our charity by proxy?" "No!" he thundered, and went on to insist that Buffalo citizens become "personal workers" concerned with more than "the mere relief of bodily wants." Another magazine about charity, *Lend a Hand*, regularly reminded readers that they could not "discharge duties to the poor by gifts of money alone....Let us beware of mere charity with the tongs." *Charities Review* emphasized the importance of understanding "charity in its original meaning of 'love,' not charity in its debased meaning of 'alms.'"

Philanthropic groups such as the Associated Charities of Boston saw their role not as raising more money, but as helping citizens to go beyond "tax-bills [or] vicarious giving" by serving "as a bureau of introduction between the worthy poor and the charitable." Managers at New York's 1,288 charitable organizations a century ago had as their major task the coordination of tens of thousands of volunteers who provided food, clothing, fuel, shelter, and employment, supported free schools and kindergartens, organized sea excursions and summer camps, staffed free hospitals and dispensaries, and constructed missions, reformatories, libraries, and reading rooms. The goal was always personal contact.

"Unworthy, Not Entitled to Relief"

But such contact was not naive. Volunteers—typically, middle-class church members—were helped by the careful *categorization* that charities required upon initial contact with applicants. Charities did not treat everyone equally—and, because they were private, they did not have to. Instead, charity organization societies considered "worthy of relief" only those who were poor through no fault of their own and unable to change their situation quickly. In this category were orphans, the aged, the incurably ill, children with "one parent unable to support them," and adults suffering from "temporary illness or accident." Volunteers who were tender-hearted but not particularly forceful were assigned to this category of the needy.

Other applicants for aid were placed in different categories and received different treatment. Jobless adults who showed themselves "able and willing" to work, or part-time workers "able and willing to do more," were sent to employment bureaus and classified as "Needing Work Rather Than Relief." Help in finding work also was offered to "the improvident or intemperate who are not yet hopelessly so." However, the "shiftless and intemperate" who were unwilling to work were categorized as "Unworthy, Not Entitled to Relief." In this group were "those who prefer to live on alms," those with "confirmed intemperance," and the "vicious who seem permanently so." Volunteers who agreed to visit such individuals had to be of hardier stock and often of rougher experience; often the best were ex-alcoholics or ex-convicts.

"You can judge the scale on which any scheme of help for the needy stands by this single quality, Does it make great demands on men to give themselves to their brethren?"

Work Before Eating

How would agencies know the categories into which applicants fell? Background checks helped, but "work tests" were a key self-sorting device, and one that also allowed the dispensing of aid while retaining the dignity of the recipient. When an able-bodied man asked an agency for relief, he often was asked to chop wood for two hours or to whitewash a building. A needy woman generally was given a seat in the "sewing room" (a child-care room often was nearby) and asked to work on garments that would be donated to the helpless poor or sent through the Red Cross to families suffering from the effects of hurricanes or tornadoes. Woodyards next to homeless shelters were as common in 1890 as liquor stores are in 1990: charity managers could see whether applicants were willing to work, and the applicants could earn their keep.

The "work test" occasionally received criticism from those who insisted that charity should be "unconditional," but minister Gurteen argued that it was not "a very hard-hearted thing for the public to require an equivalent of labor, from those who are able to give it, in return for the relief which they receive." He asked, "Is it not in the sweat of his brow that man is to eat his bread? Is not the Commandment, 'Six days shalt thou labor'?" He then quoted the Apostle Paul's injunction that "If a man will not work, he shall not eat," and noted that experience supported revelation: "When the managers of a Boston charity attached thereto a woodyard, and announced that relief would be given to no able-bodied man, unless willing to do a certain amount of work, the daily number of applicants fell off at once from 160 to 49. In every city, in which the test has been applied, it has been eminently successful."

The work test, along with teaching good habits and keeping away those who did not really need help, also enabled charities to teach the lesson that those who were being helped could also help others. The wood was often given to widows or others among the helpless poor. At the Chicago Relief and Aid Society woodyard in 1891, 872 men reportedly chopped wood and, while receiving 6,337 tickets for meals and lodging, also earned enough income for the woodyard that 2,396 tickets could be given free to invalids and others unable to work. In Baltimore, the Friendly Inn gave free room and board to those unable to work, but for the able "sawing and splitting four sticks entitles to a meal, ten sticks to a lodging." The inn stated that 24,901 meals were earned in 1890 and 6,084 given without work.

Discernment against Fraud

Categorization went along with *discernment*, which grew out of the benign suspicion that came naturally to charity workers who had grown up reading the Bible. Aware from their theology of the deviousness of the human heart, 19th-century charity workers were not surprised when some among the poor "preferred their condition and even tried to take advantage of it." The St. Louis Provident Association noted that "duplication of alms is pursued with cunning and attended most invariably with deceit and falsehood." One magazine reported that a "woman who obtained relief several times on the ground that she had been deserted by her husband, was one day surprised at her home with the husband in the bedroom. She had pretended that the man was her boarder." The husband turned out to have a regular income. Jacob Riis noted that some claims of illness were real, but other times a background check revealed "the 'sickness' to stand for laziness, and the destitution to be the family's stock in trade."

Only discernment on the part of charity workers who knew their aid-seekers intimately could prevent fraud. Baltimore charity manager Mary Richmond wrote that her hardest task was the teaching of volunteers "whose kindly but condescending attitude has quite blinded them to the everyday facts of the neighborhood life." To be effective, volunteers had to leave behind "a conventional attitude toward the poor, seeing them through the comfortable haze of our own excellent intentions, and content to know that we wish them well, without being at any great pains to know them as they really are." Volunteers had to learn that "well-meant interference, unaccompanied by personal knowledge of all the circumstances, often does more harm than good and becomes a temptation rather than a help."

Discernment by volunteers, and organizational barriers against fraud, were important not only to prevent waste but to preserve morale among those who were working hard to remain independent. One charity worker noted, "Nothing is more demoralizing to the struggling poor than successes of the indolent or vicious." The St. Louis Provident Association solution was to require volunteers to abide by set rules of giving:

• To give relief only after personal investigation of each case....

• To give necessary articles and only what is immediately necessary....

• To give what is least susceptible of abuse....

• To give only in small quantities in proportion to immediate need; and less than might be procured by labor, except in cases of sickness....

• To give assistance at the right moment; not to prolong it beyond duration of the necessity which calls for it....

• To require of each beneficiary abstinence from intoxicating liquors....

• To discontinue relieving all who manifest a purpose to depend on alms rather than their own exertions for support.

Doles without discernment not only subsidized the "unscrupulous and undeserving" but became a "chief hindrance to spontaneous, free generosity," and contributed to "the grave uncertainty in many minds whether with all their kind intentions they are likely to do more good than harm." Only when "personal sympathy" could "work with safety, confidence, and liberty," would compassion be unleashed.

Compulsory Employment

The next key element in the fight against poverty was long-term *employment* of all able-bodied household heads. *Charities Review* stressed the importance of work, and proclaimed, "Labor is the life of society, and the beggar who will not work is a social cannibal feeding on that life." Indiana officials declared, "Nothing creates pauperism so rapidly as the giving of relief to [able-bodied] persons without requiring them to earn what

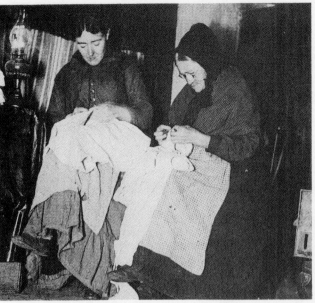

Jacob Riis/The Library of Congress

When an able-bodied woman sought relief, she was given a seat in the "sewing room" (a child-care room was often nearby) and asked to work on garments given to the helpless poor.

Women volunteers by day and men by night worked out of cramped offices and church basements to raise the poor from pauperism to independence.

---

they receive by some kind of honest labor." An emphasis on work would have been savage had jobs not been available—but, except during short-lived times of "business panic," they were. A single-minded work emphasis also would have been unfair if alternatives to begging did not exist during short-lived periods of unemployment—but private charities in every major city provided the opportunity to work for food and lodging.

Most of the able-bodied poor accepted the work obligation, partly because of biblical teaching and partly because they had little choice. S. O. Preston in New Haven reported that fewer than one out of a hundred refused to work in the woodyard or sewing room, perhaps

because "there is no other institution in this city where lodging can be secured except by cash payments for same." The New Orleans Charity Organization Society reported that it provided lodging to 6,000 persons one year but turned away 143 who were "shiftless" and unwilling to work; its motto was, "Intelligent giving and intelligent withholding are alike true charity."

Had there been alternatives, bad charity might have driven out good. After several years of easy-going charity in Oregon, N. R. Walpole of Portland "found among the unemployed a reluctance to work, and regarded compulsory work as the only solution of the problem." New York charity leader Josephine Lowell wrote, "The problem before those who would be charitable, is not how to deal with a given number of poor; it is how to help those who are poor, without adding to their numbers and constantly increasing the evils they seek to cure."

Jacob Riis agreed; when the tough standards of some New York groups appeared to be weakening, Riis foresaw a tribe of "frauds, professional beggars...tightening its grip on society as the years pass, until society shall summon up pluck to say with Paul, 'If a man will not work neither shall he eat,' and stick to it." Riis, like other Christians a century ago, kept returning to the apostolic teaching. Jewish leaders, meanwhile, emphasized that a person unwilling to work could not justify his conduct even by citing a desire to study the Bible: they quoted a Talmudic saying, "All study of the Torah that is not accompanied by work must in the end be futile and become the cause of sin." Within the Talmudic tradition, avoiding dependency was so important that even work on the Sabbath was preferable to accepting alms: one rabbi said, "Make thy Sabbath a weekday and do not be reduced to need the help of human beings."

Jacob Riis/The Library of Congress

Volunteer "slum angels" minded babies, helped wash clothes, and made food for the sick.

The Right to Work

Along with an emphasis on employment came a focus on *freedom*—which was defined by immigrants not as the opportunity to do anything with anyone at any time, but as the opportunity to work and worship without governmental restriction. Job freedom was the opportunity to drive a wagon without paying bribes, to cut hair without having to go to barbers' college, and to get a foot on the lowest rung of the ladder, even if wages for that job were low. Freedom was the opportunity for a family to escape dire poverty by having a father work long hours and a mother sew garments at home.

The goal of charity workers was to show poor people how to move up while resisting enslavement to the charity of governmental or private masters. Church programs were devoted to the attainment of economic freedom through the acquisition of job skills. A check of 112 Protestant churches in Manhattan and the Bronx alone shows that among them were 92 industrial, evening, or sewing schools, 45 libraries or reading rooms, and 50 employment offices or small-sum savings banks often called Penny Provident Funds (pennies add up, the ministers preached). St. Bartholomew's, an Episcopalian church located in an area of New York City to which immigrants from the Middle East were flocking, sponsored a tailor shop that provided work for 35 women and produced 3,600 garments for needy children. Its employment bureau filled over 2,500 jobs annually. Its volunteers, fluent in Armenian, Syriac, and Turkish, staffed special job-finding and evangelism programs for

immigrants. The church had 2,000 evening students taking free classes in English composition, dressmaking, embroidering, sewing, and cooking, along with classes (for a small fee) in stenography and bookkeeping.

Charity leaders and preachers frequently spoke of freedom and showed how dependency was slavery with a smiling mask. Minister Joseph Crooker noted that "it is very easy to make our well-meant charity a curse to our fellow-men." Social worker Frederic Almy argued that "alms are like drugs, and are as dangerous," for often "they create an appetite which is more harmful than the pain which they relieve." Governmental welfare was "the least desirable form of relief," according to Mary Richmond, because it "comes from what is regarded as a practically inexhaustible source, and people who once receive it are likely to regard it as a right, as a permanent pension, implying no obligation on their part." If charity organizations were to do better, they had to make sure the poor understood that "dirt and slovenliness are no claim to help; that energy and resource are qualities which the helper or helpers will gladly meet half-way."

"Revere the Precepts of the Bible"

The seventh principle of the social covenant of the late 19th century was an emphasis on *God*, and religious faith and duty. "True philanthropy must take into account spiritual as well as physical needs," one charity magazine proposed. Poverty will be dramatically reduced if "the victims of appetite and lust and idleness...revere the precepts of the Bible and form habits of industry, frugality, and self-restraint," Pennsylvania state charity commissioners declared. The frequent conclusion was that demoralized men and women needed much greater help than "the dole of organized charities."

There were some differences between Christians and Jews as to what that help was. The biblically orthodox Christians of the late 19th century worshipped a God who came to earth and showed in life and death the literal meaning of compassion—*suffering with*. Christians believed that they—creatures made after God's image—were called to suffer with also, in gratitude for the suffering done for them. Jewish teaching emphasized the pursuit of righteousness through the doing of good deeds, particularly those showing loving-kindness (*gemilut chasadim*). The difference was significant—but both approaches led to abundant volunteering. Furthermore, similarities in theistic understanding led both Christians and Jews to emphasize the importance of personal charity. The Good Samaritan in Christ's story bandages the victim's wounds, puts him on a donkey (the Samaritan walks alongside), takes him to an inn, and nurses him there. The Talmud also portrayed personal service as "much greater than charity," which here is defined as money-giving.

The religious underpinning of compassion in America was in place as early as 1725 when Puritan minister Benjamin Colman told his congregation that "compassion and Mercy to the poor is Conformity to God." Colman emphasized that he was talking about personal involvement, and not mere monetary transfer: "Christ seeks not yours but you. God values our *Hearts* and *Spirits* above all our Silver or Gold, our Herds and

Flocks. If a Man would give all the Substance of his House instead of Love, the Loves of his Soul and the Souls of his House, it would be contemned."

Bluebird's Salvation

Christians and Jews both read an Old Testament that depicts compassion not as an isolated noun, but as the culmination of a process. Repeatedly in Judges and other books, the Bible tells of how when the Israelites had sinned they were to repent and turn away from their sin—only then, as a rule, would God show compassion. Late-19th-century Americans who read the Bible regularly did not see God as a sugar daddy who merely felt sorry for people in distress. They saw God showing compassion while demanding change, and they tried to do the same. As the *Saint Vincent De Paul Quarterly* explained,

> The Vincentian must be prepared to discipline, admonish, and encourage....[Most of the poor] must be disciplined into providence, for they are seldom provident for themselves. To be their true benefactor, the visitor must admonish them to know and appreciate their high destiny.

Groups such as the Industrial Christian Alliance noted that they used "religious methods"—reminding the poor that God made them and had high expectations for them—to "restore the fallen and helpless to self-respect and self-support."

In addition, Christians believed that the Holy Spirit could and would rapidly transform the consciences of all those whom God had called. Those who believed in fighting poverty through salvation were delighted but not surprised to read in the *New York Herald* of how "the woman known as Bluebird up to a year ago was one of the worst drunkards in the Lower East Side....Scores of times she had been in the police courts." Then she was counseled by an evangelist and agreed to go to the Door of Hope rescue home. She was converted and the *Herald* reporter told what happened:

> I went to 63 Park Street, the Five Points Mission Hall. A big crowd of ragged, bloated, and generally disreputable looking men and women were seeking admission....A very pleasant looking young woman dressed neatly in black and having a bunch of flowers at her waist...spoke to them of love and hope. The crowds kept coming until the break of day. No one would ever think that the neatly attired young lady speaking so appealingly had once been the terror of the slums, always alert to get in the first blow.

Some 100 of Bluebird's former gang associates changed their lives over the next several years as, in the words of the *New York Times*, she was "transformed into one of the most earnest and eloquent female evangelists who ever worked among the human derelicts in dark alleys and dives" and "threw her whole soul in the work of evangelism among her former associates." Most of those 100 conversions were permanent, a follow-up years later concluded.

Abandonment of Categorization

In 1890 Jacob Riis combined realism and optimism. New York's "poverty, its slums, and its suffering are the result of unprecedented growth with the consequent disorder and crowding," he wrote. "If the structure shows signs of being top-heavy, evidences are not wanting—they are multiplying day by day—that patient toilers are at work among the underpinnings." The good news was that, through many charitable efforts, "the poor and the well-to-do have been brought closer together, in an every-day companionship that cannot but be productive of the best results, to the one who gives no less than to the one who receives." Riis concluded that, "black as the cloud is it has a silver lining, bright with promise. New

> **"A handful of noble women...accomplished what no machinery of government availed to do. Sixty thousand children have been rescued by them from the streets."**

York is today a hundredfold cleaner, better, purer, city than it was even ten years ago....If we labor on with courage and patience, [these efforts] will bear fruit sixty and a hundred fold."

As the 1890s wore on, however, many well-meaning people were not content with laboring on patiently. Washington Gladden, Walter Rauschenbusch, and other leaders of the Social Gospel movement began to argue that good charity must be universalistic and unconditional. Part of their new thinking was based on a changed view of the nature of God and the nature of man. The older view saw God as both holy and loving; the new view tended to mention love only. The older anthropology saw man as sinful and likely to want something for nothing, if given the opportunity. The new view saw man as naturally good and productive, unless he were put in a competitive environment that warped finer sensibilities. In the new thinking, the work test was cruel, because a person who has faced a "crushing load of misfortunes" should not be faulted if he does not choose to work: "We ask ourselves whether we should have done any better if we had always lived in one room with six other people." Change would not come when a person was challenged, but only when he was put into a pleasant environment so that his true, benevolent nature could come out.

Materialism of the Social Gospel

It soon became customary for leading journalists and academics to argue that only the federal government could create a socioeconomic environment that would save all, and that those who were truly compassionate should rally behind the creation of new programs. Some had faith that governmental construction of housing projects could bring about the new day. B. O. Flower, editor of the popular magazine *The Arena*, envisioned in 1893 "great buildings, each covering a square block and from six to eight stories high." Professor Richard Ely, founder of the American Economic Association, argued that only "coercive philanthropy"—taxation of all, like it or not—would "establish among us true cities of God." In 1899, the nation's most-read newspaper, the *New York Journal*, ran columns that purported to show how every problem of "social misery and wrong" could be solved by officials with "a genuine and earnest and passionate

---

The 19th-century war on poverty was undermined by the insistence of the Social Gospel movement that charity be universalistic and unconditional.

---

desire for the betterment of mankind." Welfare programs could "become the outer form of the altruistic spirit—the unselfish, loving, just nature of the new man."

Ironically, what was called the "Social Gospel" brought with it a materialist emphasis that led some new philanthropists to exhibit embarrassment and annoyance with the evangelical emphases of the older programs. Why did the Magdalene Benevolent Society have to use "Christian principles" in its "work among fallen women"? Why did leaders of the New York Christian Home for Intemperate Men think it vital to embrace "distinctly Christian" principles of "physical, moral, and spiritual restoration" in order to help inebriates and opium addicts? The Social Gospel-oriented *Encyclopedia of Social Reform* suggested that such emphases were wrongheaded, for university-educated people now knew that "social wrongs" caused individual problems that would readily disappear as the poor were placed in a better material environment.

Decline of Personal Involvement

Those who had volunteered to save souls as well as bodies (and who believed that saving souls was the way to save bodies) found the new emphases frustrating, and often retreated from social work. Personal involvement tended to decrease. Previously, volunteers who became impatient were asked to remember how patient God was with them as He forgave their sins: "If every time a family under our treatment backslided, we should give up in despair," one charity group commented, "little permanent good could be accomplished." But as the ideas of affiliation, bonding, and so forth were deemphasized,

professionals trained in social work "efficiency" began to dominate agencies. They often had neither the time nor patience to bond with applicants, yet they did not want amateurs to complicate matters. At the United Charities of Chicago by 1915, for example, "interested laymen were as likely to be consigned to a desk job as they were to be assigned to a family." When volunteers at one charity organization wanted more involvement, its president announced that his staff was "so well organized" that there was little for volunteers to do.

As the new materialistic, professionalized, and government-focused thinking became imbedded in academic thought, private charities even began to be portrayed as the villains because they made it "easy for the state to evade responsibility." One new thinker, Frank Dekker Watson, praised a Philadelphia group's announcement that it would no longer help widows, for only when private charity shrank would pressure to increase "public funds" grow. Increasingly, some saw the existence of points of light as a token of governmental weakness rather than a sign of social strength. Furthermore, as personal involvement and commitment became less expected and less praised, the move to equate compassion with cash picked up speed. In 1929, just before the stock market crash, the *Literary Digest* described the "habit" among the wealthy of "flinging purses and crying: 'Spend this for me!'" One wealthy Chicagoan, when asked why her peers were not involved in person-to-person activity, said, "Organizations look after everything, and they give to them, so why think about it?"

Entitlement Rather Than Need

The result of these and other changes was that when a major economic crisis emerged in the early 1930s, it seemed not only natural but inevitable to rely on governmental programs run by professionals and emphasizing material transfer rather than individual challenge and spiritual concern. During the Depression, when millions of individuals were not responsible for their plight, and jobs were not readily available, many governmental programs made moral sense as temporary expedients (although some may have prolonged overall economic misery). The continuation of some New Deal relief programs during the postwar return to prosperity then set the stage for the modern crisis of the welfare state—although in the '50s, most poor families remained intact and most people still saw benefits not as rights but as backups only for use during dire emergencies.

It was in the 1960s, under conditions of prosperity rather than duress, that a cultural revolution led to attacks on any kind of categorization and investigation of welfare applicants. Lyndon Johnson's War on Poverty was a disaster not so much because of its new programs but because of their administered emphasis on entitlement rather than need. Opportunities to give aid with discretion disappeared as welfare hearings became legal circuses and depersonalization triumphed. Talk of affiliation and bonding was seen merely as an attempt to fight wars on poverty cheaply. Small efforts at categorization and discernment were seen as plots to blame the poor rather than the socioeconomic system that trapped them. "Freedom" came to mean governmental support rather than the opportunity to work and move up the employment ladder. A *Time* magazine cover asked whether God was dead. He certainly seemed that way in much of what went by the name of philanthropy, even in many churches and synagogues.

It is now widely recognized that the entitlement revolution of the 1960s has not helped the poor. More women and children have been abandoned and impoverished. Crime and drugs have destroyed the economies and the communities of the inner cities. The poor generally, and homeless individuals specifically, are treated like zoo animals at feeding time. Rarely are they treated as men and women created in the image of God with moral responsibilities.

To see firsthand what homeless individuals could receive and were expected to do, I recently spent a couple of days dressed as a homeless person in Washington, D.C. I was given or offered lots of material at shelters and agencies, both government-supported and private—lots of food, lots of medicine, and lots of clothes (even a bathing suit so I could use a free swimming pool). But not once was I asked to do anything—not even to carry away my tray after a meal.

An able-to-work, homeless person in 1890 would have been asked to take some responsibility for his own life, and to help others as well, by chopping wood or cleaning up trash. Then he would have had to make contact with other people, whether relatives or former colleagues. Now he is free to be a "naked nomad," shuffling from meal to meal.

Demoralization among the poor in 1990 is matched by "compassion fatigue" among the better-off, whether on the political left or the right. The liberal columnist Ellen Goodman recently described the "slow process" by which "generosity can turn into resentment and sympathy can turn hard. . . . I wonder what personal price we pay for disillusionment." Mickey Kaus in *The New Republic* has pointed out that since we now have "no principle to tell us when our abstract compassionate impulses should stop," we are supposed to have "compassion for the unmotivated delinquent who would rather smoke PCP than work." He concluded in frustration that "we are left with the indiscriminate dispensing of cash in a sort of all-purpose socialized United Way campaign." Kaus is right about what we are left with—but that frustration could equally well lead to a backlash in the form of a neo-Social Darwinist dismissal of the poor.

The alternative to indiscriminate handouts from the left hand or a right-handed return to Social Darwinism is now, as in the late 19th century, a moral realism based on belief in God and the high destiny of each man and each woman—for each is created in God's image. We have seen from the failure of the Great Society that there are no shortcuts in fighting poverty. There are no rational alternatives to investigating the claims of applicants, to requiring work, to demanding that fathers provide for their children. There is no good substitute for personal contact. The struggle against poverty requires time and moral judgment. As Professor Robert Thompson of the University of Pennsylvania put it in 1891: "You can judge the scale on which any scheme of help for the needy stands by this single quality, Does it make great demands on men to give themselves to their brethren?"

Flight from Responsibility

The lessons of charity in the 1890s can be applied to the 1990s. Today, when confronted with a needy individual, do we find out "who is bound to help in this

The Jacob Riis Collection/The Library of Congress

Charities routinely used work tests and background checks to distinguish between the deserving and undeserving poor.

case," or do we immediately proffer aid? Studies show that many homeless alcoholics have families—they just do not want to be with them. Often, those who have been married have abandoned their wives and children. Many of the homeless have had jobs, but they just do not want to stick to them. When we hand out food and clothing indiscriminately, aren't we subsidizing disaffiliation? Do government and private programs increase the likelihood that a pregnant, unmarried teen-ager will be reunited with those on whom she actually is dependent, whether she wishes to admit it—parents, the child's father—or do they offer a mirage of independence? Do programs encourage single-parenting? Do fathers now effectively have the choice of providing or not providing?

On the subject of bonding, let's look particularly at

The crisis of the modern welfare state is not just a crisis of government. Too many private charities dispense aid indiscriminately—ignoring the moral and spiritual needs of the poor and, in so doing, treating them more as animals than as people.

what many religious institutions do. Are boards of deacons often mere distributors of a "deacon's fund" of cash donations and cans of food—or do they act as a switchboard to connect better-off congregation members with the needy? Nathaniel Rosenau of the United Hebrew Charities noted a century ago, "If every person possessing the capability should assume the care of a single family, there would not be enough poor to go around." Individuals and families all have different callings—some may adopt hard-to-place children, others may provide rooms of refuge for abandoned women persevering through crisis pregnancies, and so on—but everyone can do something. Do churches and synagogues convey through both words and programs the biblical messages of personal involvement and mutual obligation?

Are there ways that governmental programs can encourage bonding? Cash contributions are now tax deductible, but what about the offering of a room to a homeless person or to a pregnant and abandoned woman? Going back to the 17th century, town councils sometimes covered the out-of-pocket expenses of those who took in the destitute, and a tax deduction of this kind—carefully designed to avoid creating a new victim class or widespread fraud—could be useful. Similarly, when farmers took in older orphans they provided care but also received work, and there was nothing wrong in that economic tradeoff, which benefited all. The economy today does not allow the same agricultural incentives, but tax deductions for all adoption expenses similar to those for the medical expenses of birth, and significant tax credits for the costs of adopting hard-to-place children, could be another way to lower economic barriers to bonding. Government action can be only a secondary affecter of attitudes, of course, but if political leaders want to do something useful, they may consider such ideas.

Updating the Work Test

We could also use some of the categorizing sensibility of a century ago. One *Charities Review* article described

the "floating population of all large modern cities" as including some "strangers seeking work" and needing temporary help, but a larger number of "victims of intemperance and vice." That's not all that different from today, with studies showing a majority of the homeless in major cities suffering from alcohol or drug abuse. What we have often forgotten in our rush to help "the homeless" generally is the Baltimore Charity Organization Society's warning that the worst kind of "wastefulness" is that which "squanders brotherly love in the doing of useless or mischievous work." Don't we need to stop talking about "the homeless" in abstraction and start distinguishing between those who need a hand (such as the mentally ill, and abandoned women with small children) and those who desperately need a push?

Work-test requirements for the able-bodied at each shelter, if alternative handouts were not available, would have the same effect as those of a century ago. Only the truly needy would come, and the few malingerers would be quickly exposed. Most would learn to help themselves and others, not by chopping wood these days, but by cleaning up streets and parks or working at other tasks. Thousands of crack babies, born addicted to cocaine and deserted by mothers who care only for the next high, are languishing with almost no human contact under bright lights in hospitals. Some volunteers already hold the trembling, sometimes twitching babies, but there are not enough. Why shouldn't homeless women and men who are gentle and healthy enough be assigned to hold a baby for an hour in exchange for a meal?

The work test can be updated in many other useful ways. Yet, instead of developing ways to change behavior, some homeless advocates so lack discernment that they fight even small standard-setting attempts. In New York last year, a shelter administrator was reprimanded after he wrote a memo proposing that residents of a men's shelter not be allowed to wear dresses, high heel shoes, and wigs. An official of the Coalition for the Homeless argued that "the memo is evidence of a real misconception of what the shelters are all about. Trying to curtail freedom of expression, trying to shape the behavior of clients, is completely inappropriate." A century ago, the major task of shelters was to shape behavior in positive ways. Now, a director of Chicago's Center for Street People says the center's role is "to be supportive, not of a particular life-style in the sense of endorsing it, but supporting people." But is the center, by not supporting any particular life-style, truly supporting people, or is it helping to perpetuate their problems?

The Need for Spiritual Revival

In a way, our ideas about poverty reflect our ideas about the nature of man, which in turn are tied to ideas about the nature of God. New ways of fostering affiliation, bonding, categorization, discernment, employment, and freedom are important—but in the end, not much will be accomplished without a spiritual revival that transforms the everyday advice people give and receive, and the way we lead our lives. Two stories—one from a Christian source, one from a Jewish source—may illustrate this point.

Jacob Riis/The Library of Congress

**A Jacob Riis photo of the New York Foundling Asylum, 1888.
Riis called New York at that time the most charitable city in the world.**

The Christian story was told by John Timmer, a minister in Michigan who was a child in Holland half a century ago. His parents at that time hid Jews from the Nazis. Earlier this year he asked, "Why did my parents do it? Why did they risk their own lives and possibly those of their six children? What madness possessed them to take such risks?" Timmer wrote, "The only reason I remember my father giving was this: 'As God shows compassion to us, so we must show compassion to others.'" Timmer added, "These are words in which rescuers make themselves the equal of the rescued because both are equally dependent on the compassion of God." That realization suffused American charity a century ago. Without it, the will to put up with all the problems of dealing with poverty, and the will to maintain moral realism, disappear.

The Jewish story was told by concentration camp survivor Joseph Horn. He discussed his reactions when a black teen-ager recently stole several hundred dollars from him and was later arrested. Horn thought back to

1945 and how, shortly after deliverance from camp, he stole a German bicycle and was arrested by English military police. When a Jewish chaplain came to visit, Horn told him the theft was justified: The Germans had killed the other members of his family and taken his possessions. "And then I asked, why am I not entitled to this miserable bike?"

The chaplain's answer was that we are made in God's image and should not spit on that reflection by stealing or acting in other disgraceful ways. Horn noted that the teen-ager who stole his money in 1990 "may have been convinced, just as I was, that he was simply taking back what his peers tell him was justifiably his, if it had been properly distributed in the first place." Every time we tell someone he is a victim, every time we say he deserves a special break, every time we hand out charity to someone capable of working, we are hurting rather than helping. Horn concluded, "My question is this: Will this young man meet a real chaplain who will help him, the way I was helped?"

Limits of Public Policy

When I walked around Washington as a homeless person, I met people who felt they were doing good, but no real chaplains. No one even pointed me in the right direction, even when I hinted at where I wanted to go.

Isn't it time we realized that there is only so much that public policy can do? That only a richness of spirit can battle a poverty of soul?

Once, at a very good free breakfast spot, when the kind young waitress asked me for the fourth time if she could bring me anything more to eat, I asked (with my homeless mumble), "Could I have a...Bible?" Puzzled, she asked, "You want a bagel? a bag?" I said, "Bible." She answered, "I'm sorry, we don't have any Bibles." Isn't it time we moved beyond bread and bags, beyond the material?

Certainly, our political leaders can break down some programmatic barriers to compassion, but isn't it time we realized that there is only so much that public policy can do? Certainly it's good to "empower" the poor so they are not in thrall to the welfare establishment, but isn't it time to realize that only a richness of spirit can battle a poverty of soul?

The crisis of the modern welfare state is not just a crisis of government. Too many private charities dispense aid indiscriminately—ignoring the moral and spiritual needs of the poor and, in so doing, treating them more as animals than as people. The government of a pluralistic society is inherently incapable of tending to these spiritual needs, so the more effective provision of social services will ultimately depend on their return to private and especially to religious institutions. We need to make sure that our alternative points of light provide light and not just another shade of darkness. The century-old question—does any given "scheme of help...make great demands on men to give themselves to their brethren?"—is still the right one to ask. Most of our 20th-century schemes have failed. It's time to learn from the warm hearts and hard heads of the 19th.

EDUCATION
IDEAS & STRATEGIES FOR THE 1990s

HOW THE STATES CAN DO A WORLD OF GOOD

Denis P. Doyle, Bruce S. Cooper, and Roberta Trachtman

THE HARD FACT IS THAT AS THE 1990s BEGIN OUR SCHOOLS LOOK MORE LIKE THOSE OF THE EARLY 1980s THAN UNLIKE THEM.

Denis P. Doyle is a senior fellow at Hudson Institute. Bruce S. Cooper is a professor and Roberta Trachtman is an associate professor, both in education administration and policy at Fordham University Graduate School of Education. This article is adapted from their book Taking Charge: State Action on School Reform in the 1980s *published in February 1991 by Hudson Institute and is printed with permission. Doyle's first book in this area,* Excellence in Education: The States Take Charge, *was published by AEI in 1985.*

During the 1980s, all 50 states made important changes in their schools. Fourteen completely reorganized their education systems, and another five are doing so now. More than 40 states raised their requirements for high school graduation, and 19 added a minimum-competency test to their requirements.

Forty-six states mandated competency tests for new teachers, and 23 allowed teachers alternative routes to certification. States also raised teachers' salaries dramatically in the decade, with top pay surpassing $50,000 a year in many districts. Starting salaries improved, too, rising at twice the rate of inflation and now averaging around $24,000.

Over 1,000 school districts experimented with "controlled-choice" plans of one kind or another: open enrollment, magnet schools, metro transfers, admission zones, and regional second-chance schools.

Many states made dramatic breaks with tradition during the 1980s. Mississippi, one of the nation's poorest states, increased funding significantly and established statewide kindergartens. Minnesota, one of the most affluent, adopted a statewide system of choice, with open enrollment and regional magnet schools, and tax breaks for parents of private, parochial, and public school students.

Yet even with these improvements, recent studies indicate that America's schools are still woefully inadequate. We score at or near the bottom, on average, in international tests of mathematics and science achievement. And although we spend over 30 percent more than in the 1980s (in constant 1980 dollars), our rate of improvement is nearly flat, as seen by comparing SAT scores over the years. In more schools than not, the reforms of the 1980s did not mean fundamental change. They meant stricter state requirements and greater control. These are traditional responses to the criticisms of our schools. States easily raised requirements for course content and high school graduation, for teacher training and licensing, until they realized that more of the same was not enough. The hard fact is that as the 1990s begin our schools look more like those of the early 1980s than unlike them. Why has the pace of change been so slow? The first

From *The American Enterprise*, March/April 1991, pp. 25-33. Adapted from *Taking Charge: State Action on School Reform in the 1980s* by Denis P. Doyle, Bruce S. Cooper, and Roberta Trachtman. Published by Hudson Institute, Fall 1991.

reason is that schools are conservative institutions, slow to change in the best of times. They do not lead, they follow, and they follow long-term secular trends. Schools respond to demographic, legal, economic, and cultural changes that are themselves slow to evolve. Unlike the best colleges and universities, where new ideas are generated, schools are mainly repositories of information that they attempt to transmit to students. Thus, schools stick to what they have long known: standard day-to-day practices, schools organized around state and local regulation, and systems that are best described as insulated, even isolated, from changes around them.

Second, while the evidence is clear that our schools are in trouble, the voting public is not convinced that *their* schools are in trouble. The trouble is in someone else's school, or school district, or state. Reformers get general support for school improvement that tends to evaporate when families realize that these changes will affect their own schools. The so-called reform movement, therefore, is rather thin; it lacks drive and support that real grass-roots indignation would fuel.

Third, school organization and governance—based on local school districts and neighborhood assignment of students—has produced perverse consequences. The affluent, the discerning, and the ambitious are able to escape the tender mercies of the local monopolies: they change residence, or they pay tuition to private or parochial schools.

Fourth, and perhaps most distressing, America's educators act as though they have no stake in the movement for educational excellence. It is a supreme irony that educators and their professional associations are, by and large, in the rear guard of academic improvement. They are not pushing the cause of higher standards; on the contrary, they often object both to the changes and to the people who want to make them.

And finally, the politics of education has remained unchanged in many states and localities. The essential framework of those who make the decisions and those who live with them is still in place. The 1980s saw the preservation, and in some cases expansion, of government control which cast the parents as passive actors in the schooling of their children. School systems still cling to their bureaucracies and their regulations, and parents are still excluded from making real decisions about the schools and teachers to which their children are assigned. Efforts to restructure schools have run headlong into powerful vested interests. Any proposal to fund families rather than systems, for example, is immediately suspect because it might lead to vouchers for enrollment at any school; this defensiveness engenders incredible unity among the otherwise divided groups that make up the education establishment. In the absence of strong, unified groups in favor of fundamental change, the school bureaucracy continues to behave as it always has—institutional inertia prevails.

And now change will come even harder. In the past decade, efforts to improve schools came as part of a wave of prosperity. The 1990s will be different. Schools will have more-limited resources and even stronger mandates. They will be called on to do even more, with less. But using the positive changes of 1980s as a strong beginning, the states can push our schools toward real excellence. The unfinished agenda is discussed below.

Teachers

The 1980s saw most states attacking the problem of improving teacher training and competency. Certification and teacher preparation have, of course, long been state responsibilities. Raising teacher standards was easily accomplished, and most states attempted it, although the results did not measure up to expectations. The teacher employment market—the supply of and demand for teachers in various locations, subject areas (math, science, technology), and skills (bilingual teachers, special education teachers)—had more to do with who was hired than changes in teacher requirements and training policies. Many states realized that to improve teaching they would need to enhance, improve, and even empower teachers through better conditions of employment. In the 1980s, several states changed the very basis of teacher remuneration. In fact, according to a Rand Corporation study, by 1986 all but seven of the states had introduced some form of performance-based compensation, including career ladders, master teachers, various teacher-incentive programs, and the once-unacceptable merit pay.

We have learned much from the 1980s that will help us in the decades ahead. Schools will need teachers, lots of them. Schools will see an aging teacher work force—even now the average age is 47 years old. And the nation has realized, finally, that without improved classroom practices little reform will work anyway. Following are some concrete suggestions for states and localities.

The states can play an important role in attracting young people with high potential into teaching. New Jersey, for example, has created alternate routes into teaching for college graduates who want to work in schools but have no formal teacher training or state-

SCHOOLS WILL NEED TEACHERS, LOTS OF THEM. SCHOOLS WILL SEE AN AGING TEACHER WORK FORCE—EVEN NOW THE AVERAGE AGE IS 47 YEARS OLD. AND THE NATION HAS REALIZED, FINALLY, THAT WITHOUT IMPROVED CLASSROOM PRACTICES LITTLE REFORM WILL WORK ANYWAY.

issued licenses. States should form interstate compacts to help one another locate good candidates for the teaching profession and help teachers, once they gain experience and prove their ability to teach, find jobs in other states.

The states must find more teachers in some fashion, because a million new teachers will be needed in our nation's schools in the next twelve years. The federal government, universities and colleges, and states jointly could create a "teacher brigade," a major effort to attract, prepare, and train the next generation of teachers. Teach for America, a volunteer effort organized by a Princeton University undergraduate, shows that there are bright, able undergraduates who are willing to choose education as a career and that there is demand for these young adults in our schools. Another incentive might be forgiveness of college loans for graduates willing to work off their indebtedness by teaching.

Better yet, why not give teaching scholarships, much as the military now awards tuition and fees to Reserve Officers Training Corps (ROTC) members in their undergraduate years, in exchange for four years of active service upon college graduation? The cost of training teachers, as part of undergraduate or postgraduate (fifth year) programs is small, and the benefits are large. School districts, too, should work closely with their states to create new, exciting kinds of teacher preparation and improvement plans.

One idea, called the Mentor Program, is as simple as it is economical. Let's say a school district has a job opening—as thousands currently do. Instead of filling it with one experienced teacher from a diminishing supply of veteran teachers at a salary of perhaps $30,000 including fringe benefits, why not hire two teacher interns who are enrolled in a preparation program in a nearby university to co-teach the open classroom slot? Using the same $30,000, the school district would get two new staff trainees, and the trainees would get a job, a stipend, and a year's professional training "free," which would include the following:

• *Mentoring.* A full-time mentor would work with a group of 12 or so such interns and help these new teachers navigate their first year in the classroom.

• *Licensing.* Participants would take the courses required for a state license while they were teaching.

• *Accumulated benefits.* At the end of the first year, these new teaching professionals would have a year's teaching experience, a state teacher's certificate, and a master's degree (usually required for permanent certification) from the cooperating university, all at no cost to the trainee. In fact, they would have received a $6,000 tax-free stipend, plus the equivalent

of a $10,000 master's degree and certification program.

What better way to train, build, and improve the work force? We know already that school districts often hire graduates who have done their student teaching in district schools. A year's work in a school is excellent training and economical. Mentoring programs are now working well in New York City and White Plains, New York, in cooperation with the Fordham University Graduate School of Education.

Students

States have also concentrated their efforts on improving the quality of school programs in hopes of improving student performance. By and large, the 1980s was a period of increased demand for academic attainment but few breakthroughs in instructional technology and process. The schools have expanded the requirements for courses, the numbers and types of students to be served, and the time in school without improving the classroom activities and programs.

Sadly, in many cities class size has increased just at the time when the numbers of minority, non-English-speaking students—many of whom have special needs—are increasing. Our schools performed no better in the 1980s than before in reaching these children who need more help.

A few areas have improved, however. Early-childhood programs, kindergartens, child care, and latchkey programs have been expanded in many states. Twenty-six states, according to a *Phi Delta Kappan* article by Anne Mitchell, now have public school child-care programs, responding to the demands of changing families. Two particular trends—working mothers and teenage parents—have made expanded day care and kindergarten programs essential.

Special education has been broadened, though at times it appears that children are being dumped into this category to get them out of regular classrooms. States have taken steps to reverse this trend, now pressing for mainstreaming and more integrated programs. Certainly, this trend should continue into the 1990s, with the states and localities reviewing their procedures and freeing special education from the heavy restrictions of federal and state regulation.

• **Second-Chance Schools.** Dropout programs spread too, with some interesting new approaches. Minnesota created "second-chance" regional high schools for young people wishing to return to school outside

DROPOUT PROGRAMS SPREAD TOO, WITH SOME INTERESTING NEW APPROACHES. MINNESOTA CREATED "SECOND-CHANCE" REGIONAL HIGH SCHOOLS FOR YOUNG PEOPLE WISHING TO RETURN TO SCHOOL OUTSIDE THEIR IMMEDIATE COMMUNITIES.

their immediate communities. These programs hold great promise, and are natural avenues for state intervention. Since individual schools often have trouble serving these dropouts, regional schools become more like colleges and are less painful for students to attend.

Thus, states need to take the lead in teaching the hard-to-serve student. A number of other programs, broader in design, are succeeding, and they provide useful models for other states:

• **Regional/Statewide Magnet Schools.** States should consider, as many have, supporting regional specialized schools to reach students underserved by local high schools. These might include schools of music and the arts, technical schools, and advanced academic schools (in areas such as the humanities, math, science, design, and computer sciences).

• **Cooperative College/High School Programs.** Several states now have high schools located on the campuses of local universities. These "middle colleges," as they are called in New York City, give high school students the opportunity to use the resources of a nearby college and even take courses for college credit. These joint ventures give school principals extra leverage with their local school bureaucracies, allowing them to innovate and improve programs, working around the rules and regulations of their districts.

States are in a good position to broker such university/high school ventures because so many local colleges are state-supported. Models exist in a number of settings (the New World School of the Arts in Miami, a music and art high school located at the Dade County Community College, and a number of middle colleges on the campuses of the City University of New York); other states should take a hard look at, and emulate, these exciting experiments in cooperation with local schools.

• **High-Technology Schools.** A number of districts are experimenting with super high schools—schools using the newest technology. The seeds of another revolution, a postindustrial, knowledge-based one, are embedded in our society. For the first time in our history—at least on a large scale—what people know and are able to do is the key economic variable. No longer are strong backs and deft hands the *sine qua non* of economic vitality. In a wholly new way, knowledge is power.

The contours of the information society are already in place: virtually unlimited access to information; instantaneous data exchange across groups, schools, boundaries. In fact, the ease of access to information fueled the revolutions in Eastern Europe and elsewhere. And in education, the rapidity of technological change, once started in school, will spread as rapidly as television, video games, and the PC.

In the 1980s, schools have been slow to apply the realities of the postindustrial world, though some progress has been made. Imagine schools that would make use of the latest technology: personal computers, fiber optics, HDTV, satellite communications, VCRs, CD-ROMs, high-speed copiers, facsimile transmission, hand-held videocameras, compact audio recorders and players, networking, and nearly limitless software development. What if all this technology were put together and dedicated to teaching children? Various plans, such as the Education Utility, a privately funded venture that has proposed to provide a computer network for schools, could bring all this technical power to the fingertips of teachers and the desktops of children. This would make a significant contribution to enriching the educational experience.

States, working closely with local districts, teachers' groups, and industry, should consider setting up model technology schools for all ages and abilities. These schools can be wired together, sharing information, ideas, curricula (electronic textbooks may replace cumbersome, expensive, and quickly out-of-date tomes). Models already exist; the new decade is the time to expand them, bringing technology, pedagogy, and excellence together in the classroom.

Parental Choice and School Governance

The 1980s were remarkable in advancing the twin notions of enhanced parental choice and local school autonomy. One may think of them as components of an equation, the demand and supply side of the school market structure. On the *demand* side, parents were supposedly given greater latitude in selecting schools, and the concept of parents as decision-makers has advanced. On the *supply* side, schools were given greater authority to shape their own programs and recruit students.

Yet by the end of the 1980s, few states had moved to replace the failing school monopolies with real market mechanisms, real choice, or real diversity. Market forces can be expanded in American education, and public interest and responsibility in education will be maintained. But states must be convinced that centralized, bureaucratic, and monopolistic systems are themselves inherently inefficient and ineffective—as the last decade of public schooling has shown.

But monopolies do not exist in a vacuum. World-renowned management analyst Peter Drucker has made an observation that has

THE 1980s WERE REMARKABLE IN ADVANCING THE TWIN NOTIONS OF ENHANCED PARENTAL CHOICE AND LOCAL SCHOOL AUTONOMY... THE DEMAND AND SUPPLY SIDE OF THE SCHOOL MARKET STRUCTURE.

clear implications for schools: a monopoly, he said, can exist only when supported by pro-monopoly laws. In the absence of statutes and practices that prohibit competition, competition will appear spontaneously. And in those circumstances, when a manufacturer or provider of a service has a natural monopoly, he will submit to the temptation to charge what the market will bear. This may take the form of high prices, excessive profits, poor service to clients, poor working conditions for employees, or most likely, all of the above.

When not protected by law or edict, however, the monopolist creates a high price umbrella under which less efficient producers can enter the market, protected initially by the artificially high prices. As the newcomers start to compete for clients, they become more efficient, cutting prices and introducing real competition into the market. Almost without exception, this development causes the monopoly to look to the statute books for protection: import limits, tariffs, duties, and regulatory controls that inhibit, limit, and prevent market entry.

A case in point: when the state of Wisconsin broke the monopoly of the public schools by funding 1,000 low-income students in private, nonsectarian schools in Milwaukee, the Wisconsin superintendent of schools, Dr. Herbert J. Grover, sounded the alarm the way any good monopolist would. Rather than say, "Okay, folks, we can beat these nonpublic schools at their own game!", Dr. Grover got nasty, carping, "Now we've got the president of the United States (what does President Bush have to do with the Wisconsin law?) nuking the public schools and the pluralism that ought to come out of public education. We will have everyone fleeing the public schools now that the Private-Education President says, 'Send public school money to private schools.'"

Note what the chief executive officer of the Wisconsin Public Schools is saying: that given half a chance, children will leave the public schools; that once the figurative Berlin Wall between public and private comes down, the prisoners will escape to the other side. By implication, public policy should force the poor (since the middle class can exit by paying for private schools or moving to a middle-class suburban district) to stay in a system against their will.

The architect of the Milwaukee plan, State Representative Polly Williams, herself a black woman and a parent, explained that this choice plan permits the poor family to exercise the same rights and responsibilities as the middle-class one by leaving the bankrupt public school system. She argues, persuasively, "This system

MARKET FORCES CAN BE EXPANDED IN AMERICAN EDUCATION, AND PUBLIC INTEREST AND RESPONSIBILITY IN EDUCATION WILL BE MAINTAINED.

is not doing its job. We can't keep funding the failure we are funding."

States should challenge the school monopolies, inducing demand by putting purchasing power in the hands of consumers (parents and students) and increasing supply by making entry into the local school market as direct and simple as possible. Two simple, practical, and related reforms are a good place to begin. Both are possible now, through pilot efforts. Both improve, not destroy, the common school experience in the United States. Both allow parents, particularly those with the fewest resources and the greatest deficits, opportunities previously enjoyed by the middle class. Both give schools the resources and autonomy they require. Each innovation supports the other.

First, states should create vouchers for low-income students—as a step in expanding equal opportunity, choice, and empowerment. Second, states should set individual schools free from their local bureaucracies to pursue excellence as autonomous, responsible institutions. Both these ideas are being tried with some success in the United States and Great Britain, offering examples of what happens when states and localities attack the ineffective school monopolies and engage schools in the process of real reform.

Helping Poor Families

The toughest problem in most states today is the growing group of students, largely poor, who are alienated from the school experience. These pupils elude conventional school reform. The federal, state, and local governments have poured millions of dollars into compensatory education, dropout prevention, drug education, and other schemes, most of which have failed. The programs have often become employment devices for specialists, but few of the resources reached the students and their families.

Examples of what happens when resources do reach students are heartening. A Wall Street millionaire "adopts" a whole classroom of students in Harlem, guaranteeing them what every middle-class child has by birthright: funds for further and higher education. Suddenly, these students attend school, most graduate from high school, and a majority go on to college. Nothing so mystical here: people with opportunities and options behave differently from those trapped in a system of denigration, poverty, and poor services.

Vouchers for the poor leave the local school markets in interesting ways. Suddenly, parents have school money and can shop around. In Kansas City in 1990, a group of lawyers proposed that the state pay tuition for students to attend local integrated private schools, as part of a federal court-mandated desegregation plan (*Jenkins et al. v. State of Missouri*). Rather than bus students into the suburbs, why not let them walk to the nearby private schools, which are convenient, racially diverse, and of high academic quality? In fact, these parochial schools could offer a better (and integrated) education for *half* the tuition costs of the segregated, failing public schools. Russell Clark, the federal judge in the *Jenkins* case, refused the motion as being unnecessary, even though the court-approved remedy of public magnet schools had failed to attract many whites into the system. In fact, the public-school-only approach had kept blacks *out* of the better magnet schools, since to maintain racial balance more whites and fewer blacks were needed in the schools. By August 1990, over 4,000 black children were still awaiting school assignment, because so few whites had applied—and racial balance was not possible.

Why not issue vouchers and let poor families enjoy the same access as middle-class families? All the hokum about poor families not caring, not knowing, not participating reminds one of the classic arguments about consumers. Given no choices, no resources, and no future, people behave as though they have no interest and purpose. Given resources, they demonstrate enlightened consumerism. In eastern Germany, citizens are beginning to distinguish among goods and services again, and are willing to invest time and energy in making informed choices—a big change from their listless reaction to long lines for rotten meat and stale bread in premarket days.

In Milwaukee's limited voucher plan for poor students to attend nondenominational private schools, poor parents, traditionally given few options, are suddenly able to select from a range of public and private schools. Other cities and states should try similar programs, to see if resources, so long wasted on programs for the disadvantaged, might work if the families themselves had some say.

Several sad stories illustrate the point. Kansas City spent $600 million on dressing up its inner-city schools to attract white suburbanites. Fewer than 100 showed up. That's $6 million per student, a lot of vouchers. In New York City, the Board of Education spent $68 million on dropout prevention, and the dropout rate rose 5 percent. Give potential dropouts a $5,000 reward for staying in school, redeemable in a local public or private school, college, or trade school, and see the results.

Without regulations and bureaucracy, the school could help these students directly.

Opting Out

States should consider allowing schools to become self-governing—with their own boards of trustees, like colleges—and then fund them directly, rather than through the local school bureaucracy. This idea is as simple as it is revolutionary. Stand each school on its own two feet: give it resources, freedom, authority, and opportunity to run its own affairs. It would be accountable to its families and in the final analysis to the state for productivity. But the day-to-day operation would be its own.

Several recent studies and experiments point the way. In a paper presented to the American Educational Research Association, Robert Sarrel and Bruce Cooper found in New York City that nearly $2.00 per pupil is spent on overhead for every $1.00 that reaches the classroom. That is, in 1989, of the average $6,107 per student that the system spends, less than $2,000 goes into the direct instructional program. *Forbes* reported from this study, "Much of the money stayed in the Board's own eight buildings, which house a staff of over 4,000." Michael Fischer reported similar findings in the Milwaukee public elementary schools in a paper prepared for the Wisconsin Public Policy Research Institute in 1990.

What would happen if the full $6,000 were given to the school itself for more teachers, guidance, materials, equipment, and paper and pencils, rather than having the money spent supporting the overhead function of education? The school would get the funding first, would purchase the services it needs from the central office, and could even accept bids to buy goods and services from the outside market. Imagine a system in which the teachers get the funding, attention, and time, and the central office must scrounge around for equipment and pencils (as many teachers must now do).

Great Britain has given the concept a try. In 1988, as part of the Education Reform Act, the nation created a whole new category of schools, labeled "grant-maintained" because they were maintained by direct grants from the central government, setting them free from political and bureaucratic constraints of local authorities. Under this program, any state-run schools could, with a majority vote of its parents and trustees, apply to the national government to "opt out" of its local school district and become an independent school, with the same level of funding by the central government.

GIVEN NO CHOICES, NO RESOURCES, AND NO FUTURE, PEOPLE BEHAVE AS THOUGH THEY HAVE NO INTEREST AND PURPOSE. GIVEN RESOURCES, THEY DEMONSTRATE ENLIGHTENED CONSUMERISM.

Suddenly, these grant-maintained schools receive their full share of local expenditures, not what's left after the various administrative offices and functions have extracted their overhead costs. Schools themselves determine what's important to them—not bureaucrats miles away. The results are interesting. David Brooks reported in the *Wall Street Journal* last June, for example, that Britain's "opt-out" schools had more resources than regularly run schools, since money bypassed the local bureaucracy and was channeled directly into the school. *Opt-outs have found themselves with, on average, between 15 percent and 20 percent more money to spend, and with more discretion to channel the money the way they wish. At the Hendon School in London, for example, there has been a 58 percent increase in expenditure on books and teaching materials, a 400 percent increase in classroom equipment, a 25 percent increase in tuition for music lessons and improvements in the school meal provisions. Bankfield High in Cheshire hired six extra teachers and increased per-pupil spending on books form $50 to $160. Other schools are simply glad to be free from the political meddlings of the local councils.*

The school establishment in Britain has resisted change, too. Opting out threatens to make bureaucrats obsolete, and opposition has been keen. Rather than compete honestly and attempt to make other schools in the system more efficient, the local school managers have fought hard and dirty. In one case, the school board tried to sell the school and its grounds rather than have the school opt out. Parents have been threatened; black parents were told that the new school would discriminate against them. One local school district even took out ads in newspapers urging parents not to vote to become grant-maintained. Another ruled that the sports teams at the opt-out school could no longer compete against teams from the district. Petty bureaucrats can be pretty petty.

At least, one might argue, the monopoly is alive and active if for no other purpose than to protect its captive clientele. But what do bureaucrats have to offer?—the exact "services" that opt-out schools seek to escape in the first place: controls, standardization, regulations. What parents seem to want is a good school, with a responsive, high-quality program, not a team of bureaucrats sitting at desks miles from the school.

Opting out has two particularly attractive features. First, schools will have more resources. Consider, for example, a typical large public high school with 2,000 pupils in a U.S. city. Each of these students is worth about $7,000 from federal, state, and local sources—for a total of $14 million ($7,000 × 2,000 students). Under the current arrangement, the 110 teachers in that single school are paid, on average, about $50,000 including benefits, for a total of $5.5 million (110 teachers × $50,000 total salaries and fringes in that school building). Thus, even though the students are worth $14 million citywide, only about 40 percent ($5.5 million) of the money goes for teachers.

What if almost the full $14 million went to the school, and the school leaders, teachers, parents, and others closest to the classroom decided what external services to buy back from the system? With the same allocation per pupil, each school will be more fully funded, and staff will have more autonomy and resources. True, some in the system will scream, particularly the displaced bureaucrats who are offered a job teaching in a school or none at all. True, some functions will be added in the school building (business manager, curriculum people), but at least these functions will be accountable to the school, not the hierarchy; to the demands of parents and teachers, not the politics of the system.

Second, with need for little or no new money, states could make the schools once again the center of school reform. We are reminded of Eastern Europe. As Brooks concludes, "In many ways, the opt-out campaign resembles modernization efforts in Eastern Europe. Rather than try to reform or shrink stagnant bureaucracies, it is easier [and more efficient] simply to bypass them."

The states are at a crossroads in their important responsibilities in education. The 1980s saw intense interest in school reform—indeed, intense activity—but the results were often sparse. For the most part, change took place at the margin, although the decade did witness some significant reform with promising results. In the 1990s, the states will need to be bold to challenge the lethargy of local school systems and educational establishments. The 1980s demonstrated the need for change and pointed the way. But it was only the beginning. More challenges, more choices, and more competition will be the keys to enabling the states to make an enormous difference in the education of our children.

STATES SHOULD CONSIDER ALLOWING SCHOOLS TO BECOME SELF-GOVERNING—WITH THEIR OWN BOARDS OF TRUSTEES, LIKE COLLEGES—AND THEN FUND THEM DIRECTLY, RATHER THAN THROUGH THE LOCAL SCHOOL BUREAUCRACY.

Infrastructure: America's Third Deficit

*America's economy suffers a crippling deficit in spending
on vitally needed public works. Declining U.S. public investment
is a major cause of our economy's faltering productivity, profitability,
and private sector capital formation.*

DAVID ALAN ASCHAUER

*David Alan Aschauer is the Elmer W. Campbell Professor
of Economics at Bates College in Lewiston, Maine. This
article is adapted from his 1990 study published by the
Economic Policy Institute, Washington, D.C. and is
printed here with their permission. The concepts and
results in this paper will be expanded in a book sponsored
by the Twentieth Century Fund.*

In the past few years, a number of tragic incidents have focused attention on the disrepair of the nation's public infrastructure:

• a bridge collapses on the NY State Thruway, taking the lives of ten motorists;

• a dam bursts in Georgia, flooding a bible school and drowning school-aged children;

• medical debris washes up on the shores of Long Island, posing a health risk to millions of people.

Concern has also grown over the less dramatic but pervasive congestion of our streets, highways, and air routes. Delays proliferate in a transportation network that is apparently insufficient to meet the needs of a growing economy. The U.S. Department of Transportation has estimated that in 1985, total vehicle delays on the highways exceeded 722 million hours; it is projected that this alarming number will skyrocket to 3.9 billion hours by the year 2005 if improvements to the nation's freeway system are not forthcoming. While these cars and trucks sat in traffic, they wasted nearly 3 billion gallons of gasoline, almost 4 percent of annual consumption in the United States. The total cost of this congestion was estimated at $9 billion.

According to the Federal Aviation Administration, air travel delays in 1986 resulted in $1.8 billion in additional airline operating expenses and $3.2 billion in time lost by travelers.

Underlying these headlines, anecdotes, and cost estimates is a larger question: To what extent has the decline of investment in public infrastructure affected the performance of the U.S. economy as a whole?

This article will show that the reduction of public investment spending in the United States over the past twenty-five years played a central role in a number of our long-term economic ills. If the United States had continued to invest in public capital after 1970 at the rate maintained for the previous two decades, we could have benefited in the following ways:

• Our chronically low rate of productivity growth could have been up to 50 percent higher—2.1 percent per year, rather than the actual rate of 1.4 percent;

From *Challenge* Magazine, Vol. 34, No. 2, March/April 1991, pp. 39-45. Reprinted by permission of M. E. Sharpe, Inc., Armonk, New York 10504.

• Our depressed rate of profit on nonfinancial corporate capital could have averaged 9.6 percent instead of 7.9 percent;

• Private investment in plants and equipment could have increased from the sluggish historical rate of 3.1 percent, to 3.7 percent of the private capital stock.

These results indicate that close attention should be paid to the critical role played by public infrastructure in augmenting overall economic performance.

U.S. productivity slump

A number of signs indicate that the United States' economy has not performed as well in recent years as in the so-called "golden age" of the 1950s and 1960s. For two decades the economy has experienced a *continuing slump in the growth rate of economic productivity,* measured either conventionally as output per labor hour (labor productivity) or alternatively as output per unit of combined private labor and private capital services (called total factor or multifactor productivity). Beginning sometime in the early 1970s—the specific date is much debated—productivity growth fell by some 1.4 percent per year. In the case of labor productivity, the drop was from 2.8 percent to a much lower 1.4 percent. This was clearly an important development. It meant that labor productivity would no longer double every twenty-six years; under the new trend we could only expect labor productivity to double once every fifty-one years. This implies that on a per capita basis, our future income must rise much more slowly, thereby generating a wide variety of concerns on issues such as the viability of our national social insurance programs and our national security.

Low productivity growth was reflected in a 3.3 percent decrease in the real average hourly wage between 1979 and 1987. Annual average wages and salaries only held up in this period because people were working 5.8 percent more hours per year. The typical worker in the factory, on the construction site, and behind the check-out counter increasingly feels the bite as wages fail to keep up with inflation.

Not only has productivity growth fallen over time in the United States, it has been low for the past three decades relative to our major international competitors. For example, from 1965 to 1985, Japan and West Germany achieved labor productivity growth rates in excess of 3 and 2 percent per year, respectively. One reflection of our low productivity growth, when coupled with persistently high consumption growth, is the yawning trade deficit and the switch, during the 1980s, from our nation's position as the world's largest creditor to the world's largest debtor.

A second dimension of poor economic performance which is related to low productivity growth is a *low profit rate.* During the 1970s and 1980s, the profit rate was depressed to a considerable amount below its level in the 1950s and 1960s—from about 11 percent to about 8 percent.

A third indicator of poor economic performance which is closely linked to the fall-off in the profit rate is a *low rate of net private investment.* For instance, the growth rate of the private capital stock (the value of capital assets) has been about 3 percent per year in recent years, down from about 4 percent in the 1950s and 1960s. Of course, there is much controversy about the validity of these facts as well as about their appropriate interpretation. For instance, some argue that no true productivity slowdown has occurred; instead, what we have in this regard is "a case of statistical myopia." Others, such as Martin Feldstein and Lawrence Summers, argue that there is really no long-term downtrend in the corporate profit rate. And there is much controversy about whether investment really has been depressed during the 1980s. Paul Craig Roberts, for example, chooses to emphasize gross, as opposed to net, investment rates, and gross investment has been relatively stable during recent years. Finally, it is necessary to be careful about interpreting movements in productivity, profit rates, and investment—or, for that matter, other variables such as the current account deficit—as indicators of economic *malaise.* The appropriate, or optimal, rates of national savings, investment, and productivity growth are inherently unobservable and may well be changing over time. It seems clear, nevertheless, that the economy has not been performing well of late and that the typical person in the street is rightly concerned about our long-term economic prospects. (See Michael Darby in For Further Reading.)

Fall-off in public investment

The reasons for our low productivity growth, our low profit rate, and our low net investment rate—in general, our state of economic *malaise*—have so far resisted explanation by economists. Many obvious culprits have been brought to trial in the economics literature and, for one reason or another, all have been found largely innocent.

For example, the Bureau of Labor Statistics came to the conclusion that at most one-half of the total fall-off in productivity growth can be explained by obvious suspects such as oil price hikes during the 1970s, a decline in research and development spending after the mid-1960s, and mismeasurement of labor input.

This article brings another suspect before the bench:

public infrastructure capital. What role did movements in the amount of public infrastructure capital play in the evolution of the macroeconomy over the past forty years?

To be potentially important for explaining shifts in the performance of the aggregate economy, the public capital stock must be large relative to the private capital stock,

Table 1   **Private and Public Capital Stock, 1987**

Capital Stock	Billions of Dollars	Percent of Total
Total	$6,487.3	100
Total Private	4,142.8	64
Nonfarm Business	3,974.6	61
Farm	168.2	3
Total Public	2,344.5	36
Military	457.7	7
Nonmilitary	1,886.8	29
Core Infrastructure	1,195.7	18
Education, Hospital, & Other Buildings	535.9	8
Conservation & Development	155.2	2

Source: Bureau of Economic Analysis.

and it must display variable trends over time. Table 1 provides 1987 data on the levels of total, private, and public stocks of fixed reproducible capital. It can be seen that of the total physical capital stock of $6.5 trillion, $2.3 trillion (36 percent) is held by the public sector. For every $2 of private capital, there is $1 of public capital.

While military capital makes up the bulk of the federal capital stock, it only amounts to 7 percent of the nation's total (public and private) stock of capital. Nonmilitary capital accounts for 29 percent of the national stock of tangible capital. Finally, the stock of "core infrastructure capital" (streets and highways, water and sewer systems, mass transit, airports, and electrical and gas facilities) comprises nearly 20 percent of the nation's stock of physical capital. Moreover, because the elements of core infrastructure are intrinsic to almost every sector of private production, they are especially influential in the determination of total national economic output. Clearly, the public capital stock has sufficient magnitude to influence the behavior of the private economy in a meaningful way.

Setting military spending to one side, the bulk of the public capital stock resides in the state and local government sector. For instance, in 1985 the total federal net stock of public capital, excluding military equipment and facilities, was $247.1 billion in 1985 dollars. But the state and local counterpart to this amount was $1,518.7 billion. Thus, the state-local component of total civilian public capital was roughly 86 percent (Bureau of Economic Analysis, 1987).

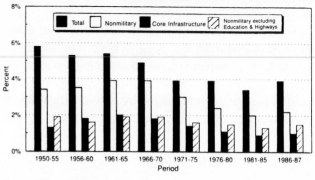

Figure 1   **Trends in Public Investment Relative to GNP 1950 to 1987**

Source: Bureau of Economic Analysis.

Not only is the public capital stock large, but it also has evolved in a marked pattern over the post-World War II period, as shown in Figure 1. The level of nonmilitary public investment generally rose during the 1950s and 1960s, reaching some 3.9 percent of GNP in the latter decade. It then fell during the 1970s and the early 1980s. While in recent years public investment has rebounded slightly, it remains far below levels attained during the mid-1960s. This striking pattern prevails for nearly all functional categories of public capital investment. Relative to output, the level of investment in core infrastructure peaked within a year of the peak in nonmilitary public capital spending, and it has risen only modestly in the last half-decade. Nonmilitary public investment minus spending on educational structures and highways displays similar trend behavior.

Note that the levels depicted in Figure 1 pertain to gross investment in nonmilitary capital; no deduction has been made for the physical wear and tear on the nation's total stock of public capital. Once the public stock is adjusted for depreciation, the negative trend becomes even more disturbing. As shown in Figure 2, by 1982 *net* public investment in core infrastructure had nearly ground to a halt in the United States, coming in at less than 0.5 percent of total output. This means that the United States was doing little more than replacing the existing public capital

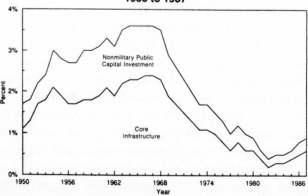

Figure 2   **Net Public Investment Relative to GNP 1950 to 1987**

Source: Bureau of Economic Analysis.

stock; almost nothing was being added, despite the needs of the growing private economy.

This fall-off in public investment is reflected in a similar fall-off in the amount of infrastructure capital available to each worker in the economy. After climbing from around $8,500 per worker in 1950 to $15,000 per worker in the early 1970s, the public capital stock tumbled to some $13,000 per worker by the end of 1987.

At the same time, the dollar value of private plants and equipment per worker has continued to climb throughout the post-World War II period, from about $16,000 in 1950 to roughly $34,000 by the end of 1987. Thus, while the *private* sector has largely, though not completely, been doing its job in equipping workers with adequate tools and work environments, the public sector has been negligent in providing the appropriate amount of infrastructure, the necessary foundation to the private economy.

U.S. economy's third deficit

It is common for economists to talk about the "twin deficits" of the 1980s: the federal government budget deficit; and the trade or current account deficit. But in a sense, the last decade has also witnessed a third deficit: a deficit in spending on vitally needed public works. Indeed, the fundamental thesis of this article is that this third deficit is central to some of our most important long-term economic difficulties: our declining private profit rate on machinery and structures; our overall failure to invest adequately in our future; and our sluggish growth in productive efficiency.

Recent empirical evidence indicates that the public capital stock is an important factor of production; the slowdown in public investment can help explain a significant portion of the slump in productivity growth in the past two decades. Historical statistical (time series) evidence for the post-World War II period in the United States demonstrates that the "core infrastructure" bears a substantially positive and statistically significant relationship to both labor productivity and multifactor productivity. (See Aschauer [1989a] in For Further Reading.) The core infrastructure category is the most statistically significant of the various categories of public capital. By these estimates, a one percent increase in the stock of infrastructure capital will raise productivity by 0.24 of one percent.

Figure 3 illustrates the close relationship estimated between total factor productivity and the nonmilitary public capital stock. To highlight the link between longer-term movements in total factor productivity and the public capital stock, the measures have been adjusted for business cycle effects.

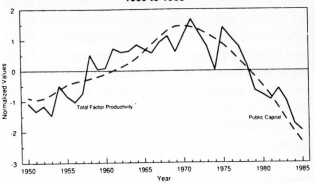

Figure 3   **Public Capital and Productivity 1950 to 1985**

Source: Author's calculations.

The graph shows how that portion of total factor productivity which *cannot* be explained by technological progress (proxied by time) or by the state of the business cycle (proxied by the capacity utilization rate) *can* be explained by movements in the public capital stock. One can see the close association between changes in productivity and public capital; indeed, the empirical estimates in my paper (1989a) suggest that of the total 1.4 percent annual fall-off in productivity growth during the 1970s and 1980s, fully 57 percent—or 0.8 percent per year—can be attributed to the downturn in public investment spending. The levels of productivity and public capital stock peaked in the late 1960s to the early 1970s and during the mid-1960s, respectively.

Certain refinements of my paper (1989a) by Munnell (1990) entailed adjusting the standard Bureau of Labor Statistics measure of labor input to account for changes in the age/sex composition of the labor force and updating the sample period to 1987. Munnell obtained strong parallel results on the importance of public capital in private sector production. Munnell also computed adjusted measures of multifactor productivity growth, and found that after accounting for changes in the quality of the labor force and for changes in the growth rate of the core infrastructure capital stock, the fall-off in multifactor productivity growth during the 1970s and 1980s relative to the 1950s and 1960s was "much more in line with expectations . . . [Much] of the drop in published multifactor productivity numbers may reflect the omission of public capital from the calculations of inputs rather than a decline in technological innovation" (See Munnell [1990] in For Further Reading.)

Of course, from a policy standpoint it would not be prudent to rest such strong conclusions solely on the basis of aggregate historical data from one country. It should be very instructive to examine cross-sectional evidence by comparing states, industries, or countries. In fact, additional empirical results buttressing the case for expanded public spending on infrastructure are available.

Analysis shows that public investment in streets, highways, and water and sewer systems is an important factor in explaining the variation in levels of productivity across states. Also, the level of such public spending is lower than would be chosen by optimizing governmental bodies. Indeed, the inefficiency of our existing allocation of investment resources is underlined by the finding that increases in GNP resulting from increased public infrastructure spending are estimated to exceed those from private investment by a factor of between two and five. This means that a shift from private to public investment would increase GNP substantially; it reflects the dearth of resources presently committed to infrastructure. Munnell estimates the sizes of state-area public capital stocks and finds that public infrastructure capital is an important factor of production determining the level of state-area productivity. The categories of public capital bearing the most importance for private productivity turn out to be streets and highways and water and sewer systems; other public capital facilities have little or no explanatory power in private sector output regressions. (See Aschauer [1991]; Munnell [1991] in For Further Reading).

Further substantiation of these findings emerges in studies using comparative historical (pooled time series) data from national comparisons for the Group of Seven nations (Canada, France, Germany, Italy, Japan, Great Britain, and the United States) over the period 1965 to 1985. Upon controlling for private investment and employment growth, public nonmilitary investment bears a significantly positive relationship to growth in gross domestic product per employed person. This is a noteworthy result because a number of researchers have pointed out that the productivity slump was not a disease unique to the United States; on the contrary, it had epidemic-like proportions, affecting nearly all industrialized economies. The explanation for the productivity slowdown "is unlikely to lie in the special circumstances of a single country" (see Stanley Fischer in For Further Reading). In that regard, it is interesting to note that public investment spending as a share of gross domestic product fell during the late 1960s and early 1970s in five of the seven countries in the Group of Seven. Furthermore, the ratio of public investment to total government spending declined during this period in all the Group of Seven countries.

Clearly, the size of the public capital stock is an inescapable feature of the explanation for national productivity trends. This conclusion holds when considering the evolution over time of productivity in the United States; it holds when comparing disparate productivity levels in the states; and it holds when comparing the productivity performance of major industrial nations.

Furthermore, changes in the *public* capital stock may influence the marginal productivity of *private* factors of production. For example, a better transportation network would allow Federal Express to make better use of additional trucks and airplanes which, in turn, would raise profit rates on such private capital goods. Historical statistical analysis (aggregate time series) suggests that the rate of return to private capital in the nonfinancial corporate sector is positively affected by changes in the stock of public capital per worker. Data on manufacturing firms over the period 1970 to 1978 show similarly strong effects from public capital (highways, sewers, water facilities) as well as the total of these. In particular, there is evidence of a complementary relationship between public and private capital. In short, public capital is "profitable" because it boosts the returns to private capital. (See Kevin T. Deno in For Further Reading.)

Public capital promotes private growth

The evidence appears to support overwhelmingly the proposal that investing in public infrastructure directly augments private sector production. Therefore, a valid case can be made for a significant increase in public investment spending. But what impact would an increase in public capital spending have on private investment? If the public investments merely displace private investments in plant and machinery—economists call this a complete "crowding out" of private capital accumulation—then national investment (private plus public) would be left unchanged and relatively minor productivity gains could be expected.

An increase in public investment can be expected to have two basic effects on private investment activity. One is the positive effect on the profitability or the rate of return to private capital. The theory of the firm suggests that firms will respond to heightened profit rates by expanding the pace of capital investment. But if we assume that the private sector profit rate remains constant, the second effect of greater public capital investment would be to reduce private investment as national investment (private plus public) is pushed beyond the level which optimizing agents would choose.

Historical data for the United States suggest that both types of effects may well be operative. More specifically, results indicate a nearly one-to-one "crowding out" of private by public investment (holding fixed the rate of return to private capital) as well as a "crowding in" of private by public investment—as the rate of return to capital responds over time to the increases in the public capital stock which are brought about by higher public investment. In the long run—in this case four or five years—the "crowding in" effect dominates and overall private investment is stimulated; *indeed, for every dollar increase in public investment, private investment rises by approximately 45 cents.*

Simulation data

It is instructive to bring together some of these empirical results to consider how large an effect public investment has on crucial dimensions of economic performance: investment, profits, and productivity. This is accomplished by utilizing empirical estimates to construct a minimal model capable of simulating the effect of higher public investment on the aggregate economy. The increase in public investment hypothesized for the purpose of the simulation is consistent with what the United States would have experienced if the actual historical rate of public investment from roughly 1950 to 1970 had held up for the following two decades, rather than falling off as it did.

The simulation exercise conducted below depicts an increase in the level of public nonmilitary investment by one percent of the private capital stock during the period from 1970 to 1986, an amount 125 percent greater than the actual level of public investment in this time period, so that the rate of public investment since 1970 is comparable to that of the 1950s and 1960s. By incorporating the effects of the greater public investment, Table 2 provides data on actual and simulated levels of the rate of return to private nonfinancial corporate capital, on net private investment in nonresidential structures and equipment, and on private business sector productivity growth.

The actual data document that between 1970 and 1988, inferior economic performance was experienced relative to the 1953–1969 period, along with a lower rate of return to private capital (7.9 percent as opposed to 10.7 percent), lower private investment (3.1 percent of the private capital stock rather than 3.8 percent), and lower labor productivity growth (1.4 percent per annum as opposed to 2.8 percent).

The simulation data also reveal relationships between public nonmilitary investment, private profitability, private investment, and private sector productivity growth. Figure 4 shows that in the first five years of the hypothetical expansion in public investment, the rate of return to capital rises by 2 percentage points over its actual level, remaining at its 1953-1969 level of 10.7 percent instead of falling to 8.7 percent. This is due to the cumulative positive effect of the rising public capital stock on the productivity of private capital. During the same period, the private investment rate averages 3.9 percent of the

Table 2

Simulated Impact of Public Investment on Private Economy

	Return to Private Capital (%)		Private Investment (% of Private Capital Stock)		Productivity Growth (% per Annum)	
	Actual	Simu-lated	Actual	Simu-lated	Actual	Simu-lated
1953–69	10.7	—	3.8	—	2.8	—
1970–74	8.7	10.7	3.9	3.9	1.5	1.9
1975–79	8.5	9.9	3.2	4.2	1.3	2.2
1980–84	6.7	8.4	2.7	3.0	1.1	1.9
1985–88	7.8	9.6	2.8	3.8	1.8	2.7
1970–88	7.9	9.6	3.1	3.7	1.4	2.1

Source: Author's methodology.

private capital stock, the same as in the actual data. This reflects two offsetting forces: In the first three years of the higher public investment, private investment is pushed lower due to the direct crowding out effect of higher public investment, while in the next two years private investment is brought above its historical level by the higher rate of return to private capital. In the same period, private sector productivity growth is enhanced by 1.5 to 1.9 percent per year. As the private investment rate (as a percent of the capital stock) is seen to remain steady, this enhancement of productivity growth reflects the direct, positive effect of a growing public capital stock on the productivity of labor.

In the later years of increased public investment, the simulation results show that the rate of return to private capital could have held up to between one and two percentage points more than the historical levels. At the same time, productivity growth would then rise by a more substantial amount (nearly one percent per year above historical values) because the direct effect of growth in

Figure 4   **Actual and Simulated Impact of Rate of Return to Private Capital**

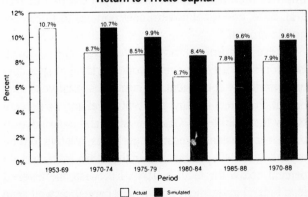

Source: Author's calculations.

the public capital stock is augmented by the indirect effect of a higher return to capital, raising private investment which, in turn, stimulates productivity growth.

On the whole, the simulation exercise suggests the possibility that the performance of the economy might have been greatly improved by an increased investment in public facilities. Comparing the 1970–1988 period to the 1953–1969 period, the rate of return to private capital could have been only 1.1 percentage points lower (instead of 2.8 percentage points); private investment could have been only 0.1 percentage points lower (rather than 0.7 percentage points lower); and annual productivity growth could have been 0.7 percent per year lower (instead of 1.4 percent lower).

Present policy

President George Bush, Secretary of Transportation Samuel Skinner, Budget Director Richard Darman, and Council of Economic Advisers Chairman Michael Boskin are all well aware of these arguments for the importance of a sound infrastructure to our economic vitality. In his introduction to Secretary Skinner's recent report on the nation's transportation needs, President Bush said that "our competitive success in the global economy depends [on preparing] our transportation system to meet the needs of the 21st Century." Similarly, in the President's proposed Fiscal 1991 Budget, Richard Darman wrote that "it is intuitively apparent that some public investments—particularly those of infrastructure such as streets, highways, airports, and water and sewer systems—provide direct productive services and are complementary with private capital. Comparisons over time and across countries seem to indicate that some relationship may exist between additions to such capital and growth." In the 1990 *Economic Report of the President*, Michael Boskin asserted that "inadequate government infrastructure can impede improvements in productivity growth" and that "taking advantage of productive opportunities to maintain and improve the infrastructure is an important part of federal, state, and local government policies to raise economic growth."

These sentiments notwithstanding, the Administration's FY 1991 budget involved a level of spending on nonmilitary equipment and structures, relative to total output, 26 percent below the 1960 level and 24 percent below the 1980 level. Grants to state and local governments for physical investment purposes, relative to total output, were 40 percent under the 1960 level and 43 percent below the level in 1980. Likewise, the level of total federal investment (in physical capital, as well as in research and development, and education) lay 33 percent below its 1960 level and 10 percent under its 1980 level.

Of course, it is highly unlikely that the mix and level of public investment spending which was chosen over the past forty years will be preferred in the future. Even if, for instance, it were established beyond a shadow of doubt that the Interstate Highway System was a key determinant of productivity growth in the 1960s and 1970s, such a discovery would not necessarily imply that a similar effect on productivity would be obtained from the construction of another 40,000 miles of controlled access highways. We live in a dynamic economy which changes constantly in response to technological progress, foreign competitive pressures, and alterations in the demographic characteristics of the domestic workforce. In the future, infrastructure needs may well shift from surface to air transportation, from the transport of goods to that of ideas, and from a national to an international focus. Potentially large efficiency gains are best to be expected, therefore, from improved air and seaport facilities and from telecommunications networking, among other things.

The evidence surveyed in this article, along with the related simulation results, suggest that the neglect of the quality and quantity of our nation's infrastructure facilities will act as a severe drag on our overall economic performance. Unless we address our public capital needs immediately, we can expect a continuation of lackluster productivity growth, low profit rates on the existing private capital stock, stagnant real wages, and sluggish private net investment.

The United States should directly augment its public capital stock through a stepped-up rate of infrastructure investment. Following this course will help equip the nation to compete effectively in the international arena and, at a minimum, it offers some hope for a partial reversal of our sliding economic fortunes.

For Further Reading

Kenneth J. Arrow and Mordecai Kurz, *Public Investment, the Rate of Return, and Optimal Fiscal Policy*, Johns Hopkins Press, Baltimore, 1970.

David A. Ashauer, "Is Public Expenditure Productive?" *Journal of Monetary Economics*, Vol. 23, 1989a.

———, "Public Investment and Productivity Growth in the Group of Seven," *Economic Perspectives*, Vol. 13, No. 5, 1989b.

———, "Why Is Infrastructure Important?" in *The Third Deficit: The Shortfall in Public Capital Investment*, Federal Reserve Bank of Boston, Conference Series, No. 34, 1991 (forthcoming).

DAVID A. ASHAUER AND JEREMY GREENWOOD, "Macro-economic Effects of Fiscal Policy," in Karl Brunner and Allan H. Meltzer, eds., *The "New Monetary Economics," Fiscal Issues and Unemployment,* North-Holland, Amsterdam, 1985.

MICHAEL R. DARBY, "The U.S. Productivity Slowdown: A Case of Statistical Myopia?" *American Economic Review,* Vol. 74, 1984.

KEVIN T. DENO, "The Effect of Public Capital on U.S. Manufacturing Activity: 1970 to 1978," *Southern Economic Journal,* Vol. 55, No. 2, 1988.

STANLEY FISCHER, "Symposium on the Slowdown in Productivity Growth," *Journal of Economic Perspectives,* Vol. 2, No. 4, 1988.

LAWRENCE MISHEL AND DAVID M. FRANKEL, *The State of Working America, 1990–91 Edition,* Economic Policy Institute, Washington, D.C., 1991.

ALICIA H. MUNNELL, "Why Has Productivity Growth Declined?" *New England Economic Review,* January/February, 1990.

———, "How Does Public Infrastructure Affect Regional Economic Performance?" In *The Third Deficit: The Shortfall in Public Capital Investment,* Federal Reserve Bank of Boston, Conference Series, No. 34, 1991 (forthcoming).

ENERGY FOR THE NEXT CENTURY

All signs seem to indicate we're heading—however slowly—toward a post-petroleum society. The policies we craft in the next decade might well determine whether it will be like Mad Max or Ecotopia.

Will Nixon

WILL NIXON *is Associate Editor of* E Magazine.

Just when the peace movement had run low on placard slogans—"No Blood For Oil" having lost some of its octane as the Gulf War wound down—George Bush announced his long-awaited National Energy Strategy (NES) at lunchtime on February 20. Not since Jimmy Carter had a president decided that energy planning should involve more than checking the gas gauge before heading off on a long trip. Indeed, Carter had donned a cardigan sweater, turned the White House thermostat down to 68, and solemnly told the nation that his energy policy was "the moral equivalent of war." Cynics now quipped that George Bush had dropped the equivalency part. But the NES was much more than that. It admitted that the United States couldn't kick the foreign oil habit, which was the great dream of presidents in the 70s, but offered almost 100 ways to increase our own energy production. It recommended opening up Alaska's Arctic National Wildlife Refuge for oil and gas exploration, reviving the nuclear energy industry by eliminating some of those pesky public hearings, freeing the oil and gas industries from some cumbersome regulations, and burning more garbage for energy. As for encouraging us to use less energy to begin with, well, better luck next time. The NES virtually ignored better car mileage standards and mass transportation. It dropped tax breaks for renewable energy and federal lighting standards. And, perhaps most negligent of all, it never got around to the reason we need an energy policy in the first place—to stop the flood of carbon emissions into our atmosphere which cause global warming. "When people talk about the need for a national energy policy, they don't mean writing down the mistakes of the past 10 years, which is what the Bush Administration has done," said Alexandra Allen of Greenpeace.

The next morning, a handful of Greenpeacers went to the Senate offices where Admiral James Watkins, secretary of the Department of Energy (DOE) was due to appear before the Energy Committee. Senator Albert Gore of Tennessee had already promised a "battle royal" on Capitol Hill over Bush's energy plan. The Greenpeacers arrived at 7:30 AM, but the Washington media pack had already claimed the room. So they stood out front, holding a "Reality Check" for Bush and Watkins. It was made out for "Untold Billions" for "Oil Wars, Oil Spills, Global Warming and Nuclear Waste."

In the gray and white world of Washington, Greenpeace provides the most color, but they were hardly alone in their outrage at the President's energy plan. Only a year ago the DOE had suggested that its plan would be almost the reverse of what Bush finally announced. Deputy Secretary Henson Moore had said, "Energy efficiency and renewables are basically the cleanest, cheapest and safest means of meeting our nation's growing energy needs in the 1990s and beyond."

"Based on comments by the DOE last year," said Scott Denman of the Safe Energy Communications Council, "and based on George Bush's claims in his State of the Union address that his strategy would support conservation, efficiency and alternative fuels, what we've been given is a cruel hoax. It's not an energy strategy, it's an energy tragedy."

Out in San Francisco, Chris Calwell of the Natural Resources Defense Council (NRDC) said, "The themes that emerge are simple and familiar: drill more, nuke more, pay more, save less." His group released an analysis entitled: "Looking for Oil in All the Wrong Places," with some math to show just how wrongheaded the NES was. If we drilled the Arctic Refuge and the Outer Continental Shelf, as the NES proposed, we might produce a little more than six billion barrels of oil or its equivalent in natural gas, and these areas would be drained dry by the year 2020. But if we used our renewable energy supplies— the sun, wind, rivers that flow into hydroelectric dams, and plants and trees that can be turned into biomass fuels—and we made our world far more energy efficient, we would have the equivalent of 66 billion barrels of oil. As Robert Watson, the author of this report says, "We *will* have a post-petroleum society. The question is whether it will be like Mad Max or Ecotopia."

The NES hadn't always looked so grim. For more than a year, the DOE had held hearings across the country, patiently listening to an army of experts who hadn't found a sympathetic ear in the executive branch since Ronald Reagan took office and put the DOE under the sleepy care of dentist James Edwards. Admiral Watkins had made his name in Washington, DC by taking over Reagan's troubled AIDS commission and producing a good report. "He showed he has a good ear. He's receptive to contrary points of view," says Scott Denman, who spoke at two hearings late in 1989. "He heard from every energy expert in the country."

These experts had a remarkable story to tell: the United States, with what scrambled energy policies we do have, already saves an estimated $160 billion a year in energy costs compared with 1973. "The really interesting thing is that total energy consumption was virtually identical in 1973 and 1986," says

> "There are all sorts of incentives for fossil fuels which, to be fair, should be eliminated or applied to energy efficiency and renewables."

John Morrill of the American Council for an Energy-Efficient Economy. "And yet our GNP grew by 40 percent during those years."

Until the 70s, conventional wisdom had insisted that energy growth was synonymous with economic growth, but changes wrought by the oil shocks of 1973 and 1979 tied that thinking in a knot. The Corporate Automobile Fuel Efficiency (CAFE) standards passed in 1975 pushed cars from 13 miles per gallon to 27.5 in 1986, and now save us five million barrels of oil a day. Utilities dropped oil for cheaper coal. Homes were weatherized. Some states took action, such as California, which required 1980 refrigerators to use 20 percent less electricity than the 1975 models, causing an entire industry to change. (By the mid-80s refrigerators, the biggest energy drains in most homes, had improved by 35 percent.) Not until 1985 when President Reagan

Bush's National Energy Strategy

President Bush's National Energy Strategy (NES) includes almost 100 proposals for increasing our domestic energy production. Among his major initiatives are:

• Offering 1.5 million acres of the Arctic National Wildlife Refuge for oil and gas exploration. The Department of the Interior also announced plans to lease thousands of square miles on the outer continental shelf for similar exploration, from the Beaufort and Chuckchi Seas off Alaska, to the Gulf of Mexico, to large tracts off Southern California and the Eastern Seaboard.

• Reviving nuclear power by shortening post-construction public hearings and by transferring the problem of permanent radioactive waste disposal to an independent corporation not subject to the public constraints on a governmental agency. The NES would also extend the life of

currently operating plants to 60 years from their current 40.
• Amending the Public Utility Holding Act to allow utilities to expand across state lines and to allow private power plants to compete with utilities. This change could spur the private development of nuclear power plants regardless of public utilities' desires.
• Reducing regulations on natural gas pipelines and eliminating Federal review of natural gas imports or exports.
• Requiring the owners of fleet vehicles, such as taxis or delivery vans, to switch to alternative fuels: alcohol, natural gas or electricity. By the year 2000, ninety percent of the new fleet vehicles must run on an alternative fuel.
• Continuing the present tax breaks for energy conservation.

An Alternate National Energy Strategy

Numerous groups have called upon the country to adopt energy policies that

would increase our energy savings—an approach which they believe will be faster, cleaner and cheaper than increasing our energy production. Among their major proposals are:

• Improving our energy efficiency by two to three percent a year, the rate we achieved in the late 70s and early 80s.

• Increasing automobile fuel efficiency standards to 45 mpg for cars and 35 mpg for light trucks by the year 2001.

• Raising the federal gasoline tax by 50 cents a gallon to help finance mass transit and other energy efficiency programs.

• Adopting "least cost" planning methods that include energy savings and environmental effects when making all of our energy decisions.

• Increasing the funds for federal research on energy conservation and renewable energy until they are at least equal with those for nuclear power.

• Creating new tax credits for renewable energy and a carbon tax on fossil fuels.

rolled back the CAFE standards and oil prices dropped, did our energy savings stall.

One after another people appeared before the DOE with ideas on how to get us back on the savings track. After all, we still have a ways to go—Japan and Germany use half as much energy per dollar of economic output as we do. "The message from elected officials, citizens groups and energy related businesses was conservation, conservation, conservation," Denman says.

"What we've been given is a cruel hoax. It's not an energy strategy, it's an energy tragedy."

The DOE listened. "Admiral Watkins looked at the issue, and he began to say the one thing that's loud and clear is that improved conservation and energy efficiency are where the most gains can be made and the government can do a lot more than it has," said Christopher Flavin of Worldwatch who testified at the first hearing in August 1989. In April 1990 the DOE released an interim compendium of what it had heard so far which was dominated by conservation and energy efficiency. But then the report left the DOE for the White House.

"President Bush knows as much about energy as anyone we've ever had in the White House," says one DOE official. What Bush knows, though, is producing energy, not saving it. His home state, Texas, is the worst energy hog in the country. It can't even fill up its own gas tanks, importing 48 thousand barrels of oil in 1989 on top of 736 thousand barrels from its own wells. "Texas has 42 percent fewer citizens than does California," reports a study by the consumer advocacy group, Public Citizen, "but it uses 37 percent more energy." California has a state energy department and Texas doesn't, which just shows what a little planning can do.

"The implicit assumption of the NES is that the market runs at top efficiency," says Michael Brower of the Union of Concerned Scientists (UCS). "Any conservation or renewable energy we have is the amount we should be getting because we have a free market. Our point is that the market is not really free. There are all sorts of incentives for fossil fuels which, to be fair, should be eliminated or applied to energy efficiency and renewables. And the free market doesn't take into account the cost to the environment." This spring the UCS, NRDC, and the Boston-based nonprofit environmental research group, the Tellus Institute, released an alternative national energy strategy to show what we can do by taking conservation and efficiency seriously. "Nobody has ever made this serious an effort to meet the skeptics on their own ground," Brower says.

More than a dozen states now give serious consideration to energy efficiency and the environmental costs of fossil fuels when planning out their needs. Rather than simply worrying about energy supply, they consider demand, and often find that the cost of reducing the demand is a lot cheaper than increasing supply. This new approach, labeled "demand side" or "least cost" planning, now dominates on the West Coast and in New England where states have to import fossil fuels. States that produce coal and oil, though, tend to stick to the "supply side" view.

"If every state took the least cost approach there would be no reason to build any new power plants—coal or nuclear—in this decade," says Michael Totten of the International Institute for Energy Conservation. And if we took this approach in all of our energy decisions, we could be using seven percent less energy by the year 2000, instead of 34 percent more, as we would on our present course. In the next century, after we've captured these savings, renewable energy sources such as windmills, photovoltaics that turn sunlight into electricity, and turbines that run on biomass fuels could be competitive with fossil fuels.

But the NES took the supply side view. And many observers laid the blame on John Sununu more than on George Bush. "Sununu has always been hostile to demand side measures," Robert Watson says. "We both think the other's solution is a drop in the bucket. He dismisses conservation out of hand as being irrelevant. We dismiss nuclear power as largely being irrelevant. But I think we have the better basis for dismissing it."

After President Bush's announcement, the NES became just another influential sheaf of paper on Capitol Hill where Congress was moving into full gear to make 1991 the year for energy. The President was doing his part in the Persian Gulf, said one Republican staffer, now Congress had to do its part at home. The legislators introduced some 80 bills on energy, including one by Senators Bennett Johnston (D-LA) and Malcolm Wallop (R-WY) that was an oil and gas industry dream. But Senator Richard Bryan (D-NV) reintroduced his bill to improve auto fuel efficiency standards by 40 percent to 40 miles per gallon by 2001. It had been defeated the previous year, but now he had 35 co-sponsors. In the House, Representative Barbara Boxer (D-CA) offered an even better bill to push the standards to 45 mpg. And Representative Philip Sharp (D-IN) came up with a bill to make the federal government a major champion of energy efficiency. The battle had indeed come home.

One More Final Showdown at the Arctic Refuge

The Exxon Valdez spill seemed to save the Arctic Refuge, but the Gulf War put it right back into play. To the oil and gas industry, the Refuge could provide one tenth of our country's future production. To environmentalists, the Refuge is the last untouched

> "If Detroit was really smart they'd go into the mass transit business—most of our roads will not be able to handle many more cars. And in many places there's just no more room to build new roads."

corner of North America with the full spectrum of arctic and subarctic ecosystems.

"It's the only one up there," says Mike Matz, of the Sierra Club office in Washington, DC. "The oil industry has the rest of the North Slope, and all of the offshore areas, so there's no reason they need it." In fact, nearby Prudhoe Bay has 27 billion barrels of oil of which nine billion can be recovered, but another field nearby has 15 to 20 billion barrels. The oil industry is simply waiting until it is more profitable to drill. The Department of the Interior has done seismic testing of the Arctic Refuge and estimated a one in five chance of finding oil. They then estimated that *if* oil is found the field could yield maybe 3.2 billion barrels.

"We use 18 million barrels a day, so that's about a 180 day supply," Matz says. And it would take a minimum of seven years to begin shipping oil from the Refuge. So why do the oil companies want it so badly? "The financial health of the oil companies depends not on production, but on how much oil they have access to," Matz says. A gusher in the Arctic Refuge would immediately improve any company's financial standing even if they didn't drill it for years. "So all of this shouting about needing it for our national energy security is bogus," Matz concludes. He believes that, after a close debate, the Senate will kill the idea.

Arctic Refuge or not, the United States remains an oil power on its last legs. The average Saudi oil well pumps 9,000 barrels a day, while ours pump 15. Our domestic reserves could easily be dry by 2020 at our present rate of consumption. But the world's known oil reserves jumped from 615 to 917 billion barrels between 1985 and 1990, mostly in the Persian Gulf where it's cheaper to drill. During the late 80s we stopped producing two million barrels a day—as much as we imported from Kuwait—because the price fell too low. "A lot of the stripper wells, ten barrels a day or less, were shut down because they were just not economical," Watson says. "But if we kept eking out that stuff from already existing fields we'd have a lot of little wells that could add up to something big. We'd prefer that to sinking new wells in Alaska. But we'd need incentives for oil recovery

No Blood For Oil

All of those working for a renewable energy future are hoping that the public disquiet over the Persian Gulf War will create the political momentum needed for change, from support for better car fuel mileage standards to more funding for solar power. Before the Iraqi invasion of Kuwait our energy debate had revolved around the impact of fossil fuels on global warming. War made the issue much more personal. In late January, Dave Kraft of the Illinois-based Nuclear Energy Information Service said, "Two years ago we were arguing from abstractions, but recently we've been arguing about preventing piles of body bags."

Such major environmental groups as the Natural Resources Defense Council, the Sierra Club and the National Audubon Society, want to capitalize on the public mood for change, but they avoided any real stand on the war itself. They are not in the business of foreign affairs, they say. Mike McCloskey, chairman of the Sierra Club, said that the group "doesn't have a position on this war—or past wars," though it did issue statements about "extending warfare to birds, shrimp and

sea life." McCloskey said he is "gravely concerned about the oil spills," but he added that he "wouldn't want to characterize the whole war" as an attack on Gulf ecology.

Some groups, though, saw the Persian Gulf War as *the* environmental crisis of the moment. They weren't about to keep quiet. Bill Walker, media director of Greenpeace's office in San Francisco, says Greenpeace "was the first major environmental group to overtly oppose the war. As environmentalists, we had to take a stand against the war, which was being fought over a resource, oil, which we knew to be toxic to the planet." Walker points out that Greenpeace, which had significant contingents at both major peace marches in Washington, DC last January, "was founded on principles of non-violence. We believe that the planet cannot support armed conflict. We don't know how you can call yourselves environmentalists and not oppose war."

At the Earth Island Institute, also in San Francisco, Gar Smith, editor of *Earth Island Journal*, said, "We suspended a lot of our ordinary work, and used our expertise to get information out." The group even shut its offices on

occasion to go to teach-ins and demonstrations. Both Greenpeace and Earth Island say they lost members and publication subscribers because of their stand against the war.

The Washington, DC-based Friends of the Earth (FOE) also took an early and firm stand against the war. FOE warned of the environmental consequences of the Gulf War in early January; its releases, predicting oil spills and well fires, later proved highly accurate. "Unfortunately, nobody paid any attention until it actually started occurring," said Dr. Brent Blackwelder, vice president of policy, who noted that FOE had "postponed or reduced in intensity" some of its other campaigns to concentrate on the war. "The war essentially laid waste to the entire Fertile Crescent," said Blackwelder. "We essentially poisoned the Persian Gulf and obliterated Kuwait to 'save' it."

Like many of the activist spokespersons, Blackwelder is critical of the richer, more established groups that were slow to respond to the war crisis. "A lot of the groups regarded it as too controversial," he said. "They didn't want to take a stand."
— *Jim Motavalli*

in these fields because things like injecting steam to melt the thick globby oil or sideways drilling add five or ten bucks for each barrel of oil recovered."

"The fact is, oil is too cheap in this country," he continues. "It's simultaneously one of the most valued and one of the least valued commodities we have. It's valuable enough to send half a million people over to the Middle East—and our citizens are probably the most precious resource we have—yet we're not willing to spend an extra buck per gallon, or to require the auto industry to increase its fuel economy."

Car Wars

"The biggest untapped oil field in America is riding 18 inches off the ground in our gas tanks," says Paul Allen, communications director of the NRDC. Allen didn't invent this wonderful soundbite, nor will he be the last to use it as Congress begins debating new CAFE standards in one of the major energy battles of the session. "CAFE was one of the best energy policies we ever had," Watson adds. Passed in 1975 when new cars averaged 13 mpg, these standards pushed the standards up to 27.5 mpg in 1985 when Reagan rolled them back to 26 mpg, basically because Ford and GM couldn't make the higher standard and wanted to avoid the fines.

New standards have been contemplated for a while, but the Persian Gulf War gave momentum to the issue. After all, two thirds of our oil goes to transportation. "It's become much more politically mainstream," says Deborah Bleviss, author of *The New Oil Crisis and Fuel Economy Technologies.* "It has a good chance in the House, but in the Senate it's much more iffy because of John Dingell, who single-handedly held up the Clean Air Act for years." Dingell, who runs the Energy and Commerce Committee, represents Dearborn, Michigan and the auto industry. A new CAFE law would cost Detroit billions and probably add $500 to the price of a new car.

Detroit's old counterattack against CAFE is safety: when the head-on collision comes, do you want to be in a 27.5 mpg tank or a 40 mpg sardine can? "The real irony is that they've never really cared about safety," Bleviss replies. As for the big car/little car scenario, nobody really knows, she adds. The only tests we have, crashing a speeding car into a flat wall, simulate the impact of a car hitting its own weight. And the land rovers and mini-vans that are selling so well these days do poorly in these tests. Smaller cars can be built more safely, but Bleviss says, "The question is, do we want to?"

"If Detroit was really smart they'd go into the mass transit business," Watson says. "Our roads just won't be able to handle many more cars. And in many places there's no more room to build new roads." Our cars are indeed crowding in on themselves like lemmings—each day Californians lose a total of fifty years in traffic delays. Many feel we need to forgo the old suburban ideal of a quarter acre for every home and a car in every garage, and

adopt a clustered, European style of life. But Watson warns, "What we're talking about is changing the American Dream, and that isn't going to happen anytime soon. Our conception is still of your big tailfin car driving out to your suburban home on empty freeways. But we haven't seen that since 1965, if we ever really saw it at all."

Power to the Future

Some say our energy future will become a showdown between solar power and nuclear energy. They're related, of course, since the sun is a giant fusion reactor—but solar power leaves the problems with fusion 93 million miles out in space. But all the problems we've created with fossil fuels have revived the nuclear alternative. The NES calls for increasing our nuclear power capacity by 30 to 80 percent over the next three decades.

Dr. Jan Beyea of the National Audubon Society, sometimes cast as an apostate for not rejecting the nuclear idea out of hand, says, "When we talk about global warming, we mean that if we don't take steps now, in 50 years the die will be cast; there will be no hope of preventing global warming from then on." Our planet releases six billion tons of carbon into the atmosphere each year; Beyea and many other scientists believe we must cut back by 20 percent by the year 2010 to avoid the greenhouse crisis.

"We need energy conservation in the short run, but in the long run we have solar and nuclear," Beyea continues. "Both are problematic. The price of solar power during the day isn't bad, but at night it gets very expensive because of storage. Although I'm skeptical, Dr. Larry Lidsky at MIT says that an 'idiot proof' nuclear reactor can be built, so I think we should give him the dollars to see if that's true."

Unlike the nuclear proponents of the early 50s who promised energy "too cheap to meter" Beyea comes to his view out of pessimism. "The public has a choice," he says. "They can choose solar, or they can slip back into nuclear. I detest nuclear power, but I don't think one stone can be left unturned. This is no joke. This is the final environmental battle."

For now, though, nuclear power is one of the great white elephants of our industrial history. The United States has 111 plants which produce 25 percent of our electrical power, but nobody has ordered a new plant since 1978. The NES includes some band-aids for the industry, such as speeding the post-construction approval process, but one Congressional staffer doesn't take them seriously. "Even if they had a majority in Congress, which they don't, the industry still wouldn't get an order."

"You show me one utility that is really hot about nuclear, and I'll show you two dozen that wouldn't touch it with a ten foot pole," says NRDC's Watson. "When we've got reams of material that show the cost of saving electricity is one or two cents per kilowatt hour, why would anyone spend ten cents—25 in the case of Seabrook—for electricity from nuclear power?" These days many utilities meet

"The United States—so huge, so sunny, so windy, and so dotted with geothermal hotspots like those already heating homes in Boise, Idaho—has renewable energy supplies that dwarf our oil and gas reserves."

their needs with energy savings campaigns supplemented by new 250 megawatt combined cycle plants that use oil or natural gas. Like many, Watson believes that natural gas will be our transition fuel to a renewable energy future.

The United States—so huge, so sunny, so windy, and so dotted with geothermal hotspots like those already heating homes in Boise, Idaho—has renewable energy supplies that dwarf our oil and gas reserves. And renewable sources, mostly from hydroelectric dams and wood burning power plants, already produce eight percent of our energy compared to the seven percent from nuclear power. Back in the late 70s the DOE created great expectations, confidently predicting that by the year 2000 twenty percent of our power would come from the sun. But Ronald Reagan wasn't interested. He took down the solar panels Carter had installed on the White House roof. He slashed the DOE's research and development budget for renewable energy from $557 million in 1981 to $78 million in 1989. And in 1985 he let the 40 percent solar tax credit for homeowners expire. A $700 million solar industry, which had installed solar water heaters in a million homes, preventing the need for a 1,000-megawatt power plant, rapidly became a $70 million one. Scott Sklar of the Solar Energy Industries Association says, "We lost 35,000 people in 1985, which was more than the U.S. auto industry."

California alone refused to give up the dream. Today it has become the world's showcase for solar and wind power. The parabolic mirrors of Luz International in the Mojave Desert produce 90 percent of the solar electricity generated in the world today—194 megawatts a day—or one percent of Southern California Edison's peak supply. The wind farms that stretch across the passes at Altamont, Tehachapi, and San Gorgonio, looking like crops of airplane propellers, can generate 1,500 megawatts. The first wind farm built in 1981 was quickly dubbed a "tax farm" because it seemed to produce more writeoffs than electricity. But Randall Swisher, executive director of the American Wind Energy Association, says those bad old days are long gone. "The cost of wind energy was 25 cents per kilowatt hour at the first wind farms in California in 1981, but it's between five and nine cents today, and we expect that to decline at least another 40 percent." And California is only the 14th windiest state in the country. Now that these technologies are proving themselves, proponents believe the federal government should get back in the business of supporting them with new tax breaks and research funds.

"If we get everything we think we can," Sklar says, referring to the energy legislation now pending in Congress, "solar and renewable energy could be producing 20 percent of our country's power by 2000."

"If we stop fooling ourselves that nuclear is only eight cents a kilowatt hour and coal four to six, instead of 12, 14, or 16 like it should be," says Robert Watson, referring to the environmental costs of those industries, "and we had the same level of effort going into solar and alternative technologies that we have going into the moribund nuclear industry, then we would have a very viable industry within ten years."

ABORTION IN A NEW LIGHT

*Treating abortion as a public health problem, rather than a
criminal act or ideological flashpoint, will actually
reduce its incidence.*

JODI L. JACOBSON

*Jodi L. Jacobson is a senior researcher working on
population, family planning, and women and development at the Worldwatch Institute.*

Among the first actions taken
by Romania's provisional government following the execu-
tion of dictator Nicolae Ceausescu in December 1989 was a
repeal of the ban on abortion. The 14-year-
old edict, created by Ceausescu in a fruitless
attempt to raise the nation's birthrate, outlawed contraceptives and made abortion a
criminal offense punishable in some instances by death.

Some six months earlier, the United States,
a country with one of the world's most liberal
abortion policies, took a step backward on
reproductive rights. Last July's U.S. Supreme Court ruling on *Webster v. Reproductive Services* in effect flashed a green light to
those states seeking to strictly regulate abortion procedures. In *Webster,* the court threw
out the trimester framework established in
the landmark 1973 *Roe v. Wade* decision,
which permitted states to regulate abortions
only after the first trimester, and to ban them
only in the last. The case upholds Missouri's
law declaring that life begins at conception
and that physicians must carry out extensive
tests before performing many second trimes-

ter abortions. Furthermore, *Webster* extended government control of private abortion facilities by upholding Missouri's ban on
the use of public facilities for abortion.

Not since the Vietnam era has a single
issue so polarized public opinion in the United
States. For abortion-rights activists, *Webster*
has been the equivalent of the Tet Offensive,
galvanizing supporters in much the same way
that battle rallied opponents of the Vietnam
War. State election gains in November 1989
by candidates supporting abortion rights
indicate that the long-somnolent pro-choice
majority may finally have awakened. But, the
zeal and dedication of a highly organized
pro-life minority ensures that the fight over
reproductive freedom is far from over.

A careful examination of trends in Romania, the United States, and other countries
illuminates several important points about
the global abortion debate. One is that,
against the backdrop of a general liberalization of abortion laws, events in several countries reveal an ominous undertow eroding
recently codified reproductive rights. Two,
abortion politics has become deadlocked in
a no-win dispute over the ideology and crim-
inology of abortion procedures, resulting in
a tug-of-war over laws that don't even begin
to address the complex social phenomenon
of abortion. Three, this dispute postpones
the day when the energies of both the pro-
choice and pro-life camps can be directed

fully toward improving the health and welfare of women and children worldwide.

The Issue that Knows No Compromise

In legalizing abortion, Romania joins some 35 other countries that have made similar changes since the late-1970s. In fact, a 30-year tide of liberalization in laws governing family planning has increased access to contraceptives and made abortions safer for millions of women worldwide. As a result, the relative number of unintended pregnancies and deaths due to illegal abortion procedures has dropped in many countries.

But groups vociferously opposed to abortion—and, in many cases, to family planning methods altogether—have kept up their fight to reverse these policies. The U.S. decision, the first major success of the "pro-life" movement, sent shock waves through the ranks of activists in Western Europe, where the abortion debate has been far less emotional than in the United States but is becoming more polarized. Europeans from both camps have described the decision as a "wind from the west." While European pro-life groups have been "in the doldrums for a number of years . . . supporters are [now] heartened by what has taken place in the United States [and are] back in business," declares Bill Sherwin, executive secretary of the International Right to Life Federation in Rome.

The struggle over abortion rights is now a cross-border affair, with money and anti-abortion protestors crossing the Atlantic from the U.S. to Europe. According to Leonora Lloyd, director of the pro-choice National Abortion Campaign in London, Operation Rescue, a group that has been linked to violent tactics, is sending its organizers to England and elsewhere. Abortion-rights activists in Canada, France, Italy, Spain, and West Germany are gearing up for renewed battle.

Pro-life activists from the U.S. and Europe are supporting the growth of parallel movements in developing countries. Their agenda focuses on maintaining or reinstating restrictive abortion laws rather than providing couples with the means to prevent unintended pregnancy. However, studies show that millions of Third World couples still lack access to birth control. Not surprisingly, poor women suffer the highest rates of death due to complications of pregnancy and illegal abortion. In 1989, the anti-abortion group Human Life International held its first international conference in Zambia, a country with one of Africa's most liberal reproductive rights policies. Representatives of this group are suspected of starting a widespread disinformation campaign about locally available contraceptives, causing a great deal of confusion and anguish on the part of women relying on these methods.

Unanswered Questions

In many ways, the goals of pro-life activists raise more questions than they answer. For example, why are so-called pro-life forces so blind to the public health toll of illegal abortion?

Illegal abortion represents a global public health problem of tremendous proportions. Estimates indicate that about 55 million unwanted pregnancies end in abortion every year, nearly half of which are illegal operations carried out mostly in the Third World. The World Health Organization (WHO) attributes the loss of roughly 200,000 women's lives annually to illegal abortions, most of which are performed by unskilled attendants under unsanitary conditions, or are self-inflicted with hangers, knitting needles, toxic herbal teas and the like. What is more, for every woman who dies, many others suffer serious, often long-term health consequences.

By contrast, modern abortion procedures performed under proper medical supervision in countries where they are legal are among the safest of all medical procedures. In the United States, for instance, an early abortion procedure is 11 times safer than a tonsillectomy or childbirth.

Why focus on banning abortions when evidence overwhelmingly indicates that this is not the answer to the problem? History has proven that laws cannot eliminate abortions, they can only make them more or less safe and costly. Try as it might, no government has ever legislated abortion out of existence.

In Ceausescu's Romania, for example, reproductive repression was as widespread as economic privation. No woman under the age of 45 with less than five children could obtain a legal abortion. A special arm of the secret police force Securitate, dubbed the "Pregnancy Police," administered monthly checkups to female workers. Pregnant women were monitored, married women who did not conceive were kept under surveillance, and a special tax was levied on unmarried people over 25 and childless couples that could not give a medical reason for infertility.

Despite the law, data show that in the 1980s Romania's birthrate fell before rising again later, and that the country outranked virtually all other European nations on rates of abortion and abortion-related maternal mortality. One survey showed that Bucharest Municipal Hospital alone dealt with 3,000 failed abortions last year; still other sources indicate that well over 1,000 women died within that city each year due to complications of botched abortions. Legalization of abortion in Western Europe, by contrast, has produced the world's lowest abortion-related mortality rates. In several of these countries, public education efforts on planned

---

Given
pro-life groups' desire to ban or restrict contraceptives, how do they propose to reduce the incidence of abortion?

---

parenthood have precipitated a fall in the number of abortions.

Why are pro-life groups opposed to programs most likely to prevent the greatest number of abortions? The best way to reduce the number of abortions and unintended pregnancies is to support a comprehensive family planning and health program that educates couples about birth control and lets them know where to get it. Epidemiological and social studies show conclusively that family planning improves the health of women and families most effectively by preventing the most dangerous pregnancies— those that occur in women too young or too old to carry safely to term, and those that come within 24 months of a prior birth.

Family planning also affords people the means with which to exercise their basic human right to determine the number and spacing of their children. The benefits extend to children because infants who are

adequately spaced tend to be better nourished and cared for than those following close on the heels of their siblings. These facts notwithstanding, pro-life groups in the United States and elsewhere have been the most vocal opponents of strategies that would reduce the number of unintended pregnancies and abortions and improve overall family health.

Politicking by pro-life groups led the United States to dramatically restructure and limit its involvement in international family planning efforts. The Reagan administration ended U.S. leadership on international family planning efforts with the announcement of a new policy stance at the 1984 International Conference on Population in Mexico City. This policy, developed under heavy lobbying from groups opposed to family planning in general, cut off U.S. funds to any private voluntary group that provides abortion services or counseling, even though a law banning the use of U.S. funds for abortions abroad was already on the books and had been stringently enforced since 1973. Blacklisted agencies include the well-respected International Planned Parenthood Federation (IPPF) and United Nations Population Fund.

Unfortunately, this turnabout has curtailed IPPF plans to expand the number of family planning clinics around the world to cope with a growing number of couples of reproductive age. At the same time, the research, development and marketing of low-cost, long-acting contraceptives, such as implants and injectables, has also been slowed. Similar efforts in the United States and Europe have resulted in costly legal battles over family planning funds, as well as research and development of drugs such as RU-486, which terminates pregnancy in its earliest stages, when abortions are least controversial.

Given the fact that many pro-life groups harbor a strong desire to ban or restrict contraceptive methods now on the market, eliminate contraceptive research and development, and scuttle family planning altogether, just how would they propose to reduce the incidence of abortion?

If the pro-life lobby were successful in severely restricting birth control and abortion in many countries, how would it propose to deal with the regional disparities between population and resources? Without abortion as a backup to the failure, ineffective use, or total lack of birth control methods, just how would the world deal with 55 million additional (and unwanted) pregnancies each year? More fundamental to the debate perhaps is the question of how will women, forced to bear children they do not want, ever really achieve their potential as individuals?

Abortion Laws, Worldwide

"Pro-choice" or "pro-life," few people would disagree with the idea that reducing the number of unintended pregnancies and abortions worldwide, and attempting to ensure that the largest share of abortions are carried out in the first trimester, when they are safest and least controversial, is a desirable public policy goal. Ironically, few countries have worked wholeheartedly towards this end.

The majority of the world's people now live in countries that have moved from blanket prohibition of abortion to a more reasoned acceptance of its role as a backup to contraceptive failure and unwanted pregnancy. The debate in these countries has evolved from whether or not to legalize abortions to just under what circumstances they should be available. Still, most countries relegate abortion to the criminal code, rather than dealing with it comprehensively as a public health problem.

The trend toward liberalization began in full force in the 1950s, as recognition of the need to reduce maternal mortality and promote reproductive freedom became widespread. Social justice was also an issue. Bringing abortion into the public domain reduced the disparity between those who could afford adequate medical care and those forced to resort to unsafe practitioners.

Most countries have enacted abortion laws within their criminal codes, using traditional legal justifications to indicate the actual circumstances under which abortions can be legally performed. Countries with the narrowest laws restrict abortion to cases where pregnancy poses a risk to a woman's life, although most include cases of rape or incest. Other laws consider risks to physical and mental health; still others the case of a severely impaired fetus. Some societies condone abortion for what are known as "social" reasons, as in cases where an additional childbirth will inflict undue burdens on a woman's existing family. Broadest are the laws that recognize contraceptive failure, or a simple request (usually within the first trimester), as

sound basis for abortion. Most governments leave specific interpretations (how to define "health") up to the discretion of the medical community.

According to Rebecca Cook, professor of law at the University of Toronto, several of the 35 countries that liberalized their laws since 1977 created new categories, such as adolescence, advanced maternal age, or infection with the AIDS virus, as a basis for legal abortion. Cyprus, Italy and Taiwan, for example, all broadened their laws to consider "family welfare," while Hong Kong recognized adolescence. France and the Netherlands have included clauses pertaining to pregnancy-related distress. In Hungary, one of the first Eastern European countries to liberalize abortion laws, abortion rights are extended to pregnant women who are single or have been separated from their husbands for a period of six months, to women over the age of 35 with at least three previous deliveries, and to women caught in economic hardship, such as the lack of appropriate housing.

Even countries with the most liberal laws recognize some constraints on a woman's right to abortion. Generally speaking, abortions are least regulated during the first trimester of pregnancy, during which most liberal codes permit abortion on-request. In Singapore, for example, abortions are available upon request until the 24th week of pregnancy, while in Turkey only until the 10th week. A woman seeking to terminate a pregnancy after this period must show just cause under the law.

A recent review of international abortion policy data by the Washington-based Population Crisis Committee indicates that about 75 percent of the world's population (3.9 billion out of 5.2 billion people) live in countries that permit abortion on medical or broader social and economic grounds. In Ethiopia and Costa Rica, for example, abortion is legal only in cases of risk to the woman's health, while in Tunisia it is available on-request until the 12th week of pregnancy and in Taiwan on-request until the fetus can live outside the womb (otherwise known as viability, the stage between the 24th and 28th weeks of pregnancy).

Another 20 percent live in 49 countries in which abortion is totally prohibited or is legal only to save the life of the mother. The category includes much of Africa, Latin America and Muslim Asia. Unfortunately, these are also countries where women have the least access to safe, affordable means of contraception. The remaining 5 percent of the world's people are governed by laws that have added rape and incest to this fairly restrictive list.

Bucking the liberalization trend are Finland, Honduras, Iran, Ireland, Israel, New Zealand and now the United States. Abortion laws in this group have become more restrictive since 1977. A Honduran law permitting abortions in cases where they would protect the life and health of the mother and in cases of rape and fetal deformity was rejected because it was perceived to conflict with constitutional provisions stating that the "right to life is inviolable."

Likewise, changes in the constitutions of Ecuador (1978) and the Philippines (1986) incorporated provisions according the right to life "from the moment of conception." Some of these changes have ambiguous implications. Chile's constitution, for example, protects not only the right to life and to physical and psychic integrity of individuals, but also of those "about to be born." Whether or not an embryo or 10-week-old fetus is "about to be born" remains unclear.

Because many nations' legal codes reflect social ambivalence about abortion, what happens in practice often does not reflect the law on the books. In some countries where abortion is illegal in principle, it is carried out quite freely in practice. Conversely, in other countries where women hold the legal right to abortion on demand, they find it difficult to actually procure one because of local opposition or reluctance to carry out national laws. Such is the case in the Bavarian region of West Germany, where local officials have sought to circumvent national abortion rights laws.

"Liberal" laws themselves do not always safeguard a woman's ability to exercise abortion rights. A pervasive problem is that while many countries have liberalized their laws, they have not gone so far as to commit public resources to providing safe abortion services, nor do most countries mandate widespread access.

Some laws work against the goal of ensuring that when abortions do occur they are carried out at the earliest possible point. New laws in Bermuda, Kuwait, the Seychelles and Qatar include hospital committee authorization requirements before an abortion can be performed. Yet, in most cases,

these regulations, strongly supported by the pro-life community, act only to delay abortions until later stages of pregnancy, when procedures are riskier and the fetus is more developed. Such institutional and third-party authorization requirements have come under legal attack in many countries and been struck down in several, including Canada and Czechoslovakia. Unfortunately, several U.S. states may soon enact such restrictions.

The resolution of other issues under debate in countries throughout the world could have a negative effect on abortion rights. They are: when and to what extent government health-care programs should cover the costs of legal abortion; whether or not a husband's consent or notification should be required before a married woman can obtain an abortion; and whether or not laws should condition adolescent abortions on parental notification.

The question is, Will the same forces responsible for the U.S. *Webster* decision be successful in turning back the clock in other countries? The social impacts of setting limits on family planning options are likely to be staggering. Apart from the immediate health impacts of illegal abortion, experience in a number of countries shows that forcing women to carry pregnancies to term results in higher rates of infanticide, greater numbers of abandoned and neglected children, and, particularly in the Third World, a decline in health and nutritional standards. In Romania, the numbers of abandoned and neglected children soared after abortion and contraception were outlawed. Similar trends have been documented in African and Latin American countries.

A Prescription to Reduce Abortion
Only by making contraceptives safer and more available, increasing access to family planning information and supplies, and teaching children the concept of responsible parenthood will the number of unintended pregnancies and abortions be reduced. Abortion, however, will never disappear. Activists and policymakers need to begin rejecting fixed but unfounded notions about the ideology and criminality of abortion in favor of a more rational understanding of its role in the spectrum of choices within a comprehensive family planning program. In effect, this would be a strategy based on the notion that prevention is better than cure.

The first step is to remove abortion from the criminal code and address it as a public health problem. A few countries—China, Togo and Vietnam—have already done so. In Cuba, abortion is considered a criminal offense only when it is performed for profit, by an unqualified person, in an unofficial place, or without the woman's consent.

Second, mobilize support for family planning programs. According to Rebecca Cook, a number of countries have taken this positive step by setting up programs aimed at reducing the incidence of unwanted pregnancy. Some countries now require post-abortion contraceptive counseling and education, and some mandate programs for men, too. Italy now requires local and regional health authorities to promote contraceptive services and other measures to reduce demand for abortion, while Czech law aims to prevent abortion through sex education in schools and health facilities and provides for free contraceptive and associated care. Turkish law provides access to voluntary sterilization as well as to abortion.

These efforts have been successful. On the Swedish island of Gotland, abortions were almost halved in an intensive three-year program to provide information and improved family planning services. Similar results have been shown in France and elsewhere.

Third, provide support and funding for international contraceptive research and development. Making contraceptives safer, more affordable, and more widely available will reduce the need for abortions around the world.

Fourth, target high-risk groups with education programs. In the United States, for example, lack of education on family planning methods leads to one of the highest rates of unintended pregnancy among teenagers in the industrial world. That group undergoes about one-third of all abortions each year. It's no coincidence that U.S. teens lag far behind their Western European counterparts in knowledge of contraception. A common myth perpetuated by the pro-life movement is that sex education, including family planning information, leads to teen promiscuity. Data from the Alan Guttmacher Institute and elsewhere show the reverse is true.

The impact of unwanted pregnancies extends beyond the individual to encompass public health and the question of sustainable development. An international consensus among a diverse body of policymakers already exists on the adverse effects of rapid population growth on economic performance, the environment, family welfare, health, and political stability. If minimizing population-related problems is an international priority, as has been accepted by a number of U.N. legal conventions, then it is essential that abortion be available as a birth control method of last resort.

The success of abortion-rights activists throughout the world will depend on their ability to make clear that abortion is a social reality that cannot be erased by legal code. Obviously, the ideal situation would be to eliminate all unintended pregnancies. In the real world, though, limited access to birth control and the inevitability of contraceptive failure, either through imperfect technologies or human error, means that unplanned pregnancies will continue to occur.

PROBLEMS THAT GROW BIGGER AND BIGGER

Big Messes

Kenneth W. Hunter

Kenneth W. Hunter is a senior faculty member of the Training Institute, U.S. General Accounting Office, 441 G Street, N.W., Washington, D.C. 20548. He is also treasurer of the World Future Society and co-editor of *Futures Research Quarterly.*

World War II left the United States with a storehouse of technology ready for use, an underemployed labor force, a huge pent-up economic demand, and no strong economic competitors in the global marketplace. Under these conditions, the United States was launched forward on a massive wave of economic growth that did not begin to lose its force until the 1970s. The events that signaled this turning point are all familiar: Vietnam, Watergate, the end of the Bretton Woods agreement, Nixon's opening to China, the entry of Japan Inc. into the global marketplace, and the rise of OPEC.

These events have put Americans into a state of shock and denial. U.S. leaders and citizens alike have been denying that these changes are significant and that they require changes in our own behavior. Only in the past few months have events forced the United States to examine the nature of the major shifts taking place in the world, and so far that examination has been very superficial. The majority of Americans remain focused on their own needs and desires, continuing the high-consumption lifestyle that they can now maintain only through credit and sales of assets. Little or no attention is paid to the future.

What's been going on in Washington all the while? Not much. The electorate is denying that serious problems exist, and the political consensus basically favors the policies that were created between the 1930s and the 1960s. So the nation's elected representatives have a mandate only to oversee the administration of government operations and to maintain the status quo by making the marginal changes required by external forces.

TODAY'S ISSUES HAVE BECOME "BIG MESSES," WHICH SHARE THREE COMMON CHARACTERISTICS: THEY'RE GLOBAL, CROSS-CUTTING, AND LONG TERM.

Lacking any big assignments, they have taken on many little assignments, mostly on behalf of individual constituents and special-interest groups.

From Issues to Big Messes

As the decades of denial have rolled on, the imbalances and conflicts we generally call "issues" have grown into big messes. These messes share several characteristics. One is longevity: It took years of neglect to create the big messes that exist in the environment, in drug addiction and the illegal industry that supports it, in the nation's financial institutions, in its education system, in infrastructure, and in housing. Again and again, technical analysts and auditors have reported internally on deteriorating conditions, but policy officials failed to take action at a time when the needed corrections would have been easier and cheaper to make than they are now or will be in the future.

This pattern of neglect appeared in both the savings-and-loan industry and the weapons-production industry. The thrift industry began deteriorating after the laws regulating it were changed in the early 1980s. By 1985, the U.S. General Accounting Office (GAO) had assessed the industry's condition and alerted Congress that the industry had problems with the quality of its assets as well as with interest rates. It took four more years for the situation to get bad enough that any action was taken.

Reprinted with permission from *The Futurist,* January/February 1991, pp. 10-17. *The Futurist,* published by the World Future Society, 4916 Saint Elmo Avenue, Bethesda, Maryland 20814.

In the case of the nuclear weapons production industry, by the early 1980s GAO had reported that the federal government's nuclear facilities had safety and health problems and that the Department of Energy's oversight was inadequate. GAO discovered more and more problems as the 1980s progressed; it continued to report on them and to increase its estimates of the cleanup costs. As these estimates passed the $100-billion mark — nearly a decade after GAO began examining the problems — the issue finally got onto the nation's policy agenda. The search for solutions is now under way.

I expect the same pattern of events to emerge in other areas during the 1990s. Major water-supply systems will continue to deteriorate and may collapse. The existing system of financial markets will be increasingly unable to effectively handle the global flow of transactions in stocks and commodities while at the same time serving as the primary source of capital financing. Health care in inner cities and rural communities will keep deteriorating, and there will be increased conflict among those who provide services, as well as those who finance services, consumers, and regulators, with no real mechanism for resolving these disputes. Environmental damage will continue, and it may become clear that some of this damage is not reversible and that the world must adapt to permanently deteriorated living conditions. In addition, there will be the wild cards — problems that we cannot foresee today.

Besides longevity, the big messes are alike in being global in scope. Political borders have proven almost irrelevant to the flow of pollution, communications, money and credit, technology, weapons, and migrants.

A third characteristic of the big messes is that they are also cross-cutting: Such problems as the trade deficit, the underclass, and the deterioration of the nation's infrastructure don't fit into the prescribed domains of existing legislative committees, executive departments,

"AMERICANS GENERALLY HAVE A BASIC OPTIMISM, A PENCHANT FOR HIGHLIGHTING GOOD NEWS AND DENYING INDICATIONS OF PROBLEMS."

academic disciplines, industry associations, or long-established interest groups, so they are automatically kicked upstairs and become the responsibility of the leadership.

Fighting Shortsighted Optimism

Unfortunately, America's political institutions have great difficulty dealing with issues that are long term, global, or cross-cutting. Americans generally have a basic optimism, a penchant for highlighting good news and denying indications of problems. Americans also tend to be shortsighted, favoring actions that have short-term benefits and long-term costs and opposing actions whose initial costs are clearly defined but whose benefits are unclear or off in the future. For example, the compromise strategy to address the savings-and-loan crisis was crafted to fit the industry's immediate needs and the government's immediate budgetary constraints; it will be up to future generations to pay off the long-term debts that are being incurred to cover payments to individuals who had money in the failed institutions.

Similarly, a natural protectionist bias emerges in any issue that involves international relationships. Jobs for American workers automatically become a major factor to be considered. If the issue is aid to developing countries, the question is, "How much of it will be used to buy goods and services from U.S. suppliers?" If the issue is intellectual property rights, the question is, "How can we protect the rights of Americans who hold pat-

ents, trademarks, or copyrights?" If the issue is the structure of regional trade arrangements, such as those emerging in Europe and Asia, the question is, "How can U.S. companies be guaranteed access to these markets?"

The fact that the issues tend to be cross-cutting brings out the worst bureaucratic instincts of even the best-intentioned people. All the issues tend to be forced onto top leaders, who must deal with petty bickering as well as substantive problems. For instance, to address the nation's drug-abuse problem it became necessary to install a new White House official with a strong personality who could coordinate the wide array of actions under way in law enforcement, the military, foreign diplomacy, and health and social services. Each sector has its own view of the problem and its own approach — a situation that, if not handled skillfully, can become totally chaotic.

Despite these impediments to real progress on major problems, people continue to seek elected office in the United States. But they have learned to keep their campaigns free of any real examination of the big messes, which cannot be discussed in 20-second sound bites and about which people really don't want to hear anything, anyway. Not having campaigned for any substantive policy changes, elected officials have no mandate for advocating such changes or for even raising fundamental questions. Their only mandate is to seek marginal changes that will make the problems go away for now. So that's basically what Washington has been up to.

Looking to the 1990s

How long can the United States continue to avoid these unresolved issues while other countries have accepted the need for action and begun the process of reform? How might the dynamics of public policy in the United States change in the 1990s? What might trigger such a change?

It appears that America can maintain its addiction to high consumption and low investment as long as the Japanese and Germans are willing to accept U.S. credits and to defer their own consumption. Both countries have been content to do so, until recently when Japanese interest rates began rising and reunified Germany became involved in reviving the former East German economy. Certainly some change in America's relationships with those two countries now seems inevitable: Sooner or later the World-War-II residue of fear and suspicion must be confronted, and this decade seems likely to see some restructuring of global military relationships. But it's difficult to say whether such a restructuring would result in a major reduction of the U.S. share of the defense bill in the Far East and Europe, or in Japan and Germany increasing their militaries beyond narrowly defined defensive forces. Neither Japan nor Germany seems likely to force these issues anytime soon, since they are sensitive domestically and could create a great deal of conflict.

So one must look elsewhere for forces that might drive the United States to change its behavior and its policies. What about the American people? In general, there seems to be little interest in how the government operates or in the processes of change. The individuals who will have to pay the bills for the country's current excesses, and whose standard of living will as a result be lower than that of their counterparts in Germany and Japan, are now too young to vote or else don't vote in large numbers. Therefore, they are not likely to force change through the electoral process — but they would be quick to take their protests into the streets if some event pushed them beyond their threshold of tolerance.

What else might trigger change? Existing businesses and interest groups have invested so much time and energy in gaining influence in the current system that they are among the strongest advocates of maintaining the status quo. Entrepreneurs are too few and too detached from the policy process to have much impact on it. And the majority of people in political leadership positions developed their values and approaches to public

NEW YORK STOCK EXCHANGE

policy during the boom years. The president and most of the congressional leaders started their work in public office well before the major changes of the late 1960s and early 1970s. Back then, leading and legislating — designing and implementing new programs — were fun.

Today's leaders still remember the good old days and seem to resent the politics of limits and survival. They seem to be having as much trouble as the public in accepting that changes need to be made.

Stock markets seem to have become detached from the real economy. They dropped substantially in 1987 without affecting the economy in any major way, author Hunter says. A recession might be rationalized as inevitable after so many years of growth and so would not spur fundamental changes in economic policy.

Crisis as Catalyst

Major changes can always be triggered by crises. But what kind of crisis might bring such change in the 1990s? Sudden military threats still have the capacity to effect rapid change, as the Iraqi invasion of Kuwait has demonstrated. But in the post-Cold-War era, the conflicts that endure are increasingly being shifted to the agendas of international organizations. A stock-market crash? The stock markets seem to have become detached from the real world of investment and the economy: The market can drop substantially without affecting the economy in any major way. A severe recession? A recession as severe as that of 1982 could be rationalized as inevitable after so many years of growth. How about the collapse of a major system — such as a communications system, air-traffic control, the water supply to a major city, or an energy supply — that would cause serious economic and social disruption? These systems are so decentralized that they would deteriorate rather than collapse completely. Therefore, the impact of a system's deterioration would be local and varied.

If there is no triggering event to make the United States examine its behavior and its consequences, the nation will have great difficulty cleaning up the big messes and will miss some big opportunities. The United States will continue its slide downward relative to other nations that are conserving, saving and investing, and strengthening their long-term economic capabilities.

In addition, the consequences of long-term neglect of crucial problems will begin to mount up. Employers will continue to encounter new entrants into the labor market who lack the skills to become effective workers. Environmental damage will continue to lower living conditions. Homeless, drug-addicted, mentally ill, and unskilled individuals will continue to live below the safety net; some of them will continue to resort to drugs and crime as escapes, however temporary, from their hopeless lives.

As the decade drifts on, the American people's threshold of tolerance for relative discomfort may be approached or even passed. Parents will become troubled that they cannot be sure their children's living standard will be higher than theirs was; many will conclude that it will be lower. It will become more

> "TODAY'S LEADERS . . . SEEM TO BE HAVING AS MUCH TROUBLE AS THE PUBLIC IN ACCEPTING THAT CHANGES NEED TO BE MADE."

Soil erosion—another long-term and avoidable problem—can permanently degrade land if not curbed and can cause silting of rivers downstream.

apparent that the entry of women into the labor market since the early 1970s was not just a matter of choice but was in many cases the only way for families to make ends meet. People will become aware that the Japanese and the Europeans are living better than Americans are — and they'll wonder how that could have happened. The United States has demonstrated a high tolerance for ineffectiveness and inefficiency, but one has to believe that at some point there's a limit.

The mounting level of concern will probably translate into a shift

AGRICULTURAL RESEARCH SERVICE, USDA

in voter attitudes and expectations. The campaigns for the 1992 or 1996 elections may begin to address questions about the future and about the changes that need to be implemented now to make that future better for the American people and their children. Interestingly, most of today's leaders who got their starts in the good old boom days will be out of active politics. The debates will be among candidates who entered politics during the last turning point — the 1968-1973 period — when they ran for office as environmentalists, anti-Vietnam-War advocates, and post-Watergate political reformers. They gained office because, for that very brief period, voters were hungry for real reforms. Some of these representatives fought for those reforms, but as their constituents' hunger for change has dissipated, they have settled for marginal adjustments, quick fixes, and numbers games year after year. How these politicians handle shifts in voter attitudes and shape them into mandates for real change will be one of the critical variables in this decade's political landscape. My hunch is that enough of them will take advantage of the opportunity to launch a real reform effort.

Such a grass-roots-driven modernization movement would include an array of policy changes. It could be directed at creating a government that is not just smaller, as the budget deficit dictates, but that is also smarter. In other words:

● A sharp reduction in subsidies to obsolete and inefficient producers.

● A big investment in education and training, in infrastructure, science, and technology — but with a focus on modernization.

● Revisions in accounting and financial practices that would force current producers and consumers to pay for the costs of environmental cleanup and protection rather than passing them on to future generations.

● Restructuring of organizations, simplification of computer software, and widespread training so that there will finally be some real benefits from the massive investments that have been made to bring

---

"THE UNITED STATES [CANNOT] SAIL THROUGH THE 1990s WITHOUT BEING AFFECTED BY THE STORM OF CHANGE OCCURRING AROUND IT."

---

computer technology into the workplace.

● Creating information services that cut through the information glut (which makes managing more difficult than ever) and enable people to see and deal with problems effectively.

● A new social contract that reflects the realities of the two-earner family.

● A shift in the formal and continuing education of the nation's leaders that emphasizes global, long-term, and cross-cutting ways of thinking rather than the currently prevalent short-term, narrow, discipline-based approaches.

● An acceptance of the constant need to monitor changes occurring in the world so that normal problems can be dealt with before they become big messes that can be fixed only through herculean efforts.

Unfortunately, to anticipate that such a transformation could take place quickly and directly is wishful thinking. I do not believe that the United States can sail through the 1990s without being affected by the storm of change occurring around it. How would the nation respond if the Japanese and Germans really acted like its bankers (which they are) and began dictating the terms of U.S. fiscal, monetary, and industrial policies? How would it respond to widespread wars throughout Africa and the Middle East that included the use of tactical nuclear, chemical, and biological weapons? How would it respond to the accidental detonation of a single nuclear weapon? How would it respond if the AIDS virus threatened to spread broadly among the white, heterosexual, non-intrave-

nous-drug-using population? How would it respond to evidence that environmental damage in some parts of the world might take hundreds of years to reverse and that millions of people should be relocated? How would it respond to a really big earthquake — much bigger than the one that hit San Francisco in 1989?

In my opinion, the United States has not prepared well for such contingencies. So far, however, it has been exceptionally lucky, and it has become fairly good at managing crises — at least one at a time. Therefore, it seems likely that the 1990s will not see a cataclysm but rather a long, drawn-out process of gradual change. The country's bankers in Tokyo and Frankfurt will continue to support it, and over the course of the decade the nation will face several discrete and reasonably manageable crises.

This is about as optimistic as I can be. Of course, there is always the threat that the nation's luck could fail and that several crises could converge at once, overwhelming its leaders and political institutions and forcing major changes under adverse conditions, as in the 1930s.

Actions Today

The United States should follow a basic strategy of keeping the current big messes from getting totally out of hand and of acting on opportunities whenever possible. As it makes policy decisions in pursuit of this strategy, three simple, overarching ideas can serve as "guiding principles."

The first need is a way of thinking about and acting on problems that is global, long term, and cross-cutting — to match the nature of the big messes. The second need is to keep in mind that education and training are the keys to success, so when in doubt the country should invest more in learning. The third need is to hold elected leaders personally accountable for managing change in society — for the results both of their actions and of their decisions not to take action.

The need to develop new ways of thinking — my first guiding principle — is critical. The solutions to problems do not lie in the traditional, narrowly defined boxes such as academic disciplines, but in the gaps between them. The flexibility, capacity, and know-how to take the ideas from one box and merge them with those from another are needed. Information systems and reporting procedures that highlight problems before they become big messes are needed. Today, America learns by trial and error — a risky and time-consuming process that requires a long-term perspective and a lot of patience.

Consider, for example, the restructuring of European political, military, and economic relationships that is now going on. This appears to be one of the most complex sets of social changes ever undertaken. One of its remarkable features is that the leaders who are guiding the reform process seem to be attempting to respond in moderation to each other and to each new phase of the situation. This contrasts sharply with the traditional process of change through war or revolution, with whoever wins getting to redesign the social and political institutions. Most individuals involved in Europe's current transition seem to understand that they have made a major shift to a new set of rules and that they are now at the very frontiers of social change, where each day's events must be evaluated to plan the next day's actions. In other words, Europeans are now fully engaged in creating their own future.

The second of my guiding principles for the 1990s — that education is of paramount importance — touches on all areas of U.S. life. Why is learning so important? For the individual, it creates more choices about what kind of work one does and for whom one works, about how one spends one's leisure time, and about how one deals with the growing complexities of everyday life. For employers and for the economy, learning determines the quality of the work force and the company's — or the nation's — relative competitiveness in the marketplace. For society, learning affects the diversity and quality of the organizations, products, and services that are available. For the polity, it sets the electorate's intellectual level and degree of participation, the quality of the candidates, and the richness of the policy choices that are laid out. My approach would be to build into all education programs not only a core of basic knowledge, but also a set of skills that would enable people to keep learning new material and solving new problems throughout their lives.

The third of my guiding principles — that the leader of any type of organization needs to know how to manage change — is likely to become more and more important as the major transitions occurring in the world continue to unfold. Leaders tend to spend most of their time juggling the many current issues — the problems and opportunities — that must be dealt with if their organizations are to operate smoothly and perform a societal function effectively. A leader's job is to understand the forces that are driving the need for change; to sort out those issues that require fundamental change from those that call for only marginal adjustments; to have a sense of the organization's capacity to tolerate shocks and stress and to respond to crises and challenges; to jettison the formula approaches — such as the indexing of benefits to inflation — that have substituted for decision making in the past few decades; and to manage both fundamental and marginal changes in such a way that the short-term and long-term strategies are consistent and mutually reinforcing and comprise a clear and coherent vision of the organization's future.

Although I'm frustrated sometimes by the slow pace at which America deals with the big messes and potential opportunities, each day I read about people and organizations that are taking outstanding and innovative actions along the lines I've advocated here. I am encouraged that, in some places at least, new strategies and techniques are being implemented. I have to hope that these developments will spread and that from the ranks of doers and thinkers will emerge the leaders needed for the nation to navigate safely into the twenty-first century.

National and Global Economy

What do trends in the economy have to do with understanding social problems? Plenty! Economy is society's power to self-heal. With resources of money, materials, and educated specialists available, we can accomplish a great deal. With these resources in short supply, we must choose which programs to promote and which to forgo. In poor nations where people simply do not have resources, social problems must go unattended.

Even though the United States is one of the world's richest nations, its economy shapes the resolve to attack national problems. When economic hard times are anticipated, resources are directed to increasing profits and jobs while denying social needs. How the economy is viewed has a great deal to do with the national attitude for or against spending for social programs.

We begin our readings by taking a look at ourselves as economists. How much economic understanding do you possess? "The High Cost of America's Economic Ignorance" cautions that what we do not know can affect our quality of life. For example, did you realize that during the 1980s, while the rich were prospering, the lowest 25 million members of our society lost 10 percent of their incomes? "The Income Distribution Disparity" tells us that understanding how national wealth is allotted has a great deal to do with whether or not the lower classes can solve their own problems or if they must wait for help from others.

"Will the Third Great Wave Continue?" asks about the future of our nation's wealth. The first "Great Wave" long ago formed today's nations, the second created "free trade" among nations. Currently the "third wave," started after World War II, is making many nations prosperous, but if it slows, the United States might be less able to meet the needs of its own citizens.

"Deadly Migration" combines the news of our losing industry with the problems of pollution. Currently the United States has manufacturers exiting to Third World countries were wages and pollution regulations are lower. The loss of jobs at home is unwelcome news, and the impact on the environment poses international problems as air pollution blows across borders into the United States.

Looking Ahead: Challenge Questions

How well do you understand economic discussions? Where is understanding economics useful to understanding social problems?

How does income distribution relate to social problems?

Would you advocate redistributing national income if it could ease social problems?

What impact would stagnation in international trading have for the United States?

What problems are posed for our society by manufacturing jobs leaving the United States and taking their pollution with them?

Unit 5

The High Cost of America's Economic Ignorance

James A. Lee

James A. Lee is a professor of management at the College of Business Administration, Ohio University, Athens.

> *Add to the long list of subjects about which we are ignorant one more—economics.*

For 20 years I have been tracking college students' lack of knowledge of a few simple economic and related facts. Opinion Research Corporation has been tracking the general public's similar knowledge since 1945. A review of these polls is not good news, and it is especially bad news for colleges and universities. It is clear that the more people we educate, the less they know about profit rates and related economic facts (see the **Figure**).

In 1945, the American public estimated that manufacturers made 18 cents after taxes on each dollar of sales; the actual figure was seven cents. In 1945 we conferred 250,000 college degrees. Both these numbers stayed relatively constant until 1960. However, as the number of degrees conferred began climbing steeply, the American public's overestimates of profit rates also began climbing. Whereas the average estimate in 1945 was only 300 percent too high, the estimate in 1986 of the after-tax profit per dollar of sales had climbed to 32 cents while the actual was four cents, an 800 percent overestimation. The Figure looks the same if the public's profit rate estimates are plotted against the average years of schooling of American adults. In 1945 this was nine years. As average schooling grew to more than 12 years (1986), overestimates of profit rates also grew.

I will discuss how I believe this happened. First, however, what kinds of effects can we expect from such gross ignorance? Common sense tells us that from a management standpoint, if our employees already think we make too much money, they are not going to work very hard to help us make more. Even the majority of business school seniors, when asked "What is the most practical way for workers to increase their standard of living?" check the answer "For all workers to get more of the money companies are already making." The alternative answer offered is, "For all workers to produce more."

Juries would likely be inclined to more reasonable awards in liability cases if they were not so ill-informed about profit rates. And corporations would not have to lobby so hard in Washington, D.C. if constituents had a realistic understanding of profit rates. Voter pressures on congressmen, based on such ignorance, cause the latter to add unnecessary restrictions and regulations on business.

This economic ignorance is not limited to profit rates on sales. Similar polls show that return-on-investment rates are overestimated nearly as much. My polls of business administration students at junior and senior levels (after having taken two courses each of accounting, finance, and economics) strongly suggest that such overestimates are more a function of emotionally guided attitudes than of exposure to samples of real income statements and balance sheets. Since 1969, my classes have variously overestimated ROI rates by several hundred percent. Typically, more than two-thirds believe that corporations make 20 percent after taxes, and one-third think the rate is closer to 40 percent! To show that there is little reasoning involved in these estimates, I typically ask a class what the return on a savings account at the local bank is. They quite accurately answer, "About five to six percent." I

Figure
Number of Degrees Conferred, Public Estimates of Profits, and Actual Profit Rates, 1945-86

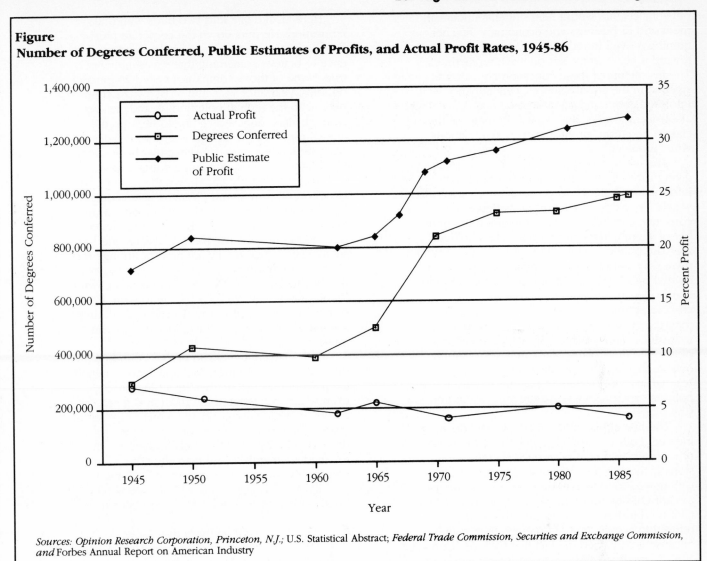

Sources: Opinion Research Corporation, Princeton, N.J.; U.S. Statistical Abstract; Federal Trade Commission, Securities and Exchange Commission, and Forbes Annual Report on American Industry

then ask, "Who, in his right mind, would put money in a savings account if he could earn 20-40 percent after taxes on General Motors stock?" It then becomes clear that the nature of the overestimate is an emotionally conditioned attitude.

It follows then that my students would underestimate the capital investment per job in American industry. They do. They also believe that a greater proportion of business and industry should be owned by the government. Flagrant overestimates fit into this cluster of emotionally loaded ignorance: They overestimate the percentage of nonfarm workers who are members of unions by about 200 percent and grossly overestimate the percentage of job vacancies that are filled by the efforts of government employment services. The directions of their estimation errors are certainly not random, as if they are simply guessing. The answers show a clear pattern.

One of the questions on my poll asks: "How do you think total wages compare with net profits for most business firms?" Answers may be

chosen from the following: "a) profits greater than wages, b) wages and profits about equal, c) wages about double profits, d) wages several times profits." Although wages generally run about nine times profits, 75 percent of my business students believe that profits are greater than wages (answer "a" above).

I cannot believe that this level of economic ignorance is healthy for America, any more than I believe that semi-literacy in language and math and ignorance in science and geography are healthy.

HOW WE ACQUIRE OUR ECONOMIC IGNORANCE

How, then, do we acquire this organized ignorance? Unfortunately, these erroneous notions are picked up from a variety of sources that are not amenable to a simple programmatic cure. Social studies additions to the curriculum over the last 40 years have crowded out subjects that would help students understand the world of business and economics. Teacher training moved to reduce subject-matter training toward a heavy emphasis on teaching methods. The instructors of these education courses are steeped in the social sciences, generally not well informed about and often hostile to such matters as business, profits, and capital. In many of their classes, the term "profit-maker" is synonymous with "profiteer."

The media foster ignorance of business by giving carefully selected scraps of dramatized information designed to get readers or viewers to watch. They typically report gross figures on corporate earnings but do not mention the number of shareholders, nor who the shareholders are. The public is generally kept unaware of who owns, say, Standard Oil of Indiana: 63 percent is owned by 21,215 institutions, including insurance companies, retirement plans, colleges, trusts, charities, foundations, banks, and religious and fraternal organizations; 30 percent is owned by individuals; and 7 percent by Standard Oil employees' savings plans. Many Americans simply believe that large corporations are owned by "capitalists," not owners of paid-up life insurance policies or workers with vested interests in pension plans.

The liberal bias of the media is well documented. Polls consistently show that 80 percent of reporters and editors vote Democratic. Occasionally this bias is not very well concealed. A CBS news (not editorial) announcer once referred to Gulf Oil's quarterly profits as "obscene." When Gulf tried to buy time to correct this image, CBS refused to accept the brief presentation, mainly because it contained the fact that CBS, ABC, and NBC all made greater profits on investment than did the oil industry.

Our universities help the media get further mileage out of their distortions by using their material in the classroom. Frederick Sturdivant's *The Corporate Social Challenge*, a text used in business ethics courses, carried a reprint of an article by Milton Moskowitz (originally published in *The Nation*) that fosters ignorance of actual profit rates. Here is an example from the piece:

> I remember once being at a conference where a corporation president bemoaned the fact that the public seemed to think that companies earned 25 percent on the sales dollar, when, in fact, the average is closer to three percent. I then asked him what about those companies—IBM, Xerox, Avon Products, for examples— which manage to net 25 percent on the sales dollar, year after year. He looked at me with a startled expression and said, "They do?"

Here Moskowitz kills two birds with one fabrication. He puts down the corporate president as ignorant, and persuades his reading audience to believe something that was simply not true. None of those companies netted 25 percent on sales, year after year. But Moskowitz's contributions to the mental pollution of students were assured, since none was going to hunt up the annual reports to verify the assertion. Besides, what student is going to believe that his instructor assigns readings containing outright lies?

Study after study has shown the most popular villain on prime-time TV is the businessman. In "Hollywood's Favorite Heavy," broadcast on March 25, 1987, the Public Broadcasting System pointed out that by age 18, "the average kid has seen businessmen on TV attempt (or arrange for) over 10,000 murders." Narrator Eli Wallach noted that businessmen on TV "seem to make an awful lot of money, without ever having to work hard or produce useful products. To succeed, all they seem to do is lie, steal, cheat, blackmail, even murder."

Both managements and unions contribute to our economic ignorance, too. Managers generally keep silent on most matters regarding profits, even when exaggerated information is given out by others. Unions typically quote earnings before taxes, compare profit gains of a good year to those of a bad year without elaboration (as do the media generally), and typically portray, in their publications, top management as a big fat man lighting his cigar with a $1,000 bill while holding his foot on the back of a worker's neck.

The sources of all these distortions do America a distinct disservice. Until Americans fully understand where jobs come from (ideas, capital, profits, or savings), and that the main source of their job security is the profits that come from the success of their companies' products or services in the market, their motivation to help improve productivity will be lacking.

Perhaps the best defense against this mental pollution lies in educating our young to be wary of these sources of disinformation—the media, social science instructors, unions—about business economics. Schools and managements could also begin by teaching them more accurately about the various roles of profits. They need to be reminded often that profits provide jobs, revenue for government programs, dividends for pension plans and insurance companies, and funds for research and development, and that they stimulate more sales for suppliers and savings for banks. We should move toward eliminating the "dirty" connotation from the word "profits" to the point where people can distinguish clearly the difference between a profit-maker and a profiteer. Many Americans can no longer do this.

The Income Distribution Disparity

Even a disastrous policy blunder is unlikely to lower the real incomes of 25 million Americans by more than 10 percent. Yet that is what happened to the poorest tenth of the population during the 1980s.

PAUL KRUGMAN

Paul Krugman is Professor of Economics at the Massachusetts Institute of Technology. This article is excerpted with permission from his book, The Age of Diminished Expectations: U.S. Economic Policy in the 1990s, *published in 1990 by The Washington Post Company.*

Although the typical American family had about the same real income in 1988 as it did in 1978, this was not true of untypical families: the rich and the poor. The best-selling novel of 1988, Tom Wolfe's *Bonfire of the Vanities*, portrayed an America of growing wealth at the top, a struggle to make ends meet in the middle, and growing misery at the bottom. The numbers bear him out. During the 1980s, the rich, and for that matter the upper middle class, became a great deal richer, while the poor became significantly poorer.

In making this comparison, it is important to be careful about starting dates. The great bulk of the population is better off now than it was in the last year of the Carter Administration or the first two years of the Reagan Administration, when the economy was in a deep recession. That recession, however, was transitory—as we will see later, it was part of a deliberate, bipartisan policy of temporarily raising unemployment in order to reduce inflation. The recession years, therefore, provide a misleading base for comparison. The

more appropriate comparison is with a time of more "normal" unemployment, which puts us back to 1979. When one does this, the growth in inequality is startling.

One recent study concludes that, after adjusting for changes in family size, the real income before taxes of the average family in the top 10 percent of the population rose by 21 percent from 1979 to 1987, while that of the bottom 10 percent *fell* by 12 percent. If one bears in mind that tax rates for the well-off generally fell in the Reagan years, while noncash benefits for the poor, like public housing, became increasingly scarce, one sees a picture of simultaneous growth in wealth and poverty unprecedented in the twentieth century. The same study estimates that the fraction of Americans who are "rich" (defined by an arbitrary but constant standard) nearly doubled from 1979 to 1987, even while the fraction of families defined by the U.S. government as living in poverty simultaneously increased by 15 percent.

Even these numbers probably fail to capture the full extent of what has happened, because they miss the real extremes. The ranks of the extremely well-off were reinforced by the vast fortunes made by traders and investment bankers on Wall Street, and by huge increases in executive compensation. Meanwhile, the amount of sheer misery in America has surely increased much faster than the official poverty rate, as homelessness and drug addiction have spread.

Long-term comparisons of income distribution are fraught with difficulties, but for what it is worth, standard calculations show that the surge in inequality in the United States after 1979 reversed three decades of growing equality, pushing the income shares of the top and bottom categories to their highest and lowest levels, respectively, since 1950. Since measures of inequality in 1950 were magnified by widespread rural poverty, it is probably safe to say that income distribution within our metropolitan areas is more unequal today than at any time since the 1930s.

While some conservatives do not consider income distribution a valid issue for public concern, the changes in that distribution in the 1980s had a far more important effect on people's lives than any deliberate government action. After all, even a disastrous policy blunder is unlikely to lower the real incomes of 25 million Americans by more than 10 percent; yet that is what happened to the poorest tenth of the population during the 1980s. Not everyone agrees that the soaring inequality of the 1980s was a bad thing, but it is a simple fact that the growth of both affluence and poverty in the 1980s largely reflected changes in the distribution of income, rather than in its overall level.

An extra $1,000

There are at least two reasons for arguing that the increased inequality of the 1980s changed *overall* welfare for the worse. First, most Americans do care at least a little bit about how well-off others are, and it is hard to argue with the conclusion that an extra thousand dollars of income matters more to a poor family than to someone whose income is already in six digits. Second, the income distribution colors the whole tone of society: A society with few extremes of wealth or poverty is a different, and surely more attractive, place than one with a yawning gulf between rich and poor.

In the long run, income distribution is not as important a determinant of economic well-being as productivity growth, but in the 1980s increasing inequality in income distribution, rather than growth in productivity, was the main source of rising living standards for the top 10 percent of Americans. And the 1980s were the first decade since the 1930s in which large numbers of

Americans actually suffered a serious decline in living standards.

Yet income distribution, like productivity growth, is not a policy issue that is on the table. This is partly because we don't fully understand why inequality soared, but mostly because any attempt to reverse its trend appears politically out of bounds.

One reason that action to limit growing income inequality in the United States is difficult is that the growth in inequality is not a simple picture. Old-line leftists, if there are any left, would like to make it a single story—the rich becoming richer by exploiting the poor. But that's just not a reasonable picture of America in the 1980s. For one thing, most of our very poor don't work, which makes it hard to exploit them. For another, the poor had so little to start with that the dollar value of the gains of the rich dwarfs that of the losses of the poor. (In constant dollars, the increase in per family income among the top tenth of the population in the 1980s was about a dozen times as large as the decline among the bottom tenth.)

To tell the story of what happened in the 1980s, it is necessary to paint a more complicated picture. At least three separate trends have combined to make our society radically less equal. To begin with, at the very bottom of the scale, the so-called "underclass" grew both more numerous and more miserable. Entirely unrelated, as far as anyone can tell, was a huge increase in the incomes of the very rich. In between, among those who work for a living, the earnings of the relatively unskilled fell while the earnings of the highly skilled rose.

Let's start with the underclass. While there is no generally accepted statistical definition of the underclass, we all know what it means: that largely nonwhite hard core of people caught in a vicious circle of poverty and social collapse. Attempts to measure the size of the underclass, like those of Isabel Sawhill at the Urban Institute, suggest that it began growing during the 1960s, and has continued to grow, perhaps at an accelerating rate, since then. In the 1960s and 1970s, social programs were expected to cure persistent poverty; in the 1980s they were widely accused of indirectly perpetuating it. At this point it appears that if you increase spending on the poor, they have more money; if you reduce it, they have less; otherwise, it doesn't make much difference. That is, neither generosity nor niggardliness seems to make much difference to the spread of the underclass. Conservatives argue that the welfare system has reduced incentives and contributed to the growth of the underclass; liberals respond that Reagan's cuts in social spending contributed to the growth of the underclass by making it more difficult for the poor to climb out of poverty. Both could be right. The most important causes of the growth in the underclass, however, like the sources of the productivity slowdown, lie more in the domain of sociology than of economics.

The increased incomes of the rich and very well-off present less of a puzzle than the growth of the underclass. While high incomes have been made in a variety of ways, one source stands out above all: finance. The 1980s were a golden age for financial wheeling and dealing, and the explosion of profits in financial operations has helped swell the ranks of the really rich—those earning hundreds of thousands or even millions a year.

Most Americans live between the stratosphere and the lower depths, and for them the growth in inequality has been yet a different story. First, there was the yuppie phenomenon: the rise of two-income families with $50,000 or more in annual income. Second, wage differentials among occupations widened: the real wages of blue-collar workers have declined fairly steadily for the past decade, and earnings of highly educated workers have risen rapidly. (The ratio of earnings of college graduates to those of high school graduates declined during the 1970s from 1.5 to 1.3, then rose to 1.8 during the 1980s.)

What we really don't know is why these phenomena have all happened now. The rise of two-income professional couples reflects the lagged effects of the women's movement, plus the aging of the baby boom generation. The surges in pay differentials and in market manipulation are more mysterious. Politics may have had something to do with it. The Reagan years provided a tolerant climate both for tough bargaining with workers and for financial wheeling and dealing. Other forces, like the decline of smokestack America and the consequent restructuring of the U.S. economy, may also have played a role.

What to do?

Whatever the reasons for soaring inequality in the 1980s, what can policy do about it? In particular, can anything be done about the extremes of wealth and poverty that have emerged in the past decade?

The problem with poverty, as an issue, is that it has

Poverty has become so much a part of the American scene that the general public no longer has the sensitivity it did in the 1960s; at the same time, the wealthy have become wealthier. Developing a policy that will lessen the extremes of wealth and poverty appears to be the real social and economic challenge of the 1990s. (UN Photo/P. Sudhakaran)

165

basically exhausted the patience of the general public. America launched its War on Poverty in the 1960s—a time of rising incomes and widespread optimism about government activism. This "war" was supposed to be social engineering, not merely charity. It was intended not simply to raise the living standards of the poor, but to help them work their way out of poverty. Yet poverty did not decline. Despite sharp increases in aid to the poor between the late 1960s and the mid-1970s, poverty remained as intractable as ever, and the underclass that is the most visible sign of poverty grew alarmingly. Today, relatively few people believe, as so many did in the 1960s, that government can do much to help the poor become more productive; all that it seems able to do is raise their standard of living by giving them more money (and influential books, like Charles Murray's *Losing Ground*, deny even that).

But if aid to the poor is simply charity, then its political base is nothing more than public generosity. In a time of budget deficits and largely static living standards for the average American, such generosity does not come easily. There are some modest signs of a resurgence of social activism; money may eventually become available to deal with the conspicuous poverty of the homeless; and Congress has made an effort to reform the tax system to help the working poor. But any systematic initiative to raise the incomes of the poor seems unlikely for many years.

As for the rich, a few public policy initiatives might cut down on some of their sources of income. For example, tighter regulation of financial markets might limit the number of people with incomes in the tens of millions, and a cooled-off financial market might indirectly put some limits on executive pay. For the most part, however, the only way to make the rich less so is to tax them. Yet this conflicts, or is perceived to conflict, with other policy goals—such as encouraging risk-taking and entrepreneurship. Given that the deepest problem with the U.S. economy is slow productivity growth, it is difficult to argue for tax increases that might reduce incentives, even if some people make large sums in return for dubious contributions. In effect, there seems to be a public consensus that Donald Trump is the price of progress.

So income distribution, like productivity growth, is a policy issue with no real policy debate. The growing gap between rich and poor was arguably the central fact about economic life in America in the 1980s. But no policy changes now under discussion seem likely to narrow this gap significantly.

ECONOMIC INTEGRATION

WILL THE THIRD GREAT WAVE CONTINUE?

Paul W. McCracken

Paul W. McCracken, Edmund Ezra Day University Professor Emeritus at the University of Michigan, is a former chairman of the President's Council of Economic Advisers. From July to December 1986, he was interim president of the American Enterprise Institute, and he is presently a member of its Board of Trustees.

Is the third great wave of international economic integration coming to an end, or can it be extended into the decades ahead?

In an influential address over a quarter-century ago, AEI Senior Fellow Gottfried Haberler identified two earlier waves of economic integration. This underappreciated giant of economics (to use Nobel laureate Paul Samuelson's phrase) began this presidential speech to the American Economic Association with a discussion that has a surprisingly contemporary ring. "We live in the age of integration," he said. "Every conceivable—or inconceivable—combination of countries has been proposed, more-or-less seriously, as a candidate for integration. . . . With the formation of the European Economic Community, [with] the European Common Market as a going concern, integration has passed from the talking stage, where it had remained for many years, into the stage of concrete realization. The example of the Common Market, besides spawning a rival European combination (the European Free Trade Agreement), has induced the creation of similar schemes in other parts of the world—in South and Central America—and still others are on the drawing board."

Haberler did not go on to analyze the various proposals but instead stepped back to look more broadly at the earlier waves of integration and the threats to them, including constriction of a liberal trading order and slowdowns in employment and growth in the industrial countries—conditions present today. It is instructive to look back at Haberler's formulation, certainly to appreciate its sagacity, but also to review his warnings for us today, particularly for our relationship with the economic powerhouses emerging in Asia.

The Three Waves

The first great wave of economic integration was the internal integration of the economies of the present-day nation states, first in the United Kingdom in the eighteenth century, then in France and the United States, and somewhat later in many others. The second was the movement toward free trade in the nineteenth century, which crested toward the end of the 1870s.

The third wave started soon after World War II and gathered momentum quickly, and it, too, has been phenomenally successful. Throughout these years, the volume of world trade has grown more rapidly than world output, indicating that a persistently rising proportion of world output has been crossing national boundaries on its way to market. From 1950, close to the beginning of this third movement, until 1973, world output increased at the rate of 6 percent per year while the volume of trade increased more than 8 percent per year. Rates of

increase in world output and trade since 1973 have settled at somewhat more modest levels, but the proportion of world output moving in international commerce has grown steadily.

Contrary to the cliché that this growth has made the rich nations richer and the poor nations poorer, the pattern is more complex. Average per capita real income has been rising more rapidly in the low-income nations than in the middle- and high-income nations, according to the World Bank's annual *World Development Report*. There are, however, some exceptions; most are in Africa, with a few in the Western Hemisphere. Since 1965, Uganda's per capita real income has been declining by 3 percent per year. Some other names on that unfortunate list are Chad, Madagascar, Zambia, Jamaica, and El Salvador. In this year's *World Development Report*, 19 of the 121 countries listed lost ground. In his introduction to the report, Barber Conable, president of the Bank, foresees 3-percent annual growth for the industrial world but an average of better than 5 percent for the developing countries in the 1990s.

Asian Integration and Internationalization

One area of the world, Asia (particularly East Asia), has benefited more than others from the growing internationalization of the world economy, mostly from the movement toward free trade that characterized the second wave of integration. My first trip to Japan was in the 1950s. One did not need to resort to statistics to see that Japan was then a poor country. Almost all of the guests at the then-new Imperial Hotel (now an annex to a newer, larger building) were Americans. Visitors took home lacquer ware, cloisonné, silk, and other items in whose production a low-wage country had a comparative advantage. Heavy cargo carts were being drawn behind bicycles. I visited a little company in a decrepit building in the Nagoya area that produced a pathetic product that many thought would never sell outside Japan. The company was Toyota.

I have visited Japan almost annually since that time, an experience akin to looking at a motion picture one frame of film at a time. The bicycle cargo carts gave way to motorized tricycle trucks, which gave way to thoroughly modern trucks. Outside Nagoya now is Toyota City, the auto company's vast industrial complex where it manufactures its trend-setting array of products.

When we look beyond Japan, we see economies such as Korea, Taiwan, Malaysia, and Thailand now in the ranks of middle-income countries. And there are other positive developments. Indonesia, the fifth-most-populous country in the world, has reduced the incidence of poverty from 60 percent of the population to 20 percent in two decades, according to the *World Development Report* for 1990. Singapore and Hong Kong are now listed as high-income economies, with per capita GNPs that are higher than those of Israel and some members of the European Economic Community. Japan's per capita GNP is now listed as second only to that of Switzerland; it is 60 percent above that for the United Kingdom and 6 percent higher than our own.

Whose Advantage?

Clearly, this explosive pace of economic development has been good for the Asians, but has it been good for us in the Western world? Most of us, of course, live better because our shirts come from China, our microwave ovens from Korea, the semiconductor chips embedded in our equipment from Kuala Lumpur, and for some of us, our cars from Japan. No turgid research monograph is required to conclude that as consumers our material levels of living would drop sharply if we were directed to buy only products made here at home.

As these Asian economies have industrialized, however, we have found ourselves with head-to-head competition from a growing array of producers there, and that competition is producing widespread anxiety. Is the current advantage for the American consumer transitory? Does industrialization there extinguish a comparable volume of production here? Is it the cause of, or does it contribute to, the Rust Belt, the hollowing of America, deindustrialization—the ominous indications of decline we have heard discussed in recent years?

Trade and competition have clearly been good for the American economy as well as the Asian, yet we tend to see Asia's march toward industrialization as a zero-sum game. We think that if Japan produces a car and sells it here, one less car will be produced here. If Japan has more employment, we will have that much less. For understandable reasons, it would be hard to persuade an unemployed U.S. auto worker otherwise; however, this perspective ignores the dynamics of the process. How much we sell abroad depends for the most part on the prosperity of our customer countries. Rising levels of income are achieved for most countries through industrialization, which in turn leads to more opportunities for head-to-head competition with other countries.

We see how this works immediately when we look at our own trade mosaic. Our largest-volume trading partners are high-income, and therefore industrially advanced, economies like Canada, Japan, Germany, and the United Kingdom. Bangladesh does not cause us many competitive headaches, but neither is it much of a market for U.S. output. The proportion of our output of goods and services finding a market abroad has more than doubled since 1960 (see Table 1); much of the gain occurred during the 1970s when the Asian industrial economies were emerging.

Table 1: U.S. Exports and GNP
(Dollar amounts in billions)

Year	GNP	Exports(a) Amount	% GNP
1950	$288.3	$14.5	5.0%
1960	515.3	29.9	5.8
1970	1015.5	68.9	6.8
1980	2732.0	351.0	12.8
1990(b)	5409.4	660.5	12.2

Notes: (a) = Exports of goods and services, national amounts definition; (b) = First half, annual rate.

Source: U.S. Department of Commerce.

When we look at the pattern of U.S. foreign trade, we see the growing importance of Asia. Three decades ago, Asia was a market for one-fifth of our exports, and 18 percent of our imports came from there. By the late 1980s, the area accounted for almost 30 percent of our total export market, and over 40 percent of our imports came from there. The vigorous economic development of the area in recent decades that has been giving our industries so much competitive pressure has also generated the purchasing power to make them a major and rapidly growing export market for us (see Table 2).

Two centuries ago, David Hume recognized this two-dimensional nature of economic progress when he observed in "Of the Jealousy of Trade," an essay: "Not only as a man but as a British subject, I pray for the flourishing commerce of Germany, Spain, Italy, and even France itself."

How Will We Fit In?

What are the implications of an increasingly integrated world economy? Whatever the answer, history suggests that the question is an important one. This century has already seen one great spasm of international economic disintegration that began about 1930, though its roots went back to the 1920s. Worldwide depression was probably a major factor among the forces leading to World War II, but within the ambit of purely economic considerations, it was a disaster of Brobdingnagian proportions. Gottfried Haberler has calculated that the world volume of industrial production on the eve of World War II was almost double that on the eve of World War I but that the volume of industrial products in international trade was actually less. The consequences were significant: inefficient use of productive resources and unnecessarily lower material levels of living.

A continuation of the great movement toward an increasingly integrated world economy in the era ahead is going to pose more-complex problems than we have seen in the years since the end of World War II. If I were a citizen of one of the East Asian economies, I would be concerned as I look at the world economy, for several reasons.

The history of the earlier waves of international economic integration suggests that two sets of factors were particularly important in their reversal: major changes in the pattern of trade and stagnation of the domestic economies. When trading patterns shifted, displacement pressures seemed to be too large and too rapid for nations to absorb politically. The large increase in European wheat imports from America, for example, played a role in cooling sentiment for freer trade in the nineteenth century. In the second case, sluggish domestic economies in Europe in the nineteenth century brought economic integration to a halt, and we saw again the damaging effects of poor domestic economic conditions on the world economy in the two decades between the world wars, especially in the 1930s.

Both conditions are present today. The rapidity and scope of East Asia's economic development and trading influence have clearly imposed pressures and strains on export markets, generating domestic political demands here and in Europe for restrictions. And the less-optimistic outlook for the U.S. economy has accentuated pressures here for relief from foreign competition.

Moreover, the structure of the world economy that emerged after World War II—which was particularly conducive to an expanding economic order—has been changing. It was an aggregation of sovereign nations, with one, the United States, having the scope and strength to exert a hegemonic influence on the shape and direction of international economic developments and policy. This was epitomized by the international monetary system, in which all other countries defined their currencies in terms of the U.S. dollar and the dollar itself was

defined as 1/35th of an ounce of gold. Trade barriers were being worked down under the General Agreement on Tariffs and Trade (GATT) on a multilateral basis. And the results were highly promising.

For a variety of reasons (some inevitable, some unfortunate), this multilateral and hegemonic structure is becoming decidedly rickety. It was never our, nor anyone else's, objective for postwar international economic policy that per capita incomes in other countries should forever remain at low levels relative to ours. That this gap narrowed, and for Japan and Western Europe closed, simply indicated that economic policies were succeeding. A side effect, obviously, has been the inevitable diminution of our hegemony.

Unfortunately, that diminution is being exacerbated by the deteriorating performance of our own economy. Until 1972, in terms of real purchasing power, average earnings from a week of work were rising about 20 percent per decade—not a dramatic gain but enough for people to be able to assume that better days were ahead. If that trend had continued, earnings (assuming current prices) would have been about $560 per week in 1990, compared to the roughly $350 that the U.S. economy actually delivered. Indeed, the American economy is delivering today an average weekly pay envelope that has substantially less purchasing power than it did 20 years ago. The causes of this are complex and not particularly well understood. This can be explained in part by the growing practice of adding value to pay by giving nonwage benefits. But it also reflects a fundamental deterioration

of the American economy's capability to perform—a deterioration relative to its own history and relative to the rest of the industrial world.

For a concatenation of reasons, therefore, our hegemony and authority have weakened. If that simply meant that the aging ruler still has the instincts but must be content with more modest expressions of them, the American sense of machismo would be bruised, but we—and the world—could survive that. It may mean more, however. C. Fred Bergsten, director of the Institute for International Economics, warns in a recent *Foreign Affairs* article: *The world economy has enjoyed prolonged periods of stable prosperity only when under the stable leadership of a single country—the United Kingdom in the latter part of the nineteenth century and the United States in the first postwar generation. It has never experienced successful "management by committee."*

We may have no choice but to make the best of it if indeed the United States can no longer wield hegemonic authority. Furthermore, the world economy is not just a framework of individual countries and overarching organizations such as GATT, the IMF, and the World Bank. We now exist as clusters of nations, with the emergence of the European Economic Community, the Canada–U.S. Free Trade Area, and perhaps another including Mexico. (Mexico is now our third-largest export market and a middle-income economy, a fact many Americans don't know.)

How free-trade areas fit into a liberal trading order, what the internal requirements are for their success, how they can be made to move us toward rather than away from a generally liberal order—these are questions for another day. The EEC, of course, has far-larger objectives than trade and has had the basic support of the U.S. government going back to the Treaty of Rome (1957). If I were a citizen of a country in Asia, however, I would feel apprehensive about the free-trade-area momentum. These alliances can easily divert trade rather than create trade. They do not necessarily encourage a greater volume of world trade, and the two major areas are apt to divert trade away from Asia.

Another problem may be even more fundamental. Clusters of national economies work better if there is a leader. Economic success and power are constituent parts of the capability to lead,

Table 2: Pattern of U.S. Foreign Trade
(Percent of total)

	Exports			Imports		
	1929	1960	1987	1929	1960	1987
The Americas	36.9%	37.4%	37.5%	36.8%	46.9%	29.1%
Canada	18.1	18.4	23.6	11.4	19.7	17.5
Cuba	2.5	1.0	–	4.7	2.7	–
Mexico	2.6	3.9	5.8	2.7	2.7	5.0
Europe	44.7	35.9	28.7	30.6	29.3	24.0
U.K.	16.2	7.3	5.6	7.5	6.8	4.3
France	5.1	3.4	3.1	3.9	2.7	2.6
Germany	7.8	6.3	4.6	5.8	6.1	6.7
Asia	12.3	20.4	29.0	29.0	18.4	43.0
Japan	4.9	6.8	11.2	9.8	7.5	20.8
Oceania	3.7	2.4	2.6	1.3	2.0	1.0
Africa	2.5	3.9	2.5	1.5	3.4	2.9

Source: Basic data from the U.S. Department of Commerce.

but they are only part of what makes an international leader. The leader's governing ideology and culture must be attractive to others, attractive enough for others to be inclined to follow. In the European Economic Community, there is a clear leader—Germany—and economic policy in the Community is made *de facto* at the Deutsche Bundesbank. In Asia, by contrast, Japan clearly has the economic dominance and power, but it would have more difficulty with the noneconomic requirements for leadership. And the United States can play that role in an enlarged North American trade area.

Even if agreement could be reached, a Pacific Free Trade Area that would include the three major countries in North America and the industrial economies of Asia would raise a whole set of additional questions. Indeed, would the various free-trade-area clusters, under the euphemistic banner of free trade, devolve into fortresses whose relationships would move further away from a liberal world order? At this juncture,

the world economy seems to be uncertain about whether to continue moving multilaterally or to organize by free-trade areas. For the Asian industrial economies, which way decisions go is of substantial importance.

Our Resolve

How all of this works out depends importantly on whether the United States can come to grips with its own policy problems. Our basic economic problem is well known and can be stated simply. We save about 16 percent of our gross national income each year. About 90 percent of this annual savings flow is required to finance the private economy—mortgages, business borrowing, consumer financing. The remaining 10 percent (now roughly $85 billion) is available for the government. If the government deficit is larger than that, we require foreign funds to balance things out. That requires high interest rates to attract these funds, and rates

would go much higher yet if foreign investors were to conclude, as some do now, that here is not the right place for their funds.

What worries the rest of the world is the apparent erosion in our capacity to govern. Therapeutic action equal to a small percent on each side of the budget would restore equilibrium, but our institutions of governance seem incapable of this. It is sobering to note that this is the first time since World War II that foreign funds have run from, rather than turned to, the U.S. dollar.

I once alluded tongue-in-cheek to McCracken's Law, which goes something like this: "In this country, we finally turn and grudgingly do the right things, but only after trying everything else first." Therein may be cause for optimism, for we surely must be close to the end of that list.

The gains for all nations from the three waves of economic integration have been too important for any nation, including the United States, to slow the momentum.

Deadly Migration

HAZARDOUS INDUSTRIES' FLIGHT TO THE THIRD WORLD

JOSEPH LaDOU

JOSEPH LaDOU, M.D., is chief of the Division of Occupational and Environmental Medicine at the University of California, San Francisco. As a director of the International Commission on Occupational Health, he has traveled extensively to investigate working conditions and to establish training programs in occupational and environmental medicine in newly industrialized countries.

In 1988, a California manufacturer of epoxy coating materials decided that it could no longer afford to make its products in the United States. The cost of complying with new emission standards for the solvents the products contained would simply have been too high. Yet the company learned that if it set up shop in Mexico, it not only could use the same solvents but could dump wasted solvents at no cost into the arroyo behind the plant.

It's no secret that the low cost of manufacturing in Third World and newly industrialized countries has prompted thousands of First World corporations and investment groups to set up manufacturing operations there. The biggest lure, of course, is cheap labor—factory wages in countries such as Thailand, Bangladesh, Ghana, Guatemala, and Bolivia are often as low as 5 percent of those in industrialized countries. Companies also manufacture abroad to be closer to foreign markets and to overcome trade barriers. In return, the host countries reap significant benefits. According to the U.N. Environment Programme, foreign companies and investors have provided 60 percent of all industrial investment in developing countries over the past decade. For many nations, such investment is the primary source of new jobs.

But the industrial migration has a perverse side, the extent of which the California epoxy case can barely hint at. As developed nations enact laws promoting en-vironmental and occupational safety, more and more manufacturers are moving their hazardous and polluting operations to less developed countries, most of which have either no environmental and worker-safety regulations or little power to enforce those that are on the books. Hazardous industries have migrated to many parts of Africa, Asia, and Eastern Europe. Japan, for example, with its limited land and dense population, has a pressing need to export manufacturing industries such as electronics, chemical production, and metal refining. And many European nations have exported hazardous industries such as textiles, petrochemicals, mining, and smelting.

There is an ironic twist to the problem. Countries that spend little on things like sewage systems, water treatment plants, and enforcement of environmental and occupational safety can offer tax rates dramatically lower than those in the industrialized world. Foreign-based manufacturers take the bait and move in, polluting waterways and endangering workers. Yet the host government can't afford remedies because of the low tax rate.

Pollution and working conditions are so bad that, in effect, the Industrial Revolution is taking place all over again, but with much larger populations of workers and in many more countries. And many of the resulting deaths and injuries are taking place with the complicity of First World companies.

The Faces of Exploitation

The practice of using less developed nations as a dumping ground for untreated factory waste is but one of many forms the export of industrial hazards can take. Industries whose markets in developed countries are shrinking because of environmental concerns are vigorously promoting their products in the less health-conscious Third World. DDT is a compelling example. Its worldwide production, led by U.S. and European companies, is at record levels, even though it has been illegal to produce or use the pesticide in the United States and Europe since the 1970s.

Asbestos is another distressing example. To stimulate the development of companies that will produce asbestos products, Canada's government sends free samples of the material to a number of poorer countries, where many workers and communities are still unaware of the mineral's dangers. (Bangladesh received 790 tons, worth $600,000, in 1984.) Partly as a result of such promotion, Canadian asbestos exports to South Korea increased from 5,000 tons in 1980 to 44,000 tons in 1989. Exports to Pakistan climbed from 300 tons to 6,000 tons in the same period. Canada now exports close to half its asbestos to the Third World.

The First World also exports entire industries—including most lead smelting, refining, and product manufacture—that present occupational hazards. In developed nations, companies using processes that involve lead are required to take costly precautions to protect workers. U.S. lead workers must receive special training, have proper work clothes and changing facilities, and go on paid leave if tests reveal high lead levels in the blood. But in the lax regulatory climate of Malaysia, most lead-acid battery workers—at both foreign- and locally owned plants—have lead levels three times as high as allowed in U.S. workers. And lead plants exported to India continue operating even though 10 percent of the workers have lead poisoning.

Even a migrating industry that doesn't involve toxic materials can be hazardous, because First World corporations often apply a double standard to worker safety. At home, they might comply rigorously with health and safety regulations. Abroad, the same companies let safety standards plummet to the levels prevailing in the less developed host country.

Those levels are miserably low. Worker fatality rates are at least twice as high in industrializing countries, and workplace injuries occur with a frequency not seen in the developed nations since the early years of the Industrial Revolution. Workers in poor countries—usually with limited education, skill, and training—tend to labor in small, crowded factories with old, unsafe machinery, dangerous noise levels, and unsound buildings. Protective gear is seldom available. The companies also tend to be geographically scattered and inaccessible to health and safety inspectors.

On learning of such conditions in India or Malaysia, we in the First World may wince but may also be tempted to put them out of mind—to regard them as a Third World problem from which we are comfortably remote. Yet Americans need look no farther than their own southern border to find some of the worst

instances of migrating industries' disregard for human health and environmental safety. Many of the factories that U.S. and other foreign interests operate in northern Mexico freely pollute the water, the air, and the ground and subject workers to conditions nothing short of Dickensian.

The Siesta of Reason

In 1965, Mexico sought to overcome chronic unemployment through the Border Industrialization Program, designed to lure foreign manufacturing business—mainly from the United States—into Mexican border states. The country's government hoped that foreign capital would flow into the economy along with modern production methods that would help create a skilled workforce.

Under the program, manufacturers send raw materials and equipment to Mexico. If they agree to take back the finished products, they need pay taxes only on the value added in Mexico instead of on the value of the entire product. Another big draw is that factory wages average about $5.40 per nine-hour day, less than in Korea, Taiwan, Hong Kong, and other countries long favored for off-shore manufacturing. For U.S. investors, the cost of transporting goods and materials to and from northern Mexico is lower as well.

Today, nearly 1,800 factories operate under this program in northern Mexico, employing about half a million workers. The plants, known as "maquiladoras," extend from Tijuana in the west to Matamoros on the Gulf of Mexico. Their owners include some of the largest U.S. corporations: IBM, General Electric, Motorola, Ford, Chrysler, General Motors, RCA, United Technologies, ITT, Eastman Kodak, and Zenith. Japan's Sony, Matsushita, Hitachi, Yazaki, and TDK also run maquiladoras, as do numerous European companies.

Most maquiladoras are small plants with fewer than 100 workers. In the program's early years, they were largely clothing manufacturers and hand assembly operations, employing mostly women. Today maquiladoras manufacture or assemble a wide range of products, from automobile parts to high-technology electronic components. Men now account for close to 40 percent of the workforce.

No one disputes that the main goal of the Border Industrialization Program has been met. The estimated $3 billion in foreign exchange earnings that maquiladoras pump into the Mexican economy each year now exceeds revenues from tourism and is second only to Mexico's oil and gas exports. Virtually all the new manufacturing jobs created in Mexico in the past decade—and a fifth of the country's manufacturing jobs overall—resulted from the rapid growth of the maquiladoras.

Yet these benefits have come at a high cost. The Border Industrialization Program has created serious social and environmental problems in both countries, but especially in Mexico. The prospect of employment in maquiladoras has caused the populations of border towns and cities to swell. Since 1970, for example, Nogales (south of Tucson) has grown fourfold to 250,000, and Juarez (across the Rio Grande from El Paso) has grown from 250,000 to 1.5 million.

Overcrowding strains these municipalities beyond their limits. Tens of thousands of workers subsist in cardboard huts in squatters' camps without heat or electricity, and sewage is dumped into the arroyos, through which it flows to the nearest river or estuary. At least 10 million gallons of raw sewage from Mexico flows into the Tijuana River every day, polluting San Diego's beaches. The Mexican government is so hard pressed to deal with the problem that the U.S. government, the state of California, and the city of San Diego have agreed to pay most of the $192 million cost of a treatment plant on the border.

But maquiladoras do more than just overburden sewers. Many owners and managers—especially of small maquiladoras engaged in metal working, plating, printing, tanning, and dyeing—readily admit that they moved their operations to Mexico partly because hazardous processes are unwelcome in the United States and other developed countries, and that Mexico is not creating any serious obstacle to their activities. As one owner of a furniture factory explained to me, "I can find lots of Mexican workers in the United States. What I can't find here in Tijuana is the government looking over my shoulder."

Indeed, the very terms of the Border Industrialization Program seem to encourage recklessness. Many foreign companies or investment groups set up maquiladoras through the Mexican government's "shelter program," whereby the parent company—typically known only to the government—maintains control of production and a Mexican company forms to act as co-manager. This shelter firm recruits, trains, and pays all the Mexicans in the workforce. It also manages relationships with the local community and with the Mexican government. In short, foreigners run the business while their Mexican partners see to the social tasks. Because it is a Mexican corporation, the shelter operator shields the foreign company from liability in case Mexico ever cracks down on violators.

Consequently, the foreign operators have little incentive to make sure the 20 million tons of hazardous waste that maquiladoras generate each year is properly disposed of. No data are available on how much of this waste is deposited in rivers and streams, the air, or the ground, but the volumes are enormous. For example, the New River flows northward from Baja California into California contaminated by industrial wastes such as chloroform, benzene, toluene, xylene, and PCBs, and by agricultural runoff that contains various pesticides,

including DDT. The river also carries more than 20 million gallons of raw sewage each day.

California has evaluated numerous alternatives to protect community health and Imperial Valley agriculture. The cheapest solution is to provide the Mexican city of Mexicali with a wastewater collection and treatment system, following the approach proposed for Tijuana sewage. The U.S. Environmental Protection Agency may eventually have to take similar action for all the major cities and towns along the U.S.-Mexico border. In that event, the U.S. taxpayer would ultimately pay for the reduced cost to industry of manufacturing in Mexico.

Mexico's lax monitoring of industrial practices encourages dumping of hazardous waste. Under Mexican law, toxic materials brought in by plants for use in manufacturing—such as paints, cleaning solvents, oils, and acids—must be returned to the country of origin or recycled in Mexico. But according to the Texas Water Commission, only about 60 percent of these waste materials leave Mexico. The other 40 percent—much of it toxic, the commission reports—is disposed of illegally in Mexico's sewers, drainage systems, and landfills. When waste is returned to the United States, it is often transported in improperly packaged and labeled containers.

Dirty Work

Just as the amount of illegally dumped waste is difficult to pin down, so too is hard information on working conditions in maquiladoras. Not only do U.S. and Mexican maquiladora managers deny investigators access to their plants and their workers, but the Mexican government discourages inquiries and health studies. What's more, the U.S. Department of Commerce refuses to share its list of companies participating in the maquiladora program so as not to discourage them from complying with reporting procedures.

High worker turnover rates—6 to 15 percent per month in the states of Chihuahua, Sonora, and Baja California—also make it difficult to survey health effects in maquiladoras. Controlled studies are almost impossible with such an unstable employee population.

What investigators have been able to piece together is that while working conditions in the maquiladoras vary greatly, they are in most cases far inferior to those required in developed countries. Many plants are inadequately ventilated and lighted. Accidents resulting from inattention to safety procedures and the absence of safety equipment are frequent. Nogales maquiladoras reported more than 2,000 accidents in 1989—three times the accident rate of comparable factories on the U.S. side of the border. Sanitation is poor, production quotas are high, noise is often excessive, and machinery is often unsafe.

Workers also receive few rest periods and must perform long hours of microscopic assembly work. And even though many workers regularly handle hazardous materials—especially organic solvents—protective clothing, gloves, and other safeguards routinely required of U.S. industry are rare. To make matters worse, the workers lack safety instruction on the hazardous materials they are using—again a U.S. requirement.

Some plants even allow workers to take home empty contaminated steel drums that once contained hazardous chemicals such as pesticides, solvents, acids, and alkalies. Thousands of these containers are used to store water for domestic purposes throughout the industrial regions of Mexico.

Because of a dearth of studies, the amount of harm caused by such exposure is essentially unknown. But the case of Matamoros, the town where the former U.S. company Mallory Capacitors operated a maquiladora for many years, raises alarming possibilities. The Matamoros School of Special Education has identified 20 retarded children whose mothers were pregnant while employed by Mallory and required to work with PCBs, highly toxic chemicals used in the company's products. PCBs were banned in the United States in 1977 because of their toxicity.

The Matamoros exposures occurred for full workdays over many months. The women often had to reach into deep vats of PCBs with no protection other than rubber gloves. Many of the workers developed the chloracne rash these chemicals typically cause. Recent medical studies in Taiwan and Japan of pregnant women exposed to PCBs reveal the same sort of retardation as in the children of Matamoros. It is very likely that many more children damaged by their mothers' work at Mallory live in other Mexican towns that health researchers have not yet studied. And Matamoros may not be the only town in Mexico where PCBs have caused retardation.

Why does Mexico allow these environmental and occupational abuses to continue? One reason is a lack of resources to combat the problem. SEDUE (Secretariat of Urban Development and Ecology), Mexico's environmental oversight agency, faces financial constraints that limit its ability to regulate the maquiladora industry.

But political constraints play a role as well. The Mexican government enthusiastically supports the maquiladora program. Should SEDUE become too aggressive in its efforts, the government might withdraw the meager environmental funds the agency does receive. Municipal governments also operate from a precarious position. If they complain about hazardous waste dumping or unsafe working conditions—or if they press for taxes to support better sewage treatment facilities, schools, and medical care—the owners might move the plants to other cities or even other countries.

Despite these problems, Mexico has made some progress in environmental regulation. In May 1989,

SEDUE required all plants to obtain water discharge permits indicating their compliance with Mexico's rather liberal laws on toxic waste treatment. They may then dump the treated water into the sewer system. Any plant violating this requirement can be fined up to $70,000, and those responsible face a prison sentence of six years. But like most environmental laws in developing countries, this threat is made by an agency that lacks the full backing of its government and the resouces to carry out its mission. So far, this effort has produced few results, although a number of companies are now consulting with industrial hygienists and safety engineers to ensure that they will not be fined.

The U.S. government, too, is inching toward cleaning up the border—likewise with few concrete signs of progress. The federal Rio Grande Pollution Correction Act of 1988 aimed at dealing with that river's problems. But its limited scope and lack of financial support led to widespread disappointment and an array of further legislative attempts. Congress is now considering legislation to set up a permanent U.S.-Mexican environmental health commission, in which the EPA and SEDUE would work jointly to evaluate the maquiladoras and explore ways of preventing or punishing environmental abuse along the border.

Unfortunately, none of these proposals addresses the fundamental flaws of the maquiladora program, such as its failure to raise enough taxes to improve infrastructure. Given both governments' acceptance of the present system, no law that would attack the problems at their roots has any serious likelihood of enactment in the near future.

An International Approach

The slowness of the United States in dealing with abuses by the maquiladoras is typical of the way First World nations have responded to the problems caused by the export of hazardous industries. Like the EPA, which devotes only about a tenth of a percent of its budget to its Office of International Affairs, the environmental agencies of other wealthy countries are just beginning to develop concern for the consequences of industry's actions abroad. Nevertheless, it is the exporting nations that need to take the initiative.

The host countries, hungry for jobs and foreign capital, cannot be expected to make the first moves to end unsafe and polluting practices—and they often resent outside pressure to do so. Poorer nations take the position that only after they have attained the standard of living that rich countries enjoy will they adopt the restrictive environmental policies of the First World. What's more, these countries generally lack large, well-funded environmental groups like those in Europe and the United States. Popular support for actions that may impede the growth of the job market and a rise in living standards is virtually nonexistent.

Thus the world's industrialized nations will have to work together to end the shameful practice of exporting obsolete and hazardous technologies and industries. International agreements must replace the perverse incentives that threaten the world's environment.

International environmental organizations could help stem many of these problems. The U.N. Environment Programme, for example, has been working with a number of Third World countries to introduce siting requirements for hazardous industries. UNEP is also developing information centers on hazardous materials. The U.N. World Health Organization (WHO) and International Labour Office (ILO) provide some guidance to developing countries on occupational health and safety. But the combined annual budgets of these agencies is only about $3 million, severely hampering their ability to fund environmental research and provide worker education and health inspections. And WHO and ILO have confined their activities mainly to larger employers, while the vast majority of work-sites in developing countries are small.

Other global bodies have made laudable attempts to control industry's behavior. The OECD Guidelines for Multinational Enterprises, the U.N. Code of Conduct on Transnational Corporations, and the ILO Tripartite Declaration of Principles Concerning Multinational Enterprises and Social Policy attempt to provide a framework of ethical behavior. The ILO declaration of principles, for example, recommends that multinationals inform worker representatives about hazards and protective measures. But stronger medicine is needed.

When industry migrates to developing countries, governments and international lending institutions could require environmental impact assessments. The World Bank, along with other international lenders, now offers to produce such assessments when the host country can't. The bank has also taken steps toward requiring poor countries to put occupational and environmental protections in place as a condition for receiving development capital. Similarly, industrialized countries must insist that companies apply the same safety and environmental regulations to their manufacturing operations abroad as they do at home.

As part of this effort, countries need to cooperate to set global standards for occupational and environmental exposures to dangerous substances. Some newly industrialized countries have formulated lists of chemicals and metals that should receive priority regulation and enforcement. Yet these lists often contain laboratory reagents, rarely used chemicals, and other materials not likely to pose occupational and environmental problems, while omitting many highly toxic substances that see broad use. Industrialized countries therefore need to adopt one set of standards with which all companies manufacturing in poorer countries must comply.

So far, both rich and poor nations see the short-term advantages in the export of hazardous industries but turn a blind eye to long-term harm. In the Third World and the First World alike, the risk of future accidents like Bhopal, the cost of environmental cleanup, and pollution's toll on public health are seldom discussed with candor. But as the developed countries have found, the longer environmental damage and hazardous working conditions continue, the greater the cost of remedying these problems once regulations and enforcement are in place. By disregarding such concerns, First World industries are shifting substantial burdens to those least able to bear them.

Global Peace or War

Why include peace or war in a collection on social problems? Because war itself is a social problem—probably the most violent, most feared, and worse breakdown of society. Further, war clearly connects to other social problems when arms expenditures sacrifices social programs. Sociologists point out the United States' "second to none" military preparedness costs have greatly affected homelessness, inadequate schools, and decaying infrastructure. Worldwide, this connection seems especially clear as governments spend large amounts of money for weapons, while failing to address their people's needs for better standards of living.

For over forty years the United States maintained a costly military presence, mainly to contain the might of the U.S.S.R. Recently, the motives for that spending have changed. The intricate balance of world power has shifted. Eastern Europe has broken from its communist governments, and Western Europe has joined in an economic community. Where the United States will stand internationally—and how much it will need to siphon dollars for military spending—is an open question.

"America's Century Will End With a Whimper" gives an unflattering prophecy that social problems will pull the United States down to where it cannot lead internationally. If that becomes reality, it will mean that social problems are the nation's worst enemy.

By evaluating the history of Europe's behavior over the centuries, "Myths of European Unity" explores the prospects for Western Europe becoming one nation-like union. The author wonders whether old jealousies and traditional fictions might once again keep Europe disunited. The article shows Europe's long history of social unrest, and discusses whether or not the unification of Europe could have a direct impact on the economy and social policies of the United States.

"The CIA Connection" accuses an agency dedicated to the United State's foreign policy with being a prime cause of the drug problem in the nation's streets. Can foreign policy—supposedly working "outside" the nation—be involved with a social problem "inside" the nation? Read this article to learn how.

"The Roots of Muslim Rage" reminds us of the potential for peace or war in the Middle East. It stresses how important understanding local culture is when analyzing international events. Has the United States always promoted the best policies for relaxing cultural tensions when dealing with Muslim nations?

"Military Victory, Ecological Defeat" puts a definite damper on the national joy over the Persian Gulf War result. War harms the environment. To see the results, review the conditions in Kuwait and Iraq where oil spills, burning oil wells, and destroyed chemical plants continue to pollute the environment and endanger health.

Looking Ahead: Challenge Questions

How likely is it that social problems within the United States will reduce the nation's position within the world community?

What features within European culture will work against achieving strong unity in modern Europe? What does this mean for the future of the United States?

How might it be that the CIA, an instrument of U.S. foreign policy, could produce a serious drug problem in the streets of this country?

How might the United States use an understanding of Muslim values to promote peace in the Middle East?

How can the ecology be the big loser in a modern war? What international actions might be taken to protect the environment from the ravages of war?

Unit 6

America's Century Will End with a Whimper

A German forecasts the decline of a superpower

DER SPIEGEL

WERNER MEYER-LARSEN

In 1941, Henry Luce, the editor of *Time*, decided that the era now ending should be known as "the American century." He was right. Almost 50 years later, the West—above all, its ruling power—has won the cold war. "Countless people all over the world," brags Alvin Toffler, author of the best-selling book *Future Shock*, "are eager to embrace the Western, meaning the American, way of life."

And American protection. When Iraqi dictator Saddam Hussein invaded Kuwait last summer, there was only one land that the emirate's neighbors could call upon for emergency assistance: the U.S. But at home in America, everything looks very different. The American century is dragging inexorably to a close, and not a single cry of triumph can be heard. "There is a groundswell of opinion in this land," says John Chancellor, the respected television commentator, "that in recent years something has gone terribly wrong here."

The decline of America is an idea that was discussed in the U.S. for several years and then rejected. But now it seems that the great majority of Americans no longer have any confidence. Against a background of the grandiose march into the Persian Gulf, with the prospect of a real war, fear of inflation and recession is spreading.

The American people show signs of wanting to stop their country's economic, social, and political erosion. But to do so will require resolve and changes in almost every sector of the country: industry, finance, education, and government. The problems facing the country are daunting.

Superpower America can no longer pay for what it undertakes, can no longer develop what it will need in the future, can no longer produce what it needs. The nation's finances are overextended. The Gulf crisis may cost up to $100 billion, causing the federal budget deficit to zoom up to $250 billion or $300 billion. Interest must be paid on more than $3 trillion of government debt, including the cost of the savings-and-loan collapse.

From the newsmagazine "Der Spiegel" of Hamburg.

As a result, President George Bush must go begging for money to pay for his expeditionary corps. The U.S., the world's policeman, is trying to sell itself as a security-guard company.

The world power is exhausted, a nation at the end of its rope. The 40 years of cold-war militarization, superpower status, and the role of world policeman have gravely wounded the nation's economy and society. They have turned the U.S., in spite of its wealth and human capital, into a land that increasingly exhibits Third World symptoms:

• Every year, 2 million Americans leave school without having learned to read and write;

• 37 million Americans do not have health insurance;

• Almost a fourth of all children younger than six, and about half of all black children younger than six, live beneath the official poverty line. In the cities, infant mortality rates resemble those in traditionally agrarian lands.

Critics of America have fixed on a single guilty party when it comes to explaining the nation's decline: former President Ronald Reagan. But the decline began long before he took office. Only the extent of the damage is a result of the years of illusion under the Great Communicator. Reagan, with a clear grasp of what the great majority wanted, fed the nation a powerfully addictive drug: He built up the most expensive and powerful military machine in the history of the world—while pumping up endless consumption, financed through tax cuts and foreign capital. It is true that the military buildup forced the Soviet Union into an arms race that it eventually had to abandon. But domestically, the president and his California mafia opened the gates for a replay of the robber-baron years of early American capitalism.

The wartime economy unleashed by Reagan created boom and bust zones, distorting the country's industrial structure in ways as dramatic as they were dangerous. Research money was followed by streams of capital going to the military-industrial complex, and both captured the nation's top scientific talent. This slowly but surely ate away at America's industrial competitiveness. The per

From *World Press Review*, January 1991, pp. 24-29. Reprinted from *Der Spiegal*, of Hamburg, Germany.

capita investment in civilian research and development in America has been far lower, for many years, than in Japan and Western Europe. The result: American business, with the exception of perhaps space and satellite technology, is no longer leading the world as it did 20 years ago. For example, in 1975, the first 15 places on the *Fortune* 500 list of the world's largest companies included 11 American corporations. Now there are only seven. Further, in the early 1970s, America's computer industry controlled 90 percent of the U.S. market. By 1990, Japan had surpassed it in many areas.

The Japanese are eating their way up the electronics food chain," says a representative of the American Electronics Association, a trade group. Hans Wiesendanger, who works on patents at Stanford University, says that American companies are often unwilling to pay the costs of turning basic patents into production technology. This has already cost America its photo, audio, and video industries.

For almost a century, America had a balance-of-trade surplus. In 1971, the deficits returned—$2.7 billion worth. Since 1985, the trade deficit has been at that level every week. Direct American investment overseas also has not kept pace. As late as 1970, Americans invested $75.5 billion in foreign lands, while non-American companies pumped only $13.3 billion into the U.S. economy. In 1989, Americans invested $374.4 billion overseas, while foreigners brought $400.8 billion into the U.S. Because the Japanese have invested heavily in high-visibility projects, Americans are especially unnerved by Japanese investments. A Japanese car, the Honda Accord, is the most popular car in the U.S.

The fact that the Accord, produced in America, has achieved the highest quality rating in the country contradicts the popular notion that American industrial workers are careless, unwilling to work, and stupid. It is not their fault that so many defective products emerge from the assembly line—the problem is with management.

Corporate America follows different rules from those of Japanese or European firms. U.S. executives look only at quarterly financial results and pay more attention to stock prices than to investment or market share. Meanwhile, Americans save less than 6 percent of their incomes, only a third the Japanese rate and less than half of what Germans save. Further, Americans are consuming 3-4 percent more than they create in wealth.

The heads of the country's savings-and-loan institutions used the slackening of government regulation during the Reagan administration to increase their profits, legally and illegally. The losses incurred during this spree, which could rise as high as $1 trillion, will be borne by the taxpayers. On top of the disaster at the savings and loans came the blows to the commercial banks. They have been hurt by the S&L crisis, uncollectable Third World loans, and risky domestic lending. The government estimates that 35 major banks may collapse.

Along with Wall Street investment banks, the commercial banks allowed themselves to be drawn into another variant of the great American money-instead-of-productivity spectacle—the so-called Rebuilding of Corporate America. This "reconstruction" was invented by a clique, centered around financial magician Michael Milken, that bought companies with borrowed money. To secure their loans, they offered as collateral not their own fortunes, but the net worth of the company they wanted to buy. The entire deal hinged on short-term financing, which was taken care of by so-called junk bonds. The takeover artists, once successful, had two alternatives when it came to making their big profits. They could let the company they had taken over assume the debts run up during the takeover and install a management that would make Draconian cuts, or they could sell off parts of the firm.

These takeover artists tricked the public by claiming that they were forcing American industry to become more efficient. In fact, though, the companies often were forced to pay off the debts incurred by their buyers and had to sell off their major assets.

Once stagnation set in, the whole takeover game collapsed, leaving behind billions in losses. The winners were the takeover artists, stockholders, and lawyers. Even Milken, who has been sentenced to prison, still has millions of dollars from his maneuvers.

Financial adventures, the debt mentality, and the quest for quick profits have brought American industry to ruin. Banks and corporations are not able to keep up with Japanese or European competitors.

The situation for the U.S. has been made worse by the internationalization of competition. According to Jean-Claude Derian, an economic adviser to the French government, 1970 was the year "of the historical turning point when world economic competition began .... As the world's largest market for high-tech goods and the most open market in the world, the U.S. was condemned to be the arena in which the new trade war was fought."

But the American system reacted exceptionally passively to the country's loss of competitiveness. Instead of expanding internationally, many American banks closed their branches overseas. Instead of throwing themselves into new investments to yield higher productivity, entire industries in the U.S. simply gave up. Henry Luce's successor, Henry Grunwald, wrote recently, "In many ways, American business has let America down."

While finance and business have faltered, the social structure of America has been thrown into disarray. New York vividly exemplifies what the entire nation is going through. One in 100 New Yorkers is homeless; one in 300 has AIDS. Every four-and-a-half hours, someone is murdered; every six minutes, someone is robbed; every four minutes, a car disappears. To restore the city to a state of relative health, almost the entire gross national product (GNP) of the U.S. would be required: Lewis Rudin, chairman of the Association for a Better New York, estimates the cost of reconstruction at $5 trillion.

America's 50 states and thousands of counties form social islands, comprise ethnic niches, and represent particular interests. So the nation has moved toward the arithmetic average of its many identities: No new taxes, and no social redistribution, are what the broad, conservative middle class demands, thwarting any attempt even to maintain the status quo.

Twenty-five years ago, all of this was quite different. It was then that President Lyndon B. Johnson promised his citizens the Great Society: first-class schools, social support for the elderly, decent housing for the poor, health services and safeguards against disaster for everyone. But the money disappeared in the Vietnam war and its aftermath and seeped away during the economic emergency caused by the oil crisis of the 1970s. Social programs, infrastructure maintenance, and school reforms could no longer be financed and were dealt with piecemeal. Thus the rift between the rich and the poor has been widening. Nearly 13 percent of the population—31.5 million Americans—lives below the official poverty line of $12,675 annually for a household of four. Minorities are particularly affected: More than 30 percent of blacks and 26 percent of Hispanics—but only 10 percent of whites—earn less than this amount. And many of them are working at full-time jobs; about 7 million Americans do not earn enough from their jobs to lift themselves above the poverty line.

At the same time, the country has some 1.5 million millionaires. Here one finds the 800 highest-paid captains of industry, an elite group that in 1989 had an average annual income of $1.3 million and $40 million in stock holdings. In 1980, American managers earned 40 times as much as industrial workers; in 1989, they earned 93 times as much. On the other hand, the salary of the industrial worker went down. The average salary in countries such as Switzerland, Denmark, Norway, Canada, and Japan is higher than it is in the U.S.

At the same time, America allots about 48 percent of its total budget—a good seventh of the GNP—to social programs. Eight hundred billion dollars—the equivalent of nearly 70 percent of the GNP of West Germany—are earmarked for social redistribution in capitalist America. But without an effective plan, the nation is pouring a large portion of this money down the drain.

America's social policy does not have an overall structure. Instead, it has grown out of a patchwork of legislation created as the situation demanded, or by congressional representatives who sought to gain votes by giving something in return. Congressmen have passed laws on behalf of the elderly, the homeless, single mothers, and veterans. And once a program is put into effect, it is never terminated. The result: The city of New York and the nation pay up to $4,000 a month to house one family in a hotel for the homeless, where drugs and violence are rife. The rent alone is three times higher than the poverty-line income. Giving cash so that the family can move out of the city would be a better alternative.

Similar disparities exist between expenditures and results in American health care. Americans pay $600 billion a year for medical care, 50 percent more than they do for education and about twice as much as for the military. Yet compared with other countries that pay far less for their health, the U.S. gets pitifully little in return. In child mortality, life expectancy, and visits to the doctor, the U.S. occupies last place among the major industrialized countries.

The only successful assistance program is Social Security, which has provided security for working people in their retirement years. Yet the prospects for a successful life before retirement are becoming steadily worse. One important reason is that the public school system is falling apart. "If a hostile foreign power had attempted to give America the bad education that it has today," the National Commission on Excellence in Education has warned, "we would have viewed it as an act of war."

In 1989, the National Geographic Society found that 24 million adult Americans could not locate their own country on a map of the world. A survey by the National Assessment of Educational Progress revealed that 84 percent of college students knew when Abraham Lincoln died, but only 25 percent knew why he had waged the Civil War. The Council on Competitiveness has determined that 60,000 teachers of mathematics and the natural sciences are not fully qualified for their positions. Only a quarter of high-school graduates can solve a math problem that requires more than one step.

One-quarter of school-age children can neither write correctly nor read at a satisfactory level. Since 1985, every fourth student in high school has failed to earn a diploma and has dropped out of school.

According to a 1985 finding by a White House commission headed by John A. Young, chief executive of the U.S. computer company Hewlett-Packard, this is particularly bad news, because the highest dropout rate—from 40-45 percent—is found among the fastest-growing segments of the population of the U.S.: blacks and Hispanics. "It is clear that the competitiveness of American industry is threatened when many young workers lack the basic skills for productive work," he says.

Each year, the U.S. spends more than $350 billion on various school programs that, like much in the U.S., grew out of a patchwork of federal legislation. Individual school districts and their communities finance schools through property taxes. The average property tax of a rich community such as Stamford, Connecticut, amounts to $5,443 per year; that of a poor one such as Monroe, Alabama, comes to $128. Whenever the community cannot or does not want to pay, the educational system deteriorates, and the more affluent members of the community whisk their children off to private schools.

If American society is clearly divided along class lines, it is even more so within the educational system. Families from the underclass often give up any thought of getting a better education for their children, because they lack information. Blacks go into the military if they want to become something, and the middle class resorts to affordable state universities. It is mainly the children of the wealthy who attend elite colleges such as Yale, Harvard, Princeton, or Stanford. The two-tiered educational system has given rise to a superbly educated elite in positions of leadership and in the research divisions of the large corporations, but down below there gapes a dangerous abyss.

All American companies have to pay for the incompetence of their employees. "The mistakes range from the office worker who provides incorrect information to manual workers who measure things incorrectly, to the laborers who allow the machines to break down—all because they cannot read well enough," writes Leonard Lund of the Conference Board, a business-research organization.

Apart from the colossal cost of misguided social policies and the financing of the school disaster, there is another steadily rising cost factor: The U.S. leads the world in crime. There are many excuses and explanations for this: the clash of the First and Third worlds in the street; the symbiosis of poverty and poor education; the envy felt by the forgotten third of society; the collective aggression of a nation of immigrants; the drug catastrophe; and ever-present racism.

An almost erotic affection for guns, inherited from the pioneers, is responsible for the highest murder rate in all of the industrial countries. In 1989, 21,500 people were murdered in the U.S., about 60 percent by people with handguns. Over the past 15 years, more American citizens have met their death through firearms than the U.S. military lost in the second world war.

America's police forces are not lax when it comes to slapping on the handcuffs—7.3 million Americans were arrested in 1989. Some 3.7 million Americans, constituting nearly 2 percent of the adult population, are under continual supervision by prison or police authorities. The number of prisoners in federal and state penitentiaries rose from 250,000 in 1975 to 710,000 in 1989. All of this takes money, which a nation needs to maintain its productivity. The U.S. does not even have the money to maintain its infrastructure.

America's long-distance highways are dilapidated. Tens of thousands of overweight trucks and hundreds of thousands of private cars use the highways in congested metropolitan areas, yet the roads date from the Eisenhower era, when only half as many cars were on the road. Throughout the nation, some 40 percent of all river and road bridges are considered hazardous. In the San Francisco area, traffic has been hopelessly snarled since the 1989 earthquake. There is no money to rebuild.

The erosion of roads, bridges, schools, and industry in the U.S.—and of the social fabric itself—is accompanied

"An almost erotic affection for guns, inherited from the pioneers, is responsible for the highest murder rate among the industrialized countries."

by political decay. Thirty years ago, John F. Kennedy said, "Ask not what your country can do for you; ask what you can do for your country." Ronald Reagan, says television commentator Chancellor, "stood Kennedy on his head." The state, condemned as big government, became the enemy.

The Reagan revolution was not only an economic and social shock but also a political one. The motto was: a lid on charity and a free rein for Rambo. The dollar was the yardstick of political morality. The Reagan mafia undermined the pillars of democracy: Three of the four political powers—the presidency, the Congress, and the press—coalesced into a cartel that neutralized any check on the government. That the fourth power, the judicial branch, remained intact, for the most part, is due largely to the longevity of its senior justices. The power cartel posed a danger to the fundamental ideas of the constitution that made America the most modern country in the world.

The Reagan revolution, however, attempted to turn America into an oligarchy. It pushed for the rigorous leadership of an upper class: a form of rule by people who kept their money safe in numbered accounts in Switzerland. With catchy slogans about national pride, a future life of luxury, and anti-communism, Reagan's circus of illusion branded every form of opposition by the notorious East Coast intellectuals as liberal (meaning "crypto-communist"). No one who wanted to be re-elected spoke out against the dismantling of social programs. The media glossed over the creeping metamorphosis of the democracy into oligarchy. Not once did television news stars Dan Rather, Peter Jennings, or Ted Koppel, all experienced journalists, take Reagan on. Under such Byzantine circumstances, the administration of this popular president could do almost whatever it chose.

The president's game of lowering taxes and raising military expenditures was supposed to move the Democrats in Congress to bury their aspirations for social and political reform in the face of the mounting deficit. Every discussion of the deficit improved the conservatives' chances of restructuring society. Vital future programs fell by the wayside: Money was lacking for energy research, technological development, and education. "Our country used to have dreams," says Chancellor. "We dreamed of independence, and we got it. We dreamed of becoming a continental power, and we became it. Our immigrants dreamed of a different life in prosperity, and they created it. We dreamed of the moon landing and carried it out. But where are our dreams now?"

Reagan's successor provides few answers. Before he was elected president in 1988, George Bush expounded on his incomprehension of the "vision thing."

How is America supposed to reform itself without a reform president? How will the people be motivated without the "vision thing"? The U.S. is perforce giving up on its fascination with the Golden Eighties and turning its attention to being a normal democratic society. To do this, the nation must reverse the downward spiral of the dollar by removing cyclical weaknesses, doing away with waste and excess, and reforming its industry. But this puts great demands on 250 million people. To, in turn, strengthen the dollar, the country must look to its policies on energy, immigration, and industry.

For decades, America's productivity derived from its immeasurable reserves of raw materials, the speedy integration of immigrants, and the largest single market in the world. An energy policy that was maintained primarily with domestic reserves lay at the basis of postwar prosperity. Energy companies did not invest in coal, solar, or wind technology but rather bought bargain-price Arab oil. Years later, the bill arrived: Rich in raw materials, America had failed to develop energy reserves.

Likewise, in the 1960s the country lost another prerequisite of its superior productivity: Immigration policies were changed. Before this time, most immigrants were skilled Europeans who were able to work in industry right away. But farmers looking for cheap labor managed to push legislation allowing streams of uneducated Latin Americans into the country. An initiative by Sen. Edward Kennedy of Massachusetts put an end to this trend: Congress passed a bill allowing well-trained immigrants into the country.

6. GLOBAL PEACE OR WAR

Creating an industrial policy will be more difficult, however. Americans have shied away from providing federal assistance for the development of new technologies. The maxims of the free-market economy and free competition are against it. But not once have the computer companies managed to raise the necessary capital. Have American business leaders learned nothing?

The learning process is obviously difficult, and the ideas for reawakening America are generally of a speculative nature. Nonetheless, a country of 250 million people, says historian Paul Kennedy, on the basis of its human resources alone, will not sink to the level of a second-class nation.

Many Japanese agree. "America has to make its way," says Foreign Ministry official Takakazu Kuriyama, in a world "where it is no longer the dominant power, but it is still the leading power among the industrial states." And Kenneth Kaufman, a fund-raising specialist at Stanford University, foresees U.S. growth. "There will be three large economic communities," he says, "one in Europe, one centered in Japan, and one consisting of the U.S., Canada, and Mexico. We'll come off well."

For political scientist Walter Dean Burnham of the University of Texas, however, there is a great deal of cleaning up to be done before the country will shine again. Ronald Reagan waged his last campaign under the slogan, "A New Morning in America." What he had in mind was a promising beginning for a radiant future.

"Now," Burnham says, "it's the morning after."

Britain and Europe 1992

Myths of European Unity

Alan Sked

Alan Sked is senior lecturer in international history and convener of European studies at the London School of Economics. His latest book is *The Decline and Fall of the Hapsburg Empire, 1815–1918*.

A version of this article first appeared as an occasional paper published by the Bruges Group, London.

ALL NATIONALISTS require a mythological view of the past in order to sustain their political beliefs and rally support for their cause. Those Europeans who now argue the case for what is, in effect, a united European "nation" are no exception. The only difference between these European nationalists and previous ones is that they themselves repudiate nationalism even as they espouse it, doing so under the illusion that nationality as a concept presupposes linguistic and cultural unity. It does not, of course: as we shall see, cultural unity is not all that difficult to manufacture after the event, and linguistic diversity is no great obstacle.

The main instrument of contemporary European nationalism is not language but history, and it is no coincidence that the European Commission has already estab-lished a committee of historians to ensure that history in Europe is taught in the proper "European" manner—the manner, that is, that will support and strengthen the required myths. One of the most important purposes of such myths is to provide a readily available shorthand to determine what—or who—is "good" or "bad" for the cause at hand. As applied to individuals, such judgements pertain to their success or failure in living up to their allegedly proper historical roles.

This process is now underway in Europe. Today, "good Europeans" are those who support European federalism or, as it is rather peculiarly known, "*the* European Ideal." "Bad Europeans" are traitors to the embryonic European nationalism that seeks to create a European superstate, which will in turn restore Europe's natural position at the center of the world. This whole approach invokes a very particular conception of European history built around a cluster of interlocking myths. The purpose of this article is to examine those myths. I identify five of them, and in summary form they are:

Myth One: "*The* European Ideal" tran-scends nationalism. Its aim is to bring nations together and prevent war from breaking out again in Europe. Opponents of "*the* European Ideal" wish to divide Europe into antagonistic national groups.

Myth Two: Europe is not, as Bismarck said, merely a "geographical notion" but a cultural unity formed from a shared historical experience. This experience is a cumulative one which begins with the ancient Greeks and thereafter follows a peculiarly "civilized" route through history via ancient Rome, "Christianity," the Renaissance, the Enlightenment, and the French Revolution and comes to a climax with the creation of the European Community. This will soon become a federal Europe which will finally enthrone Reason in the world, thus saving it from the more primitive values of American materialism, Soviet and Chinese communism, Islamic fundamentalism, and Third World corruption.

Myth Three: Europe, in any case, has the right to stand at the center of world affairs. America, after all, is the offspring of Europe, as is Latin America. Communism in all its forms is a bastard child of European socialism, while Third World nationalism is once again the product of European thought. Finally, for most of the previous millennium Europe has dominated the world in terms of technology, ideology, and politics. Only since 1945 has it ceased to be the major actor in world affairs. It is therefore natural that Europe should once more resume a central position in world politics.

Myth Four: The creation of European unity since 1945 has been the work of a number of great idealists, headed by Jean Monnet. The idealism of these continental statesmen has been continually frustrated by Great Britain, a country led by "bad Europeans," which even today under Mrs. Thatcher is determined to stop the "inevitable" creation of a federal Europe.

Myth Five: Europe will never be able to play its true role in world affairs unless it is united. Unity will bring both strength and influence. Bigger is better. Unity will enable Europe to defend its interests in the world as well as to increase its prosperity.

Let us now examine these myths in turn to see whether "*the* European Ideal" really stands up to historical and political analysis.

The Myths Examined

MYTH ONE: "*The* European Ideal" as I have just described it is the vision of an historic civilization gaining political unity within its natural frontiers. Clearly these frontiers are not "national" ones, at any rate not in terms of linguistic unity. Nevertheless, the process envisioned is exactly the same as that which brought about the creation of nation-states such as Germany and Italy in the nineteenth century. Moreover, the examples of India, Switzerland, and the United States clearly demonstrate that it is possible to create a nationalism in a linguistically diverse population. What is needed is a sense of identity which can be manufactured using historical myths and political propaganda. This is exactly what happened with nineteenth-century European national cultures. National histories were written, often incorporating national folk-myths, and a nationalist press came into being which propagated the political cause. It is true, however, that revolutions and wars were often required before nation-states were finally established.

On the other hand, it should not be accepted that the nationalism of the nation-state inevitably leads to war and should be scorned on that ground alone. This is simply another myth. After all, nationalism has many advantages: it reconciles classes, smooths over regional differences, and gives ordinary people a sense of community, pride, and history. European nationalists are themselves seeking precisely those benefits from "*the* European Ideal." It is therefore ironic that they should blame nation-state nationalists exclusively for war, since a strict account of modern European history shows that wars were brought about largely by the refusal of supranational, dynastic states—the Ottoman, Hapsburg, and Napoleonic empires—to allow for national self-determination. Likewise, in the twentieth century, it was the Kaiser's bid for world power (*Griff nach der Weltmacht* in Fritz Fischer's famous phrase) and Hitler's racial mumbo jumbo which led to world conflict. In short, it has been the apparent redundancy of the nation-state and the yearning for continental power-bases which in previous centuries has more than once led to the negation of "European civilization."

Had Wilhelm II or Hitler—or for that matter Franz Joseph or Napoleon—been prepared to allow nation-states to exist (or come into existence peacefully), nationalism would not today have incurred such discredit and the nineteenth-century liberal ideal of free peoples living peacefully in nation-states might today still be the ideal, rather than the norm. In any case, states of all sorts—national, dynastic, communist, or other—have always found enough excuses besides nationalism to go to war. Whether it succeeds in creating a unified state, European nationalism is in itself no greater a guarantee of peace than any other political movement, cause, or ideology. Nor is it a guarantee against any future war of secession or civil war such as has happened frequently in other multinational or supranational federal states, and is now threatening to erupt in Gorbachev's Soviet Union.

MYTH TWO: For many people there exists such a thing as "European culture" or "European civilization." Ask them to define it and they are usually at a loss. Nevertheless they are likely to insist that Europeans are different from Chinese, Africans, or Arabs. At base, this concept is really just a racial or geographical notion, the same in fact which used to excite nineteenth-century explorers when they came upon other "white men" in remote lands among primitive tribes. In this sense, of course, "European" includes American, since Americans in the nineteenth century were regarded as just another branch of the white European race.

On the other hand, since America's rise to world power, Europeans have become keener to firm up their ideas about exactly what it is that makes them European—hence the much invoked historical odyssey from ancient Greece (Athens, of course, not Sparta) to modern Brussels. The objections to this way of interpreting Europe's past are fairly evident. It is so obviously selective—and on a variety of levels—that it clearly draws on propaganda rather than history. This remains true whether that history has been written by H.A.L. Fisher, H.G. Wells, or John Bowle. There really is little point in treating European history as if the Greeks existed only in ancient times; as if fascism and national socialism were not an integral part of the story; or as if Christianity did not divide Europeans as much as it united them.

It is not even plausible to claim Greece, Rome, and Christianity as essentially European civilizations. Greece and Rome were Mediterranean cultures with major centers in Africa, Asia Minor, and the Near East. Alexander the Great, it should be remembered, chose to conquer the civilized world in Egypt, Persia, and India. He was unaware that he was doing so in the cause of European civilization. Greece and Rome were followed by other Mediterranean civilizations—Byzantium and the Turks. Byzantium, like the Western Roman empire after Constantine, was a Christian power. Yet, Christianity, it should also be recalled, arose in Palestine from Jewish roots and was thus a Mediterranean religion. Although Christianity spread, it did so in a way that divided as much as united Europe. The Eastern church refused to recognize the leadership of Rome, which was also rejected by much of Western Europe after the Reformation. The result was that Russia and parts of Eastern Europe developed a different culture from that of Western and Central Europe, while for centuries religious wars and rivalries divided the Continent. Meanwhile, the Mediterranean tradition still survived. The Turks were only slowly driven out of Europe (the battle of Lepanto in 1571; the siege of Vienna in 1683; the Balkan Wars of 1912–13), although even today Turkey is a member of NATO and a candidate for full membership in the European Community. When the great French historian, Fernand Braudel, wrote on the age of Philip II, he chose the title "La Mediterraneé et le mond mediterraneén à l'époque de Philippe II." He did not write about the *European* civilization of that era.

Finally, despite the pretensions of Mitterrand's France, the legacy of the French Revolution cannot be claimed as a unifying force in European history either. As Mrs. Thatcher pointed out, that legacy was hardly liberty, democracy, and civil rights, but the opening of a Pandora's box of passionate ideologies which caused as much division as unity.

Europe, in truth, has been the home of many civilizations, often at the same time, with mixed results for the human race. It is facile and unhistorical to pretend that they have been a cumulative or a unifying force. To quote Geoffrey Barraclough, a historian who gave much thought to this matter: "Civilizations do not add up. The extraordinarily impressive portrait head of Yarim-Lun, King of Alalakh in the eighteenth-century B.C., the Hermes of Praxiteles, and Raphael's Sistine Madonna are not stages in a continuous development towards artistic perfection; each is the expression of a distinct civilization." The same is true of Egyptian pyramids, Doric temples, and Gothic cathedrals as far as architecture is concerned. And the same is true once again regarding literature. Aristophanes, Virgil, Shakespeare, Goethe, and Dostoevsky are not links in a chain. They do not add up to "European culture," but reflect different European cultures.

Today it is difficult even to talk of a contemporary European culture. Europeans read their national newspapers and watch national television programs. Over and above they may dine at Indian and Chinese restaurants (not to mention McDonald's) or watch American films, soap operas, and pop videos. They belong therefore both to their national cultures and to a cosmopolitan Western one based on jeans and junk food. To state that they belong to a specifically European culture is to indulge in an act of faith.

MYTH THREE: The relationship between Europe and the superpowers feels unnatural to many Europeans. After all, since roughly the time of the Renaissance, Europe has been at the center of world affairs—voyages of discovery, colonial acquisitions, rising living standards, agricultural and industrial revolutions, modern theories of government, the building of world empires, the spreading of "civilization," and much else. Russia during most of this time has had to "catch up" with Western Europe, not dominate or threaten it. Until recently (1917 or, better, 1945) even the United States has had only a passive role to play in world affairs, being invited to redress the balance of the Old World only when the European balance itself had spun out of control. Normally, the world was expected to revolve around a European axis.

Today many Europeans are hoping that this situation may once again prevail. Having recovered their confidence since 1945 they profess dismay at U.S. and Soviet diplomacy. It is true that the Soviet Union never enjoyed much support in the West, but since the death of Kennedy, the reputation of the United States has also suffered a great decline in Europe. The war in Vietnam, the overthrow of Allende, Watergate, the Carter years, the Iran-*contra* affair have all made Europeans decry the poor leadership and policies of successive American presidents. Whether President Bush's impressive performance in forging a coalition against Saddam Hussein in the initial stages of the Gulf crisis will do anything to modify this trend remains to be seen, and will depend on how the crisis is resolved. In any case, it is conveniently forgotten that most European countries themselves have had a similar, patchy record, with France in Vietnam, Algeria, and Madagascar; the British at Suez and in Cyprus; Spain, Portugal, and Greece suffering under dictatorships as recently as the 1970s; Italy with P–2, the Red Brigades, and the Mafia; Belgium with intractable linguistic problems; Ireland with the IRA; West Germany with the Baader-Meinhof gang and the *Berufsverbot*. European "experience," it is assumed, will do the trick. Once again it is conveniently forgotten that it was "European experience" that forced America into the role of world leader in the first place.

Finally, it is overlooked that Europeans have found it extraordinarily difficult to agree on anything. Until very recently, the Continent was divided along ideological lines. In Western Europe, only some states are members of NATO, only some members of NATO are full members, and many European states still prefer neutrality. Even on an issue such as terrorism it has proved enormously difficult to achieve any common policy. There are wide differences of opinion on economic and social policy and on the fate of different parts of the world, such as the Middle East, South Africa, and Latin America. What then does Europe really have to offer in terms of world leadership?

MYTH FOUR: For many Europeans—especially the "good" ones—the fact that European unity has not yet been achieved is due above all else to the diplomacy of the United Kingdom. This is *the* myth of the postwar European past. Continental Europe, it is said, was led by the founding fathers, Monnet, de Gasperi, Adenauer, Schuman—idealists all—while Great Britain, under Attlee and Bevin, Churchill and Eden, frustrated their work. Postwar European history, therefore, is written in much the same style as that of European Civilization or the Ascent of Man. Instead of the Stone Age leading to the Bronze Age leading to the Iron Age leading to the Machine Age, or Greece leading to Rome leading to Christianity leading to Modernity, we have the story of the Council of Europe leading to the Schuman Plan leading to the Pleven Plan leading to the Treaty of Rome leading to the Single European Act. The obvious destination of future European history is a United Europe. But although this plan has been carved out on tablets of stone in Heaven, Britain, now in the guise of Mrs. Thatcher, is once again offering satanic opposition to the forces of light.

The true history of postwar Europe is very different. For a start, the Continent was not full of idealists in the late 1940s and early 1950s and the country that pushed hardest for European unity was not France, Germany, or Italy, but the United States. Imitation is the sincerest form of flattery and Americans were convinced that if federal union could work well for them, it could also do the same for Europe. They surprisingly overlooked the fact that Europeans speak different languages, had been burning and bombing and otherwise exterminating one another for the previous six years, and that the Continent contained more war criminals than "federasts" (the term coined by Dutch foreign minister Stikker in 1948 to describe federalists). Little wonder that America's plans went askew. However, since the Americans were threatening to link Marshall aid to European unity, the Council of Europe was proposed by the French as a means of playing along with them (whilst also serving domestic political purposes). Much more significantly, the French proved highly unwilling to turn the Organization for European Economic Cooperation (OEEC) into a supranational organization and quickly agreed with the British to limit the scope of the European Assembly quite strictly.

For that matter, neither was the Schuman Plan the simple result of ideological conviction. Monnet needed access to cheap German coking coal to revive heavy industry in France and wanted control of potential German armaments production taken out of German hands. The Italians, for their part, wanted access to iron ores in French Algeria, while the Germans were happy, so soon after

the war, to be treated as anything approaching equals. Britain always rejected supranationalism, but this neither undermined, nor was intended to undermine, European cooperation. Britain had taken the lead on the OEEC in 1947, had built up the Brussels Treaty Organization in 1948, and had promoted the Western European Union in 1955 for Europe's defense. Britain had also taken the lead in persuading the Americans to defend Europe at a time when French defense and foreign affairs priorities centered around Vietnam and *Algérie française* (the latter a rather peculiar European concept which might be taken, albeit rather generously, to represent the Mediterranean tradition in European culture).

The French liked to believe that they were the key to European integration, something which they really only favored when it suited France. They could thus kill off the European Defense Community in 1954 and, between 1963 and 1969 under de Gaulle, both exclude Britain from the Common Market and stop European federalism in its tracks. They even withdrew from the integrated command system of NATO and pursued a foreign policy at odds with their European partners. However, it is Great Britain which is condemned as having been consistently anti-European. This has largely been due to British complaints about a Common Agricultural Policy which has always been recognized as profligate, but which was deliberately designed to suit French interests while keeping Britain out. Today France still attempts to present itself as more "European" than Britain, despite the fact that Great Britain has always complied with Community directives more quickly and comprehensively than France, or any other member state.

M YTH FIVE: Despite setbacks, Europe *is* now approaching the stage where an honest debate is required on its future. Supporters of "*the* European Ideal" demand a full federal superstate, but that of course is only one ideal to choose from among many. Others may prefer some sort of confederation along Swiss lines or an even looser system of cooperation such as exists today. Certainly, if the internal market is completed by 1993, the key question should be: "Is there any need to go further?" Coordination of defense and foreign policies hardly requires new institutions, whilst most other areas of government, such as health, education, and social welfare, should surely not be run from Brussels.

Federalists tend to become emotional when their case is attacked. They say they wish to outlaw war from Europe and that only a federal state will enable them to do this. In fact, peace in Western Europe is already secure under present institutional arrangements and there is no need to go further. On the larger question—whether Europe should become a superstate—federalists often become rather coy. They say they have no desire to create a superpower in Europe, yet they cannot get around the fact that a single European market with a population and GNP greater than America's would in itself transform international affairs. At this point, however, European nationalism often reasserts itself: Why should Europe not equal the superpowers in international affairs?

The question is a natural one but can be answered honestly only by examining the nature of a European superpower. To be organized properly it would require much more in the way of revenues, bureaucrats, and armed forces, as well as more regulation and uniformity. It would also have to assume more responsibilities around the world with no guarantee of being able to execute them successfully. America, after all, has a rather mixed record in international affairs since 1945. It was unable to prevent the Soviet takeover of Eastern Europe; unable to create a United Europe; unable to escape a military commitment to Western Europe; unable to prevent the communist takeover of China; unable to liberate the people of North Korea; unable to win the war in Vietnam; unable to save the Shah of Iran or to rescue American hostages in the Middle East; and more recently unable to forestall the Iraqi invasion of Kuwait. The U.S. is expected nonetheless to intervene everywhere as a world policeman and to spend millions on aiding and defending states around the world whose problems are often self-inflicted.

The Soviet Union, likewise, has a miserable record in international affairs. No advanced country in the world has freely accepted Soviet leadership and, apart from a residual presence in Eastern Europe, it has limited influence only in Cuba, Ethiopia, and North Korea. Yet the Soviet Union has bank-

rupted its economy by spending millions on armaments to protect this dismal empire.

Among the potential superstates, on the other hand, Europe is in a political and economic position similar to Japan. Europe's defense expenditure is limited and its world role is less than it might well deserve to be. Why then give up this favorable situation merely for the role of stumbling giant? The irony is that Europe can only remain really true to its past if it refuses this poisoned chalice, since, for the last five hundred years, disunity has often been its strength. According to Professor E.L. Jones's account of the "European Miracle," it was the "unity" of the Ming, Mogul, and Ottoman empires which sealed the fate of other parts of the world and allowed Europe to take the lead.[1] Professor Paul Kennedy's study of *The Rise and Fall of Great Powers* would not appear to point to any different moral. "Imperial overstretch" is looming ominously before Europe already.

Bigger then is not best. Perhaps we should recall the words of Montesquieu's *Esprit des Lois:*

> In Asia they have always had great empires: in Europe these could never subsist. Asia has larger plains; it is cut into much more extensive divisions by mountains and seas. . . . [I]n Europe, the natural division forms many nations of a moderate extent, in which the ruling by laws is not incompatible with the maintenance of the state. . . . It is this which has formed a genius for liberty, that renders every part extremely difficult to be subdued and subjected by a foreign power.

Perhaps then it is our divisions which have helped to keep us free; our rivalries which have sustained our spirits; and our differences which have contributed to our strength. Certainly, in the future, it will be our determination to remain democratic that will count for most. Our commitment to diversity in liberty must always outweigh the attractions of uniformity.

Recent events in Eastern Europe should also make us stop and think. The Soviet empire has already broken up and the Soviet Union itself may soon do so. If, after further progress in democratization, the Eastern European and Soviet peoples request admittance to the "common European home," we are faced with the prospect of a European state stretching from the Atlantic to the Pacific. To make such a state a federal one would surely be an act of madness. But to create a European Union, League, Community, or Commonwealth along lines similar to those in existence today might just belong to the realms of possibility.

Europeans should refrain from romanticizing their past and should beware of idealizing their future. They should place limits on their ambitions and recognize the advantages as well as the disadvantages of their present situation. Oswald Spengler once compared the motivation behind the construction of the Egyptian pyramids, the Doric temples of ancient Greece, and the

Gothic cathedrals of the Middle Ages. The first he attributed to "inexorable necessity"; the second to "balance and symmetry on a deliberately limited scale"; the third to a yearning for "infinite space." If we must worship at Europa's shrine, let us do so in the spirit of the ancient Greeks, rationally and in a balanced manner. The last thing Europe needs is Gothic horror.

[1]E.L. Jones, *The European Miracle, Environments, Economies, and Geopolitics in the History of Europe and Asia* (Cambridge: Cambridge University Press, 1987).

The CIA Connection

Once it is packaged in plastic envelopes, heroin from Pakistan, Burma, or Mexico is ready for its trip to the United States via an infinite variety of couriers—airline attendants, diplomats, merchants, gangsters—and almost invariably financed and organized by one of the major American distribution syndicates. To the average American who witnesses the dismal spectacle of the narcotics traffic at the street level, it must seem inconceivable that the Government is implicated. But America's heroin plague is of its own making.

Unfortunately, during the long years of the Cold War, American diplomats and CIA agents have been involved in the narcotics traffic at three levels:

¶ coincidental complicity through covert alliances with groups actively engaged in the drug traffic;

¶ support of the traffic by covering up for drug-lord allies and thus condoning their involvement;

¶ active engagement in the transport of opium and heroin.

ALFRED W. McCOY

Alfred W. McCoy is professor of history at the University of Wisconsin, Madison. This article, copyright © 1991, Alfred W. McCoy, is adapted from "The Politics of Heroin: CIA Complicity in the Global Drug Trade" (a completely revised and expanded edition of "The Politics of Heroin in Southeast Asia"), published by Lawrence Hill Books (June 1991).

Such U.S. complicity played a catalytic role in the buildup of Burma's opium trade in the 1950s and the growth of the Golden Triangle heroin traffic in Southeast Asia during the 1960s and 1970s. Official U.S. tolerance for drug dealing by our clandestine allies also occurred in the borderlands of Afghanistan and Pakistan in the early 1980s, rapidly transforming this remote region into one of the world's leading producers of heroin.

Despite the global prohibition of opium and coca sales, a vast illicit industry continues to link the highlands of the Third World with the cities of the First.

Over the past century, peasants of the Andes and the southern rim of Asia have relied on these drugs as their major source of cash. In such remote, rugged regions with costly transport and poor roads, narcotics—with their light weight and sure market—remain the only viable cash crops.

These mountain regions, moreover, provide refuge to rebels who find narcotics, with both production and marketing outside government control, an ideal economic base for revolution. The Asian and Latin American highland zones lie at the

From *The Progressive*, July 1991, pp. 20-26. Adapted from *The Politics of Heroin: CIA Complicity in the Global Drug Trade.*
Copyright © 1991 by Alfred W. McCoy. Published by Lawrence Hill Books.

intersection of trade routes, terrain, national boundaries, and ethnic frontiers that make them natural outlaw zones beyond the reach of most modern states. The merchants who control the opium or coca crop are often legitimate tribal leaders who can mobilize arms and armies to defend their trade. Whether at peace or in rebellion, many highland regions of Asia and Latin America are dominated by narcotics, which create potent political support for the survival of this lucrative trade.

As the raw drugs come down from the highlands, they usually move to centers of secondary services essential to the global traffic—processing, finance, and smuggling. Since the farmers need credit and markets for each new crop, a major expansion of drug production has three requirements—finance, logistics, and politics.

What happened in Southern Asia beginning in the late 1970s is a case in point.

By May 1980, Dr. David Musto, a Yale University psychiatrist and White House adviser on drugs, was an angry man. In late 1977, he had accepted President Jimmy Carter's appointment to the White House Strategy Council on Drug Abuse with the understanding that this statutory, policymaking body would "determine Federal strategy for prevention of drug abuse and drug trafficking."

Over the next two years, Musto found that the CIA and other intelligence agencies denied the council—whose members included the Secretary of State and the Attorney General—access to all classified information on drugs, even when it was necessary for framing new policy.

At one memorable briefing by CIA specialists on Colombia, Musto came armed with current World Bank data on the role of the U.S. dollar in the cocaine trade. The agency experts responded to his loaded questions with a direct lie about the dollar. When Musto confronted them with his World Bank data, the CIA men retracted their false statements without a blush. Musto's complaints to the White House about CIA lying produced no response.

When President Carter reacted to the Soviet invasion of Afghanistan in December 1979 by shipping arms to the muja-hideen guerrillas, Musto's disquiet grew. "I told the council," he recalls, "that we were going into Afghanistan to support the opium growers in their rebellion against the Soviets. Shouldn't we try to avoid what we had done in Laos? Shouldn't we try to pay the growers if they will eradicate their opium production? There was silence." As heroin from Afghanistan and Pakistan poured into the United States, Musto noted that the number of drug-related deaths in New York City rose by 77 per cent.

Concerned by the mounting "heroin crisis," Musto joined Dr. Joyce Lowinson, another White House Drug Council member, in writing an op-ed-page article for *The New York Times* to protest the Carter Administration's failings. The two expressed their "worry about the growing of opium poppies in Afghanistan and Pakistan by rebel tribesmen" and asked: "Are we erring in befriending these tribes as we did in Laos when Air America (chartered by the Central Intelligence Agency) helped transport crude opium from certain tribal areas?"

While the two drug experts could only guess at the reasons for the expanded opium production, they had no doubts about the consequence—a flood of heroin. "On the streets, this drug is more potent, cheaper and more available than at any time in the last twenty years," they wrote. Although denied official intelligence, these two medical doctors warned, quite accurately as it turned out, that "this crisis is bound to worsen."

At the same time that Musto was voicing his concerns about a possible flood of Afghan heroin in late 1979, field agents for the Drug Enforcement Administration (DEA) were already finding that his possibility was fast becoming their reality. Following a decade of major victories in the global drug war, the sudden surge of heroin from Southern Asia—Afghanistan and Pakistan—disheartened the drug agents. As the first shipments of the new heroin began to arrive, the DEA called a special "Middle East Heroin Conference" at New York's Kennedy Airport in December 1979.

The DEA's intelligence chief opened the gathering of his agents by introducing the "new Middle Eastern heroin threat," the agency's terminology for the Pakistan-Afghanistan heroin surge which seemed to be rising without restraint.

Flying in from the Middle East for the conference, agent Ernie Staples added to the gloom. Since the "political situations" in the region were unfavorable, he reported, the DEA's "first line of defense"—interception near the growing areas—had collapsed. In a frank admission of failure, Staples stated flatly that there were "no longer any DEA personnel working effectively in these source countries." Grown and processed without restraint, Southern Asian heroin was capturing the European market.

"Europe at present is being flooded with Middle Eastern heroin," said Staples. As supply surged, wholesale heroin prices in Europe were falling and purity had risen to a new high—a statistic confirmed by 500 recent deaths from drug overdose in West Germany.

With ample supplies of Southern Asian opium and morphine, Marseille's Corsican syndicates were cooperating with the Sicilian Mafia. Judging from a recent seizure of New York-bound heroin in Italy, Sicilian Mafia groups based in Palermo were starting to smuggle the new heroin into the United States. "All indications," concluded Staples, "point to an increase of trafficking between Europe and the United States."

As DEA agents from Boston to Chicago stood in succession, they added details that revealed a developing crisis. Responsible for the nation's premier heroin market, the New York agents had been the first to see the impact of the new Southern Asian heroin. There was every sign that the New York heroin market of some 150,000 addicts was coming out of a long drought—police exhibits showed a "dramatic increase in purity," hepatitis cases were up, and city police had recorded a sharp rise in heroin arrests.

Changes in the New York market were soon felt in the rest of the country. The DEA's Washington, D.C., office, for example, reported an "increase in overdose death statistics." Within a year, these trends, seen so clearly by both Musto and the DEA in late 1979, began to transform the nature of the U.S. drug problem.

During the 1980s, America experienced an unprecedented drug crisis. Rising from insignificant levels, cocaine use doubled between 1982 and 1985. Eclipsed by the media glare on cocaine and crack, global heroin production and U.S. consumption rose steadily as well. Between 1983 and 1986, the number of heroin-related deaths doubled. And, while casual use of drugs declined toward the end of the decade, the hard core of regular users grew steadily.

Although the drug pandemic of the 1980s had complex causes, the growth in global heroin supply could be traced, in large part, to two key aspects of U.S. policy: the failure of the DEA's interdiction efforts and the CIA's covert operations.

By attacking heroin trafficking in separate sectors of Asia's extended opium zone in isolation, the DEA simply diverted heroin exports from America to Europe and shifted opium production from Southern to Southeast Asia and back again—raising both global production and consumption with each move.

Ironically, the increasing opium harvests in Burma and Afghanistan, America's major suppliers, were in large part the product of both the DEA's ill-fated attempts at interdiction and certain of the CIA's covert operations. Just as CIA support for Nationalist Chinese troops in the Shan states had increased Burma's opium crop in the 1950s, so the agency's aid to the mujahideen guerrillas in the 1980s expanded opium production in Afghanistan and linked Pakistan's nearby heroin laboratories to the world market. After a dec-

ade as the sites of major CIA covert operations, Burma and Afghanistan ranked, respectively, as the world's largest and second-largest suppliers of illicit heroin in 1989.

In the ten years that followed his prediction, Musto's dismal vision of America's coming drug crisis has been fulfilled.

Covert CIA operations in Afghanistan transformed Southern Asia from a self-contained opium zone into a major supplier of heroin for the world market. Since the Sixteenth Century, when recreational opium-eating first developed, Southern Asia had constituted a self-sufficient drug market. In the highlands spanning Iran, Afghanistan, and northwest India (now Pakistan), tribal farmers grew limited quantities of opium and sold it to merchant caravans bound for the cities of Iran and India.

During the decade of Cold War confrontation with the Soviet Union in Afghanistan, however, CIA intervention provided the political protection and the logistics that opened that nation's poppy fields to heroin markets in Europe and America. Although Soviet forces have withdrawn and CIA aid has now slackened, there is every indication that Afghanistan, like Burma before it, will remain a major heroin supplier.

Long something of a backwater in U.S. foreign policy, Southern Asia emerged in the late 1970s as a flashpoint in the Cold War. As the United States and its allies sent in covert operatives, secret arms shipments, and military aid to meet the escalating political crises, opium production soared and heroin poured out of the region into European and American markets.

The Iranian revolution of February 1979 was the first in a series of major events that changed the character of both the region's politics and its narcotics traffic. Waves of strikes and mass demonstrations in Teheran toppled the Shah and his apparatus of repression, breaking his once-tight controls over the country's opium trade. His successor, the Ayatollah Khomeini, denounced drug dealers as "first-class traitors and a danger to society," but the new Islamic regime, reflecting Iran's traditional tolerance for the drug, did not place opium in the same forbidden category as alcohol, thereby creating an ambiguity that allowed the traffic to flourish. Six months after the revolt, the CIA reported that drugs were being sold openly on Teheran's streets and that the Revolutionary Guards, with many addicts in their ranks, did "not interfere with the dealers."

By September, CIA analysts in the U.S. embassy estimated that Iran's next poppy harvest would raise opium production from the current 200 tons to an estimated

325 tons. They argued that Iran's opium boom had "created a new 'golden triangle' comprised of Iran, Pakistan, and Afghanistan." Once the new bumper crop was harvested, Iran's opium "will join that . . . flowing over the 'silk route' of Marco Polo to Turkey and from there to Western Europe." The CIA concluded its report with a warning: "The world must brace itself for a flood of opium and heroin from Iran."

As events turned out, the CIA was half right. Beginning in 1979, Southern Asia did increase its heroin exports, but the drugs came from the Pakistan-Afghan borderlands, not Iran. As it had for two centuries, Iran showed a remarkable appetite for drugs and absorbed all of its own opium harvests, now greatly expanded under the new regime. Although Iran did not produce a surplus for export, its increased harvests now met its own needs, freeing Afghanistan's opium for export to Europe.

Initially, a peculiar twist in the global drug trade brought Southern Asia's heroin to Europe in 1979. Although the Pakistan-Afghanistan opium harvest rose steadily from 400 tons in 1971 to 1,200 tons in 1978, almost all of the increased production was consumed locally. Small quantities first appeared in Europe in 1975. But in the months following the region's bumper crop of 1978, European police still seized only forty-nine kilograms of Southern Asian heroin, a tenth of the 451 kilograms intercepted from Southeast Asia. Then the monsoon rains failed for two years in Southeast Asia, reducing Burma's opium production to a record low.

Nature, combined with covert-action nurture, soon turned Southern Asia's local opium traders into suppliers to the world. As a network of heroin laboratories opened in 1979-1980 along the Afghan-Pakistan border to service the global markets opened by Southeast Asia's drought, Pakistan's opium production soared to 800 tons, far above its 1971 harvest of some ninety tons. By 1982, the Afghan poppy fields, linked with laboratories across the border in Pakistan, supplied more than half the heroin demand in America and Europe. To cite statistics, European seizures of Pakistani heroin shot from 121 kilograms in 1978 to 880 kilograms in 1980. Only three years after the first CIA arms reached the mujahideen, Southern Asia, never before a source, supplied 60 per cent of the U.S. heroin market. Inside Pakistan itself, the number of heroin addicts soared from only 5,000 in 1980 to 1.3 million in 1985.

During the ten years of CIA covert support for the mujahideen resistance, U.S. Government and media sources were silent about the involvement of leading Afghan guerrillas and Pakistan military in the heroin traffic.

Southern Asia became the focus of a crisis in U.S. foreign policy so grave that three successive Administrations, from Carter to Bush, gave the CIA unlimited funds and unrestrained authority to do whatever had to be done. After Iranian mobs toppled the Shah in 1979, America lost its military surrogate in the Persian Gulf, gateway for the West's oil supplies. A year earlier, various communist factions of the Afghan army had overthrown the dictator Mohammad Daoud and established a pro-Soviet regime in that strategic nation, the historic threshhold for Russian expansion toward the Indian Ocean. After months of internecine fighting among Kabul's communists, Soviet troops invaded Afghanistan in December 1979, occupying Kabul, the capital, and installing a pliable Afghan communist as president.

President Carter reacted with ill-concealed rage, using his diplomatic and covert-action resources to mobilize military aid for the mujahideen guerrillas. Within weeks, massive arms shipments began—hand-held missiles and antitank weapons from China, Kalashnikov assault rifles from Egypt, munitions from Saudi Arabia, and a variety of U.S. weapons from the CIA.

But Carter's covert-aid effort was limited by the coolness of his relations with General Mohammad Zia ul-Haq, leader of Pakistan's harsh martial-law regime. Soon after President Ronald Reagan took office in 1981, however, the White House announced a $3 billion program of military aid to Pakistan, including the latest F-16 fighters.

With Pakistan now openly committed to the mujahideen, General Zia's military assumed a dominant role in supplying the Afghan resistance forces. The Saudis delivered their clandestine aid directly to client guerrilla units inside Afghanistan. But most allied agencies worked with Pakistan's Inter-Service Intelligence (ISI), Zia's chosen instrument, which he was then building into a powerful covert-operations unit with the advice and assistance of the CIA. The agency's relationship with ISI was a complex give-and-take that makes simple caricatures inappropriate—that ISI was the agency's errand runner on the Afghan border or, conversely, that ISI manipulated the CIA into writing a blank check for General Zia's own Afghan policies. Whatever the nuances of covert relations may have been, the partnership produced a transformation of Pakistan's heroin trade.

When the Soviet Union began infiltrating Afghanistan in early 1979, the CIA worked through ISI to organize the first mujahideen resistance groups. "Throughout most of the war," explains Afghanistan expert Barnett Rubin, "the United States subcontracted to General Zia and ISI the main political decision about which Afghans to support." The U.S. program to aid the Afghan guerrillas began in April 1979, eight months before the full-scale Soviet invasion.

The following month at Peshawar in Pakistan's North-West Frontier Province, a CIA special envoy from the Islamabad station first met Afghan resistance leaders, all carefully selected by Pakistan's ISI—which was in effect offering the agency an alliance with its own Afghan client, Gulbuddin Hekmatyar, leader of the small Hezbi-i-Islami guerrilla group. The CIA accepted and, over the next decade, gave more than half its covert aid to Hekmatyar's guerrillas.

It was a dismal decision. Unlike the later resistance leaders who commanded strong popular followings inside Afghanistan, Hekmatyar, by all accounts brutal and corrupt, led a guerrilla force that was a creature of the Pakistani military. After the CIA built his Hezbi-i-Islami into the largest Afghan guerrilla army, he would use his arms—with the full support of ISI and the tacit tolerance of the CIA—to become Afghanistan's leading drug lord.

Among the legion of American correspondents who covered the Afghan resistance during the 1980s, few bothered to probe the background of Hekmatyar, the CIA's chosen instrument. An Islamic militant and former engineering student, Hekmatyar had founded Afghanistan's Muslim Brotherhood and led student demonstrations in Kabul during the late 1960s to oppose the king's secular reforms. In the early 1970s, according to a 1990 report in *The New York Times*, "he had dispatched followers to throw vials of acid into the faces of women students who refused to wear veils." Accused of murdering a leftist student in 1972, Hekmatyar fled into Pakistan's North-West Frontier where, as a member of Pushtun tribes that straddle the border, he was able to continue his political work. Living in Peshawar, Hekmatyar allied himself with Pakistan's Jama'at-i Islami (Party of Islam), a fundamentalist and quasi-fascist group with many followers inside the Pakistani officer corps.

Through these contacts with the military, Hekmatyar would become commander of a Pakistani covert operation to destabilize a new government in Kabul in 1974—five years before the Soviet invasion. When Mohammad Daoud, a former prime minister, led a coup against the Afghan king and established a republic in 1973, Pakistan's Prime Minister Zulfikar Ali Bhutto ordered his military to begin training a secret force of 5,000 Afghan rebels at clandestine camps inside Pakistan.

Armed and supplied by Islamabad, Hekmatyar led these guerrillas into Afghanistan and launched a revolt in the Panjsher valley north of Kabul in July 1975. Hekmatyar's propaganda that Daoud's conservative republic was a "godless communist-dominated regime" was unconvincing, and his mercenary force found itself without popular support. The Afghan army encountered little resistance when it marched into the valley to mop up. While Kabul put ninety-three of his captured mercenaries on trial, Hekmatyar retreated into Pakistan with most of his forces intact.

A year later, a communist coup in Kabul ousted Daoud and revived the fortunes of Hekmatyar's exile army. When the CIA station chief in Islamabad met the ISI's selected Afghan leaders in May 1979 and agreed to provide arms to Hekmatyar's guerrillas, it was a momentous decision, although nobody knew it at the time. CIA covert aid would increase markedly over the next two years, but Hekmatyar remained the prime beneficiary. Similarly, in June 1981, when President Reagan and General Zia agreed to support a full-scale war inside Afghanistan, the flood of clandestine military aid still followed the same patterns set at Peshawar by the CIA, ISI, and Hekmatyar two years earlier.

With generous U.S. aid, Pakistan opened its borders to three million Afghan refugees and allowed the CIA to conduct its secret war without restraint. Along the border, American operatives ran training camps for the mujahideen; in Islamabad, the CIA maintained one of its largest foreign stations to direct the war. CIA Director William Casey gained direct access to General Zia and was warmly received on regular visits. And, unique in a region where the official attitude toward the United States ranges from the unfriendly to the hostile, Zia allowed the CIA to open an electronic intelligence station facing the Soviet Union in northern Pakistan and permitted U.S. spy flights over the Indian Ocean from his air bases near the Persian Gulf.

Aside from $3 billion in direct aid, the Pakistan military gained control over distribution of the $2 billion in covert aid the CIA shipped to the Afghan guerrillas during the ten-year war. For General Zia's loyalists within the military, these contracts were a source of vast wealth.

At an operational level, General Zia's men controlled the delivery of CIA arms shipments when they arrived in Pakistan. Once the arms landed at the port of Karachi, the Pakistan army's Logistics Cell trucked them north to the Afghan guerrillas in the North-West Frontier. The governor of this province was Lieutenant General Fazle Huq, President Zia's closest confidant and the de facto overlord of the mujahideen. Even as the ranks of the resistance swelled after 1981, the ISI still insisted that Hekmatyar receive the bulk of CIA arms shipments.

ISI also gave Hekmatyar a free hand to rule the Afghan refugee camps that sprawled around Peshawar, and he used it to run what one U.N. worker called a "reign of terror," gaining control of rival resistance groups through violence. During the decade of the Afghan resistance war, such organizations as Asia Watch and Amnesty International received numerous reports of human-rights violations by his Hezb-i-Islami guerrillas. But the American press still published positive reports about *our* mujahideen, ignoring the abuses and drug-dealing.

A year after the Soviet withdrawal in 1989, *The New York Times* finally reported what it called "the sinister nature of Mr. Hekmatyar." By then, his atrocities had caused the president of Afghanistan's new interim government to denounce Hekmatyar—his own foreign minister—as a "criminal" and a "terrorist."

As the Cold War confrontation wound down, the international press finally broke its decade of silence to reveal the involvement of the Afghan resistance and Pakistani military in the region's heroin trade. In May 1990, for example, *The Washington Post* published a front-page article charging that the United States had failed to take action against Pakistan's heroin dealers "because of its desire not to offend a strategic ally, Pakistan's military establishment." The *Post* article said U.S. officials had ignored Afghan complaints of heroin trafficking by Hekmatyar and the ISI, an allegation that at least one senior American official confirmed. And *The Post* reported that "Hekmatyar commanders close to ISI run laboratories in southwest Pakistan" and "ISI cooperates in heroin operations."

The independent Pakistani press, angered by the country's own heroin epidemic, had reported many of the details years before. But while Pakistani heroin flooded Europe and America in the early 1980s, the Western press maintained a public silence on the origins of this new narcotics supply.

As the ISI's mujahideen clients used their new CIA munitions to capture prime agricultural areas inside Afghanistan, the guerrillas urged their peasant supporters to grow poppies, thereby doubling the country's opium harvest to 575 tons between 1982 and 1983. Mullah Nasim Akhundzada, a mujahideen commander, for example, controlled the best opium lands— once the breadbasket of Afghanistan—during most of the war. He decreed that half of all peasant holdings would be planted in opium. A ruthless leader and bitter enemy of Hekmatyar, Mullah Nasim issued opium quotas to every landowner and maintained his control by killing or cas-

trating those who defied him.

In early 1986, *New York Times* correspondent Arthur Bonner spent a month traveling in the region, where he found extensive poppy fields in every town. "We must grow and sell opium to fight our holy war against the Russian nonbelievers," explained Nasim's elder brother Mohammed Rasul.

This admission contradicted the assurances the U.S. embassy in Islamabad had been giving about the Afghan drug trade. Typical of its disinformation on the subject, just two months before, the embassy had issued a formal denial that Afghan guerrillas "have been involved in narcotics activities as a matter of policy to finance their operations."

While Mullah Nasim ruled the prime opium fields of the Helmand Valley, Hekmatyar held the complex of heroin laboratories just across the border in Pakistan, operating under the protection of Governor Fazle Huq.

By 1988, there were an estimated 100 to 200 heroin refineries in the province's Khyber district alone. Trucks from the Pakistani army's logistics cell arriving with CIA arms from Karachi often returned loaded with heroin—protected from police search by ISI papers.

Writing in *The Nation* three years later, Lawrence Lifschultz cited numerous police sources charging that Governor Fazle Huq, President Zia's intimate, was the primary protector of the heroin industry. Lifschultz said that Huq "had been implicated in narcotics reports reaching Interpol" as early as 1982. Both European and Pakistani police claimed that all investigations of the province's major heroin syndicates had "been aborted at the highest level."

With seventeen agents assigned to the U.S. embassy in Islamabad, the Drug Enforcement Administration compiled detailed reports identifying "forty significant narcotics syndicates in Pakistan." Despite the high quality of DEA intelligence, not a single major syndicate was investigated by Pakistani police for nearly a decade.

In marked contrast to the seventeen DEA agents who shuffled papers without result in the U.S. embassy, a single Norwegian detective broke a heroin case that led directly to Zia's circle. Arrested at Oslo airport with 3.5 kilograms of heroin in December 1983, Pakistani trafficker Raza Qureshi traded details about his drug syndicate for a reduced sentence. After Norway's public prosecutor filed formal charges against three Pakistani heroin merchants in September 1985, Pakistan's Federal Investigation Agency ordered their arrest. When police picked up Hamid Hasnain, vice president of the government's Habib Bank, they searched his briefcase and found the personal banking records of President Zia.

There was evidence, moreover, of a major heroin syndicate inside the Pakistan military. In June 1986, police arrested an army major driving from Peshawar to Karachi with 220 kilograms of heroin. Two months later, police arrested an air force lieutenant carrying an identical amount, indications of a tidy military mind organizing uniform deliveries. Before the two could be interrogated, both officers escaped from custody under what Pakistan's *Defense Journal* called "mystifying circumstances." These were only two of sixteen military officers arrested in 1986 for heroin trafficking.

The blatant official corruption continued until August 1988, when General Zia's death in a plane crash brought an eventual restoration of civilian rule. Typical of the misinformation that had blocked any U.S. action against Pakistan's heroin trade, the State Department's semi-annual narcotics review in September called Zia—who counted the country's leading drug lords as his confidants and close allies—"a strong supporter of anti-narcotics activities in Pakistan."

Soon after assuming office through open elections, the new prime minister, Benazir Bhutto, declared war on drugs by dismissing two of ISI's top military administrators and creating a new ministry to attack the drug trade. Despite her good intentions, however, Bhutto's commitment to the drug war was soon compromised and the outlook for an effective attack on the country's highly developed heroin industry seemed bleak. After ten years of unchecked growth under General Zia, drugs were now too well entrenched in the country's politics and economy for simple police action.

Conservative economists estimated that total annual earnings from Pakistan's heroin trade were $8 billion to $10 billion, far larger than Pakistan's government budget and equal to one-quarter of its gross domestic product. With so much heroin money flowing into the country, Pakistani commentators feared that the country's politics would take on a Colombian cast—that is, that the drug lords would start using money and arms to influence the nation's leaders.

Indeed, the first signs were not long in coming. Facing a no-confidence motion in the national assembly in late 1989, Prime Minister Bhutto charged that drug money was being used to destabilize her government. When she claimed that heroin dealers had paid 194 million rupees (the U.S. equivalent of about $9 million at the time) for votes against her, many observers found the allegation credible.

Moreover, the heavily armed tribal populations of the North-West Frontier Province were determined to defend their opium harvests. Police pistols would prove ineffective against tribal arsenals that now, thanks to the CIA, included automatic assault rifles, anti-aircraft guns, and rocket launchers. "The government cannot stop us from growing poppy," one angry tribal farmer told a foreign correspondent in 1989. "We are one force, and united, and if they come with their planes we will shoot them down."

By early 1990, the CIA's Afghan operation had proved doubly disastrous. Shortly after the Soviet withdrawal from Afghanistan in early 1989, the U.S. financed a mujahideen assault on Jalalabad, confidently predicting a victory as the first step toward a communist collapse. Instead, the attack failed and the communist regime still rules Kabul today, two years later.

After ten years of covert operations at a cost of $2 billion, America was left with mujahideen warlords whose skill as drug dealers exceeded their competence as military commanders. As the Cold War ended and the Bush Administration's war on drugs began, such Afghan leaders as the opium warlord Hekmatyar became a diplomatic embarrassment for the United States.

Following the policy of radical pragmatism it had employed before in Burma and Laos, the CIA had again allied itself with an opium warlord. Despite direct complaints from other Afghan guerrilla leaders about Hekmatyar's heroin dealing, the CIA evidently refused to do anything that might lessen his effectiveness as an instrument of its covert operations.

In mountain ranges along the southern rim of Asia—whether in Afghanistan, Burma, or Laos—opium is the main currency of external trade and thus a key source of political power. Since agency operations involve alliances with local power brokers who serve as the CIA's commanders, the agency has repeatedly found its covert operations enmeshed with Asia's heroin trade.

By investing a local asset such as Hekmatyar with the authority of its alliance, the CIA draws him under the mantle of its protection. So armed, a tribal leader, now less vulnerable to arrest and prosecution, can use his American protection to expand his share of the local opium trade. Once the CIA has invested its prestige in one of these opium warlords, it cannot afford to compromise a major covert-action asset with drug investigations.

Respecting the national-security imperatives of CIA operations, the DEA keeps its distance from agency assets, even when they are major drug lords. During the ten years of the Afghan war, some seventeen DEA agents sat in the U.S. embassy at Islamabad watching—without making a single major arrest or seizure—as the flood of Afghan-Pakistan heroin captured 60 per cent of the U.S. drug market. Operating along the Afghan border, CIA agents delivered several hundred million dollars' worth of arms to Hekmatyar's heroin convoys and cooperated closely with his corrupt protectors in Pakistan's ISI.

Over the past twenty years, the CIA has repeatedly denied any involvement in the Asian opium traffic. Although admitting that some of its allies might have dabbled in drugs, the agency insists that it has always avoided direct culpability. But critics who look for the CIA's officers to actually dirty their hands with drugs in the line of duty are missing the point. In most covert actions, the CIA avoids direct involvement in combat or espionage and instead works through local clients whose success often determines the outcome of an agency operation. Thus, the CIA's involvement in drugs usually revolves around indirect complicity in the drug dealing of its assets, not in any *direct* culpability in the actual traffic.

Still, the difference is moot on the streets of America. As David Musto demonstrated with his prescient questions in 1980, CIA complicity in opium traffic has a certain predictability to it, wherever and however it occurs.

*Why so many Muslims deeply resent the West, and why their
bitterness will not easily be mollified*

THE ROOTS
OF MUSLIM RAGE

BERNARD LEWIS

BERNARD LEWIS is a professor emeritus of Near Eastern
Studies at Princeton University. He is the author of numerous
books on the Middle East, including *The Arabs in History*
(1950), *The Middle East and the West* (1964), *The Muslim
Discovery of Europe* (1982), and *The Political Language of
Islam* (1988).

IN ONE OF HIS LETTERS THOMAS JEFFERSON RE-
marked that in matters of religion "the maxim of
civil government" should be reversed and we
should rather say, "Divided we stand, united, we
fall." In this remark Jefferson was setting forth
with classic terseness an idea that has come to be regarded as essentially American: the separation of Church and
State. This idea was not entirely new; it had some prece-
dents in the writings of Spinoza, Locke, and the philosophers of the European Enlightenment. It was in the
United States, however, that the principle was first given
the force of law and gradually, in the course of two centuries, became a reality.

If the idea that religion and politics should be separated is relatively new, dating back a mere three hundred
years, the idea that they are distinct dates back almost to
the beginnings of Christianity. Christians are enjoined in
their Scriptures to "render . . . unto Caesar the things
which are Caesar's and unto God the things which are
God's." While opinions have differed as to the real meaning of this phrase, it has generally been interpreted as le-
gitimizing a situation in which two institutions exist side
by side, each with its own laws and chain of authority—
one concerned with religion, called the Church, the other concerned with politics, called the State. And since
they are two, they may be joined or separated, subordi-

nate or independent, and conflicts may arise between
them over questions of demarcation and jurisdiction.

This formulation of the problems posed by the relations between religion and politics, and the possible solutions to those problems, arise from Christian, not universal, principles and experience. There are other religious
traditions in which religion and politics are differently
perceived, and in which, therefore, the problems and the
possible solutions are radically different from those we
know in the West. Most of these traditions, despite their
often very high level of sophistication and achievement,
remained or became local—limited to one region or one
culture or one people. There is one, however, that in its
worldwide distribution, its continuing vitality, its univer-
salist aspirations, can be compared to Christianity, and
that is Islam.

Islam is one of the world's great religions. Let me be
explicit about what I, as a historian of Islam who is not a
Muslim, mean by that. Islam has brought comfort and peace
of mind to countless millions of men and women. It has given
dignity and meaning to drab and impoverished lives. It has
taught people of different races to live in brotherhood and
people of different creeds to live side by side in reasonable
tolerance. It inspired a great civilization in which others
besides Muslims lived creative and useful lives and which,
by its achievement, enriched the whole world. But Islam,
like other religions, has also known periods when it inspired
in some of its followers a mood of hatred and violence. It is
our misfortune that part, though by no means all or even
most, of the Muslim world is now going through such a
period, and that much, though again not all, of that hatred is
directed against us.

We should not exaggerate the dimensions of the problem. The Muslim world is far from unanimous in its rejection of the West, nor have the Muslim regions of the
Third World been the most passionate and the most ex-

treme in their hostility. There are still significant numbers, in some quarters perhaps a majority, of Muslims with whom we share certain basic cultural and moral, social and political, beliefs and aspirations; there is still an imposing Western presence—cultural, economic, diplomatic—in Muslim lands, some of which are Western allies. Certainly nowhere in the Muslim world, in the Middle East or elsewhere, has American policy suffered disasters or encountered problems comparable to those in Southeast Asia or Central America. There is no Cuba, no Vietnam, in the Muslim world, and no place where American forces are involved as combatants or even as "advisers." But there is a Libya, an Iran, and a Lebanon, and a surge of hatred that distresses, alarms, and above all baffles Americans.

At times this hatred goes beyond hostility to specific interests or actions or policies or even countries and becomes a rejection of Western civilization as such, not only what it does but what it is, and the principles and values that it practices and professes. These are indeed seen as innately evil, and those who promote or accept them as the "enemies of God."

This phrase, which recurs so frequently in the language of the Iranian leadership, in both their judicial proceedings and their political pronouncements, must seem very strange to the modern outsider, whether religious or secular. The idea that God has enemies, and needs human help in order to identify and dispose of them, is a little difficult to assimilate. It is not, however, all that alien. The concept of the enemies of God is familiar in preclassical and classical antiquity, and in both the Old and New Testaments, as well as in the Koran. A particularly relevant version of the idea occurs in the dualist religions of ancient Iran, whose cosmogony assumed not one but two supreme powers. The Zoroastrian devil, unlike the Christian or Muslim or Jewish devil, is not one of God's creatures performing some of God's more mysterious tasks but an independent power, a supreme force of evil engaged in a cosmic struggle against God. This belief influenced a number of Christian, Muslim, and Jewish sects, through Manichaeism and other routes. The almost forgotten religion of the Manichees has given its name to the perception of problems as a stark and simple conflict between matching forces of pure good and pure evil.

The Koran is of course strictly monotheistic, and recognizes one God, one universal power only. There is a struggle in human hearts between good and evil, between God's commandments and the tempter, but this is seen as a struggle ordained by God, with its outcome preordained by God, serving as a test of mankind, and not, as in some of the old dualist religions, a struggle in which mankind has a crucial part to play in bringing about the victory of good over evil. Despite this monotheism, Islam, like Judaism and Christianity, was at various stages influenced, especially in Iran, by the dualist idea of a cosmic clash of good and evil, light and darkness, order and chaos, truth and falsehood, God and the Adversary, variously known as devil, Iblis, Satan, and by other names.

The Rise of the House of Unbelief

IN ISLAM THE STRUGGLE OF GOOD AND EVIL VERY soon acquired political and even military dimensions. Muhammad, it will be recalled, was not only a prophet and a teacher, like the founders of other religions; he was also the head of a polity and of a community, a ruler and a soldier. Hence his struggle involved a state and its armed forces. If the fighters in the war for Islam, the holy war "in the path of God," are fighting for God, it follows that their opponents are fighting against God. And since God is in principle the sovereign, the supreme head of the Islamic state—and the Prophet and, after the Prophet, the caliphs are his vicegerents—then God as sovereign commands the army. The army is God's army and the enemy is God's enemy. The duty of God's soldiers is to dispatch God's enemies as quickly as possible to the place where God will chastise them—that is to say, the afterlife.

Clearly related to this is the basic division of mankind as perceived in Islam. Most, probably all, human societies have a way of distinguishing between themselves and others: insider and outsider, in-group and out-group, kinsman or neighbor and foreigner. These definitions not only define the outsider but also, and perhaps more particularly, help to define and illustrate our perception of ourselves.

In the classical Islamic view, to which many Muslims are beginning to return, the world and all mankind are divided into two: the House of Islam, where the Muslim law and faith prevail, and the rest, known as the House of Unbelief or the House of War, which it is the duty of Muslims ultimately to bring to Islam. But the greater part of the world is still outside Islam, and even inside the Islamic lands, according to the view of the Muslim radicals, the faith of Islam has been undermined and the law of Islam has been abrogated. The obligation of holy war therefore begins at home and continues abroad, against the same infidel enemy.

Like every other civilization known to human history, the Muslim world in its heyday saw itself as the center of truth and enlightenment, surrounded by infidel barbarians whom it would in due course enlighten and civilize. But between the different groups of barbarians there was a crucial difference. The barbarians to the east and the south were polytheists and idolaters, offering no serious threat and no competition at all to Islam. In the north and west, in contrast, Muslims from an early date recognized a genuine rival—a competing world religion, a distinctive civilization inspired by that religion, and an empire that, though much smaller than theirs, was no less ambitious in its claims and aspirations. This was the entity known to itself and others as Christendom, a term that was long almost identical with Europe.

The struggle between these rival systems has now lasted for some fourteen centuries. It began with the advent of Islam, in the seventh century, and has continued virtually to the present day. It has consisted of a long series of attacks and counterattacks, jihads and crusades, conquests and reconquests. For the first thousand years Islam was advancing, Christendom in retreat and under threat. The new faith conquered the old Christian lands of the Levant and North Africa, and invaded Europe, ruling for a while in Sicily, Spain, Portugal, and even parts of France. The attempt by the Crusaders to recover the lost lands of Christendom in the east was held and thrown back, and even the Muslims' loss of southwestern Europe to the Reconquista was amply compensated by the Islamic advance into southeastern Europe, which twice reached as far as Vienna. For the past three hundred years, since the failure of the second Turkish siege of Vienna in 1683 and the rise of the European colonial empires in Asia and Africa, Islam has been on the defensive, and the Christian and post-Christian civilization of Europe and her daughters has brought the whole world, including Islam, within its orbit.

FOR A LONG TIME NOW THERE HAS BEEN A RISING tide of rebellion against this Western paramountcy, and a desire to reassert Muslim values and restore Muslim greatness. The Muslim has suffered successive stages of defeat. The first was his loss of domination in the world, to the advancing power of Russia and the West. The second was the undermining of his authority in his own country, through an invasion of foreign ideas and laws and ways of life and sometimes even foreign rulers or settlers, and the enfranchisement of native non-Muslim elements. The third—the last straw—was the challenge to his mastery in his own house, from emancipated women and rebellious children. It was too much to endure, and the outbreak of rage against these alien, infidel, and incomprehensible forces that had subverted his dominance, disrupted his society, and finally violated the sanctuary of his home was inevitable. It was also natural that this rage should be directed primarily against the millennial enemy and should draw its strength from ancient beliefs and loyalties.

Europe and her daughters? The phrase may seem odd to Americans, whose national myths, since the beginning of their nationhood and even earlier, have usually defined their very identity in opposition to Europe, as something new and radically different from the old European ways. This is not, however, the way that others have seen it; not often in Europe, and hardly ever elsewhere.

Though people of other races and cultures participated, for the most part involuntarily, in the discovery and creation of the Americas, this was, and in the eyes of the rest of the world long remained, a European enterprise, in which Europeans predominated and dominated and to which Europeans gave their languages, their religions, and much of their way of life.

For a very long time voluntary immigration to America was almost exclusively European. There were indeed some who came from the Muslim lands in the Middle East and North Africa, but few were Muslims; most were members of the Christian and to a lesser extent the Jewish minorities in those countries. Their departure for America, and their subsequent presence in America, must have strengthened rather than lessened the European image of America in Muslim eyes.

In the lands of Islam remarkably little was known about America. At first the voyages of discovery aroused some interest; the only surviving copy of Columbus's own map of America is a Turkish translation and adaptation, still preserved in the Topkapi Palace Museum, in Istanbul. A sixteenth-century Turkish geographer's account of the discovery of the New World, titled *The History of Western India*, was one of the first books printed in Turkey. But thereafter interest seems to have waned, and not much is said about America in Turkish, Arabic, or other Muslim languages until a relatively late date. A Moroccan ambassador who was in Spain at the time wrote what must surely be the first Arabic account of the American Revolution. The Sultan of Morocco signed a treaty of peace and friendship with the United States in 1787, and thereafter the new republic had a number of dealings, some friendly, some hostile, most commercial, with other Muslim states. These seem to have had little impact on either side. The American Revolution and the American republic to which it gave birth long remained unnoticed and unknown. Even the small but growing American presence in Muslim lands in the nineteenth century—merchants, consuls, missionaries, and teachers—aroused little or no curiosity, and is almost unmentioned in the Muslim literature and newspapers of the time.

The Second World War, the oil industry, and postwar developments brought many Americans to the Islamic lands; increasing numbers of Muslims also came to America, first as students, then as teachers or businessmen or other visitors, and eventually as immigrants. Cinema and later television brought the American way of life, or at any rate a certain version of it, before countless millions to whom the very name of America had previously been meaningless or unknown. A wide range of American products, particularly in the immediate postwar years, when European competition was virtually eliminated and Japanese competition had not yet arisen, reached into the remotest markets of the Muslim world, winning new customers and, perhaps more important, creating new tastes and ambitions. For some, America represented freedom and justice and opportunity. For many more, it represented wealth and power and success, at a time when these qualities were not regarded as sins or crimes.

And then came the great change, when the leaders of a widespread and widening religious revival sought out and identified their enemies as the enemies of God, and gave them "a local habitation and a name" in the Western Hemisphere. Suddenly, or so it seemed, America had become the archenemy, the incarnation of evil, the diabolic opponent of all that is good, and specifically, for Muslims, of Islam. Why?

Some Familiar Accusations

AMONG THE COMPONENTS IN THE MOOD OF ANTI-Westernism, and more especially of anti-Americanism, were certain intellectual influences coming from Europe. One of these was from Germany, where a negative view of America formed part of a school of thought by no means limited to the Nazis but including writers as diverse as Rainer Maria Rilke, Ernst Jünger, and Martin Heidegger. In this perception, America was the ultimate example of civilization without culture: rich and comfortable, materially advanced but soulless and artificial; assembled or at best constructed, not grown; mechanical, not organic; technologically complex but lacking the spirituality and vitality of the rooted, human, national cultures of the Germans and other "authentic" peoples. German philosophy, and particularly the philosophy of education, enjoyed a considerable vogue among Arab and some other Muslim intellectuals in the thirties and early forties, and this philosophic anti-Americanism was part of the message.

After the collapse of the Third Reich and the temporary ending of German influence, another philosophy, even more anti-American, took its place—the Soviet version of Marxism, with a denunciation of Western capitalism and of America as its most advanced and dangerous embodiment. And when Soviet influence began to fade, there was yet another to take its place, or at least to supplement its working—the new mystique of Third Worldism, emanating from Western Europe, particularly France, and later also from the United States, and drawing at times on both these earlier philosophies. This mystique was helped by the universal human tendency to invent a golden age in the past, and the specifically European propensity to locate it elsewhere. A new variant of the old golden-age myth placed it in the Third World, where the innocence of the non-Western Adam and Eve was ruined by the Western serpent. This view took as axiomatic the goodness and purity of the East and the wickedness of the West, expanding in an exponential curve of evil from Western Europe to the United States. These ideas, too, fell on fertile ground, and won widespread support.

But though these imported philosophies helped to provide intellectual expression for anti-Westernism and anti-Americanism, they did not cause it, and certainly they do not explain the widespread anti-Westernism that made so many in the Middle East and elsewhere in the Islamic world receptive to such ideas.

It must surely be clear that what won support for such totally diverse doctrines was not Nazi race theory, which can have had little appeal for Arabs, or Soviet atheistic communism, which can have had little appeal for Muslims, but rather their common anti-Westernism. Nazism and communism were the main forces opposed to the West, both as a way of life and as a power in the world, and as such they could count on at least the sympathy if not the support of those who saw in the West their principal enemy.

But why the hostility in the first place? If we turn from the general to the specific, there is no lack of individual policies and actions, pursued and taken by individual Western governments, that have aroused the passionate anger of Middle Eastern and other Islamic peoples. Yet all too often, when these policies are abandoned and the problems resolved, there is only a local and temporary alleviation. The French have left Algeria, the British have left Egypt, the Western oil companies have left their oil wells, the westernizing Shah has left Iran—yet the generalized resentment of the fundamentalists and other extremists against the West and its friends remains and grows and is not appeased.

The cause most frequently adduced for anti-American feeling among Muslims today is American support for Israel. This support is certainly a factor of importance, increasing with nearness and involvement. But here again there are some oddities, difficult to explain in terms of a single, simple cause. In the early days of the foundation of Israel, while the United States maintained a certain distance, the Soviet Union granted immediate *de jure* recognition and support, and arms sent from a Soviet satellite, Czechoslovakia, saved the infant state of Israel from defeat and death in its first weeks of life. Yet there seems to have been no great ill will toward the Soviets for these policies, and no corresponding good will toward the United States. In 1956 it was the United States that intervened, forcefully and decisively, to secure the withdrawal of Israeli, British, and French forces from Egypt—yet in the late fifties and sixties it was to the Soviets, not America, that the rulers of Egypt, Syria, Iraq, and other states turned for arms; it was with the Soviet bloc that they formed bonds of solidarity at the United Nations and in the world generally. More recently, the rulers of the Islamic Republic of Iran have offered the most principled and uncompromising denunciation of Israel and Zionism. Yet even these leaders, before as well as after the death of Ayatollah Ruhollah Khomeini, when they decided for reasons of their own to enter into a dialogue of sorts, found it easier to talk to Jerusalem than to Washington. At the same time, Western hostages in Lebanon, many of them devoted to Arab causes and some of them converts to Islam, are seen and treated by their captors as limbs of the Great Satan.

Another explanation, more often heard from Muslim dissidents, attributes anti-American feeling to American support for hated regimes, seen as reactionary by radicals, as impious by conservatives, as corrupt and tyrannical by both. This accusation has some plausibility, and could help to explain why an essentially inner-directed, often anti-nationalist movement should turn against a foreign power. But it does not suffice, especially since support for such regimes has been limited both in extent and—as the Shah discovered—in effectiveness.

Clearly, something deeper is involved than these specific grievances, numerous and important as they may be —something deeper that turns every disagreement into a problem and makes every problem insoluble.

THIS REVULSION AGAINST AMERICA, MORE GENERALLY against the West, is by no means limited to the Muslim world; nor have Muslims, with the exception of the Iranian mullahs and their disciples elsewhere, experienced and exhibited the more virulent forms of this feeling. The mood of disillusionment and hostility has affected many other parts of the world, and has even reached some elements in the United States. It is from these last, speaking for themselves and claiming to speak for the oppressed peoples of the Third World, that the most widely publicized explanations—and justifications—of this rejection of Western civilization and its values have of late been heard.

The accusations are familiar. We of the West are accused of sexism, racism, and imperialism, institutionalized in patriarchy and slavery, tyranny and exploitation. To these charges, and to others as heinous, we have no option but to plead guilty—not as Americans, nor yet as Westerners, but simply as human beings, as members of the human race. In none of these sins are we the only sinners, and in some of them we are very far from being the worst. The treatment of women in the Western world, and more generally in Christendom, has always been unequal and often oppressive, but even at its worst it was rather better than the rule of polygamy and concubinage that has otherwise been the almost universal lot of womankind on this planet.

Is racism, then, the main grievance? Certainly the word figures prominently in publicity addressed to Western, Eastern European, and some Third World audiences. It figures less prominently in what is written and published for home consumption, and has become a generalized and meaningless term of abuse—rather like "fascism," which is nowadays imputed to opponents even by spokesmen for one-party, nationalist dictatorships of various complexions and shirt colors.

Slavery is today universally denounced as an offense against humanity, but within living memory it has been practiced and even defended as a necessary institution, established and regulated by divine law. The peculiarity of the peculiar institution, as Americans once called it, lay not in its existence but in its abolition. Westerners were the first to break the consensus of acceptance and to outlaw slavery, first at home, then in the other territories they controlled, and finally wherever in the world they were able to exercise power or influence—in a word, by means of imperialism.

Is imperialism, then, the grievance? Some Western powers, and in a sense Western civilization as a whole, have certainly been guilty of imperialism, but are we really to believe that in the expansion of Western Europe there was a quality of moral delinquency lacking in such earlier, relatively innocent expansions as those of the Arabs or the Mongols or the Ottomans, or in more recent expansions such as that which brought the rulers of Muscovy to the Baltic, the Black Sea, the Caspian, the Hindu Kush, and the Pacific Ocean? In having practiced sexism, racism, and imperialism, the West was merely following the common practice of mankind through the millennia of recorded history. Where it is distinct from all other civilizations is in having recognized, named, and tried, not entirely without success, to remedy these historic diseases. And that is surely a matter for congratulation, not condemnation. We do not hold Western medical science in general, or Dr. Parkinson and Dr. Alzheimer in particular, responsible for the diseases they diagnosed and to which they gave their names.

Of all these offenses the one that is most widely, frequently, and vehemently denounced is undoubtedly imperialism—sometimes just Western, sometimes Eastern (that is, Soviet) and Western alike. But the way this term is used in the literature of Islamic fundamentalists often suggests that it may not carry quite the same meaning for them as for its Western critics. In many of these writings the term "imperialist" is given a distinctly religious significance, being used in association, and sometimes interchangeably, with "missionary," and denoting a form of attack that includes the Crusades as well as the modern colonial empires. One also sometimes gets the impression that the offense of imperialism is not—as for Western critics—the domination by one people over another but rather the allocation of roles in this relationship. What is truly evil and unacceptable is the domination of infidels over true believers. For true believers to rule misbelievers is proper and natural, since this provides for the maintenance of the holy law, and gives the misbelievers both the opportunity and the incentive to embrace the true faith. But for misbelievers to rule over true believers is blasphemous and unnatural, since it leads to the corruption or religion and morality in society, and to the flouting or even the abrogation of God's law. This may help us to understand the current troubles in such diverse places as Ethiopian Eritrea, Indian Kashmir, Chinese Sinkiang, and Yugoslav Kossovo, in all of which Muslim populations are ruled by non-Muslim governments. It may also explain why spokesmen for the new Muslim minorities in Western Europe demand for Islam a degree of legal protection which those countries no longer give to Christianity and have never given to Judaism. Nor, of course, did the governments of the countries of origin of these Muslim spokesmen ever accord such protection to religions other than their own. In their perception, there is no contradiction in these attitudes. The true faith, based on God's final revelation, must be protected from insult and abuse; other faiths, being either false or incomplete, have no right to any such protection.

THERE ARE OTHER DIFFICULTIES IN THE WAY OF accepting imperialism as an explanation of Muslim hostility, even if we define imperialism narrowly and specifically, as the invasion and domination of Muslim countries by non-Muslims. If the hostility is directed against imperialism in that sense, why has it been so much stronger against Western Europe, which has relinquished all its Muslim possessions and dependencies, than against Russia, which still rules, with no light hand, over many millions of reluctant Muslim subjects and over ancient Muslim cities and countries? And why should it include the United States, which, apart from a brief interlude in the Muslim-minority area of the Philippines, has never ruled any Muslim population? The last surviving European empire with Muslim subjects, that of the Soviet Union, far from being the target of criticism and attack, has been almost exempt. Even the most recent repressions of Muslim revolts in the southern and central Asian republics of the USSR incurred no more than relatively mild words of expostulation, coupled with a disclaimer of any desire to interfere in what are quaintly called the "internal affairs" of the USSR and a request for the preservation of order and tranquillity on the frontier.

One reason for this somewhat surprising restraint is to be found in the nature of events in Soviet Azerbaijan. Islam is obviously an important and potentially a growing element in the Azerbaijani sense of identity, but it is not at present a dominant element, and the Azerbaijani movement has more in common with the liberal patriotism of Europe than with Islamic fundamentalism. Such a movement would not arouse the sympathy of the rulers of the Islamic Republic. It might even alarm them, since a genuinely democratic national state run by the people of Soviet Azerbaijan would exercise a powerful attraction on their kinsmen immediately to the south, in Iranian Azerbaijan.

Another reason for this relative lack of concern for the 50 million or more Muslims under Soviet rule may be a calculation of risk and advantage. The Soviet Union is near, along the northern frontiers of Turkey, Iran, and Afghanistan; America and even Western Europe are far away. More to the point, it has not hitherto been the practice of the Soviets to quell disturbances with water cannon and rubber bullets, with TV cameras in attendance, or to release arrested persons on bail and allow them access to domestic and foreign media. The Soviets do not interview their harshest critics on prime time, or tempt them with teaching, lecturing, and writing engagements. On the contrary, their ways of indicating displeasure with criticism can often be quite disagreeable.

But fear of reprisals, though no doubt important, is not the only or perhaps even the principal reason for the relatively minor place assigned to the Soviet Union, as compared with the West, in the demonology of fundamentalism. After all, the great social and intellectual and economic changes that have transformed most of the Islamic world, and given rise to such commonly denounced Western evils as consumerism and secularism, emerged from the West, not from the Soviet Union. No one could accuse the Soviets of consumerism; their materialism is philosophic—to be precise, dialectical—and has little or nothing to do in practice with providing the good things of life. Such provision represents another kind of materialism, often designated by its opponents as crass. It is as-

sociated with the capitalist West and not with the communist East, which has practiced, or at least imposed on its subjects, a degree of austerity that would impress a Sufi saint.

Nor were the Soviets, until very recently, vulnerable to charges of secularism, the other great fundamentalist accusation against the West. Though atheist, they were not godless, and had in fact created an elaborate state apparatus to impose the worship of their gods—an apparatus with its own orthodoxy, a hierarchy to define and enforce it, and an armed inquisition to detect and extirpate heresy. The separation of religion from the state does not mean the establishment of irreligion by the state, still less the forcible imposition of an anti-religious philosophy. Soviet secularism, like Soviet consumerism, holds no temptation for the Muslim masses, and is losing what appeal it had for Muslim intellectuals. More than ever before it is Western capitalism and democracy that provide an authentic and attractive alternative to traditional ways of thought and life. Fundamentalist leaders are not mistaken in seeing in Western civilization the greatest challenge to the way of life that they wish to retain or restore for their people.

A Clash of Civilizations

THE ORIGINS OF SECULARISM IN THE WEST MAY be found in two circumstances—in early Christian teachings and, still more, experience, which created two institutions, Church and State; and in later Christian conflicts, which drove the two apart. Muslims, too, had their religious disagreements, but there was nothing remotely approaching the ferocity of the Christian struggles between Protestants and Catholics, which devastated Christian Europe in the sixteenth and seventeenth centuries and finally drove Christians in desperation to evolve a doctrine of the separation of religion from the state. Only by depriving religious institutions of coercive power, it seemed, could Christendom restrain the murderous intolerance and persecution that Christians had visited on followers of other religions and, most of all, on those who professed other forms of their own.

Muslims experienced no such need and evolved no such doctrine. There was no need for secularism in Islam, and even its pluralism was very different from that of the pagan Roman Empire, so vividly described by Edward Gibbon when he remarked that "the various modes of worship, which prevailed in the Roman world, were all considered by the people, as equally true; by the philosopher, as equally false; and by the magistrate, as equally useful." Islam was never prepared, either in theory or in practice, to accord full equality to those who held other beliefs and practiced other forms of worship. It did, however, accord to the holders of partial truth a degree of practical as well as theoretical tolerance rarely paralleled in the Christian world until the West adopted a measure of secularism in the late-seventeenth and eighteenth centuries.

At first the Muslim response to Western civilization was one of admiration and emulation—an immense respect for the achievements of the West, and a desire to imitate and adopt them. This desire arose from a keen and growing awareness of the weakness, poverty, and backwardness of the Islamic world as compared with the advancing West. The disparity first became apparent on the battlefield but soon spread to other areas of human activity. Muslim writers observed and described the wealth and power of the West, its science and technology, its manufactures, and its forms of government. For a time the secret of Western success was seen to lie in two achievements: economic advancement and especially industry; political institutions and especially freedom. Several generations of reformers and modernizers tried to adapt these and introduce them to their own countries, in the hope that they would thereby be able to achieve equality with the West and perhaps restore their lost superiority.

In our own time this mood of admiration and emulation has, among many Muslims, given way to one of hostility and rejection. In part this mood is surely due to a feeling of humiliation—a growing awareness, among the heirs of an old, proud, and long dominant civilization, of having been overtaken, overborne, and overwhelmed by those whom they regarded as their inferiors. In part this mood is due to events in the Western world itself. One factor of major importance was certainly the impact of two great suicidal wars, in which Western civilization tore itself apart, bringing untold destruction to its own and other peoples, and in which the belligerents conducted an immense propaganda effort, in the Islamic world and elsewhere, to discredit and undermine each other. The message they brought found many listeners, who were all the more ready to respond in that their own experience of Western ways was not happy. The introduction of Western commercial, financial, and industrial methods did indeed bring great wealth, but it accrued to transplanted Westerners and members of Westernized minorities, and to only a few among the mainstream Muslim population. In time these few became more numerous, but they remained isolated from the masses, differing from them even in their dress and style of life. Inevitably they were seen as agents of and collaborators with what was once again regarded as a hostile world. Even the political institutions that had come from the West were discredited, being judged not by their Western originals but by their local imitations, installed by enthusiastic Muslim reformers. These, operating in a situation beyond their control, using imported and inappropriate methods that they did not fully understand, were unable to cope with the rapidly developing crises and were one by one overthrown. For vast numbers of Middle Easterners, Western-style economic methods brought poverty, Western-style political institutions brought tyranny, even Western-style warfare brought defeat. It is hardly surprising that so many were willing to listen to voices telling them that the old

Islamic ways were best and that their only salvation was to throw aside the pagan innovations of the reformers and return to the True Path that God had prescribed for his people.

Ultimately, the struggle of the fundamentalists is against two enemies, secularism and modernism. The war against secularism is conscious and explicit, and there is by now a whole literature denouncing secularism as an evil neo-pagan force in the modern world and attributing it variously to the Jews, the West, and the United States. The war against modernity is for the most part neither conscious nor explicit, and is directed against the whole process of change that has taken place in the Islamic world in the past century or more and has transformed the political, economic, social, and even cultural structures of Muslim countries. Islamic fundamentalism has given an aim and a form to the otherwise aimless and formless resentment and anger of the Muslim masses at the forces that have devalued their traditional values and loyalties and, in the final analysis, robbed them of their beliefs, their aspirations, their dignity, and to an increasing extent even their livelihood.

There is something in the religious culture of Islam which inspired, in even the humblest peasant or peddler, a dignity and a courtesy toward others never exceeded and rarely equalled in other civilizations. And yet, in moments of upheaval and disruption, when the deeper passions are stirred, this dignity and courtesy toward others can give way to an explosive mixture of rage and hatred which impels even the government of an ancient and civilized country—even the spokesman of a great spiritual and ethical religion—to espouse kidnapping and assassination, and try to find, in the life of their Prophet, approval and indeed precedent for such actions.

The instinct of the masses is not false in locating the ultimate source of these cataclysmic changes in the West and in attributing the disruption of their old way of life to the impact of Western domination, Western influence, or Western precept and example. And since the United States is the legitimate heir of European civilization and the recognized and unchallenged leader of the West, the United States has inherited the resulting grievances and become the focus for the pent-up hate and anger. Two examples may suffice. In November of 1979 an angry mob attacked and burned the U.S. Embassy in Islamabad, Pakistan. The stated cause of the crowd's anger was the seizure of the Great Mosque in Mecca by a group of Muslim dissidents—an event in which there was no American involvement whatsoever. Almost ten years later, in February of 1989, again in Islamabad, the USIS center was attacked by angry crowds, this time to protest the publication of Salman Rushdie's *Satanic Verses*. Rushdie is a British citizen of Indian birth, and his book had been published five months previously in England. But what provoked the mob's anger, and also the Ayatollah Khomeini's subsequent pronouncement of a death sentence on the author, was the publication of the book in the United States.

It should by now be clear that we are facing a mood and a movement far transcending the level of issues and policies and the governments that pursue them. This is no less than a clash of civilizations—the perhaps irrational but surely historic reaction of an ancient rival against our Judeo-Christian heritage, our secular present, and the worldwide expansion of both. It is crucially important that we on our side should not be provoked into an equally historic but also equally irrational reaction against that rival.

Not all the ideas imported from the West by Western intruders or native Westernizers have been rejected. Some have been accepted by even the most radical Islamic fundamentalists, usually without acknowledgment of source, and suffering a sea change into something rarely rich but often strange. One such was political freedom, with the associated notions and practices of representation, election, and constitutional government. Even the Islamic Republic of Iran has a written constitution and an elected assembly, as well as a kind of episcopate, for none of which is there any prescription in Islamic teaching or any precedent in the Islamic past. All these institutions are clearly adapted from Western models. Muslim states have also retained many of the cultural and social customs of the West and the symbols that express them, such as the form and style of male (and to a much lesser extent female) clothing, notably in the military. The use of Western-invented guns and tanks and planes is a military necessity, but the continued use of fitted tunics and peaked caps is a cultural choice. From constitutions to Coca-Cola, from tanks and television to T-shirts, the symbols and artifacts, and through them the ideas, of the West have retained—even strengthened—their appeal.

THE MOVEMENT NOWADAYS CALLED FUNDAMENtalism is not the only Islamic tradition. There are others, more tolerant, more open, that helped to inspire the great achievements of Islamic civilization in the past, and we may hope that these other traditions will in time prevail. But before this issue is decided there will be a hard struggle, in which we of the West can do little

or nothing. Even the attempt might do harm, for these are issues that Muslims must decide among themselves. And in the meantime we must take great care on all sides to avoid the danger of a new era of religious wars, arising from the exacerbation of differences and the revival of ancient prejudices.

To this end we must strive to achieve a better appreciation of other religious and political cultures, through the study of their history, their literature, and their achievements. At the same time, we may hope that they will try to achieve a better understanding of ours, and especially that they will understand and respect, even if they do not choose to adopt for themselves, our Western perception of the proper relationship between religion and politics.

To describe this perception I shall end as I began, with a quotation from an American President, this time not the justly celebrated Thomas Jefferson but the somewhat unjustly neglected John Tyler, who, in a letter dated July 10, 1843, gave eloquent and indeed prophetic expression to the principle of religious freedom:

> The United States have adventured upon a great and noble experiment, which is believed to have been hazarded in the absence of all previous precedent—that of total separation of Church and State. No religious establishment *by law* exists among us. The conscience is left free from all restraint and each is permitted to worship his Maker after his own judgement. The offices of the Government are open alike to all. No tithes are levied to support an established Hierarchy, nor is the fallible judgement of man set up as the sure and infallible creed of faith. The Mahommedan, if he will to come among us would have the privilege guaranteed to him by the constitution to worship according to the Koran; and the East Indian might erect a shrine to Brahma if it so pleased him. Such is the spirit of toleration inculcated by our political Institutions. . . . The Hebrew persecuted and down trodden in other regions takes up his abode among us with none to make him afraid. . . . and the Aegis of the Government is over him to defend and protect him. Such is the great experiment which we have tried, and such are the happy fruits which have resulted from it; our system of free government would be imperfect without it.
>
> The body may be oppressed and manacled and yet survive; but if the mind of man be fettered, its energies and faculties perish, and what remains is of the earth, earthly. Mind should be free as the light or as the air.

MILITARY VICTORY, ECOLOGICAL DEFEAT

*Iraq was not the only loser in the Persian Gulf War.
The region's air and water quality, along with its plants and animals,
may not soon recover.*

MICHAEL G. RENNER

Michael G. Renner is a senior researcher at the Worldwatch Institute. His work focuses on the links between military activities and the environment.

Military historians are likely to remember the recent Gulf War as a modern-day *blitzkrieg*, a triumph of "smart bombs" and other high-tech wizardry. However, while the fighting was brought to a swift conclusion, the onslaught against the environment continues with undiminished ferocity. The Gulf War now ranks among the most ecologically destructive conflicts ever.

Kuwait is liberated, but the region has been transformed into a disaster zone. Hundreds of oil fires are severely polluting the atmosphere; oil deliberately spilled onto the ground and into the Persian Gulf is tainting aquifers and poisoning marine life; attacks on refineries, petrochemical plants, and chemical and nuclear facilities have likely released substantial quantities of toxic materials; damage to public utilities and roads could trigger health epidemics and famine; the massive movement of troops and their heavy equipment has imperiled an already fragile desert ecology. Kuwaiti officials think the environmental damages may be more severe than the material losses of the war.

But the disparity in the response to the military and environmental aspects of the conflict could hardly be more pronounced. To force Iraq out of Kuwait, no expense or effort was spared. An alliance of more than two dozen countries was carefully crafted, the United Nations machinery for collective security was thrown into high gear, and hundreds of thousands of soldiers and huge amounts of equipment were ferried halfway around the globe.

By contrast, assessing and tackling the ecological consequences of the conflict has been a much lower priority. For example, the effort to contain and clean up the massive oil spill in the Gulf in February was hampered by lack of money and poor coordination among various Saudi government agencies. Attempts to monitor the impacts of oil fires and to put them out also seem woefully inadequate. An air-quality testing lab in Kuwait has not been repaired, and fire-fighting equipment has been slow in coming.

The Gulf War demonstrates the need for the international community to set up a mechanism to cope with the ecological damage arising from armed conflicts. In a broader sense, though, it shows that wars and environmental protection are incompatible. Although international environmental-protection agreements are necessary, the most important step that can be taken is to work for peaceful means of resolving conflicts.

Towering Inferno

Kuwaiti officials estimate that as many as 6

From *World•Watch*, July/August 1991, pp. 27-33. *World•Watch*, published by Worldwatch Institute, Washington, D.C.

million barrels of oil are going up in flames every day—almost four times the country's oil production per day prior to the Iraqi invasion, or 9 percent of the world's petroleum consumption. Some scientists, includ-

R*oughly*
10 times as much
air pollution was being emitted
in Kuwait as by all U.S.
industrial and power-
generating plants
combined.

ing Paul Mason of the British government's Meteorological Office, believe the volume of burning oil is smaller. Beyond dispute, however, is the fact that immense clouds of smoke block the sunlight and turn day into night. In April, daytime temperatures in affected areas were as much as 27 degrees Fahrenheit below normal.

Fire fighters have never confronted so many fires burning simultaneously and in such close proximity. By May, workers had put out only 60 of the 500 to 600 fires, primarily the smaller and more accessible ones. Experts estimate that it will take at least two years to extinguish all of the blazes. By that time, Kuwait may have lost as much as 10 percent of its 92 billion barrels of proven oil reserves—either through combustion or structural damage to its oil reservoirs.

The atmospheric pollution resulting from these fires is almost unprecedented, comparable only to large-scale forest fires and volcanic eruptions. Assuming a burn rate of 6 million barrels per day, as much as 2.5 million tons of soot may be produced in a month—more than four times the average monthly emissions in the entire United States in 1989 (the last year for which data are available). In addition, more than 1 million tons of sulfur dioxide and approximately 100,000 tons of nitrogen oxides may be released each month.

The clouds of oil smoke also contain large amounts of toxic and potentially carcino-

genic substances such as hydrogen sulfide, benzene, and other hydrocarbons. Overall, according to a U.S. Environmental Protection Agency (EPA) estimate in March, roughly 10 times as much air pollution was being emitted in Kuwait as by all U.S. industrial and power-generating plants combined.

The stew of contaminants makes breathing a hazardous undertaking. Rare is the news story about postwar Kuwait that does not mention the sore throat from which virtually everyone seems to suffer. Kuwaiti hospitals are filled with people fallen ill from exposure to the air pollution, and doctors advise those with chronic respiratory problems not to return to Kuwait. Although considerable uncertainty persists concerning the long-term toll on human health, many air pollutants are thought to cause or aggravate a wide range of conditions, including blood disorders, respiratory problems such as asthma and bronchitis, coronary ailments, cancer, and possibly genetic damage. Scientists now acknowledge that prolonged exposure to even low levels of smog—the product of reactions between nitrogen oxides and hydrocarbons in the presence of sunlight—may cause irreparable lung damage. Young children and the elderly are particularly at risk.

Because Kuwaiti oil has a high sulfur content, acid rain—of which sulfur dioxide is a principal component—is expected to afflict the Gulf region and adjacent areas. Acid deposition (which does not always require rain) is known to destroy forests and reduce crop yields. It can also activate several dangerous metals normally found in soil—including aluminum, cadmium, and mercury—making them more soluble and therefore more of a threat to water supplies and edible fish. "Black rain"—soot that is washed out of the skies or eventually falls back to the ground—is coating people, animals, buildings, and crops with an oily, black film.

The effects of air pollution depend not just on the quantity of contaminants released, but on atmospheric conditions that change with the seasons. Summer is a particularly bad time for pollution in the Gulf because of diminished air-cleansing winds and rains, and increased atmospheric inversions that trap pollutants under stagnant layers of air.

The Geography of Pollution
The densest smoke is found over Kuwait,

eastern Iraq, and western and southern Iran. In Kuwait, scientists with the British Meteorological Office recorded 30,000 soot particles per cubic meter of air, 1,000 parts per billion of sulfur dioxide and 50 parts per billion of nitrogen oxides at an altitude of 6,000 feet—about 30, 20, and 10 times, respectively, the levels in a typical city plagued by air pollution.

As far as 1,000 miles away—in parts of Bulgaria, Romania, Turkey, and the Soviet Union that border on the Black Sea—smog levels caused by the oil fires are as serious as the smog found anywhere in Europe under normal conditions, according to Paul Mason. A much larger area—from the waters of the Nile to the snows of the Himalayas—is susceptible to acid rain and soot fallout, according to the Max Planck Institute for Meteorology in Hamburg, Germany (see map).

The burning of such large amounts of oil over long periods could generate enough soot and smoke to diminish solar radiation, thereby lowering daytime temperatures and reducing the amount of rainfall. One ounce of soot can block about two-thirds of the light falling over an area of 280 to 340 square yards. In Kuwait, the amount of solar energy reaching the ground is at times reduced by more than 90 percent. Reduced photosynthesis combined with the deposition of soot and other toxic materials could imperil crops.

Whether such an effect would extend beyond the Gulf region depends on how high the soot climbs and how long it remains there. That, in turn, depends on a range of factors, including the combustion characteristics of the oil fires, the size of the soot particles, and general atmospheric conditions. Intense fires, such as those involving hydrocarbons, create convective currents that give smoke a strong updrift. The finer the particles, the higher they rise, the longer they stay aloft, and the more efficient they are at blocking sunlight, according to Paul Crutzen, director of atmospheric chemistry at the Max Planck Institute for Chemistry in Mainz, Germany. Many small particles appear to be present in the smoke clouds, according to scientists from the British Meteorological Office who gathered samples from a plane in April.

The soot would need to rise to about 35,000 feet for the jet stream to pick it up and carry it around the globe. During April,

the smoke plume was reported to be hovering at altitudes of no more than 12,000 feet, with small quantities found as high as 20,000 feet. But the same hot summer weather that helps create temperature inversions near the ground could cause greater updrafting and thus make some of the smoke climb higher. By early May, the U.S. National Oceanic and Atmospheric Administration (NOAA) reported that soot levels at about 20 times above normal readings were recorded at the Mauna Loa Observatory in Hawaii. Presumably, the Kuwaiti oil fires, some 8,000 miles away, are the source of the soot. Despite the elevated soot levels, NOAA does not expect any "significant" environmental impact in North America.

At the same time that it is potentially causing a short-term cooling, the Kuwaiti oil conflagration is also contributing to the long-term phenomenon of global warming. It may add as much as 240 million tons of carbon to the atmosphere in the course of a year—about 4 percent of the current global annual carbon release. This is comparable to the amount produced by Japan, the world's second-largest economy and fourth-largest emitter of carbon dioxide from fossil fuels. Since carbon emissions need to be slashed by at least 20 percent by the year 2005 just to slow climate change, the Kuwaiti oil fires send us another step in the wrong direction.

Nothing in human experience could help model and predict the precise consequences of the Kuwaiti oil blaze. The Gulf region thus has become a huge air pollution laboratory. Unfortunately, the subjects of these dangerous pollution experiments are people, plants, and animals.

Oil on the Water

The oil spilled into the Gulf waters is posing a severe test for marine ecosystems. Estimated at more than 3 million barrels by the Saudi Meteorology and Environmental Protection Administration, the Persian Gulf oil spill roughly equals the largest in history—the Ixtoc well blowout in the Gulf of Mexico in 1979—and is 10 times the size of the Exxon Valdez accident.

Following spills during the eight-year Iran-Iraq war, the Persian Gulf was already a highly stressed environment in poor condition to withstand additional ecological assaults. A relatively shallow sea, it is essentially a closed ecosystem with only a narrow outlet to the Arabian Sea through the Strait of

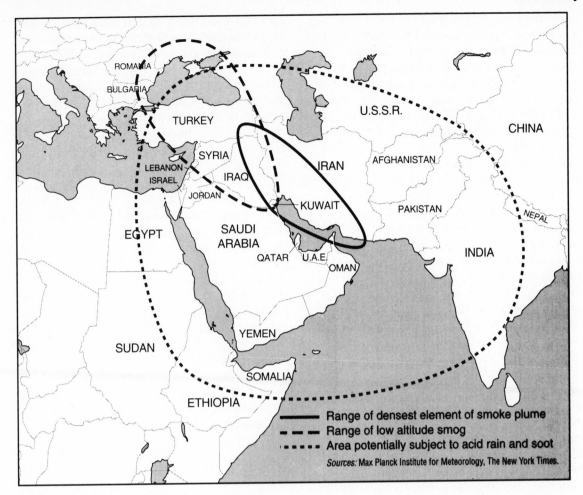

Range of densest element of smoke plume
--- Range of low altitude smog
····· Area potentially subject to acid rain and soot
Sources: Max Planck Institute for Meteorology, The New York Times.

Hormuz. Because Kuwaiti oil is of a "light" variety, up to 40 percent of it may have evaporated. The warm waters of the Gulf allow the remaining oil to decompose fairly rapidly, but significant amounts will foul shorelines or poison the sea bottom. The Saudi government was apparently ill-prepared for dealing with a disaster of such magnitude. By early April, only about half a million barrels of oil had been recovered, and it was clear the focus of the effort was to protect the country's desalination plants.

Considerable harm to Gulf fish and other wildlife—including porpoises, turtles, and seabirds—seems inevitable since many nesting and spawning grounds have been soaked in oil. At least 14,000 birds were killed along the Saudi shore. Some areas are so contaminated that they had to be declared off-limits to fishing, threatening the livelihoods of commercial and subsistence fishers. The Saudi shrimp industry, for example, has been wiped out and is considered unlikely to recover before the end of the decade. Extensive damage to coral reefs and sea grasses also has occurred, according to the EPA. If large

quantities of plankton are killed, the entire ecosystem may be threatened.

Desert Wasteland
The presence of more than 1 million soldiers with their immense arsenals has placed severe strains on the already fragile desert ecology of Kuwait, Saudi Arabia, and Iraq. Normally inhabited only by Bedouins, the desert of the Arabian peninsula cannot bear such a massive burden. Desert vegetation is sparse, but it helps to stabilize and protect the soil. Tanks and other vehicles have disrupted and compacted the soil and destroyed plants whose root systems are often close to the surface. As a result, the ground in many areas has been rendered susceptible to accelerated erosion. Seeds that lie dormant for large parts of the year, but which spark to life during spring rains, were likely affected.

If a significant portion of the desert vegetation is destroyed, dry spells might be lengthened and the ecological balance could be tipped into long-term decline. It may take hundreds of years for the desert to recover from the massive pre-war maneuvers and the tank battles, according to John Cloudsley-Thompson, an expert on desert ecology at the University of London. The Libyan desert, for example, still bears heavy scars from World War II combat, as do portions of the Negev in Israel from fighting in 1967 and 1973, and parts of the Mojave in southern California from maneuvers in the early 1940s.

The military presence has additional consequences. The armed forces routinely handle massive amounts of highly toxic materials to maintain and operate their tanks, jet fighters, and other pieces of equipment. Experience on U.S. military bases suggests that these substances could severely contaminate underground water supplies (see "War on Nature," [World • Watch] May/June 1991) if they're not properly handled. The inhospitable Saudi environment, with its blistering heat and gritty sand, forced the allied troops to use special lubricants of a more toxic nature, according to the U.S. Congressional Research Service, and generally larger amounts of hazardous materials than in more moderate climates. Exposure to even trace amounts of these chemicals through drinking, skin absorption, or inhalation can cause cancer, birth defects, and chromosome damage, and may seriously impair the function of the liver, kidneys, and central nervous system.

Another long-term peril stems from unexploded bombs and mines littering large parts of Iraq and Kuwait. The U.S. Air Force says it dropped 88,500 tons of explosives. The Pentagon generally assumes a 10-percent dud rate, meaning that almost 9,000 tons of explosive material must be cleared. Even an intensive recovery effort will likely fail to detect many of them, as experience from previous wars suggests. Gar Smith reports in *Earth Island Journal* that as much as 20 percent of the 1 million land mines laid by Iraq may remain undetected after cleanup efforts. Clearing the bombs is extremely difficult. Some of the "smart bombs" can only be disarmed with special tools and techniques that may be unavailable to Iraq. According to a report by the San Francisco-based Arms Control Research Center, some of these bombs are magnetically triggered. Any metal tool, such as a farmer's hoe or plow, could detonate them.

Chemical Warfare

The veil of military secrecy and post-war chaos in Iraq have precluded a full assessment of the effects of allied air attacks on Iraq's chemical, biological, and nuclear facilities and its refineries and petrochemical plants. Many of these facilities are located close to civilian population centers along the Tigris and Euphrates rivers. The incineration of materials produced and stored at these installations may well have generated a variety of deadly toxins, including cyanide, dioxin, and PCBs.

Reports in the German press, including such well-respected newspapers as *Frankfurter Rundschau* and *Handelsblatt*, suggest that toxic vapors escaped following air raids on chemical facilities, killing scores of Iraqi civilians. The nerve gases tabun and sarin, which Iraq has admitted possessing, evaporate rapidly and thus do not pose a persistent hazard. But another agent in the Iraqi arsenal, mustard gas, which is a mutagen and a carcinogen, is much longer-lived. A spokesman for the Patriotic Union of Kurdistan, an Iraqi opposition group, asserted in early February that allied attacks against chemical and ammunition plants led to widespread contamination of water resources.

Victor or Vanquished?

Sadly, the environmental disaster in the Gulf was preventable. In the months leading up to the outbreak of armed conflict, the alternatives of resorting to military force or relying on economic sanctions were debated, but the latter option was given too little time to work. Sanctions may have been less swift and certain than force, but would likely have spared many lives and avoided the tragic environmental effects.

That Saddam Hussein would set the torch to Kuwait's oil wells was no secret; he repeatedly threatened to do so if attacked by the U.S.-led coalition. The U.S. and British governments even commissioned studies about the potential environmental impact of such an act, but proceeded with their military plans anyway. The responsibility for the environmental destruction lies with Saddam Hussein's regime, but the devastation was either underestimated by the allied governments or considered an acceptable price of victory.

With such results, it is difficult to distinguish between victor and vanquished. Indeed, the war's ecological impact extends far beyond the battlefield, blurring the distinction between the combatants and countries that were not party to the conflict and had no say over its course.

In light of the Gulf War's ecological devastation, the time has come for the world community to consider creating a stronger convention for the protection of the environment in war. The existing United Nations "Convention on the Prohibition of Military or Any Other Hostile Use of Environmental Modification Techniques" is tailored to proscribe use of the environment as a weapon. A 1977 amendment to the 1949 Geneva Protocols prohibits means of warfare that are intended or expected to damage the environment and, in consequence, jeopardize the health and lives of the civilian population.

Neither agreement, however, includes any enforcement mechanisms and both were ignored by the belligerents in the Gulf War. Establishing such mechanisms, including trade embargoes and other nonviolent sanctions against offenders, would be an important first step. Next, lowering the threshold at which the prohibitions apply and making more explicit what acts they cover would give them more practical meaning.

But even a strengthened international code is of limited value. The conduct of war and the protection of the natural environment are fundamentally incompatible objectives. War on the environment is, unfortunately, nothing new. From the Punic Wars in the third century B.C. on, armies have poisoned wells, salted soils, and destroyed crops to foil the enemy. However, over time, the environmental impact of warfare has grown as sophisticated technology has boosted the firepower, range, and speed of weapons. In addition, modern industries present many high-profile targets whose destruction can wreak environmental devastation on a vast scale.

It was after the dawn of the atomic age that nations gradually came to realize that nuclear arsenals, if used, would destroy what they were supposed to defend. Now, in the wake of the Gulf War and its immense environmental toll, conventional warfare, too, may come to be seen as a less-acceptable means of settling conflicts.

Global Environment

We all live on just one planet! How simplistic: What a truism the foregoing statement seems! Yet thoughts of an Earth-wide social problem stuns the imagination. Our beautiful Earth is being damaged by the social careless-ness of modern peoples in pursuit of the good life. Yet the truth must be faced. As we have worked toward the betterment of global societies, collectively we have strained the Earth's capacity faster than it can recover. All plans for human improvement will need to think first of the Earth as a partner in solving social problems.

Society worldwide now pursues a better standard of living through four loosely interconnected global revolu-tions. Population growth has significantly increased the number of people using Earth's resources. Population implosion, a tendency for people to crowd together into cities, further compounds the burden. Industrialization provides the technological potential for each person to receive expanded material goods. And an international increase in human expectations adds zealous craving for exploiting the environment.

Global society demands modernization and a higher standard of living. The more these standards rise and the population increases, the greater the amount of pollution. Can Earth's natural systems survive the demands of its human inhabitants? Which will have to acknowledge de-feat first, the environment or society's plans for progress?

Our opening selection, "World Population Continues to Rise," presents a scary outlook. Another population equal to China within this decade? How will the Earth ever find the necessary resources to feed so many people? "Enough Is Enough" makes matters seem worse by telling us that people want more goods and resources than ever before. More people demanding more re-sources—think of the strain on the environment.

Our next article focuses on specific environmental problems with global implications. "Deforestation in the Tropics" explains how working to save the world's great forests has a great deal to do with understanding how local and international politics work.

"Rethinking the Environment" tells us that our tradi-tional belief that nature knows best is a myth. By itself, nature does poorly and it is time humans were aware of this truth. If we are to succeed in the future, we must correct our thinking about how the environment operates.

Looking Ahead: Challenge Questions

What is the connection between industrial advances, rising population, and danger to the environment?

What will the rapid growth in world population mean for U.S. society and its position among the peoples of the world?

Are you ready to change your socially conditioned love for consumerism in order to save the Earth's resources?

To correct tropical deforestation, why is it important to understand how governments operate?

How could the attitude that nature knows best be incorrect?

World Population Continues to RISE

NAFIS SADIK

Nafis Sadik is executive director of the United Nations Population Fund, 220 East 42nd Street, New York, New York 10017. This article is adapted from the Fund's *The State of World Population 1990*.

The executive director of the United Nations Population Fund outlines the current world population trends and suggests strategies for curbing population growth rates.

The 1990s will be a critical decade. The choices of the next 10 years will decide the speed of population growth for much of the next century; they will decide whether world population triples or merely doubles before it finally stops growing; they will decide whether the pace of damage to the environment speeds up or slows down.

The world's population, now 5.3 billion, is increasing by three people every second — about a quarter of a million every day. Between 90 and 100 million people — roughly equivalent to the population of Eastern Europe or Central America — will be added every year during the 1990s; a billion people — a whole extra China — over the decade.

No less than 95% of the global population growth over the next 35 years will be in the developing countries of Africa, Asia, and Latin America.

It has been more than 20 years since the population growth rate of developing countries reached its peak in 1965-70. But it will be during only the last five years of this century that the additions to total numbers in developing countries will reach their maximum. This 35-year lag is a powerful demonstration of the steamroller momentum of population growth.

Racing to provide services to fast-growing populations is like running up the down escalator: You have to run very fast indeed to maintain upward motion. So far, all the effort put into social programs has not been quite enough to move upward in numerical terms. The absolute total of human deprivation has actually increased, and unless there is a massive increase in family planning and other social spending, the future will be no better.

Population Trends

Southern Asia, with almost a quarter of the current total world population, will account for 31% of the total increase between now and the end of the century; Africa, with 12% of the world's population today, will account for 23% of the increase. By contrast, eastern Asia, which has another 25% of the current world population, will account for only 17% of the total increase.

Similarly, the developed countries — Europe (including the Soviet Union), North America, and Japan, which represent 23% of the current world population — will account for only 6% of the increase. The remaining 15% of the world's population, living in developing countries, will produce 23% of the increase.

By and large, the increases will be in the poorest countries — those by definition least equipped to meet the needs of the new arrivals and invest in the future.

Because of the world's skewed growth patterns, the balance of numbers will shift radically. In 1950, Europe and North America constituted 22% of the world's population. In 2025, they will make up less than 9%. Africa, only 9% of the world population in 1950, will account for just under a fifth of the 2025 total. India will overtake China as the world's most populous country by the year 2030.

Toward the end of the twenty-first century, a number of countries seem set to face severe problems if populations grow as projected. Nigeria could have some 500 million citizens — as many as the whole African continent had around 1982. This would represent more than 10 people for every hectare of arable land. Modern France, with better soils and less erosion, has only three people per hectare. Bangladesh's 116 million inhabitants would grow to 324 million, with density on its arable land more than twice as high as in the Netherlands today. This does not take into account any land that may be lost to sea-level rises caused by global warming.

It should be emphasized that these are not the most-pessimistic projections. On the contrary, they assume steadily declining fertility during most of the next 100 years.

Food

Between 1979-81 and 1986-87, cereal production per person actually declined in 51 developing countries and rose in only 43. The total number of malnourished people increased from 460 million to 512 million and is projected to exceed 532 million by the end of the century.

Developing countries as a whole have suffered a serious decline in food self-sufficiency. Their cereal imports in 1969-71 were only 20 million tons. By 1983-85, they had risen to 69 million tons and are projected to total 112 million tons by the end of the century. These deficits have so far been met by corresponding surpluses in the industrialized countries — of which the overwhelming bulk comes from North America.

World food security now depends shakily on the performance of North American farmers. Following the drought-hit U.S. harvest of 1988, world cereal stocks dropped from 451 million tons in 1986-87 to only 290 million tons in 1989, down from a safe 24% of annual consumption to the danger level of 17%.

Poverty

The world produces enough food to feed everyone today — yet malnutrition affects as many as 500 million people. The problem is poverty and the ability to earn a livelihood. The total numbers of the poor have grown over the past two decades to around one billion now.

Absolute poverty has shown a dogged tendency to rise in numerical terms. The poorest fifth of the population still dispose of only 4% of the world's wealth, while the richest dispose of 58%. Economic recession, rising debt burdens, and mistaken priorities have reduced social spending in many countries.

But population growth at over 2% annually has also slowed social progress. So much additional investment has been required to increase the quantity of health, education, and other services to meet the needs of increased populations that the quality of service has suffered.

In many sectors, the proportion of deprived people has declined. But this is a reduced proportion of a higher total population swelled by rapid growth. As a result, the total numbers of deprived people have grown.

The growth of incomes may be affected by population growth. On a regional basis, there is an inverse relationship between population growth and growth of per capita income. There is a lag of 15–20 years between the peak of population growth and the peak growth in the labor force. Already there are severe problems in absorbing new entrants to the labor force in regions such as Africa or South Asia. Yet, in numerical terms, the highest rates of labor-force growth in developing countries lie ahead, in the years 2010–2020.

The labor force in developing countries will grow from around 1.76 billion today to more than 3.1 billion in 2025. Every year, 38 million new jobs will be needed, without counting jobs required to wipe out existing underemployment, estimated at 40% in many developing countries. Complicating the issue will be the spread of new, labor-saving technologies.

The land still provides the livelihood of almost 60% of the population of developing countries. But most of the best and most-accessible land is already in use, and what is left is either less fertile or harder to clear and work. The area available per person actually declined at the rate of 1.9% a year during the 1980s.

Urban and Education Issues

In recent decades, urban growth in developing countries has been even more rapid than overall population growth. Town populations are expanding at 3.6% a year — four and a half times faster than in industrialized countries and 60% faster than rural areas. Rural migrants swell the total, but an increasing share of this growth now comes from natural growth within the cities themselves.

The speed of growth has outpaced the ability of local and national government to provide adequate services. The number of urban households without safe water increased from 138 million in 1970 to 215 million in 1988. Over the same period, households without adequate sanitation ballooned from 98 million to 340 million.

The total number of children out of school grew from 284 million in 1970 to 293 million in 1985 and is

A woman in Lesotho shovels earth while carrying her baby on her back. Ninety percent of the labor force here is women. In many cultures, women do much of the labor while rearing children. A key to success in reducing overpopulation, according to author Sadik, lies in reaching women in developing countries.

projected to rise further to 315 million by the end of the century. Also between 1970 and 1985: The total number of illiterates rose from 742 million to 889 million, and the total number of people without safe sanitation increased from about a billion to 1.75 billion.

Eating Away at the Earth

These increasing numbers are eating away at the earth itself. The combination of fast population growth and poverty in developing countries has begun to make permanent changes to the environment. During the 1990s, these changes will reach critical levels. They include continued urban growth, degradation of land and water resources, massive deforestation, and buildup of greenhouse gases.

Many of these changes are now inevitable because they were not foreseen early enough, or because action was not taken to forestall them. Our options in the present generation are narrower because of the decisions of our predecessors. Our range of choice, as individuals or as nations, is narrower, and the choices are harder.

The 1990s will decide whether the choices for our children narrow yet further — or open up. We know more about population — and interactions among population, resources, and the environment — than any previous generation. We have the basis for action. Failure to use it decisively will ensure only that the problems become much more severe and much more intractable, the choices harder and their price higher.

At the start of the 1990s, the choice must be to act decisively to slow population growth, attack poverty, and protect the environment. The alternative is to hand on to our children a poisoned inheritance.

Danger Signals

Just a few years ago, in 1984, it seemed as if the rate of population growth was slowing everywhere except Africa and parts of South Asia. The world's population seemed set to stabilize at around 10.2 billion toward the end of the next century.

Today, the situation looks less promising. Progress in reducing birth rates has been slower than expected. According to the latest U.N. projections, the world has overshot the marker points of the 1984 "most likely" medium projection and is now on course for an eventual total that will be closer to 11 billion than to 10 billion.

In 15 countries — 13 of them in Africa — birthrates actually rose between 1960-65 and 1980-85. In another 23 nations, the birthrate fell by less than 2%.

If fertility reductions continue to be slower than projected, the mark could be missed yet again. In that case, the world could be headed toward an eventual total of up to 14 billion people.

Why should we be worried about this? At present, the human race numbers "only" 5.3 billion, of which about a billion live in poverty. Can the earth meet even modest aspirations for the "bottom billion," let alone those of the better-off and their descendants, without irreparable damage to its life-support systems?

Already, our impact has been sufficient to degrade the soils of millions of hectares, to threaten the rain forests and the thousands of species they harbor, to thin the ozone layer, and to initiate a global warming whose full consequences cannot yet be calculated. The impact has greatly increased since 1950.

By far the largest share of resources used, and waste created, is currently the responsibility of the "top billion" people, those in industrialized countries. These are the countries overwhelmingly responsible for damage to the ozone layer and acidification, as well as for roughly two-thirds of global warming.

However, in developing countries, the combination of poverty and population growth among the "bottom billion" is damaging the environment in several of the most sensitive areas, notably through deforestation and land degradation. Deforestation is a prime cause of increased levels of carbon dioxide, one of the principal greenhouse gases responsible for global warming. Rice paddies and domestic cattle — food suppliers for 2 billion people in developing countries — are also major producers of methane, another of the greenhouse gases.

Developing countries are also doing their best to increase their share of industrial production and consumption. Their share of industrial pollution is rising and will continue to rise.

At any level of development, larger numbers of people consume more resources and produce more waste. The quality of human life is inseparable from the quality of the environment. It is increasingly clear that both are inseparable from the question of human numbers and concentrations.

A Case for Change

Redressing the balance demands action in three major areas:

1. A shift to cleaner technologies, energy efficiency, and resource conservation by all countries is necessary, especially for the richer quarter of the world's population.

Carbon-dioxide emissions will be hardest to bring under control. If the atmospheric concentration of carbon dioxide is to be stabilized, cuts of 50% to 80% in emissions may be required by the middle of the next century. These will be

difficult to achieve even with the most-concentrated efforts.

Four major lines of action will produce the greatest impact, especially if they are pursued in parallel. The first is improved efficiency in energy use. The second is a shift from fossil fuels, which currently account for 78% of the world's energy use, to renewable sources such as wind, geothermal, and solar thermal. The third is halting deforestation. The fourth is slowing population growth.

There are no technological solutions in sight for methane emissions from irrigated fields and livestock. They have both expanded in response to growing rural populations and to meet expanding world demands for cereals and meat. The irrigated area has grown by about 1.9% a year since 1970, slightly faster than world population. Livestock and irrigation will both continue to expand

A literacy class for mothers at a social center in Chad. Achieving literacy for women gives them access to new information, which in turn gives them more choices regarding children and family planning. Literacy programs are one of the main components of international organizations' outreach to developing countries to stem the world's population growth rates.

FAO PHOTO BY F. MATTIOLI

in line with populations in developing countries. Reducing population growth is the only viable strategy to reduce the growth in methane emissions from these sources.

2. A direct and all-out attack on poverty itself will be required.

3. Reductions are needed in overall rates of population growth. Reducing population growth, especially in the countries with the highest rates of growth, will be a crucial part of any strategy of sustainable development.

Reducing the rate of population growth will help extend the options for future generations: It will be easier to provide higher quality and universal education, health care, shelter, and an adequate diet; to invest in employment and economic development; and to limit the overall level of environmental damage.

What Needs to Be Done?

Immediate action to widen options and improve the quality of life, especially for women, will do much to secure population goals. It will also widen the options and improve the quality of life of future generations.

Education is often the means to a new vision of options. It encourages a sense of control over personal destiny and the possibility of choices beyond accepted tradition. For women, it offers a view of sources of status beyond childbearing. Because of this, education — especially for girls — has a strong impact on the health of the family and on its chosen size.

Women assume the burden of childcare along with their other tasks. They are in charge of nutrition, hygiene, food, and water. As a result, the effect of women's education on child survival is very marked.

Education's impact on fertility and use of family planning is equally strong. Women with seven or more years of education tend to marry an average of almost four years later than those who have had none.

Yet, there remains a great deal to be done in women's education, even to bring it level with men's. Women make up almost two-thirds

of the illiterate adults in developing countries. The importance of literacy programs for adult women goes far beyond reading and writing: It also allows access to practical information on such matters as preventive health care and family planning, which are often part of the programs themselves.

Sustained improvements in health care give people a sense of control over their lives. With adequate health care, parents develop the sense that they have some choice over their children's survival. Parents' feeling of control over their lives is extended by modern family planning; they can protect the health of both mother and child by preventing or postponing childbirth. Preventive measures that the family itself can apply assist the process.

Support for Family-Planning Efforts

Political support from the highest levels in the state is essential in making family planning both widely available and widely used. Political backing helps to legitimize family planning, to desensitize it, and to place it in the forum of public debate. It helps win over traditional leaders or counter their hostility. It also helps to ensure that funding and staffing for family planning are stable and protected against damaging budget cuts or the competing demands of rival departments.

Support must extend far beyond the national leadership before programs take off. It may be necessary to involve a wide range of religious and traditional leaders in discussions before introducing population policies and programs on a wide scale. If these leaders feel that they have been sidestepped, their opposition may become entrenched. If they are consulted and involved, on the other hand, they may often turn into allies. In Indonesia, for example, Muslim religious leaders were consulted at national and local levels; they not only withdrew their opposition, but have added their voices to the government's call for family planning.

Four main barriers block the way to easy access to family planning. The most obvious is geographical:

FAO PHOTO BY F. BOTTS

An outdoor class in a rural primary school in Swaziland. The Swazi government, assisted by international organizations, delivers advice on family planning through maternal and child-health centers.

How long do people have to travel to get supplies, and how long do they have to wait for service when they get there?

The second barrier is financial: While many surveys show that people are willing to pay moderate amounts for family-planning supplies, most poor people have a fairly low price threshold. Costs of more than 1% of income are likely to prove a deterrent.

Culture and communication are a third barrier: opposition from the peer group, husband, or mother-in-law; shyness about discussing contraception or undergoing gynecological examination; language difficulties; or unsympathetic clinic staff.

A fourth barrier is the methods available: There is no such thing as the perfect contraceptive. Most people who need one can find a method suited to their needs — if one is available. However, if high contraception use is to be achieved, suitable services must be not only available, but accessible to all who need them.

Suitable services mean high-quality services. In the long run, the quantity of continuing users will depend on the quality of the service.

Service providers do not need to be highly educated, but they should be sympathetic, well informed, and committed to their work. The service must be reliable, so that users can count on supplies when they need them. Good counseling is one of the most important aspects of quality. Family planning is loaded with emotional, social, and sometimes religious values. It is vulnerable to poor information, rumor, and outright superstition. Along with reliable supplies and a good system for referral in problem cases, good counseling can make a big difference to continuation rates.

Two other channels are useful in broadening the base and increasing the appeal of family planning: community-based distribution and social marketing.

Community-based distribution (CBD) programs use members of the community — housewives, leaders, or members of local groups — to distribute contraceptives. Older married mothers who are themselves contraceptive users have proved the best candidates.

Maturity, tact, perseverance, and enthusiasm are essential requirements for the good distributor.

After many years of relying only on clinic and health workers to deliver services, family-planning programs are discovering the uses of the marketplace. The private sector provides contraceptives to more than half the users in many developing countries.

Social-marketing programs reduce the cost to the user and increase sales by subsidizing supplies. These two aspects — the integration of suppliers with regular health services through training and the subsidization of supplies — are felt to combine the ease of access of the market with the sense of social responsibility of service programs.

The potential of community-based distribution and social marketing has not been exploited in most countries. Out of 93 countries studied for one survey, only 37 had a CBD or social-marketing project. There is clearly a considerable potential for expansion as an essential complement to integrated health services.

The technology of contraception is usually thought of in terms of safety and reliability. But it should also be seen as another important aspect of improving access and choice in family-planning programs.

Currently, the most popular method worldwide is sterilization, with around 119 million women and 45 million men in 1987. Next in popularity was the intrauterine device (IUD), with 84 million users, followed by the pill, with 67 million. The pattern of use differs considerably from one country to another and between developing countries and developed. Sterilization is by far the most common method in developing countries, with 45% of users, though only one-quarter of these were male. The IUD comes next in popularity, with 23%. In the North, sterilization accounts for only 14% of users and IUDs for 8%.

Users balance all the advantages and disadvantages they are aware of before deciding on a method —

FRONTIERS OF TECHNOLOGY

Research must continue for the ideal method of contraception: cheap, totally effective, risk-free, reversible, without undesirable side effects, and simple enough for use without medical provision or supervision.

No such method is yet on the horizon. But research continues to push forward the frontiers, under conditions that have become more and more difficult.

The business of developing new contraceptives has changed radically. Tighter controls on testing and rising risks of costly lawsuits have made drug companies wary. The leading role has been assumed by the World Health Organization (WHO) and by nonprofit organizations such as the Population Council and Family Health International. But real spending on contraceptive research and development has not increased.

Some promising new candidates have been developed. Norplant, already approved for use in several countries, is probably closest to wide dissemination. It consists of six tiny rods containing the progestin hormone levonorgestrol. These are implanted under the skin of a woman's inside arm. Norplant, particularly suitable for women who have completed their families, prevents pregnancies for five years before it needs replacing. A two-rod version providing protection for three years is being developed. Norplant is highly effective, and unlike the injectable Depo-Provera, its contraceptive effect ends soon after it is removed. The drawback for some situations is that it requires a physician to insert and remove. The cost, at $2.80 per year of protection, is more than the pill at $1.95, but less than Depo-Provera at $4 per year.

Other long-acting hormonal methods may be introduced during the 1990s. They include biodegradable implants, providing 18 months of protection, and injectable microspheres lasting between one and six months. Vaginal rings containing levonorgestrol, which can be inserted and removed by the woman, are also being tested. And the Population Council is researching a male contraceptive vaccine.

— **Nafis Sadik**

or no method. If they do not like the available alternatives, they will simply drop out and use no method at all, or revert to less reliable traditional methods. One recent study in East Java found that, among women who were not given the method they preferred, 85% had discontinued use within one year. Where women were given the method they wanted, the dropout rate was only 25%.

Diversity, then, is the key to providing options. Diverse channels of distribution create the widest possible access to contraception. Diverse technology offers the widest possible choice of methods. The combination maximizes use.

Developing Human Resources

Investment in human resources provides a firm base for rapid economic development and could have a significant impact on the environmental crisis. It is essential for global security. But in the past, it has often commanded a lower priority than industry, agriculture, or military expenditure.

It is time for a new scale of priorities: There is no other sphere of development where investment can make such a large contribution both to the options and to the quality of life, both in the present and in the future. Whatever the future returns, investment is needed now.

Enough is Enough

Assessing global consumption

Alan Durning

ALAN DURNING is a senior researcher at the Worldwatch Institute. This article is adapted from "Asking How Much Is Enough," Chapter Nine, in *State of the World 1991*.

"Our enormously productive economy ... demands that we make consumption our way of life, that we convert the buying and use of goods into rituals, that we seek our spiritual satisfaction, our ego satisfaction, in consumption. ... We need things consumed, burned up, worn out, replaced, and discarded at an ever increasing rate."

Victor Lebow, U.S. retailing analyst, 1955

Across the country, Americans have responded to Victor Lebow's call, and around the globe, those who could afford it have followed. And many can: Worldwide, on average, a person today is four-and-a-half times richer than were his or her great-grandparents at the turn of the century.

Needless to say, that new global wealth is not evenly spread among the earth's people. One billion live in unprecedented luxury; one billion live in destitution. Overconsumption by the world's fortunate is an environmental problem unmatched in severity by anything except perhaps population growth. Surging exploitation of resources threatens to exhaust or unalterably disfigure forests, soils, water, air, and climate. High consumption may be a mixed blessing in human terms, too. Many in the industrial lands have a sense that, hoodwinked by a consumerist culture, they have been fruitlessly attempting to satisfy social, psychological, and spiritual needs with material things.

Of course, the opposite of overconsumption—poverty—is no solution to either environmental or human problems. It is infinitely worse for people and bad for the natural world. Dispossessed peasants slash and burn their way into Latin American rain forests, and hungry nomads turn their herds out onto fragile African range land, reducing it to desert. If environmental destruction results when people have either too little or too much, we are left to wonder how much is enough. What level of consumption can the earth support? When does having more cease to add appreciably to human satisfaction?

From *Dollars & Sense*, June 1991, pp. 15-18. *Dollars & Sense* is a monthly progressive economics magazine published in Somerville, Massachusetts. First-year subscriptions cost $16.95 and may be ordered by writing *Dollars & Sense*, One Summer St., Sommerville, MA 02143.

THE CONSUMING SOCIETY

Consumption is the hallmark of our era. The headlong advance of technology, rising earnings, and cheaper material goods have lifted consumption to levels never dreamed of a century ago. In the United States, the world's premier consuming society, people today on average own twice as many cars, drive two-and-a-half times as far, and travel 25 times further by air than did their parents in 1950. Air conditioning spread from 15% of households in 1960 to 64% in 1987, and color televisions from 1% to 93%. Microwave ovens and video cassette recorders reached almost two-thirds of American homes during the 1980s alone.

Japan and Western Europe have displayed parallel trends. Per person, the Japanese today consume more than four times as much aluminum, almost five times as much energy, and 25 times as much steel as they did in 1950. They also own four times as many cars and eat nearly twice as much meat. Like the Japanese, Western Europeans' consumption levels are only one notch below Americans'.

The late 1980s saw some poor societies begin the transition to consuming ways. In China, the sudden surge in spending on consumer durables shows up clearly in data from the State Statistical Bureau: Between 1982 and 1987, color televisions spread from 1% to 35% of urban Chinese homes, washing machines quadrupled from 16% to 67%, and refrigerators expanded their reach from 1% to 20%.

Meanwhile, in India, the emergence of a middle class, along with liberalization of the consumer market and the introduction of buying on credit, has led to explosive growth in sales of everything from automobiles and motorbikes to televisions and frozen dinners.

Few would begrudge anyone the simple advantages of cold food storage or mechanized clothes washing. The point, rather, is that even the oldest non-Western nations are emulating the high-consumption lifestyle. Long before all the world's people could achieve the American dream, however, we would lay waste the planet.

The industrial world's one billion meat eaters, car drivers, and throwaway consumers are responsible for the lion's share of the damage humans have caused common global resources. Over the past century, the economies of the wealthiest fifth of humanity have pumped out two-thirds of the greenhouse gases threatening the earth's climate, and each year their energy use releases three-fourths of the sulfur and nitrogen oxides causing acid rain. Their industries generate most of the world's hazardous chemical wastes, and their air conditioners, aerosol sprays, and factories release almost 90% of the chlorofluorocarbons destroying the earth's protective ozone layer. Clearly, even one billion profligate consumers is too much for the earth.

Beyond the environmental costs of acquisitiveness, some perplexing findings of social scientists throw doubt on the wisdom of high consumption as a personal and national goal: Rich societies have had little success in turning consumption into fulfillment. Regular surveys by the National Opinion Research Center of the University of Chicago reveal, for example, that no more Americans report they are "very happy" now than in 1957.

Likewise, a landmark study by sociologist Richard Easterlin in 1974 revealed that Nigerians, Filipinos, Panamanians, Yugoslavians, Japanese, Israelis, and West Germans all ranked

Many in the industrial lands have a sense that, hoodwinked by a consumerist culture, they have been fruitlessly attempting to satisfy social, psychological, and spiritual needs with material things.

themselves near the middle of a happiness scale. Confounding any attempt to correlate affluence and happiness, poor Cubans and rich Americans were both found to be considerably happier than the norm.

If the effectiveness of consumption in providing personal fulfillment is questionable, perhaps environmental concerns can help us redefine our goals.

IN SEARCH OF SUFFICIENCY

By examining current consumption patterns, we receive some guidance on what the earth can sustain. For three of the most ecologically important types of consumption—transportation, diet, and use of raw materials—the world's people are distributed unevenly over a vast range. Those at the bottom clearly fall below the "too little" line, while those at the top, in the cars-meat-and-disposables class, clearly consume too much.

Approximately one billion people do their traveling, aside from the occasional donkey or bus ride, on foot. Unable to get to jobs easily, attend school, or bring their complaints before government offices, they are severely hindered by the lack of transportation options.

Another three billion people travel by bus and bicycle. Kilometer for kilometer, bikes are cheaper than any other vehicle, costing less than $100 new in most of the Third World and requiring no fuel.

The world's automobile class is relatively small: Only 8% of humans, about 400 million people, own cars. The automobile makes itself indispensable: Cities sprawl, public transit atrophies, shopping centers multiply, workplaces scatter.

The global food consumption ladder has three rungs. According to the latest World Bank estimates, the world's 630 million poorest people are unable to provide themselves with a healthy diet. On the next rung, the 3.4 billion grain eaters of the world's middle class get enough calories and plenty of plant-based protein, giving them the world's healthiest basic diet.

The top of the ladder is populated by the meat eaters, those who obtain close to 40% of their calories from fat. These 1.25 billion people eat three times as much fat per person as the remaining four billion, mostly because they eat so much red meat. The meat class pays the price of its diet in high death rates from the so-called diseases of affluence—heart disease, stroke, and certain types of cancer.

The earth also pays for the high-fat diet. Indirectly, the meat-eating quarter of humanity consumes nearly 40% of the world's grain—grain that fattens the livestock they eat. Meat production is behind a substantial share of the environmental strains induced by agriculture, from soil erosion to overpumping of underground water.

In consumption of raw materials, such as steel, cotton, or wood, the same pattern emerges. A large group lacks many of the benefits provided by modest use of nonrenewable resources—particularly durables like radios, refrigerators, water pipes, tools, and carts with lightweight wheels and ball bearings. More than two billion people live in countries where per capita consumption of steel, the most basic modern material, falls below 50 kilograms a year.

Roughly 1.5 billion live in the middle class of materials use. Providing each of them with durable goods every year uses between 50 and 150 kilograms of steel. At the top of the heap is the industrial world or the throwaway class. A typical resident of the industrialized fourth of the world uses 15 times as much paper, 10 times as much steel, and 12 times as much fuel as a Third World resident.

In the throwaway economy, packaging becomes an end in itself, disposables proliferate, and durability suffers. Americans toss away 180 million razors annually, enough paper and plastic plates and cups to feed the world a picnic six times a year, and enough aluminum cans to make 6,000 DC-10 airplanes. Similarly, the Japanese use 30 million "disposable" single-roll cameras each year, and the British dump 2.5 billion diapers.

THE CULTIVATION OF NEEDS

What prompts us to consume so much? "The avarice of mankind is insatiable," wrote Aristotle 23 centuries ago. As each of our desires is satisfied, a new one appears in its place. All of economic theory is based on that observation.

What distinguishes modern consuming habits, some would say, is simply that we are much richer than our ancestors, and consequently have more ruinous effects on nature. While a great deal of truth lies in that view, five distinctly modern factors play a role in cultivating particularly voracious appetites: the influence of social pressures in mass societies, advertising, the shopping culture, various government policies, and the expansion of the mass market into households and local communities.

In advanced industrial nations, daily interactions with the economy lack the face-to-face character prevailing in surviving local communities. Traditional virtues such as integrity, honesty, and skill are too hard to measure to serve as yardsticks of social worth. By default, they are gradually supplanted by a simple, single indicator—money. As one Wall Street banker put it bluntly to the *New York Times*, "Net worth equals self-worth."

Beyond social pressures, the affluent live completely enveloped in pro-consumption advertising messages. The sales pitch is everywhere. One analyst estimates that the typical American is exposed to 50-100 advertisements each morning before nine o'clock. Along with their weekly 22-hour diet of television, American teenagers are typically exposed to three to four hours of TV advertisements a week, adding up to at least 100,000 ads between birth and high school graduation.

Marketers have found ever more ways to push their products. Ads are piped into classrooms and doctors' offices, woven into the plots of feature films, placed on board games, mounted in bathroom stalls, and played back between rings on public phones in the Kansas City airport. Even the food supply may go mass media: The Viskase company of Chicago now offers to print edible ad slogans on hot dogs, and Eggverts International is using a similar technique to advertise on thousands of eggs in Israel.

Advertising has been one of the fastest growing industries during the past half-century. In the United States, ad expenditures rose from $198 per capita in 1950 to $498 in 1989. Worldwide, over the same period, per person advertising expenditures grew from $15 to $46. In developing countries, the increases have been astonishing. Advertising billings in India jumped fivefold in the 1980s; newly industrialized South Korea's advertising industry grew 35-40% annually in the late 1980s.

Shopping, particularly in the United States, seems to have become a primary cultural activity. Americans spend six hours a week shopping. Some 93% of American teenage girls surveyed in 1987 deemed shopping their favorite pastime.

Government policies also play a role in promoting consumption and in worsening its ecological impact. The British tax code, for example, encourages businesses to buy thousands of large company cars for employee use. Most governments in North and South America subsidize beef production on a massive scale.

Finally, the sweeping advance of the commercial mass market into realms once dominated by family members and local enterprise has made consumption far more wasteful than in the past. More and more, flush with cash but pressed for time, households opt for the questionable "conveniences" of prepared, packaged foods, miracle cleaning products, and disposable everything— from napkins to shower curtains. All these things cost the earth dearly, and change households from productive units of the economy to passive, consuming entities.

Like the household, the community economy has atrophied—or been dismembered—under the blind force of the money economy. Shopping malls, superhighways, and strips have replaced corner stores, local restaurants, and neighborhood theaters—the very places that help create a sense of common identity and community. Traditional Japanese vegetable stands and fish shops are giving way to supermarkets and convenience stores, and styrofoam and plastic film have replaced yesterday's newspaper as fish wrap.

All these things nurture the acquisitive desires that everyone has. Can we, as individuals and as citizens, act to confront these forces?

THE CULTURE OF PERMANENCE

The basic value of a sustainable society, the ecological equivalent of the Golden Rule, is simple: Each generation should meet its own needs without jeopardizing the prospects of future generations to meet theirs.

For individuals, the decision to live a life of sufficiency—to find their own answer to the question "how much is enough?"—is to begin a highly personal process. Social researcher Duane Elgin estimated in 1981—perhaps optimistically—that 10 million adult Americans were experimenting "wholeheartedly" with voluntary simplicity. India, the Netherlands, Norway, Western Germany, and the United Kingdom all have small segments of their populations who adhere to a non-consuming philosophy. Motivated by the desire to live justly in an unjust world, to walk gently on the earth, and to avoid distraction, clutter, and pretense, their goal is not ascetic self-denial but personal fulfillment. They do not think consuming more is likely to provide it.

Realistically, voluntary simplicity is unlikely to gain ground rapidly against the onslaught of consumerist values. And, ultimately, personal restraint will do little if not wedded to bold political and social steps against the forces promoting consumption. Commercial television, for example, will need fundamental reorientation in a culture of permanence. As religious historian Robert Bellah put it, "That happiness is to be attained through limitless material acquisition is denied by every religion and philosophy known to humankind, but is preached incessantly by every American television set."

Direct incentives for overconsumption are also essential targets for reform. If goods' prices reflected something closer to the environmental cost of their production, through revised subsidies and tax systems, the market itself would guide consumers toward less damaging forms of consumption. Disposables and packaging would rise in price relative to durable, less-packaged goods; local un-processed food would fall in price relative to prepared products trucked from far away.

The net effect might be lower overall consumption as people's effective purchasing power declined. As currently constituted, unfortunately, economies penalize the poor when aggregate consumption contracts: Unemployment skyrockets and inequalities grow. Thus arises one of the greatest challenges for sustainable economics in rich societies— finding ways to ensure basic employment opportunities for all without constantly stoking the fires of economic growth.

In the final analysis, accepting and living by sufficiency rather than excess offers a return to what is, culturally speaking, the human home: to the ancient order of family, community, good work, and good life; to a reverence for excellence of skilled handiwork; to a true materialism that does not just care about things but cares for them; to communities worth spending a lifetime in. The very things that make life worth living, that give depth and bounty to human existence, are infinitely sustainable.

Deforestation in the Tropics

Government policies that encourage exploitation—in particular excessive logging and clearing for ranches and farms—are largely to blame for the accelerating destruction of tropical forests

Robert Repetto

ROBERT REPETTO is director of the program in economic policies and institutions at the World Resources Institute in Washington, D.C. A 1959 graduate of Harvard College, he went on to get an M.Sc. from the London School of Economics and a Ph.D. in economics from Harvard University. Repetto was an economist in India, Pakistan and Indonesia, associate professor of economics and population at the Harvard School of Public Health and a consultant to a number of U.S. and multinational development-assistance agencies before joining the institute in 1983.

Tropical forests are disappearing at the rate of tens of thousands of square miles per year. The deforestation is laying waste a valuable natural resource throughout much of the developing world and is driving countless plant and animal species to extinction, and it may well have significant effects on world climate.

Among the agents of the devastation are inefficient commercial logging operations and the conversion of forested areas to cattle ranching and agriculture. Data collected by numerous investigators and evaluated by my colleagues and me at the World Resources Institute indicate that both the logging and the conversion are largely the result of government policies. Many of those policies are driven by the severe economic pressures afflicting debt-burdened underdeveloped countries. Those pressures in turn are exacerbated by certain practices of developed countries and their national and international financial institutions. Hence the causes as well as the effects of tropical-forest degradation should elicit worldwide concern.

The destruction of tropical forests is a more serious problem than it was thought to be only a decade ago, judging by recent estimates based on remote sensing from satellites and on careful field surveys [*see illustration on page 228*]. In India, for example, studies by the National Remote Sensing Centre lead to an estimated deforestation rate for the early 1980's of 1.5 million hectares (3.7 million acres) per year, some 10 times an earlier estimate by the Food and Agriculture Organization; the satellite imagery showed that large areas legally designated as forestland were already in fact virtually treeless.

Deforestation at this rate poses extreme risks to natural systems. The consequent release of carbon dioxide to the atmosphere is estimated to account for from 15 to 30 percent of annual global carbon dioxide emissions, and so it contributes substantially to the buildup of greenhouse gases. Moreover, the loss of tropical forests is rapidly eliminating the habitat of large numbers of plant and animal species. About half of the world's species inhabit tropical forests; in 10 biologically rich and severely threatened regions that account for 3.5 percent of the remaining tropical-forest area, 7 percent of all plant species will probably go extinct by the end of the century, if current trends continue.

A sense of crisis is emerging in the tropics as governments recognize that the rapid deforestation represents a waste of valuable resources and a severe economic loss. In some cases governments have taken action. In Thailand commercial logging was recently banned, over the protests of influential concession holders, when surveys showed that forest cover there had declined from 29 to 19 percent of the land area between 1985 and 1988 and after landslides from deforested hillsides cost 40,000 people their homes. In the Philippines, where undisturbed forests containing one valuable family of tall trees, the dipterocarps, have shrunk from 16 million hectares in 1960 to less than a million hectares left standing in remote hill regions, logging has been suspended in most provinces; as a result, mills in the Philippines are closing or are importing logs from Sabah and Sarawak, two states in Malaysia.

Mills in the once rich Indonesian production centers of Sumatra and Kalimantan are also experiencing shortages of accessible high-quality timber and are importing logs from Sabah, Sarawak and the Indonesian province of Irian Jaya. Government officials have begun to realize that Indonesia's ambitious plans for developing its timber industry could be thwarted by a lack of timber. Even Sabah and Sarawak, currently the major sources of logs in Asia, are harvesting almost twice the sustained yield of their forests, which are being depleted rapidly.

In the Ivory Coast, where forest cover has decreased by 75 percent since 1960, an estimated 200 million cubic meters of commercial timber has simply been burned to clear the land for agriculture, incurring a loss of perhaps $5 billion. In Ghana, where 80 percent of the forests have disappeared, the forest department estimates that only 15 percent of the timber was harvested before the land was cleared. In Brazil, where little timber is extracted before forestland is cleared by burning, the resulting loss in commercial timber approximates $2.5 billion annually.

Burning valuable timber in the course of clearing forests is only one obvious kind of wastage. The loggers themselves destroy enormous quantities of timber through careless use of equipment and inefficient logging practices. If loggers extract 10 percent of the timber in an area, selecting mature trees of the most valuable species, they typically destroy at least half of the remaining stock, including immature trees of the valued species as well as harvestable stocks of somewhat less desirable varieties. Loggers often keep reentering partially harvested areas to extract more timber before stands have recovered, inflicting heavy damage on residual trees each time and making regeneration impossible. In Ghana and the Ivory Coast, some stands have been reentered as often as three times in 10 or 15 years as concessionaires obtained sales contracts for logs of lesser-known species.

According to a recent study commissioned by the International Tropical Timber Organization, not even one tenth of 1 percent of remaining tropical forests are being actively managed for sustained productivity. Moreover, in most countries, forests designated for logging are left virtually unprotected from encroachment by settlers and shifting cultivators after a timber harvest and are thus exposed to burning and clearing. Surveys in the Amazon make it clear that deforestation is particularly rapid where roads for logging or other purposes have opened up a region.

The biological degradation of tropical forests carries a high and escalating price tag. The timber cost alone has been unexpectedly high, because tropical-timber prices have bucked the general downward trend of commodity prices and many previously uncommercial species now find ready markets. Countries where loggers have been allowed to extract as few as two or three trees per hectare, destroying the rest as uncommercial, now regret their shortsightedness. The upward trend in tropical-timber prices is likely to continue as supplies

are depleted in Asia, Central America and West Africa over the next decade; the timber in the Amazon Basin, which is now being recklessly burned, will become increasingly valuable.

Potential revenues from timber sales are by no means the only economic losses in deforested countries. Probably 70 percent of the wood harvested in tropical countries is used locally, mainly for fuel. As forests recede, severe fuelwood shortages loom. Other forest resources become unavailable to local residents, including animals killed for meat, fruits, oils, nuts, sweeteners, resins, tannins, fibers, construction materials and a wide range of medicinal compounds. In Indonesia the value of exported nontimber forest products had climbed to $123 million by 1986.

Recent studies have shown that the capitalized value of the income derived from such nontimber forest products—readily renewable resources that can be extracted sustainably—may greatly exceed that of the timber harvest. Moreover, the incomes so derived are the livelihoods of local residents, whereas the profits from timber operations are typically captured by distant elites or foreign corporations. Logging operations have sparked some violent protests by villagers in Sarawak and in the Philippines and other countries.

Quite aside from the loss of timber, deforestation often has a severe environmental impact on soil, water quality and even local climate. Shallow, easily leached soils are damaged by heavy equipment, and when they are exposed to heavy tropical rains, they can quickly erode or at least lose any remaining nutrients. Studies in Ghana showed that elimination of savanna forest raised soil-erosion rates from less than a ton to more than 100 tons per hectare per year, with a consequent nutrient loss 40 percent higher than what is being supplied by the application of chemical fertilizer. Riverine fisheries have been damaged by the increased sedimentation that results from erosion or by deforestation in floodplains that provide critical seasonal habitats for fish. Large-scale deforestation interrupts moisture recycling, thus reducing rainfall, raising soil temperatures and perhaps promoting long-term ecological changes.

Logging is often the first step in deforestation: it may be followed by complete clearing of trees and a deliberate shift to land uses—typically cattle ranching and inappropriate modes

of agriculture—that not only are unsound environmentally but also result in direct economic loss. For example, studies in the rapidly deforesting Brazilian state of Acre show that because pastures quickly lose productivity and can carry few cattle, the present per-hectare revenue from the collection of wild rubber and Brazil nuts is four times as high as the revenue from cattle ranching.

All in all, both experience and analysis reinforce the argument that deforestation has not been a path to economic development; in most tropical countries it has instead been a costly drain on increasingly valuable resources. Moreover, deforestation is not inevitable. It is largely the consequence of poor stewardship, inappropriate policies and inattention to significant social and economic problems whose true locus is outside the forest sector.

To begin with, in the developing countries most governments—which are the proprietors of at least 80 percent of the mature closed-canopy tropical forest—have not put an adequate value on that resource. As proprietors, they could capture the entire resource value of the forests' timber, except for the cost of the labor and capital committed to managing and harvesting it, by charging high enough royalties and taxes or by selling harvesting rights to the highest bidders. Instead, with very few exceptions, governments have allowed most of these resource rents to flow to timber concessionaires and speculators, who are often linked to foreign enterprises.

In the Philippines, for example, if the government had been able to collect the full resource value of the roughly three million cubic meters of timber harvested in 1987, its timber revenues would have exceeded $250 million—more than six times what was actually collected. Low royalties and taxes, combined with widespread log smuggling and tax evasion, left much of the excess profits in the hands of timber-concession holders, mill owners and timber traders. The Asian Development Bank has estimated that total profits averaged at least $4,500 per hectare harvested.

Governments have created such windfalls as these by keeping royalties and fees charged to timber-concession holders low, reducing export taxes on processed timber to stimulate domestic industry and granting income-tax holidays to logging companies. Moreover, governments have failed even to enforce the modest official charges effectively. (Between 1979 and 1984 in Indonesia, 125 million hectares were harvested, but taxes and royalties were collected on only 86 million.) As a consequence, few tropical countries have limited timber exploiters to a normal rate of profit and thereby captured the value of the forest resource for the public treasury.

The resulting bonanza atmosphere has sparked timber booms throughout the tropics, drawing both domestic and foreign entrepreneurs—many with little forestry experience—into the search for quick fortunes. Under their pressure, governments have awarded timber concessions that cover areas far greater than they can effectively supervise or manage and that sometimes extend beyond designated production forests into protected areas and national parks. In the Ivory Coast concessions were let for two thirds of the nation's production forests in just seven years. Of 755 politically favored concessionaires, only 51 actually log their holdings themselves; most of them merely sell their cutting rights, profiting as middlemen. In Indonesia, Thailand and the Philippines, the areas under concession exceed the total area of production forest.

The opportunity for private gain has attracted politicians as well as businessmen. In Thailand, Sarawak, Sabah, the Philippines and other places, cabinet ministers, senators and other senior politicians are involved in the timber industry. In the Philippines, for example, Senator Juan Ponce Enrile, the principal opposition leader, holds extensive timber concessions he acquired under the Marcos regime. In Indonesia most of the 544 concession holders are retired military or government officials who can bring pressure in Djakarta to halt investigations into violations of forestry regulations. Effective supervision by forestry-department personnel, often low-ranking officials, is virtually impossible.

While they sacrifice enormous sums in potential forest revenues, governments in the tropics are failing to invest enough in stewardship and management of the forest. In Indonesia nearly half of all trained foresters work in Djakarta, hundreds of miles by sea from the forests; those who do get out into the field find themselves dependent on concession holders for shelter and transportation. A study in Ghana found that 66 percent of all govern-ment posts for professional foresters, 54 percent of the posts for junior professionals and 43 percent of the technical-grade positions were vacant. Gabon has enough forestry personnel, but there is no way for them to do their job in the field: the departmental budget was reduced by 75 percent between 1984 and 1988. All of this means that although in many countries forestry codes and concession agreements are worded to ensure sustained productivity over at least several cycles, almost nowhere are forests being managed to achieve that goal.

Ineffective government supervision is compounded by the perverse incentives established for timber companies by the terms of concession agreements, which actually discourage any possible interest loggers might have in management for sustained yield. Even though intervals of 25 to 35 years are prescribed between successive harvests in selective-cutting systems—and longer intervals in monocyclic systems (when all salable timber is extracted at once)—most agreements run for 20 years or less, some for less than five years. Concession holders are given little reason to care whether or not productivity is maintained for future harvests.

Again, relatively undifferentiated fees are often levied, based simply on the volume of wood extracted. This encourages "high-grading," a practice in which loggers take out only logs having the highest value and do so over large areas and at minimum cost. Because trees whose standing value is less than the royalty rate can be destroyed with impunity, extensive damage is often inflicted on residual stands. In Sabah, Indonesia and the Philippines, from 45 to 75 percent of residual trees are destroyed or seriously damaged during harvesting operations. Royalties based not on what is extracted but on the size of the concession and on the total salable timber it contains would encourage more complete utilization of the timber within a smaller harvesting area; ad valorem royalties (based on the value of extracted logs) would also encourage fuller utilization.

Distorted incentives also reduce the efficiency of wood-processing industries. Many countries seek to increase both employment and the value added to forest products domestically by encouraging processing rather than the exporting of logs. They must provide strong incentives to local mills to overcome high rates of protection against the importation of processed wood in Japan and Europe. Extreme measures, such as bans on log exports or export quotas based on the volume of logs processed domestically, have created inefficient local industries, which are sometimes set up only to preserve valuable log-export rights.

In the Ivory Coast such quotas have created a large processing industry requiring 30 percent more logs than efficient mills would consume to produce the same output. This inefficiency is supported by the sale of rights—worth as much as $15 per cubic meter on the open market—to export high-value logs. In Zaire concessionaires must process 70 percent of their harvest domestically. The requirement has increased timber cutting, because profitable export of prized species supports inefficient sawmilling, which dumps low-value output domestically at prices about 30 percent below production costs.

Such extreme protection can create powerful local industries able to resist regulation. Indonesia has successfully captured between 70 and 80 percent of the world's hardwood plywood market by banning log exports and providing generous industrial incentives. The rapidly expanding but inefficient processing industry now consumes 35 million cubic meters of logs annually, more than previous peak exports, and current plans call for doubling capacity during the 1990's.

Countries sheltering inefficient processing industries can incur heavy economic and fiscal losses. In the Philippines each log exported as plywood is worth from $100 to $110 less per cubic meter than it would be if exported without processing or as sawed timber; the government sacrifices more than $20 million annually in forgone export taxes to encourage these plywood exports.

Industrialized countries have contributed to—and profited from—these forest-policy problems in the tropics. European and U.S. companies have held interests in logging and processing enterprises, especially in tropical Africa and Latin America, but Japanese business now heavily outweighs its rivals in the tropical-timber trade. Japan is the largest importer, accounting for 29 percent of the tropical-timber trade in 1986, roughly the same share as the European Economic Community. Imports (which, unlike those of the EEC, are mostly of unprocessed logs) were 30 percent higher in 1987, mainly because of a construction boom in Japan, where most tropical-hardwood

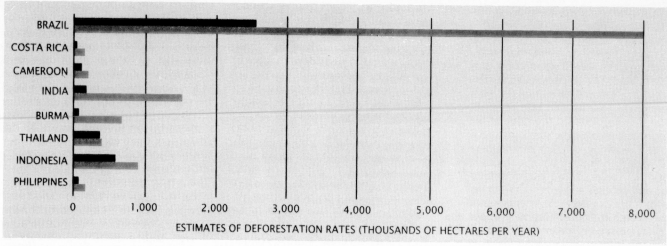

RATES OF DEFORESTATION appear to be increasing. Here estimates made by the Food and Agriculture Organization in the early 1980's (*black*) are compared with more recent estimates (*gray*) based on satellite imagery and field surveys.

imports are processed into construction plywood, primarily as disposable forms for molding concrete.

Large Japanese trading companies are involved in all stages of exploitation, as partners and financiers of logging concessionaires, as exporters and importers, and as processors and distributors. As log supplies were successively depleted, Japanese firms have shifted their attention from the Philippines to Indonesia, then to Sabah and Sarawak, and now they are interested in Amazonian forests. François Nectoux and Yoichi Kuroda find that the Japanese have shown little interest in sustained management of their holdings; their highly leveraged operations have harvested as much as possible as fast as possible in order to pay off financing charges. Moreover, Japanese firms have participated in the bribery, smuggling and tax evasion that make tropical timber cheap to import and at the same time deprive exporting countries of much of the value of their resource.

Inadequate forest policy and management are often abetted by misguided agricultural policy. Many countries actively encourage the conversion of tropical forests to other uses. Rules of land tenure in many states, such as Sabah, allow private parties to obtain title to forested land by showing evidence of "improving" it—by clearing away the trees, for example. In the Philippines, Brazil and elsewhere, recognized rights of occupancy or possession are awarded on the basis of the area of land cleared. Such provisions often become a mechanism for privatizing land from the public forest estate. Those who obtain

ownership soon sell out to larger capitalists, who consolidate the land to establish private ranches and accumulate speculative holdings.

In many cases such activities would be uneconomic without heavy government subsidies. In the Brazilian Amazon, road-building projects financed by the federal government and multinational development banks have fueled land speculation. More than 600 cattle ranches, averaging more than 20,000 hectares each, have been supported by subsidized long-term loans, tax credits covering most of the investment costs, tax holidays and write-offs. The ranches proved to be uneconomic, typically losing more than half of their invested capital within 15 years.

Indeed, surveys showed that meat output averaged only 9 percent of what was projected and that many ranches were reorganized and resold repeatedly, having served only as tax shelters. (In that respect, they were unquestionably productive, generating returns of up to 250 percent of their owners' actual equity input.) Although the Brazilian government has suspended incentives for new cattle ranches in Amazonian forests, supports continue for existing ranches, covering 12 million hectares, that have already cost the treasury more than $2.5 billion in lost revenue.

More general agricultural policies contribute indirectly to deforestation. In Latin America and the Philippines the aggregation of the better agricultural land into large, generally underutilized estates pushes the growing rural population into forested frontiers and upper wa-

tersheds. The extreme concentration of landholdings is supported by very low agricultural taxes that make farms and ranches attractive investments for people in upper-income brackets, for whom it costs almost nothing to keep extensive holdings that generate relatively little income.

Subsidized rural-credit programs also promote land concentration: ceilings on interest rates inevitably lead banks to ration credit in favor of large landholders who have ample collateral and secure titles. Particularly in inflationary settings in which land provides security, large landholders with access to virtually free credit can easily buy out small farmers who cannot finance investments to raise agricultural productivity. Many of the recent migrants into Rondônia and Acre in Brazilian Amazonia are small farmers and farm laborers who have been displaced from Paraná by large-scale mechanized cultivation.

In many countries, deforestation has provided a temporary escape valve—a respite from development pressures that can be dealt with effectively only at a more fundamental level. In the Philippines, population growth rates in the forested uplands are even higher than the high national average of 2.5 percent per year, resulting in high rates of deforestation and soil erosion. Yet the government has been reluctant to address population control directly or to attack highly skewed patterns of landholding in the lowlands.

The Indonesian government's ambitious "transmigration" program, which has so far resettled about a million families from crowded Java to the outer islands—80 percent of them to sites cleared in primary or secondary forest—was largely an attempt to provide employment and livelihoods. At a cost of $10,000 per household (in a country that invests only $125 per capita annually), transmigration could obviously not compensate for slow employment growth on Java itself, and it has been sharply curtailed in recent budget cuts necessitated by lower petroleum prices.

Indeed, rapid deforestation in the tropics during the 1980's has generally been linked to the exceptionally difficult economic conditions most tropical countries face. Indonesia's drive to export timber products is a conscious effort to offset its lower petroleum earnings and protect its development program from further cutbacks. Many of the most heavily debt-burdened countries are coincidentally those with most of the remaining tropical forests. The 1980's were the first period in 40 years when economic growth in those countries failed to outpace the increase in the labor force. Employment in the organized urban sector stagnated and declined; real wages plummeted in the informal urban labor market. Instead of the usual rural-to-urban migration, there was a pileup in agriculture.

In Brazil, for example, the agricultural labor force grew by 4 percent a year between 1981 and 1984, compared with a growth rate of only .6 percent between 1971 and 1976; agricultural wages fell almost 40 percent in real terms between 1981 and 1985. With no alternative, given the concentration of agricultural land in large holdings and the absence of jobs, rural households migrated to the frontier in increasing numbers. A more favorable economic climate could reduce the pressures of unemployment, poverty and population growth on the remaining tropical forests.

Is there hope for improvement? There are, in fact, signs of a new approach to forest policy reflecting increasing awareness of the national and global significance of tropical forests.

Many countries are taking steps to capture resource rents at full value. The government of the Philippines has imposed partial bans on logging, cracked down on illegal logging and raised timber royalties. It plans to increase timber taxes further and is considering assigning harvesting rights on the basis of competitive bids. The Ivory Coast also expects to move to competitive bidding.

Indonesia has raised timber taxes substantially. Ghana, with World Bank assistance, has doubled timber royalties to an average of 12 percent of export value and plans a further 50 percent increase by 1992.

A number of governments are now strengthening their forest-management capability with the help of development-assistance agencies. The World Bank and the Asian Development Bank now have loans for forest-management improvement in the pipeline for a dozen countries. Most of these loans support forest-policy reform as well as institutional strengthening. Under the aegis of the Tropical Forestry Action Plan, sponsored by the World Resources Institute, the World Bank, the U.N. Development Program and the Food and Agriculture Organization, more than 50 countries are preparing national action plans to conserve and manage their forests.

International interest in tropical forests has bloomed, accompanied for the first time by a willingness to contribute to their maintenance. Several voluntary organizations in developed countries have raised money for debt-for-nature swaps: a bit of the external debt of a tropical country is bought up at a discount and then exchanged for a local-currency fund (usually to be managed by a local voluntary agency) that will finance forest-conservation programs. Some business groups have

also taken an active interest. Associations of tropical-timber traders in the Netherlands and the U.K. have proposed that all importing countries levy a surcharge on tropical-timber imports to create a fund for forest conservation.

There remains a great deal more that the world outside the tropics might do. Inappropriate consumption of tropical hardwoods (for disposable concrete molds, for example) contributes to deforestation. Some businesses in industrialized countries are still taking part in forest destruction. Barclays Bank was recently found to be the majority owner, through its Brazilian subsidiary, of two huge Amazonian cattle ranches that have burned half a million acres of forest to create pasture. (The *Sunday Times* of London reported that the bank's chairman, on learning of this involvement, declared, "Being personally an extremely keen gardener and botanist...I was extremely cross.")

Development-assistance agencies are still financing activities that are destructive to tropical forests. The African Development Bank has recently agreed to a project that will run a road through one of the Ivory Coast's few remaining tracts of rain-forest and mangrove habitat. Another of its projects would develop sawmilling capacity affecting more than 800,000 hectares of virgin forest in the Congo,

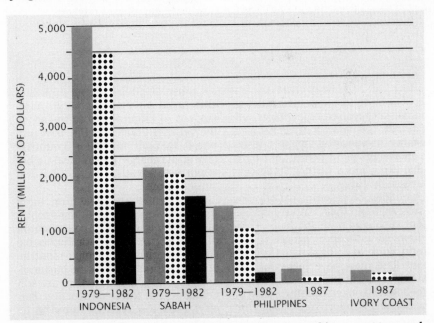

TROPICAL COUNTRIES have generally failed to collect (in royalties, export taxes and other fees) the full resource value of timber taken from their forests. The grey-colored bars show, for four-year periods or for single years, the "potential rent": what might have been collected if harvested logs had been disposed of (exported as logs, sawed or further processed) to yield the highest possible net return. The dot patterned bars show the "actual rent" that could have been collected given the actual disposal of the harvest. What the governments did in fact collect is shown in black.

7. GLOBAL ENVIRONMENT

even though the country has no forest-management capability and the area in question is the home of Pygmy communities. Such projects should be supplanted by others designed to improve forest management and step up the pace of reforestation.

The potential scope of international cooperation to halt the destruction of tropical forests is large. The Tropical Forest Action Plan provides one useful framework. The Montreal Protocol for protection of the ozone layer and a proposed conven-

tion to mitigate global climate change could also be powerful mechanisms for international cooperation. Fees levied on chlorofluorocarbons and taxes on fossil-fuel and other greenhouse gases in industrialized countries would help to reduce emissions and also provide funds needed to implement national programs formulated under the Tropical Forest Action Plan. Programs in which debt reduction is linked to improved resource management and conservation could be expanded substantially.

New forms of international cooperation would reflect the world's growing awareness that the disappearing tropical forests are not only national treasures but also essential elements of the biosphere on which everyone, everywhere, depends.

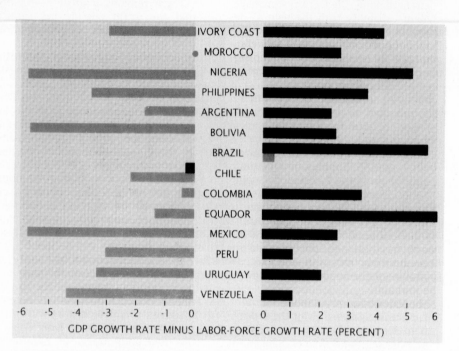

GOVERNMENT POLICIES that promote deforestation are often motivated by economic pressures. One such pressure is illustrated. From 1965 to 1980 (*black-bars*), economic growth (measured by gross domestic product) generally outpaced the growth of labor forces, but from 1980 to 1986 (*grey-bars*), labor forces grew faster than most economies, generating unemployment and reducing government revenues.

FURTHER READING

THE PRIMARY SOURCE: TROPICAL FORESTS AND OUR FUTURE. Norman Myers. W. W. Norton & Co., Inc., 1984.

THE FOREST FOR THE TREES? GOVERNMENT POLICIES AND THE MISUSE OF FOREST RESOURCES. Robert Repetto. World Resources Institute, 1988.

PUBLIC POLICIES AND THE MISUSE OF FOREST RESOURCES. Robert Repetto and Malcolm Gillis. World Resources Institute, 1988.

TIMBER FROM THE SOUTH SEAS: AN ANALYSIS OF JAPAN'S TROPICAL ENVIRONMENTAL IMPACT. François Nectoux and Yoichi Kuroda. Gland, Switzerland, World Wildlife Fund International, 1989.

Rethinking the Environment

The United States stands on the threshold of its third great era of environmentalism. The new age lacks heroes like the conservationists who put their stamp on the first, or a signal event like Earth Day 1970, which defined the second. It may be a pivotal moment in history. Today's opportunity to forge a genuine environmental ethic could well be wasted, for Americans are as confused about the environmental as they are eager to protect it. . . . Biologist Daniel Botkin says they hold ancient and sentimental misconceptions of nature, and of man's place in it, that could stifle the emerging new environmentalism.

A NEW BALANCE OF NATURE

Daniel B. Botkin

Daniel B. Botkin, a former Wilson Center Fellow, is professor of biology and environmental studies at the University of California, Santa Barbara. He recently published Discordant Harmonies: A New Ecology for the Twenty-first Century *(1990), and is the 1991 recipient of the Mitchell Prize for Sustainable Development.*

L ast June, California voters tried to strike a blow for the state's endangered mountain lions when they passed Proposition 117, protecting all but the most aggressive cats from human beings. Anybody caught killing, trapping, or transporting a mountain lion in the state now faces one year in jail and a $10,000 fine. The Wilderness So-ciety, Defenders of Wildlife, and the Sierra Club all lined up behind the measure, and there was nothing in the debate (such as it was) to suggest that Proposition 117 was anything but the epitome of the "good cause." State Attorney General John Van de Kamp invoked an emotional roll call of vanished species in support of the proposition, writing, "Although our state symbol, the grizzly bear, no longer roams the wild lands of California and the condor no longer soars over our mountains, we still have areas where one remaining symbol of our wilderness heritage, the mountain lion, is free to live . . . . Mountain lion hunting is cruel and unnecessary."

Americans at the end of the 20th century seem to believe that they have finally learned to confront environmental problems such as the threat to the mountain lion rationally, that only a lack of information and political consensus limits their ability to solve problems. The logic of Proposition 117 seems self-evident: Mountain lions will do best if left completely alone. Their population will grow to an optimum size, then stabilize, threatening neither their own existence nor that of other species. But the general view on Proposition 117, like much of our thinking about the environment today, is based on a myth, the myth that nature left to itself will find a perfect balance, that "nature knows best." It is a myth that has led to unfortunate, sometimes even disastrous, results.

A classic example of the failure of the balance-of-nature myth is Kenya's Tsavo National Park. Landsat satellite images taken over Kenya in the late 1970s show a curious geometric feature—two straight lines stretching 50 miles or more and converging at an obtuse angle. To the east, inside the 5,000 square miles of the park, a dull brown signifies vegetation so thin that most of the light detected by Landsat is reflecting off bare soil. Outside the park, a garish red signifies dense vegetation. A visitor at Tsavo would have seen that the park was indeed desert-like, a thin scattering of live and dead shrubs and trees surrounded by dense thickets of vegetation beyond its borders. Tsavo was a photographic negative of one's expectation of a park: barren inside, green outside.

After Tsavo became a park in 1948, its first warden, David Sheldrick, spent years building roads, providing year-round water for wildlife, and eradicating poaching. Sheldrick apparently was convinced that he was only giving nature a benign helping hand. Indeed, the elephants flourished. So much so that they began consuming leaves, fruits, and twigs so quickly that the trees and shrubs started to die off. By 1959, much of the park began to resemble a "lunar landscape," Sheldrick's wife Daphne later wrote in *The Tsavo Story* (1973).

In the mid-1960s, a Ford Foundation study concluded that some 3,000 elephants should be shot to keep the population within limits of its food supply. Sheldrick at first agreed, but then reversed himself. He decided, as his wife put it, that "the conservation policy for Tsavo should be di-

rected towards the attainment of a natural ecological climax, and that our participation towards this aim should be restricted to such measures as the control of fires, poaching, and other forms of human interference." To conservationists, the phrase "natural ecological climax" meant nature in a mature condition, which, once attained, persists indefinitely without change. Sheldrick and other specialists regarded the "climax" condition as the truly natural and most desirable state of wilderness. It is much the same idea that underlies California's Proposition 117: Left to itself, nature will achieve a balance.

But Tsavo was struck by a severe drought in 1969 and '70, and as some 6,000 elephants starved to death, they destroyed many of the park's remaining trees and shrubs, producing the devastation still painfully visible from space many years later. (Lately, the park has enjoyed the beginnings of a recovery.) Elephants and human beings together had drafted the lines on the Landsat image.

The elephants at Tsavo, like California's mountain lions and virtually all wildlife today, live in a fragment of what used to be large, often continuous habitats. In today's "ecological islands," a species can easily increase rapidly, exhaust its food supply, starve, and suffer a rapid decline, meanwhile causing many kinds of harm, sometimes even endangering the survival of other species.

The final act of the tragedy at Tsavo was being played out even as the first Earth Day in 1970 was bolstering the comforting illusion that there are only two sides to any environmental issue, pitting environmentalists against their pro-development foes. But the disagreement at Tsavo was among conservationists who shared basic goals.

Sheldrick's views were consistent with contemporary theories about population growth and the development of forests and other communities of organisms. From these theories come such concepts as "carrying capacity" and "maximum sustainable yield," terms that are now regularly bruited about in newspapers and popular magazines. The theories have their origins in the mid-19th century, when the new science of ecology was born amid—and influenced by—the flowering of the machine age. Until recently, population theory relied almost exclusively on two formal models that were heavily influenced by machine-age thinking. One, called "the logistic," which was first proposed in 1849 by a Belgian scientist named Pierre-Francois Verhulst, described the growth of a single population; the other, called the Lotka-Volterra equations, cast predator-prey relationships in terms of predictable oscillations of population.

The logistic was explained by Alfred Lotka in his 1925 book, *Elements of Physical Biology*: Keep a population of flies in a cage with a constant food supply, he said, and a predictable pattern will be followed. When there are few flies, food is not a limiting factor and the flies will reproduce rapidly. But eventually they begin to exceed their food supply; deaths gradually rise to equal births and the population arrives at a steady size, its "carrying capacity." These ideas can be expressed with a simple equation in calculus that produces an elegant, S-shaped growth curve.

The logistic had another elegant quality: If a population at carrying capacity strayed from that balance, it would smoothly return to it. In short, the logistic seemed to show once again that there is a balance of nature.

It also relied upon assumptions that have proved to be false. The logistic assumes that all flies or elephants or mountain lions are identical, each contributing equally to reproduction, mortality, growth, and reduction in available resources. And although the logistic is supposed to be an ecological formula, it does not explicitly take account of changes in environment, such as variations in the availability of food and water. According to the logistic, the elephant population at Tsavo should have grown smoothly to an equilibrium.

It is one thing to err in the management of African elephants or California mountain lions. But the logic of the S-shaped curve has also been taken literally by, among others, the specialists who manage the world's fisheries directly, such as those at the U.S. National Marine Fisheries Service, and through international treaties. From the logistic comes the concept that wildlife biologists call the "maximum sustainable yield population," which says that a population

grows fastest when it is at exactly one-half of its carrying capacity. So fisheries managers the world over have made it their goal to allow just a large enough catch every year to maintain this ideal population.

A photographic negative of our expectations: A view from the air in 1977 of Kenya's Tsavo National Park (at right), a virtual desert after nearly 30 years of careful conservation efforts.

Then, they believe, the fish population will grow at its maximum rate every year, like a jet engine at "best power" cruising speed.

A classic example of the failure of this idea is the Peruvian anchovy fishery, once the world's largest commercial fishery. In 1970, fishermen caught eight million tons of anchovies off Peru, but two years later the catch plummeted to only two million tons, and it continued to shrink. Yet this fishery was actively managed according to international agreement for a maximum sustainable yield. This failure has been repeated over and over again.* When Congress enacted a forward-looking piece of legislation to "save the whales" in 1972, the Marine Mammal Protection Act, the effort fell victim to the same faulty concepts during international negotiations to determine the permissible whale catch. Gradually, however, administrators have since remedied that mistake.

I have searched the scientific literature for 10 years and found no cases where a population outside a laboratory followed the S-shaped curve. Only microbes or flies

---

*Likewise, Pacific sardines, once a major species off the California coast, suffered a catastrophic decline in the 1950s that continued through the 1970s. The Atlantic menhaden catch peaked at 785,000 tons in 1956, and dropped to 178,000 tons in 1969. Atlantic herring and Norwegian cod experienced the same kind of decline. The North Atlantic haddock catch, which had averaged 50,000 tons for many years, increased to 155,000 tons in 1965 but then crashed, reaching a mere 12,000 tons by the early 1970s.

THE FIRST ENVIRONMENTALISTS

Most historians see early environmentalism as a reaction to Western industrialization. Britain's Richard Grove, in an essay adapted from Nature *(May 3, 1990), proposes a new view.*

Anxieties about soil erosion and deforestation are to be found in the literature of classical Greece, imperial Rome, and Mauryan India, and in a sporadic fashion in the annals of the early Spanish and Portuguese empires. But it was not until the mid-17th century that awareness of the ecological price of capitalism started to grow into a fully fledged theory about the limits of the natural resources of the Earth.

Some historians have argued that European colonialism was not only highly destructive in environmental terms but that its very destructiveness stemmed from "imperialist" attitudes toward nature. But that hypothesis does not stand up. Ironically, a new sensitivity to the environment developed as a product of the specific, and ecologically destructive, conditions of the commercial expansion of the Dutch and English East India Companies and, a little later, of the Compagnie des Indes.

Colonial expansion also promoted the rapid diffusion of new scientific ideas by a coterie of committed professional scientists and environmental commentators. In India, for example, in 1838, there were over 800 surgeons. During the early 18th century the need to understand unfamiliar floras, faunas, and geologies, both for commercial purposes and to counter environmental and health risks, propelled many erstwhile physicians and surgeons into consulting positions and employment with the trading companies as fully fledged professional and state scientists long before such a phenomenon existed in Europe. By the end of the 18th century their new environmental theories, along with an ever-growing flood of information about the natural history and ethnology of the colonies, quickly diffused through the meetings and publications of a whole set of academies and scientific societies throughout the colonial world.

The first of these societies appeared in the island colonies. This was no accident. In many respects, the isolated oceanic islands stimulated a detached self-consciousness and a critical view of European origins and behavior, of the kind dramatically prefigured by Daniel Defoe in *Robinson Crusoe* (1719). Such islands became, in practical as well as mental terms, an allegory of a whole world, and observations of their ecological demise were easily converted into premonitions of environmental destruction on a wider scale.

It was on the French island colony of Mauritius that the early environmental debate came to a head. Between 1768 and 1810, the island was the location for some of the earliest experiments in systematic forest conservation, pollution control, and fisheries protection. These initiatives were carried out by scientists who, characteristically, were both followers of Jean-Jacques Rousseau and adherents of the kind of rigorous empiricism associated with mid-18th-century French Enlightenment botany. Their conservation measures stemmed from an awareness of the potentially global impact of modern economic activity, from a fear of the climatic consequences of deforestation and, not least, from concern over species extinctions. The "Romantic" scientists of Mauritius, and above all Pierre Poivre, Philibert Comerson, and Bernardin de St. Pierre can, in hindsight, be seen as the pioneers of modern environmentalism.

After the British annexed Mauritius in 1810, these environmental prescriptions were transferred to St. Helena and eventually to India itself. From 1820, they were strongly reinforced by the writings of Alexander von Humboldt, who strove in successive books to promulgate a new view of the relations between man and the natural world which was drawn almost entirely from the holist and unitary thinking of Hindu philosophers. His subordination of man to other forces in the cosmos formed the basis for a wide-ranging and scientifically reasoned interpretation of the ecological threat posed by the unrestrained activities of man.

This interpretation became especially influential among the Scottish scientists employed by the East India Company. Several of them, in particular Alexander Gibson, Edward Balfour, and Hugh Cleghorn, became enthusiastic proselytizers of a conservationist message which provided the basis for the pioneering of a forest conservancy system in India. For example, in 1847 the directors of the East India Company indicated their conversion to the need for conservation with a remarkable circular on the dangers of artificially induced climate change. The subject, they said, "is one having strong practical bearing on the welfare of mankind, and we are anxious to obtain extensive and accurate information in regard to it."

Time and again, from the mid-18th century onward, scientists discovered that the threat of artificially induced climatic change, with all it implied, was one of the few really effective instruments that could be employed in persuading governments of the seriousness of environmental change. The argument that rapid deforestation might cause rainfall decline and, eventually, famine, was one that was quickly grasped by the East India Company, fearful as it always was of agrarian economic failure and social unrest. Unfortunately, the argument often required an initial famine to lend credibility to scientists. In India, for example, serious droughts in 1835–39, the early 1860s, and 1877–78 were all followed by the renewal of state programs designed to strengthen forest protection.

The question of climatic change had thus become international in scope by the mid-1860s. It was reinforced by more detailed research that raised the possibility that the very constitution of the atmosphere might be changing. Such views found an early supporter in J. Spotswood Wilson, who presented a paper in 1858 to the British Association for the Advancement of Science on "The General and Gradual Desiccation of the Earth and Atmosphere." Wilson stated that upheaval of the land, "destruction of forests and waste by irrigation" were not sufficient to explain the available facts on climate change, and that the cause lay in the changing proportions of oxygen and carbonic acid in the atmosphere. Their respective ratios, he believed, were connected to the relative rates of their production and absorption by the "animal and vegetable kingdom." The author of this precocious paper concluded with a dismal set of remarks. "As inferior races preceded man and enjoyed existence before the earth had arrived at a state suitable to his constitution," he warned, "it is more probable that others will succeed him when the conditions necessary for his existence have passed away."

The raising, as early as 1858, of the specter of human extinction as a consequence of climatic change was clearly a shocking psychological development. But it was consistent with fears that had been growing within the scientific community. Awareness of species rarity and the possibility of extinction had existed since the mid-17th century as Western biological knowledge started to embrace the whole tropical world. The extinction of the auroch in 1627 in Poland and the dodo by 1670 in Mauritius had attracted considerable attention.

The appearance in 1859 of Darwin's *Origin of Species*, with its emphasis on the place of extinction in the dynamics of natural selection, helped make species protection a more valid concept in the eyes of government, and the period 1860–70 produced a flurry of attempts to legislate for the protection of threatened species. Once more, the initial locale was an island colony, Tasmania, where a comprehensive body of laws, designed mainly to protect the indigenous birds, was introduced in 1860.

So, by the early 1860s, anxieties about artificially induced climatic change and species extinctions had reached a climax. The subsequent evolution of the awareness of a global environmental threat has, to date, consisted almost entirely of a reiteration of a set of ideas that had reached full maturity over a century ago. The pity is that it has taken so long for them to be taken seriously.

or bees grown in a laboratory do that. And the regular oscillations predicted for predator and prey by the companion Lotka-Volterra model have *never* been sustained,

The S-Shaped Curve

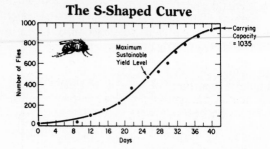

even in the laboratory. Yet these flawed models are still used by a surprising number of fish and wildlife conservation authorities throughout the world. They are not products simply of flawed mathematics or incorrect calculations but of a fundamentally mistaken view of how nature works, a view that, as we shall see, is increasingly being undercut by new findings.

Forestry is a very different field, but the underlying mythology is the same. George Perkins Marsh (1801–82), the intellectual father of conservation in America, was struck while serving as U.S. Ambassador to Egypt and Italy by the impact of man on the environment in these ancient countries. "Nature, left undisturbed," he wrote in *Man and Nature* (1864), perhaps with his native Vermont in mind, "so fashions her territory as to give it almost unchanging permanence of form, outline, and proportion, except when shattered by geologic convulsions; and in these comparatively rare cases of derangement, she sets herself at once to repair the superficial damage, and to restore, as nearly as practicable, the former aspect of her dominion."

From Marsh and others came the idea of "ecological succession": A clearing in a forest would grow back through a series of regular and predictable stages to a final, constant, stable "climax" forest. The climax forest was believed to have the greatest amount of organic matter, the greatest diversity of species. Although forest biologists have rarely relied upon mathematical formulas, the climax forest had the elegant qualities of a logistic population: undisturbed it was constant, and when disturbed it grew back to its prior constant condition.

The climax forest represented the balance of nature.

It was, in a sense, a walk in the woods as a graduate student during the 1960s that led me to question this idea of a climax forest and all that it implied. The woods was New Jersey's Hutcheson Memorial Forest, established as a natural preserve in 1954 when Rutgers University was given a 65-acre tract of woodland known to have been intact—not clearcut or burned—since 1701. The creation of the preserve became a minor media event. Sinclair Oil, which had helped purchase it for Rutgers, placed a major national magazine advertisement that made much of the conventional wisdom, referring to the woods as a place where "nature has been working for thousands of years to perfect this 'climax' community in which trees, plants, animals, and all the creatures of the forest have reached a state of harmonious balance with their environment. Left undisturbed, this stabilized society will continue to perpetuate itself century after century." *Life* and *Audubon* also took note of the remarkable "climax forest."

But like the Peruvian anchovy fishery and Tsavo National Park, Hutcheson Memorial Forest did not remain constant. Originally filled with oaks, hickories, and chestnuts, it was by the 1970s becoming a forest of sugar and Norway maples in the mature stands, with Japanese honeysuckles and Asian trees of heaven in the gaps. It now appears that the sugar maple was artificially suppressed in the climax forest prior to 1701 by frequent fires, which were probably started by Indians. Two hundred years after these outbreaks of fire ceased, the woodlands began to change. Modern human influences, of course, contributed: The Norway maple, for example, was introduced into North America by Europeans.

Hutcheson Forest is not unique. Written histories, fire scars in trees, and fossil pollen deposited in lakes provided evidence in the 1960s and '70s to show that all forests are continually changing, and have done so since the ice ages. But ecologists and conservationists continued—and, to a surprising extent, still continue—to use the old theories to write laws, set policies, and manage natural resources.

One reason for our reluctance to part with these theories is that they grow out of very deeply rooted notions about nature. "Everything in the world is marvelously ordered by divine providence and wisdom for the safety and protection of us all.... Who cannot wonder at this harmony of things, at this symphony of nature which seems to will the well-being of the world?" wrote Cicero in *The Nature of the Gods* (44 B.C.). The idea is repeated throughout Western history. Nature was perceived as perfectly ordered and stable, constant unless disturbed, and tending to recover from disturbance by returning to its former condition. This perfect order was also a primary argument for the existence of God, for only a Supreme Being could create a perfectly ordered nature.

How, then, could one explain the occasional absence of order? Western culture traditionally has given two answers, both pointing at human beings. The first blames human beings for what they have done; the second blames them for what they have *not* done. Although casting humans as the despoilers of nature may have seemed like a new idea to the environmentalists of the 1960s, who were prone to see in the West only a tradition of exploitation of the environment, it is actually quite ancient. Pliny the Elder (A.D. 23–79) long ago contrasted the beauty and bountifulness of the Earth without human interference with the imperfections of people who abused the Earth. He speculated that there was a divine purpose for beasts of the wilderness: They guarded the Earth, protecting it from human actions.

The second explanation for the absence of order—blaming humans for what they have not done—emphasizes human stewardship of nature. God put us here to complete the perfect harmony of nature. If there was disharmony, we had failed to carry out God's work. "For whom then shall we say the world was made?" asked Cicero. Why would the gods labor for trees or plants, which are "devoid of sense or feeling," or for animals, "dumb creatures who have no understanding"? Stewardship is the main idea that animates such older mainstream conservation groups as the National Wildlife Federation (founded in 1936) and the Conservation Foundation (founded in 1948, and since merged with the World Wildlife Fund).

Before the rise of modern science in the 17th century, people explained the structure of nature in terms of divine order, but they had only organic metaphors, derived from plants and animals and especially the human body, to describe its workings. The first person to descend into an active volcano and return to write about it, a 17th-century Jesuit priest named Athanasius Kircher, began his analysis by citing Virgil, who believed that the "belching rocks" of volcanoes were the torn entrails of the mountains. Water mixed with ashes, Kircher wrote in *Mundus Subterraneus* (1638), produced a continual "conception and birth" of fires in Vesuvius and Aetna. The fires grew and matured until, becoming ripe, they erupted. To Kircher, a volcano was like a rose growing into flower.

The organic view suggested that the imperfections of the environment were manifestations of the aging of Mother Earth. Mountains were her warts, infertile farmland her wasted skin. Christians tended to believe that these organic processes, the chaos of nature itself, had been set in motion by the expulsion of man from the Garden of Eden and the Flood. One of Kircher's contemporaries, a theologian named Thomas Burnet, wrote that the Flood created "the ruins of a broken world" where before had existed perfect order and harmony, a world "smooth, regular and uniform; without Mountains and without a Sea."

Beginning in the 17th century, the rise of Newtonian mechanics and the work of scientists such as Johannes Kepler (1571–1630), along with the invention of such marvelous devices as the steam engine, created a new understanding of the universe. They also bred new metaphors, fostering the idea that the Earth and the solar system operate like clockwork, like a machine. Scientific discoveries, such as the recognition that the planets do not orbit in perfect circles around the sun, overwhelmed arguments that there was a perfect order in the observable architecture of the universe. No longer was the existence of God proved by the perfect and fixed structure of the world.

Now, the *dynamism* of nature came to be seen as a demonstration of God's power. The visible physical order of old was replaced by a new conceptual order. A perfectly working, idealized machine could be seen as the product of a perfect God. "These Motions of Generations and Corruptions," wrote Sir Anthony Hale in 1677, "are so wisely and admirably ordered and contempered, and so continually managed and ordered by the wise Providence of the Rector of all things," that "things are kept in a certain due stay and equability."

The idea of order survived but the organic view of nature did not fare as well. True, in all of the arts, scientific discoveries bred a new aesthetic appreciation of the irregular and the asymmetric. English essayist Joseph Addison (1672–1719), for example, now found an "agreeable horror" in ocean storms. Later, William Wordsworth and the other 19th-century romanticists took custody of the organic metaphor.

But it was the mechanistic view that prevailed after the 17th century. A mechanistic nature—except in our own age, an oxymoron—would have the attributes of a well-oiled machine, including the capacity to keep operating, replaceable parts, and the ability to maintain a steady state, and thus to be in balance. Births and deaths, immigration and emigration, the input of sunlight and the loss of energy as heat, the intake and loss of nutrients, would always maintain life in a constant state of abundance and activity. This is the view reflected in the writings of George Perkins Marsh, in the elegance of the S-shaped population curve, and in the management of Tsavo National Park.

But if nature is a machine, then the flipside is that human beings ought to be able to re-engineer nature and improve it. This is the side that has dominated much of our management of natural resources and the environment during the 20th century. It is reflected in the approach of the lumber company that clearcuts a diverse tropical forest and replants it with a single species of tree, and in a U.S. Army Corps of Engineers project that makes a meandering river into a straight canal. The ultimate irony is that the mechanistic view unites the most extreme preservationists, who believe that the machinery of nature functions perfectly without human intervention, and nature's most extreme exploiters.

I believe that we are living through a time of change, a transition from the mechanical age to a new era that appears to us as the space and computer age. We are gradually moving away from the mechanical view of nature, toward a different set of perceptions and assumptions that will blend the organic and the inorganic. But we have not yet settled on the right metaphors, images, and symbols.

The scientific basis of this new understanding was prepared almost a century ago by a Harvard biological chemist named Lawrence Henderson in *The Fitness of the Environment* (1913). Henderson was struck by the unique set of circumstances that made life on Earth possible. The planet is endowed with water, for example, which "possesses certain nearly unique qualifications which are largely responsible for making the earth habitable." Its high specific heat means that oceans, lakes, and streams tend to maintain a constant temperature; such bodies of water also moderate summer and winter temperatures on land.

During the last two decades, scientists such as James Lovelock and Lynn Margulis have begun to appreciate that the environment is "fit" for life in part because life has evolved to take advantage of the environment and has also altered the environment. Lovelock and Margulis have taken this insight to an extreme, reviving organic thinking about nature. Lovelock argues in *Gaia: A New Look at Life on Earth* (1979) that "the biosphere is a self-regulating entity with the capacity to keep our planet healthy by controlling the chemical and physical environment." The Gaia hypothesis—named after the Greek goddess of the Earth—suggests that nature is akin to a sentient being. One problem with this view—as with the mechanistic view of old—is that nature never achieves the self-regulating "steady state" of perfection that Gaia's advocates imagine.

But the notion that life and environment interact is important. The traditional view in science is that the Earth changes slowly and evenly, and is very little affected by the life—plants, animals, fungi, bacteria, and protists—that it hosts. After all, the total mass of all living things on Earth is a tiny fraction—two-tenths of one part in one billion—of the mass of the planet. But now even geologists, who study the least changeable face of the planet, are seeing connections. The theory of plate tectonics shows that the gradual shifting of plates has redistributed life around the globe, and that some forms of life have evolved to capture the benefits of geologic change. The Earth's major iron ore deposits are, in turn, the result of global environmental changes caused by bacteria on the early Earth. Likewise, atmospheric scientists have found that the evolution of plant life has greatly influenced the composition of the atmosphere.

From these and other findings a new view of nature is gradually emerging. No longer is it possible to see nature as a stately clock-like mechanism, slow, deliberate, static. Nature as we are coming to know it is a patchwork of complex systems with many things happening at once and with each system undergoing changes at many scales of time and space. Human beings, far from being alien interlopers who disturb the timeless rhythms of nature, are intrinsic elements of the natural order. Chance events seem to play an important role.

This is a very different nature from the simple, one-thing-at-a-time, nothing-left-to-chance, everything-calculable-exactly nature of the machine age. Complexity, chance, simultaneity of events, history, and change are the qualities of nature.

Perhaps the hardest of these ideas for us to accept is that of natural change. Do we open a Pandora's Box by admitting some kinds of change? How do we manage something that is always changing? If we concede that some kinds of change are good, how can we decide which kinds are not?

We are learning, however, that we have no choice but to accept change and to distinguish the good from the bad. Nature itself must be our guide. Changes that we impose on the landscape that are natural in quality and speed are likely to be benign. Rapid changes, or those that are novel in the history of biological evolution—such as the introduction of many new chemicals

into the environment—are likely to cause problems. Global warming, for example, poses a challenge to us not so much because of the size of the change that is in the offing but because of the unprecedented speed with which it may occur.

On a practical level, this new view of nature leads to several possibilities for the management of natural resources. Consider the Kirtland's warbler, a small songbird that nests only in young jack pine woodlands in the coarse, sandy soils of Central Michigan. A friendly, pretty animal once proposed as the state bird, the warbler was the first songbird subject, in 1951, to a complete census. By the early 1960s, the population had fallen by half, leaving only about 200 males. Conservationists and scientists realized that the warbler was in trouble because its habitat, the jack pine forest, was disappearing. The reason, ironically, was that well-intentioned authorities were suppressing forest fires in Central Michigan. But jack pines require such blazes to reproduce; their cones release seeds only after they have been heated by fires, and the seeds germinate only in the sunny clearings created by fires.

It was not easy for scientists to persuade government conservation authorities that they would have to start controlled forest fires to save the warbler. That flatly contradicted cherished beliefs about the pristine balance of nature. Learning to manage the environment is in many cases like learning the lesson Alice did in trying to reach a looking-glass house in the Lewis Carroll classic: Sometimes the only way to reach a thing is to walk away from it.

Conservationists in Michigan learned that lesson. Today, the warbler survives in a preserve of 38,000 acres where since 1976 it has been government policy to set controlled fires periodically. This small episode may mark a turning point in the modern understanding and management of nature. The warbler population is not managed to obtain some magical number—a carrying capacity or maximum sustainable yield—but merely to be sizeable enough to minimize the chance of extinction. The idea is to move beyond constancy and static stability—to manage for the recurrence of desirable conditions.

Another goal can be the persistence over time within some desirable range. We could manage elephants at Tsavo so that they are reasonably visible to tourists yet allow their number to vary with changes in climate and other conditions. Gone are the stringent goals of a single carrying capacity, a perfectly constant climax ecosystem, a maximum sustainable production.

This emerging perspective can be applied to a variety of environmental problems. For example, it suggests that on the nation's farms, integrated pest management, with its mix of biological controls and some benign artificial chemicals, should be preferred over intense use of chemical pesticides. Flood control projects should no longer include the straight-line canals of machine-age surveying; designers should try to maintain the mixture of habitats that a natural flood plain has (as Frederick Law Olmstead did a century ago in Back Bay Boston). Commercial foresters should adapt to local conditions, clearcutting on a limited scale in regions (such as New England) where disturbances are normal, the soil is fertile, and forests grow back relatively quickly, but selectively logging other areas. And all logging should be avoided in certain tropical forests and other areas that have been untouched and where, because of poor soil, the prospects for regeneration are bad.

Some of these ideas are familiar; what they still lack is a truly unifying vision and rationale. At the level of ideas and metaphors, our culture is in a transition, and where we will come out cannot easily be foreseen. The science of ecology lacks the equivalent of a Newtonian physics—a coherent set of laws that explain the *dynamics* of nature rather than its structure. It awaits a genius on the order of Newton or Einstein to create a new "mathematics of complex systems" that renders nature in all of its complexity, capturing the play of chance, randomness, and variability. And ecologists are hardly alone in appreciating the need to come to terms with such factors. Some physicists, astronomers, paleobiologists, climatologists, and others recognize that the natural processes they study are not simple, regular, or certain, that what some now call "chaos" is ever present.

As we search for new ways to understand nature, we need not throw out the machine and organic metaphors completely. From the machine metaphor we need the notion that systems can be analyzed, cause and effect understood, and repairs made. From the organic metaphor we need the idea of history, and of a beginning and end, of individuality. Computers suggest one avenue toward a new understanding. Computer games children play make familiar complexity, surprises, randomness, and the simultaneity of events in a rapidly changing situation. Our children will have an easier time conceiving of the nature we know from scientific observations than those of us who grew up building erector-set towers and cranes driven by electric motors—simple machines with a single equilibrium. Perhaps one of these children will become the Einstein of ecology.

Credits/ Acknowledgments

Cover design by Charles Vitelli.

1. Close to Home
Facing overview—United Nations photo by L. Barnes. 14-15—Humanities Press International, Inc., Atlantic Highlands, N.J.

2. Racial and Ethnic Diversity
Facing overview—AP/Wide World photos.

3. Nonethnic Minorities
Facing overview—United Nations photo by John Isaac.

4. Politics, Public Policy, and Priorities
Facing overview—United Nations photo by D. Otfinowski.

5. National and Global Economy
Facing overview—United Nations photo by Shelley Rotner. 165—United Nations photo by P. Sudhakaran.

6. Global Peace or War
Facing overview—U.S. Air Force photo.

7. Global Environment
Facing overview—United Nations photo. 216—FAO photo. 233—Photo courtesy of Daniel B. Botkin. 236—Revised from D. B. Botkin and E. A. Keller, *Environmental Studies: Earth As a Living Planet.* Originally revised and reprinted by permission of Yale University Press from *An Introduction to Population Ecology* by G. E. Hutchinson, 1978, Fig. 12, p. 25.

ANNUAL EDITIONS ARTICLE REVIEW FORM

■ NAME: _____ DATE: _____

■ TITLE AND NUMBER OF ARTICLE: _____

■ BRIEFLY STATE THE MAIN IDEA OF THIS ARTICLE: _____

_____

_____

_____

_____

■ LIST THREE IMPORTANT FACTS THAT THE AUTHOR USES TO SUPPORT THE MAIN IDEA:

_____

_____

_____

_____

_____

_____

■ WHAT INFORMATION OR IDEAS DISCUSSED IN THIS ARTICLE ARE ALSO DISCUSSED IN YOUR TEXTBOOK OR OTHER READING YOU HAVE DONE? LIST THE TEXTBOOK CHAPTERS AND PAGE NUMBERS:

_____

_____

_____

_____

_____

_____

■ LIST ANY EXAMPLES OF BIAS OR FAULTY REASONING THAT YOU FOUND IN THE ARTICLE:

_____

_____

_____

_____

■ LIST ANY NEW TERMS/CONCEPTS THAT WERE DISCUSSED IN THE ARTICLE AND WRITE A SHORT DEFINITION:

_____

_____

_____

_____

_____

*Your instructor may require you to use this Annual Editions Article Review Form in any number of ways:
for articles that are assigned, for extra credit, as a tool to assist in developing assigned papers, or simply
for your own reference. Even if it is not required, we encourage you to photocopy and use this page;
you'll find that reflecting on the articles will greatly enhance the information from your text.

ANNUAL EDITIONS: SOCIAL PROBLEMS 92/93

Article Rating Form

Here is an opportunity for you to have direct input into the next revision of this volume. We would like you to rate each of the 38 articles listed below, using the following scale:

1. **Excellent: should definitely be retained**
2. **Above average: should probably be retained**
3. **Below average: should probably be deleted**
4. **Poor: should definitely be deleted**

Your ratings will play a vital part in the next revision. So please mail this prepaid form to us just as soon as you complete it.
Thanks for your help!

Annual Editions revisions depend on two major opinion sources: one is our Advisory Board, listed in the front of this volume, which works with us in scanning the thousands of articles published in the public press each year; the other is you—the person actually using the book. Please help us and the users of the next edition by completing the prepaid article rating form on this page and returning it to us. Thank you.

Article	Rating	Article	Rating
	1. America's Family Time Famine		20. Beyond the Stingy Welfare State
	2. Divorce: Sometimes a Bad Notion		21. Education: Ideas & Strategies for the 1990s
	3. Unplanned Parenthood		22. Infrastructure: America's Third Deficit
	4. What Triggers Their Drinking?		23. Energy for the Next Century
	5. Beyond the Melting Pot		24. Abortion in a New Light
	6. America the Multicultural		25. Big Messes: Problems That Grow Bigger and Bigger
	7. A New Black Politics		26. The High Cost of America's Economic Ignorance
	8. Immigration Reform: Overview of Recent Urban Institute Immigration Policy Research		27. The Income Distribution Disparity
	9. Japan's Influence on American Life		28. Will the Third Great Wave Continue?
	10. 'Return' of Native Americans Challenges Racial Definition		29. Deadly Migration
	11. Why Is America Failing Its Children?		30. America's Century Will End With a Whimper
	12. Children in Peril		31. Myths of European Unity
	13. Everyday Life in Two High-Risk Neighborhoods		32. The CIA Connection
	14. The Feminization of Poverty: Myth or Reality?		33. The Roots of Muslim Rage
	15. The Prejudice Against Men		34. Military Victory, Ecological Defeat
	16. The Story of a Nursing Home Refugee		35. World Population Continues to Rise
	17. Rights Issues Split Protestant Churches; More Battles Expected		36. Enough Is Enough: Assessing Global Consumption
	18. American Nightmare: Homelessness		37. Deforestation in the Tropics
	19. Rural Poverty: The Forgotten Poor		38. Rethinking the Environment: A New Balance of Nature

(Continued on next page)

ABOUT YOU

Name_____ Date_____

Are you a teacher? ☐ Or student? ☐

Your School Name _____

Department _____

Address _____

City _____ State _____ Zip _____

School Telephone # _____

‖‖‖

YOUR COMMENTS ARE IMPORTANT TO US!

Please fill in the following information:

For which course did you use this book? _____

Did you use a text with this Annual Edition? ☐ yes ☐ no

The title of the text? _____

What are your general reactions to the Annual Editions concept?

Have you read any particular articles recently that you think should be included in the next edition?

Are there any articles you feel should be replaced in the next edition? Why?

Are there other areas that you feel would utilize an Annual Edition?

May we contact you for editorial input?

May we quote you from above?

‖‖‖

ANNUAL EDITIONS: SOCIAL PROBLEMS 92/93

BUSINESS REPLY MAIL

First Class   Permit No. 84   Guilford, CT

Postage will be paid by addressee

The Dushkin Publishing Group, Inc.
Sluice Dock
DPG **Guilford, Connecticut 06437**

No Postage
Necessary
if Mailed
in the
United States